Britain and Ireland

'The book provides a stimulating survey of historical developments in British and Irish civilizations through the centuries. It is an example of stunning scholarship and a treasure of information and it gives a better understanding of the complexities and the diversity of contemporary cultures in Britain and Ireland. The needs of all readers, from scholars to pupils and students to the interested layman/-woman, are met.' Joachim Schwend, *Leipzig University*

'Jürgen Kramer's text provides an instructive, pedagogically alert, and engaging overview of the making of the British nation from earliest times to the present. Underscoring Britain's historic links with the Continent and exchanges with non-Western cultures, it is well-calculated to appeal to teachers and students of English as a foreign language.' Joyce Senders Pedersen, *University of Southern Denmark at Odense*

Britain and Ireland: A Concise History is a handbook on the history of the British Isles for students of British studies all around the world. It recounts the history of the two states – the United Kingdom of Great Britain and Northern Ireland and the Republic of Ireland (Eire) – and four nations – the Irish, the Welsh, the Scottish and the English – from prehistory to the present.

The book has a unique approach that presents not only the story of what happened in the British Isles, but also its interdependence with Europe and the rest of the world. The historical narrative is accompanied by numerous illustrations and information boxes, and also an extensive selection of documents with questions to challenge readers.

With chapters organised chronologically, and including a glossary and selected further reading, this is a must for all students of British studies.

Jürgen Kramer is Professor of British Cultural Studies at the University of Dortmund. He is the author of *Culture and Intercultural Studies* (1990) and *British Cultural Studies* (1997), and is co-editor of the *Journal for the Study of British Cultures*.

Britain and Ireland

A Concise History

Jürgen Kramer

LONDON AND NEW YORK

First published 2007
by Routledge
2 Park Square, Milton Park, Abingdon, Oxon OX14 4RN

Simultaneously published in the USA and Canada
by Routledge
711 Third Avenue, New York NY 10017

Routledge is an imprint of the Taylor & Francis Group, an informa business

Typeset in Dante by
RefineCatch Limited, Bungay, Suffolk

British Library Cataloguing in Publication Data
A catalogue record for this book is available from the British Library

Library of Congress Cataloging in Publication Data
Kramer, Jürgen, 1946–
    Britain and Ireland: a concise history / Jürgen Kramer.
        p. cm.
    Includes bibliographical references.
    1. Great Britain—History.   2. Ireland—History.   I. Title.
    DA27.5.K73 2006
    941—dc22
    2006014044

ISBN10: 0–415–31195–0 (hbk)
ISBN10: 0–415–31196–9 (pbk)

ISBN13: 978–0–415–31195–3 (hbk)
ISBN13: 978–0–415–31196–0 (pbk)

Contents

List of Illustrations

Figures

Maps

Tables

Acknowledgements

I should like to thank my research assistants Lisa Gajewski, Daniel Kramer (no relation), Monika Schulze and Anika Steffenhagen, whose contributions to the boxes and the selection of pictures I deeply appreciate. Ellen Grünkemeier has been a particularly inspiring and reliable collaborator. Her stimulating contributions to the selection of documents and pictures, to the boxes and to the working questions have been invaluable, and so has been her technical expertise with scanner and computer. Bernd Lenz (Passau), Edzard Obendiek and Hans Peters (both Dortmund) read most of the chapters and kindly let me profit from their comprehensive knowledge and astute criticism. At Routledge, I owe a huge debt to Gillian Oliver for lively discussions and for commissioning the book, to two generous anonymous readers whose great expertise saved me from some embarrassing slips and errors and provided useful hints for improvement, to Margaret Hill for expert proof-reading, and to Eve Setch and Katherine Davey for safely seeing the book through its production.

I dedicate this book to my Dortmund colleagues and students who have talked, discussed, joked and put up with me since 1997.

The author and publishers wish to thank the following for their permission to reproduce material from the following works:

Tacitus, 'Civilization or Servitude' from K. Morgan, *The Oxford Illustrated History of Britain* (1993), by permission of Oxford University Press. D. Whitelock's *English Historical Documents*, Vol. I (1996), reproduced by permission of Taylor & Francis Books UK. L. B. Smith and J. R. Smith, *The Past Speaks*, Vol. I, *To 1688*, Copyright © 1993 by Houghton Mifflin Company. D. C. Greenaway and G. W Greenaway, *English Historical Documents*, Vol. II (1993), reproduced by permission of Taylor & Francis Books UK. H. Rothwell, *English Historical Documents*, Vol. III (1996), reproduced by permission of Taylor & Francis Books UK. J. Tetzel, *The Spark for the Reformation: Indulgences*, 1465, reprinted by the Department of History of the University of Pennsylvania. C. H. Williams, *English Historical Documents*, Vol. V (1996), reproduced by permission of Taylor &

ACKNOWLEDGEMENTS

Francis Books UK. U. Sauerbaum, *Das elizanbethanische Zeitalter*, permission granted by Reclam A. Browning. Isaac Newton, *Mathematical Principles of Natural Philosophy*, 1687 (1962), reproduced by permission of the University of California Press. *English Historical Documents*, Vol. VI (1996), reproduced by permission of Taylor & Francis Books UK. W. L. Arnstein, *The Past Speaks*, Vol. 2, *Since 1688*, Copyright © 1993/by Houghton Mifflin Company. *The Declaration of the Rights of Man and Citizen*, 1789, prepared by Gerald Murphy (The Cleveland Free-Net – aa300), distributed by the Cybercasting Services Division of the National Public Telecomputing Network [NPTN]). Trevor May, *The Victorian Workhouse* (2000), permission granted by Shire Publications.

While every effort has been made to trace and acknowledge ownership of copyright material used in this volume, the publishers will be glad to make suitable arrangements with any copyright-holders whom it has not been possible to contact.

Introduction

This book is aimed at students, particularly students of English as a foreign language, who want an introduction to the history of that part of the world from which the language they are learning originates. *Britain and Ireland* claims to offer *A Concise History*. What does this mean? 'Britain and Ireland' stands for the whole of the British Isles. It refers to the two bigger and many smaller islands off the north-west coast of the European continent which today comprise two states – the United Kingdom of Great Britain and Northern Ireland, and the Republic of Ireland (Eire) – and four nations: the Irish, the Welsh, the Scottish and the English. The history of these islands is followed in its main outline from the very beginning to the present time. It is not, however, followed in isolation: wherever necessary, its interdependence with European and world history is given particular attention. As thousands of volumes have been published on this subject, which nobody can hope to read in a lifetime, it seemed justifiable to provide a concise introductory version for students (and the interested general reader) which follows the main historical events and developments but also makes certain choices in emphasis.

For this reason, in Chapters 1 and 2 I have concentrated on the ways in which different people, from the 'original' Britons to the Normans, have invaded, settled and made their mark in the Isles. In contrast to this, Chapter 3 focuses on the way in which the Isles, for more than three centuries, were intimately connected to and intermittently dominated by the Continent. Chapter 4 describes the long, complex and sometimes tortuous process by which the four nations of the Isles constituted themselves as political entities – mostly in opposition to each other and eventually in subordination to England. Chapters 5 and 6 outline the processes of further domestic integration and consolidation of the United Kingdom of Great Britain and Ireland (as in the unions of 1707 and 1800 and the subsequent widening of the franchise) and of colonial expansion (of the British Empire), while Chapter 7 focuses on the social and political upheavals as well as the progressive remedies of the twentieth century, including the devolutionary processes within the Isles and the break-up of the British Empire.

The method I follow is to switch from continuous narrative to structural analysis and back (with, at times, extended 'footnotes' on particular events, ideas and persons in separate boxes). Many of the events, processes and arguments described in the main text are amplified and illustrated, but also qualified, criticised and sometimes contradicted by the historical documents which make up the second part of the book. They may help to demonstrate, I hope, that history is not a unified or linear process, although the chronology (at the end of the book) will, again, stress the linear perspective. The glossary may help the uninitiated to grapple with those terms for which we have no (or almost no) modern equivalents.

However, I should like to add a word of caution. Historical overviews (such as this book offers) have their advantages – a quick, unobstructed and apparently objective view of what we always wanted to know – but they also have their disadvantages which, although they cannot altogether be avoided, should at least be pointed out. The idea that it might be possible to cross the territory of history from A to B as if it were a passage from one place to another is not only seductive but also deceptive: what may be useful if we are going from one classroom to another – namely to opt for the shortest way and stick to it – will allow only a very blinkered view of history. More specifically, in history the interesting question is perhaps less of how to make a beeline from A to B as of how many different possibilities have existed of getting from A to B, and why one was chosen and others were discarded. Moreover, whichever passage from A to B we use – i.e. which narrative of historical events and developments we follow – it is always influenced by the benefit of hindsight. That is to say, all the accounts we have of past events are already informed by our knowledge of what came after them – a fact which does not leave untouched our perception (as well as our narrative) of the events themselves. On the contrary, we tend to make more sense of them than they perhaps had when they happened. Finally, our accounts are severely (and perhaps unduly) influenced by our own concerns: because of our sympathies with (and antipathies to) certain social, political and cultural ideas in our present societies, we tend to favour (and disfavour) particular views of past events and developments.

While these dangers cannot altogether be avoided, what we can do is keep in mind the following caveats. History should not be expected to have a specific goal which it tries to reach. It should not be compared to a train moving on tracks according to a timetable. Looking at historical events and processes, we should not count on cause and effect. Things never turn out the way we expect. Perhaps history is best described as the unintended result of many different intentions which merge, mingle and mix with, but also contradict and deflect from, each other. Consequently, human beings do not so much make history as become entangled or entwined in parallel, combined or competing histories and, reacting to them, create new ones. History consists of a multitude of histories and is, because of this, notoriously confused. And, as we all are involved in this confusion, we have to bid farewell to the illusion of some commanding height from which we could obtain what I called a quick, unobstructed and apparently objective view of the historical process. We rather have to make do with informed but limited individual points of view. Which brings me to my last piece of advice. We should always read *more than one* book (or article) on any historical topic we are interested in. There is always another story, another perspective, another history to be discovered. I consulted perhaps some hundred books to write this one; if I had consulted a hundred more, it might look differently.

If this book encourages its readers to go on reading, to go on looking for new materials and perspectives, I, for one, will be quite happy. However, as I also conceive of myself as a life-long learner, I should appreciate it very much if those who are not satisfied with it (and, perhaps, would like to suggest improvements) could let me know (juergen.kramer@udo.edu). I promise to consider each and every suggestion seriously and, if I am persuaded, to take account of it in a new edition.

1 Britons, Celts and Romans, c.4000 BC–AD 410

It is reckoned that about 5 billion years ago our planet – as one of nine bigger ones in a remote corner of the Milky Way galaxy – came into existence, about 3 billion years ago its crust hardened, and about a billion years ago rudimentary forms of flora and fauna emerged. Some 500 million years later the first vertebrates (small fish) swam in the sea, but it took another 250 million years until vertebrates had developed to such an extent that they could also live on land. Some 200 million years ago we find the first mammals, and 100 million years ago the first ape-like beings. Some 2 million years ago their descendants – we may as well call them humans (*Homo habilis*) – had learned to walk upright: their heads were no longer needed to grasp and to hold (because their hands had taken over this function) and had become free to think. Some 800,000 years ago these humans began to make tools; 300,000 years later they learned to tame the fire; and when, another 200,000 years later, the sounds by which they communicated had been transformed into languages this unique development became the basis of the 'ascent' of mankind. Some 80,000 years ago humans began to protect their bodies against the weather; 30,000 years later they started to build shelters, huts and houses instead of living in caves, and another 20,000 years later they created their first works of art. Having survived so far as hunters and gatherers, 20,000 years ago humans started to domesticate animals and, another 10,000 years later, began to till the soil.

PREHISTORIC EUROPE AND THE BRITISH ISLES

Over the last 800,000 years, the part of the world which later came to be called Europe has experienced a number of climatic changes: intensely cold periods – ice ages – alternating with warmer ones. Since the last glaciation about 15,000 years ago the average temperature has constantly (but by no means evenly) risen and is likely to continue to rise. In the course of these ice ages, the human colonisation of Europe took place wherever the climate was sufficiently

Map 1 Human fossils in Europe, from *The Penguin Atlas of British and Irish History* by Simon Hall and John Haywood (Penguin Books, 2001. Copyright © Penguin Books, 2001), p. 14

hospitable, and human evolution progressed through the stages of *Homo erectus* (arriving in Europe 800,000 years ago), *Homo heidelbergensis* and *Homo neander-thalensis*, while our ancestor, *Homo sapiens (sapiens)*, arrived from Eurasia some 40,000 years ago. In Britain the oldest remains of humans (teeth, bones, but also tools) were found in the south (near Boxgrove) and stem from *Homo heidelber-gensis*, who lived there about 500,000 years ago. They were followed (and eventually replaced) about 200,000 years ago by the Neanderthals who, in turn, had eventually to give way to the modern *Homo sapiens* about 31,000 years ago. For most of the ice ages, the British Isles of today were linked to the Continent by a land-bridge and a greater part of them was covered by thick ice sheets. Some 7000 years ago, when the ice of the last glaciation melted and the sea level rose, these parts were cut off from the Continent: they became islands.

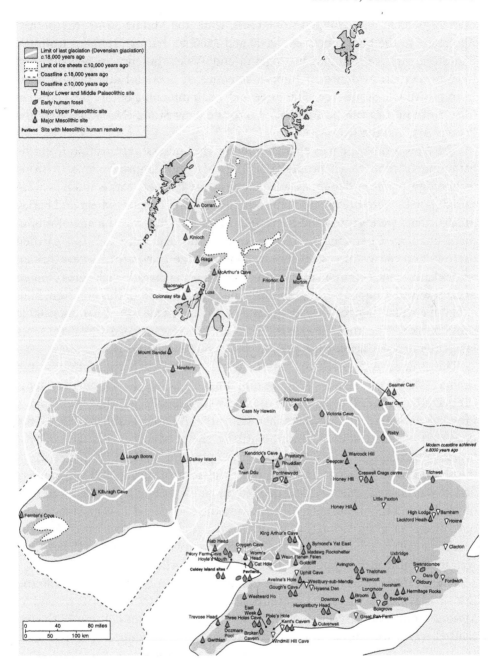

Map 2 Britain's first humans, after *The Penguin Atlas of British and Irish History* by Simon Hall and John Haywood (Penguin Books, 2001. Copyright © Penguin Books, 2001), p. 15

The human sector of Europe's prehistory is conventionally related to the three-age system of Stone, Bronze and Iron. The Old Stone (Palaeolithic) Age refers to the enormously long period before the end of the ice ages when humans worked with chipped stone tools, while the Middle Stone (Mesolithic) Age refers to the period between 8000 and 3500 BC. Human remains from the Old Stone Age were found in England and Wales (but not in Scotland and Ireland); certain evidence of human activities in Scotland and Ireland dates from the Middle Stone Age. The three and a half millennia before the Christian (or Common) Era can be subdivided into the New Stone (Neolithic) Age, the Bronze Age and the Iron Age.

The New Stone Age was characterised by the successful transition from the gathering of food to its production. Together with improvements in stone technology, plants and animals were domesticated: sheep, cattle and pigs were raised, horses were bred; woodland was cleared, and cereals (wheat and barley in particular) were grown and harvested. Moreover, this was the age of monument building. Characteristic monuments of this age were tombs – earthen barrows and cairns (in eastern Britain) and passage graves (in western Britain and Ireland) – and ceremonial centres consisting of earthwork enclosures (known as causewayed 'camps') which, especially in the second half of this era, were built either in circular (henge) or linear (cursus) form and made use of vast megalithic constructions. The most important sites are at New Grange (Ireland), Maes Howe (Orkneys), Carnac (Brittany), Avebury and Stonehenge (England).

The Bronze Age (2400 to 700 BC) was a period of both continuity and change. On the one hand, the great monuments (as well as the belief systems connected with them) remained in use and were added to; on the other hand, a growing exchange of raw materials along the Atlantic seaboard led to the flowering of new traditions and, eventually, the production of a new alloy – bronze – through the mixture of copper (90 per cent) and tin (10 per cent). In the second half of the period the agricultural control of the land was intensified: it was cleared, enclosed and divided on an increasing scale, the awareness of fertility and the importance of nurturing the soil gained in importance, and new means of grain storage (silos dug in the rock) were developed. Perhaps because of an overall increase of the population towards the end of this period, warfare became more important and the first hill-forts were built.

The greatest achievements of this era, however, were to be found not in the British Isles but at Knossos (Crete) between about 2000 and 1450 BC and at Mycenae (Greece) between 1600 and 1100 BC, where urban cultures with specialised crafts, widespread trade and written records developed. These centres

---

Stonehenge

The best-known archaeological site in the British Isles is located on Salisbury Plain, near the town of Amesbury, Wiltshire, in southern England. Probably in use between c.3100 and 1100 BC, Stonehenge's original purpose is still unclear. Opinion is divided as to whether it was a place for the worship of ancient deities, or an astronomical observatory for marking significant events (sunrise at the midsummer solstice and sunset at the midwinter solstice), or a sacred site for the burial of high-ranking people. Building Stonehenge took much time and effort. It was created in several phases with the first phase starting about 5000 years ago. At that time a low circular bank and a ditch were constructed. Inside the earth bank there was a circle of 56 'Aubrey Holes', which are invisible on the surface today. The now fallen 'Slaughter Stone' may also date from this period. Around 2100 BC, the inner ring consisting of about 80 pillars of bluestones (probably from South Wales) was constructed. A century later, the outer ring of giant sarsen (sandstone) stones (of 50 tons each) was put up, each of them accommodating a stone lintel on top. The inner horseshoe of 80 dressed sarsen blocks dates back to the same time. Stonehenge was probably completed around 1500 BC, when the so-called 'Y' and 'Z' holes were added. How these heavy stones were transported (perhaps from the Prescelly Mountains about 240 miles away) and set up is still not clear. Likewise we do not know who built Stonehenge, although we cannot but admire its ingenuity.

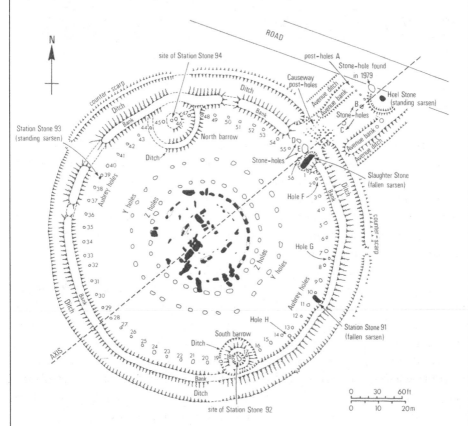

Figure 1 General plan of Stonehenge, from *Stonehenge Complete* by Christopher Chippendale (Thames & Hudson Ltd, 1994), p. 9

Figure 2 Aerial view of Stonehenge© Angelo Hornak/CORBIS

of Bronze Age Europe suffered a fatal economic, political and cultural break-down in the last quarter of the second millennium BC: Crete fell to the My-cenaean Greeks, who in turn were overrun by waves of invaders. As a con-sequence, between 1100 and 750 BC, Greece relapsed into its 'Middle Ages', which separated the period of the Trojan Wars from that of the later city-states, while continental Europe emerged from this rather passive era only when new centres of power came into being north of the Alps.

The subsequent Iron Age was the age of the Celts, who emerged at the start of the first millennium BC around the headwaters of the Rhône, the Rhine and the Danube. They were a diverse group of peoples speaking a set of related languages. Although they most probably shared a common way of life, they were not nationally, ethnically or racially unified. Theirs was a hierarchical society with a highly developed system of religious rites and rituals (adminis-tered by druids), and elaborate forms of art, music and literature. Two nine-teenth-century archaeological discoveries – in the Salzkammergut Mountains and on Lake Neuchâtel – allow us a glimpse not only of the Celtic heartland but also of two successive periods: that of Hallstatt (750 to 400 BC) and of La Tène (400 to 50 BC).

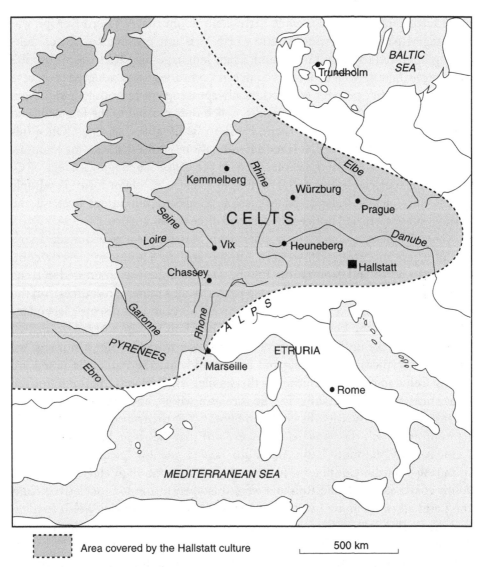

Map 3 Hallstatt culture (800–400 BC) after F. Delouche, *Illustrated History of Europe* (Weidenfeld & Nicolson, 1993), p. 41

The Celtic world expanded by means of invasions and migrations. From north of the Alps the Celts migrated to the south (capturing Rome in 390 BC), to the east (towards the Black and Caspian Seas) and towards the south-east, capturing Delphi (Greece) in 279 BC, eventually crossing the Dardanelles into Asia Minor. But Celtic influences were also spread by the export of culture and language. In Ireland and Britain, for example, the Celtic language was established by the sixth century, which means that it would probably have been known and developed there much earlier. Moreover, there is no evidence of Celtic migrants spreading westwards by the time of the migrations in the fifth

11

and fourth centuries BC. So, while there is no doubt that Western Europe was an integral part of the wider Celtic world, it is not possible to talk of Celts having migrated to Britain or Ireland. Their language may have been Europe's first *lingua franca*, which, in the course of centuries, was adopted as native language by other peoples who, ethnically speaking, were not of Celtic origin at all, but who, because of the extent to which they reacted to the linguistic and cultural influence exerted on them, came to be identified as Celts. Once this adaptation had taken place, further differentiations could ensue as, for example, in the British Isles where the earlier form of the Celtic language (Goidelic or Q-Celtic) was replaced in Britain (as well as in France) by a later form (Brythonic or P-Celtic), while Ireland did not share in this development because the east–west contacts had noticeably declined after around 600 BC.

When Pytheas, a Greek geographer from Massilia (Marseilles) made a voyage of exploration to north-western Europe around 320 BC, he cleverly combined commerce and exploration. On the one hand, he was interested in trade with the 'Tin Islands' (a clear reference to Cornwall's mineral resources); on the other hand, he wanted to explore the northern ocean and discover legendary Thule. Although the book in which he described his voyage (*On the Ocean*, 320 BC) is lost, and we only have references to it in the works of later historians, we know that Pytheas circumnavigated Britain and that the names he noted are clearly Celtic in character: Ierne for the smaller isle (Ireland), Albionon for the larger one (Britain), Pretaniké for the isles as a whole, and Prettani (or Pritani) for the peoples of the isles. Ierne (Latin Hibernia) is the transcription of a Celtic name from which the modern Eire (or Erin) may be thought to derive. The Celtic root of Albionon (Latin Albionum) is *alp*, meaning 'peak' or 'height' (as in the Alps on the Continent). It certainly refers to the high cliffs on Britain's south coast, although the Romans were mistaken in thinking it derived from the Latin *albus*, meaning 'white'. Pretaniké is cognate with the Welsh Prydain and the English Britain. Caesar used the word 'Britanni', and from the name of the people the name of the Roman province Britannia was derived. The meaning of the name is thought to be something like 'the tattooed people', although only very few of the ancient authors refer to tattooing in connection with the Britons.

The fact that a Greek geographer was the first to describe the British Isles may be attributed to the growing strength and expansive nature of Greek politics and culture after 500 BC (although Greece never formed a unitary state in those days). When the Spartans and the Athenians had jointly defeated the Persians by the middle of the fifth century BC, the spectacular rise of a number of Greek city-states began, which combined economic prosperity with the development of democratic institutions and the creation of highly complex works of philosophy, literature and art. Some twenty years later it was interrupted and endangered by the Peloponnesian War (431–404 BC). In this war between the former allies, Sparta and Athens, the latter was defeated and the

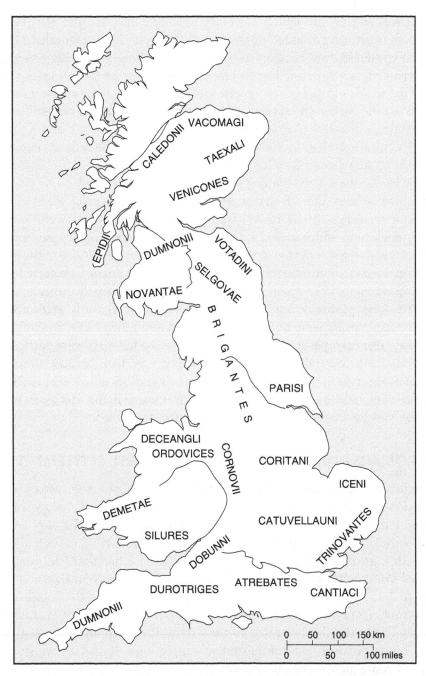

Map 4 The tribes of Britain at the start of the Roman period, from Peter Salway, *Roman Britain*, Oxford History of England, Vol. 1A (Oxford University Press, 1981). By permission of Oxford University Press

former was severely weakened. While competing empires in the east (Persia), the south (Carthage, founded *c.*814 BC) and the west (Rome, founded 753 BC) were interested in the Greek riches, Philip of Macedonia eventually conquered southern Greece in 338 BC. To this his son, Alexander the Great (356–323 BC), added the whole of the Persian Empire and led his army as far as the Indus. As he also put the Persian treasure into circulation, this gave an important boost to production and trade, establishing a common market of sorts and a shared complex culture (Hellenism). However, by the middle of the second century BC the heirs to Alexander's flowering empire could not help being conquered in turn by Rome, the up-and-coming power in the Mediterranean.

Meanwhile, in Britain's Iron Age, the first hill-forts and *oppida* (derived from the Latin *oppidum* = 'small town') were constructed. Hill-forts were fortified hill-top enclosures which served a number of social and ritual purposes (such as defence, proclamation of status, or simply stock enclosure). Many of these hill-forts consisted in an intricate combination of ramparts, ditches, protected gates and elaborate outworks which made direct approach extremely difficult. While hill-forts were primarily aimed at the enclosure of relatively self-sufficient communities, *oppida* were built as an answer to intensified trade: to command routeways (for example at river crossings). While the hill-forts were particularly numerous in the central southern part of Britain – perhaps because this was a kind of border region between the metal-producing tribes in the west and more warlike tribes in the east – the *oppida* were concentrated in the south-east where trade, in particular with Roman-occupied France, prospered.

THE ROMANS IN BRITAIN: INVASION, CONQUEST, SETTLEMENT

Traditionally, the founding of Rome is dated to 753 BC. The history of its expansion into an empire which affected the greater part of Europe can be divided into four phases. (i) When Greek culture was still flourishing (as indicated above), a small group of villages in Latium (today's Italy), in fits and starts and with a great effort, grew into the centre of an empire which eventually reached from the north of Britain to North Africa and the Near East and from Spain to Asia Minor. (ii) This empire experienced its heyday at the beginning of the second century AD, in the reign of Trajan (AD 98–117) and of Hadrian (AD 117–38). (iii) In the third century AD the extent of the empire put too great a strain on its political and administrative supply lines ('imperial overstretch') and, as a consequence, the empire was threatened from within and from without: from within by the elevation of numerous (and, quite often, competing) emperors with the local help of their loyal legions, and from without by Germanic pressure from the north. In response to this crisis Diocletian (284–305) established the Tetrarchy (i.e. the rule of four), whereby the Roman world was divided into four parts, ruled from Trier (in today's Germany), Milan, Sirmium (in today's Serbia) and Nicodemia (in today's Turkey) by four rulers – two

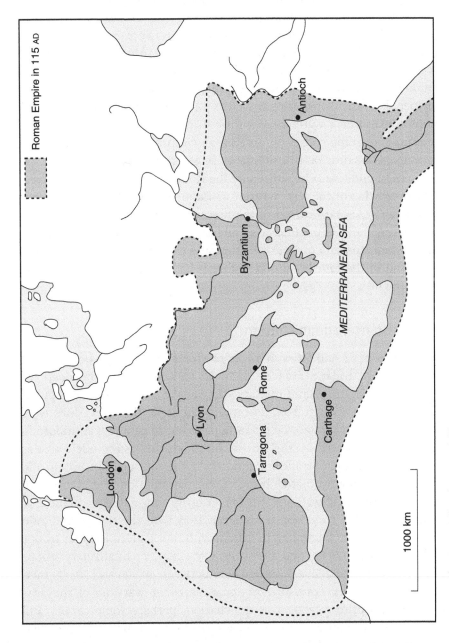

Map 5 The Roman Empire c. AD 115

Roman Empire in 115 AD

MEDITERRANEAN SEA

London
Lyon
Tarragona
Rome
Carthage
Byzantium
Antioch

1000 km

emperors (Augustuses) and two sub-emperors (Caesars). However, this system proved to be unworkable; Emperor Constantine I (312–37) re-established the empire's unity and made Byzantium (Constantinople) his capital. When Theodosius I (379–95) died, the Roman Empire was divided for the last time: the west was assigned to Arcadius, and the east to Honorius. (iv) Shortly afterwards, the western part was overrun by the invading Vandals and Goths, and its existence ended in AD 476, while the Roman Empire of the east continued to exist for another millennium until the Ottomans captured Constantinople in 1453.

For the people of the British Isles as well as for later historians, the advent of the Romans constituted a watershed: it took Britain from prehistory into history. In contrast to Celtic culture(s), to Roman culture writing was of central importance; from this time on British history ceased to be unwritten history. Of course, it was first and foremost written by the Roman victors (while the oldest indigenous British historical text, written in Latin, stems from the mid-sixth century): Tacitus' (c.55–120) record of the first forty years of Roman rule is of particular interest, and Ammianus Marcellinus (c.330–90) related its penultimate phase, when Roman control of Britain was established for the last time towards the end of the fourth century before it had to be relinquished at the beginning of the fifth.

Conquest, resistance, administration

Caesar's invasions of 55 and 54 BC were by-products of his larger undertaking of conquering Gaul (today's France) in 58–51 BC and the general need for Roman political leaders to secure military successes to maintain their popularity and their armies. Although from a Roman perspective these invasions were successful in military and economic terms (a payment of tribute was imposed), the latter was soon ignored by the British, although the lasting effect of this 'contact' on the expansion of trade and industry in the south-east of Britain and Gaul should not be underestimated. It took almost another hundred years until the Roman emperor Claudius (10 BC–AD 54) seriously considered a conquest of Britain. He also wanted to establish his reputation with the troops and gain respect at home. In AD 43 he arrived in Britain with four legions (regular troops composed of Roman citizens) and about the same number of auxiliary troops (recruited from friends and allies), somewhere between 40,000 and 50,000 men in all. The British forces, consisting of the permanent warriors of the aristocracy (whose favourite weapon was the chariot), perhaps some cavalry and the mass of levies summoned from the peasantry, were no match for the well-disciplined Roman war-machine in a pitched battle. Their successes lay, if at all, in surprise attacks and ambushes – something that we would nowadays call guerrilla tactics. Thus, Roman victory did not come as a surprise. However, at no time did the Romans succeed in conquering the whole of Britain (let alone the whole of the British Isles).

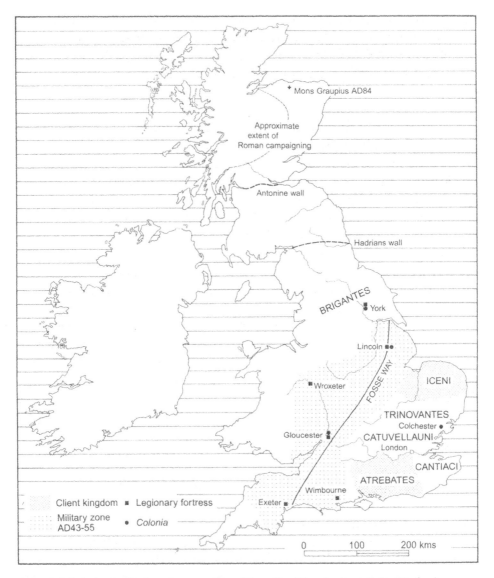

Map 6 Britain in the first century AD, from Barry Cunliffe, *Ancient Celts* (Oxford University Press, 1997), p. 253. By permission of Oxford University Press

Britannia omnis divisa erat in partes tres. First of all, there was the core of the Roman province, which consisted in a large lowland zone in the south-east (roughly south and east of a vital military road from Exeter to Lincoln, the Fosse Way) and in which London eventually became the commercial and administrative centre. Beyond this core zone there were two peripheral high-land zones in northern Britain up to the Clyde–Forth line and in the west including the south-west peninsula and Wales. Both of them, the core and the periphery, were 'Romanised', but the former much more thoroughly than the

17

latter. Finally, the north of Britain (roughly equivalent to today's Scotland) was not permanently occupied by the Romans (although at times regarded as a part of their sphere of influence), and Eire (Hibernia, today's Ireland) was left alone altogether (although invasion plans appear to have existed towards the end of the first century AD).

The Romans favoured indirect rule with the help of self-financing and self-administering local elites (men of property and influence). In the first three decades of their rule, the Romans tried to work with so-called client-kingdoms: in return for their 'friendly cooperation', the Romans backed local 'kings' (tribal chiefs) against their indigenous rivals. Typical examples were Prasutagus of the Iceni (Norfolk), Cogidubnus of the Regni (in the south), and Queen Cartimandua of the Brigantes (in the north). Later, the administration of the province was largely managed by the councils of the *coloniae* (as, for example, Camulodunum/Colchester, Lindum/Lincoln and Glevum/Gloucester), the *municipia* (as Verulamium/St Albans), and the capitals of the *civitates*. A *colonia* was a Roman city of the highest rank in which all citizens were also Roman citizens. Throughout the Empire, these *coloniae* were often created at former legionary bases and governed by a council modelled on the Roman senate. A *municipium* was a Roman city of rank below that of a *colonia*. Its organisation was similar, but its citizens were not automatically Roman citizens. Moreover, Britain was divided into districts of a kind (*civitates*) which were usually based on pre-Roman tribal territories. The capitals of these districts were organised like *municipia* but below them in rank. The Roman administration itself was split: the army was commanded by the governor (a Roman senator or former consul), but for financial matters (such as taxation and control of the mines) a provincial procurator was responsible.

Although many of the south-eastern elites led their tribes into collaboration with the Romans, there were many others who resisted the invaders (as, for example, the tribes in today's Wales). Very often maladministration was the cause of severe trouble. Boudic(c)a's revolt is a case in point. When Prasutagus, the king of the Iceni, died in AD 60, he bequeathed half of his kingdom to the Roman emperor, but the Roman administrators tried to grab the lot. When Prasutagus' widow, Boudic(c)a, protested, she was flogged, her two daughters were raped, and other nobles were mistreated. As the majority of the Roman legions were in Wales, Boudic(c)a's revolt was initially successful. She attacked, sacked and burned Colchester, London and St Albans; the total death toll was 70,000. When the Roman legions returned, they destroyed the British resisters, killing 80,000 people. Boudic(c)a is said to have killed herself. These events put back the development of the region for more than a decade.

The northern frontier was another trouble spot. Julius Agricola (40–93) became governor of Britain in 77 or 78. By the time he was recalled in 84 he had subdued a revolt in Wales, completed the conquest of the Brigantes, conquered the lowlands of Scotland and established forts there. Moreover, he had extended Roman occupation into the north of Scotland. According to Tacitus (his biographer and son-in-law), Agricola defeated a native army of some 30,000 Caledonians in a battle at Mons Graupius (perhaps in today's Aberdeenshire): 10,000 Caledonians and 360 Romans were killed. Paradoxically, Tacitus also related an 'anti-imperialist' speech of the Caledonian general Calcagus ('the Swordsman'), whose sentiments would find an echo in many later Scottish protests at English imperialist cravings:

> Here at the world's end, on its last inch of liberty, we have lived unmolested to this day, defended by our remoteness and obscurity. . . . But there are no other tribes to come; nothing but sea and cliffs and these more deadly Romans whose arrogance you cannot escape by obedience and self-restraint. Robbers of the world, now that the earth falls into their all-devastating hands, they probe even the sea; if their enemy have wealth they have greed . . . [neither] East nor West has glutted them. . . . To plunder, butcher, steal, these things they misname empire: they make a desolation and call it peace.

However, Agricola's success was not to last: within little more than two decades the army units in the north had fallen back to the Tyne–Solway isthmus. Here, following a military road (Stanegate), Hadrian's Wall was constructed in the 120s. The aim of the 73-mile-long wall was not so much to prevent raids from the north (which could only be achieved with substantial military forces) as to control the movement of people out of and into the province. A decade and a half later, another barrier further north with a length of 37 miles, the Antonine Wall on the Clyde–Forth isthmus, was constructed, but had to be given up again some twenty years later. From then on, Hadrian's Wall remained the northern frontier until the end of Roman(ised) Britain.

Roughly 10 per cent of the Roman army was based in Britain. This lent particular weight to the respective governors and induced some of them to contend for the throne of Roman emperor. This happened in AD 193 and, as a consequence, when Clodius Albinus, the governor of Britain, was eventually defeated by his competitor, Septimus Severus, the latter divided Britain into two provinces to avoid the concentration of all British legions under one governor. It happened again in the second half of the third century AD, when Britain was separated twice from the Roman Empire: in the 'Independent Empire of the Gauls' (259–73) and in a 'British' rebellion headed by two Roman military leaders (Carausius, 286–93, and Allectus, 293–6). When the latter was defeated and central government resumed, the Diocletian reforms saw to it that the two British provinces were replaced by four (subsequently five), grouped together in a *diocese* whose head, a *vicarious* (deputy) based in London, had to report to the central headquarters at Trier. And, although Constantine I (the Great), who was declared emperor by the army in York in AD 306, reintroduced unified control of the empire, fourth-century imperial politics was dominated by fragmentation: the 'Barbarian conspiracy' of AD 367, in which Picts, Attacotti and Scots attacked Britain, while Franks and Saxons attacked Gaul, although initially successful, was defeated, forts in the north and on the Saxon Shore were reorganised, and Roman order was restored. But thirty years later, in the intense struggles for supremacy after the death of Theodosius (395), the withdrawal of troops (needed elsewhere) and the breakdown of the administration (for want of economic means) signalled the beginning of the end of Roman Britain.

Economy, society, culture

Historians tend to agree that, in Roman times, Britain had as many people as in the Middle Ages at their peak: no fewer than 5 million. Four-fifths of the workforce was primarily engaged in food production, growing wheat, barley, oats and spelt (a wheat for livestock feed), but also crops like cabbages, peas, flax, celery, fennel and cucumber, and raising sheep, cattle and pigs. Those outside agriculture mined, roasted and smelted what mineral wealth there was (copper, tin and iron ore as well as a little gold and silver) or worked as small manufacturers (particularly in woollen textiles, rugs and capes) or traders. Already in pre-Roman times substantial surpluses were produced which encouraged, first, intertribal trade and, later, long-distance trading relations with tribes on the Continent. Roman occupation had at least a twofold impact on the British economy. On the one hand, the building of roads (originally constructed for the advancing armies) and towns (fundamental to Roman politics and culture) improved the ways and means of transport as well as the places of trade. On the other hand, the army was the biggest customer, always in need of food, clothes and other necessities of life for the soldiers; its demands gave an extraordinary boost to many branches of production. Although coinage had already been used in pre-Roman times, a satisfactory market economy may not have worked in the core region before the second century AD.

Although pre-Roman Britain had organised settlements, these could hardly be regarded as urban centres. However, increased contacts between the people in south-east Britain and the Romans (in Roman-occupied Gaul in particular), between Caesar's forays and Claudius' invasion, caused quite a number of transformations in the settlement areas and their social organisation: (i) trade expanded and with it the use of coinage, (ii) hill-forts were increasingly replaced by *oppida*, which were towns spread over larger areas and placed in positions advantageous for transport and communication (such as crossroads or river crossings as already indicated), (iii) smaller tribal units combined into larger ones ('early states'), dominated by powerful social elites and, increasingly, single rulers, (iv) these tribes practised shifting alliances amongst themselves and, later, with the Romans. When the Romans arrived in AD 43, they met a stratified society with a well-developed social and political structure supported in all probability by a system of tribute (which ensured that the ruling elites could live on the surpluses produced by their subordinates). This suited the Romans: they ruled indirectly through the cooperation of the local elites, who with the backing of the Romans retained and perhaps even increased their power and wealth. While the different types of cities were the centres of Roman government and administration, the countryside, at least in the core region (roughly, south and east of the Fosse Way), came to be organised around the *villa*s. These were houses in the country (built in Romanised style) at the centre of either industrial communities (e.g. producing pottery in the Nene valley) or working farms. Many of these villas were luxury houses or palaces (e.g. Fishbourne near Chichester) paid for by the agricultural surplus produced for the nearest towns.

Close to four hundred years of Roman influence decisively transformed the Celtic culture of the British Isles: while the core region experienced most of the change, in the more peripheral regions in the west and the north the impact was weaker. Roman influence in today's Scotland was only sporadic, and today's Ireland was not touched at all, if we discount trading relations (which existed). One important cultural change has already been mentioned: as no Celtic script existed, Latin and literacy went together. This also had consequences for the languages used in everyday communication: Latin was the language of the administration, the Vulgar Latin of common speech was spoken by the working population in the towns, while the rural peasantry continued to speak Celtic. Another change concerned religion: Romanised Briton was a religious kaleidoscope, which tolerantly comprised the formal rites of the official state religion (with Olympian gods such as Jupiter, Juno and Minerva), the imperial cult (which demanded sacrifices on behalf of living emperors and provided a unifying focus for loyalty to the empire), and a wide range of imported religions (such as Isis, Dionysus and Mithras cults) as well as local Celtic cults (mostly concerned with the placating of the forces of nature). Christianity probably arrived in Britain in the second century AD, but material evidence is hard to come by before the edicts of Milan (AD 313) and Arles (AD 314), which gave official toleration to Christians. (The Council of Arles was attended by the bishops of London, York and Colchester.) The chi-rho monogram representing the first two letters of 'Christ' in Greek was used for the first time by Constantine's soldiers in 312 (after he had seen a vision) and can also be found in British wall-paintings and mosaics. Third, the astonishing transformation of the physical environment with planned roads and street systems, new techniques of construction (in mortared stone and tile) and interior decoration (mosaic floors, painted plaster walls) made a vital impact, too. A fourth (and final) change affected the way of life: temples, amphitheatres, public places (forums) and town houses (not a few of them with indoor plumbing) were built and used: nobody in the British Isles was to enjoy anything remotely comparable to such a degree of hydraulic and sanitary convenience before the

Figure 3 The Christian chi-rho emblem © Copyright the Trustees of the British Museum

nineteenth century. The children of the elites obtained a Latin education, and Roman clothes and other 'civilised' allurements gained acceptance (Document 1). One of the most telling examples of Roman civilisation in the British Isles was the foundation of Aquae Sulis, today's Bath. The mineral springs in the Avon valley, which deliver almost a quarter of a million gallons of hot water (49°C) per day, attracted the Romans, who not only built a temple and dedicated it to Sulis Minerva, but also built a great bath. Perhaps it was this particular combination of the mundane (enjoying the warmth while cleaning one's body) and the sublime (purifying one's soul, being at one's devotions) which not only impressed contemporaries, but has also been a source of wonder since the demise of Roman civilisation.

2 Saxons, Danes and Normans, 410–1154

Four decisive processes were to shape the history of Western Europe in the second half of the first millennium AD: two distinct waves of migration, the growing differences between the western and the eastern halves of the Roman world, the continuing export of Christianity to non-Christian peoples, and the rise and expansion of Christianity's competitor, Islam. While many societies tried to evade, but eventually crumbled under, the pressures of the early waves of migrants (fourth and fifth centuries), others resisted the invaders before they realised the various advantages of integration. Quite often, conversions to Christianity sealed at least temporary understandings between the pagan invaders and the invaded Christians. Later waves of migration (eighth, ninth and tenth centuries) met with greater resistance, very often furthering the cooperation and eventual amalgamation of smaller social units, which then developed a complex but astonishingly resilient social, political and administrative structure (feudalism). In some cases, these processes were accompanied by (or, later, recalled in) narratives aimed at forging the people's identity (ethnogenesis).

ANGLES, JUTES AND SAXONS

Processes of migration have always been the outcome of complex situations. A certain 'push' factor (as, for example, local difficulties arising from recurring famine, war or overpopulation) may be complemented by the 'pull' factor of better living conditions elsewhere. Moreover, a certain 'shunting effect' may play a role: changes at one end of a chain of peoples may have their effect at the other end. As far as we know, a Hunnic Empire in Central Asia had been destroyed by the Chinese some thirty years BC. The Huns moved westward, basing themselves in what is today Turkestan. From there they conducted raids even further to the west, driving the (mostly Slavonic) peoples they met, robbed and raped before them. These, in turn, trying to evade the raiders,

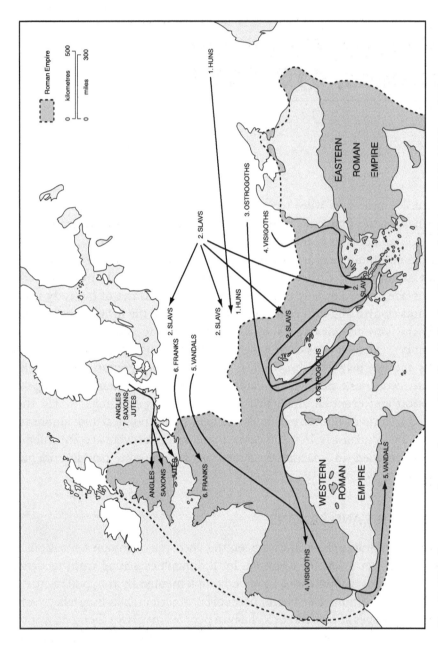

Map 7 Migrations across Europe from AD 400 after N. Davies, *Europe. A History* (OUP, 1996), p. 216

moved to the west. As a consequence, the Ostrogoths and the Visigoths, for example, moved across the Balkans to Rome (sacking it in 410), the Visigoths continuing to Spain; the Vandals migrated through the Roman dioceses of Gallia (Gaul) and Hispania to North Africa (reaching Carthage in 439), while the Franks moved into northern Gaul. Finally, the Angles, Jutes and Saxons moved from Denmark and the north of today's Germany along the Frisian coastline until they could safely cross the German Ocean (i.e. the North Sea) into Britain.

Migrants, invaders, settlers

With the demise of Rome's central authority an older political pattern began to reassert itself in the British Isles. The fundamental units both in Britain and in Ireland were petty kingdoms. Their power bases were warrior bands sustained by tribute and booty. As these warrior bands competed for wealth and power, they tried to defeat each other by forging temporary alliances not only amongst each other but also with foreign tribes. It is as good a guess as any that in this way Saxons were first invited to join the warriors of one Romano-British kingdom against its neighbouring enemies. Others arrived without invitation and in increasing numbers. As the Romans before them, these invaders came from the south and the east, penetrating deeply into those areas which had been intensely romanised before. Apparently, around 500 the westward movement of the invaders was checked by a decisive British victory at Mount Badon, the site of which cannot now be located but is thought to have been near Bath. This victory was associated with the resistance led by a certain Ambrosius Aurelianus, which gave the Britons more than a generation of peace. Moreover Nennius, the author of the very unreliable *Historia Brittonum* (c.800), refers to a *dux bellorum* ('a leader of battles') called Arthur, who may or may not have been the legendary king of the Round Table. However, the respite was short and did not lead to the expulsion of the invaders.

Although we cannot be sure if the Anglo-Saxon settlement of Britain was achieved by mass migrations and seizing of land, or by people who were warriors and settlers at the same time, or by the largely peaceful infiltrations of groups of families under the protection of either British or Anglo-Saxon chiefs (or by various combinations of all of these), we know that, as a result, three broad cultural zones came into existence: the British Isles came to be divided between (i) an English-speaking Anglo-Saxon east and (ii) a Celtic north and west, where the British (Brythonic or P-Celtic, ancestral to Welsh) and Pictish languages persisted, while in (iii) Ireland and certain small parts in western Britain (e.g. Cornwall) a different Celtic language (Goidelic or Q-Celtic, ancestral to Gaelic) was spoken. In contrast to developments on the Continent, Latin, despite its relevance as the language of scholarship, worship and law, did not become the basis of any of the vernaculars spoken in the islands. Moreover, in Britain, in

---

King Arthur (fl. sixth century)

Although Arthur is one of the most famous figures in British history, his actual existence remains in doubt. All that we can gather from historical records is that a great soldier, most probably of Romano-British origin, temporarily succeeded in stemming the tide of the advancing Anglo-Saxons. Arthur is mentioned in the *Gododdin* (a Welsh poem of *c.*600, supposedly written by Aneurin) and the not very reliable *History of the Britons*, attributed to the ninth-century Welsh scholar Nennius. The latter lists a dozen battles which Arthur supposedly won; but scholars have been unable to identify their sites, which appear to have been in England, Wales and Scotland. From the twelfth century onwards, there have been two different legends. On the one hand, there has been the Romano-British warrior with distinct Celtic features who fights the invading Anglo-Saxons and saves the oppressed Britons. This is the character created in Welsh poetry and Cornish oral traditions. On the other hand, there has been the figure of the ideal king of chivalry and courtly romance produced by Geoffrey of Monmouth in his fictional *History of the Kings of Britain* in the 1130s and embellished by the French writer Chrétien de Troyes in the 1170s and 1180s, who added the tale of the Holy Grail, of the Knights of the Round Table, and of Camelot as Arthur's capital. Although the popularity of the Arthurian legend declined in the early modern period, it was immortalised in English by Thomas Malory's *Morte Darthur*, which was completed in 1469–70 and printed by William Caxton in 1485. Malory retold the story as a tragedy which represented not only the climax but also the swan-song of the age of chivalry.

---

contrast to, for example, France, the Germanic and Celtic people did not mix. The Celts did not show any great solidarity amongst themselves, but the English surpassed them in their negative attitudes towards their neighbours.

The three – relatively reliable – sources which we possess describe the invasions from three different perspectives. St Gildas (*c.*493–570) was a Romano-British historian and monk whose tract *De Excidio Britanniae* (*On the Ruin/ Downfall of Britain*), written in the middle of the sixth century, recorded the invasions of the two preceding centuries. Gildas' narrative was prophetic rather than historical, his 'chosen people' were the Britons, and he regarded the invasions of the pagan Anglo-Saxons as a divine punishment, which the Britons deserved because their rulers had violated God's commands and neglected their calling. St Bede (672/3–735), also a monk, is usually regarded as the first English historian, not least because of his clear Anglo-Saxon focus. In his *Historia Ecclesiastica Gentis Anglorum* (*Ecclesiastical History of the English People*), finished in 731, the 'chosen people' were the Anglo-Saxon invaders who moved, as if by predestination, into Britain as their 'promised land'. And they sealed their material success with their conversion to Christianity. So, while Gildas tried to

---

St Bede ('the Venerable') (672/3–735)

Bede was given to Benedict Biscop, the founder and first abbot of the monastic community of Monkwearmouth and Jarrow, Northumbria, as a child oblate at the age of seven. He was educated by the monk Ceolfrith, who, in 688, succeeded to the abbotship of the community. Although Bede never travelled outside this area – he is known to have visited York and Lindisfarne – his breadth and depth of knowledge are astonishing. In addition to his most famous work – the *Ecclesiastical History of the English People* (completed in 731), which gained him the epithet 'Father of English History' – he contributed to biblical exegesis, science, homiletic writing, mathematics and moral criticism. His concerns were truly universal, and the quality of his scholarship places him above his contemporaries. Moreover, all his works aimed at encouraging people to imitate the moral examples of good men and to make the world a better place: 'For if history records good things of good men, the thoughtful hearer is encouraged to imitate what is good; or if it records evil of wicked men, the good, religious reader or listener is encouraged to avoid all that is sinful and perverse, and to follow what he knows to be good and pleasing to God.'

---

stem the tide of physical and spiritual defeat, Bede, who could already look back on more than a century of missionary activity in the Anglo-Saxon parts of Britain, virtually conjured up a new people (the English) and their spiritual identity. Finally, records of one kind or another of historical events were kept from the early days of Christian Anglo-Saxon England. Alfred the Great (849–99), king of Wessex (871–99), had many of these translated into vernacular Old English and brought together. They formed the *Anglo-Saxon Chronicle* and were continued in various places, in some until the twelfth century. There is no doubt that these different versions of the *Chronicle* were intended to provide (and, in fact, provided) additional legitimacy for a process which eventually resulted in the creation of one English kingdom.

Christianity

As already indicated in the previous chapter, Christianity arrived in Britain in the third century, but it suffered setbacks through revivals of heathenism and, more important, at the hands of the pagan Anglo-Saxon invaders. However, in Ireland and the western Celtic fringes of Britain, Christianity gained acceptance not only by the elites but also by the people. The idea of the withdrawal from the world (monasticism) was very important and, as a consequence, its practitioners, the monks, became the leaders of the Church. St Ninian (*c*.360–*c*.432) evangelised the Picts (Galloway), St Patrick (*c*.389–*c*.461) Ireland, and St David (*c*.530–*c*.589) Wales. St Columba (d. 597) worked in Ireland at first, founding the monasteries of Derry and, possibly, Durrow and Kells. Later he founded the monastery on Iona (563 or 565), an island on the western coast of today's Scotland (then Dalriada), which soon became the centre of Celtic Christianity. From Iona, St Aidan (d. 651) brought Christianity to Lindisfarne, a small island off the Northumbrian coast, which became another missionary centre of the north. The Book of Durrow (c.650), the Lindisfarne Gospels (early eighth century) and the Book of Kells (late eighth century) are the most impressive documents of this Celtic version of Christianity: lavishly illuminated and illustrated Latin texts of the Gospels which draw on a wide artistic repertoire from La Tène, the Mediterranean and the Germanic world. Another move to bring Christianity to the British Isles began in 597, when Roman missionaries under St Augustine (d. 604), sent by Pope Gregory I (590–604), arrived in Kent. Differences in administrative organisation as well as in details such as the date of Easter gave rise to disputes between the Celtic and Roman branches of the Church, which were eventually resolved at the Synod of Whitby (664), when Roman customs prevailed. Although it had been hoped that the resolution of these conflicts would produce a certain unity of the English church, this was not achieved before the primacy of Theodore of Tarsus (c.602–90), who was made archbishop of Canterbury in 669. In 672 he summoned the first synod of the whole English church and by the time of his death he had succeeded in creating an organised, united church.

Kingship

The origins of kingship in the different parts of the British Isles, which in due course became England, Wales, Scotland and Ireland, have some common characteristics, but they also differ decisively from each other. One common trait is that in the beginning, i.e. after the demise of the Romans and during the Anglo-Saxon invasions, the British Isles were a region of many kingdoms. In the Anglo-Saxon part of Britain, the leaders of the invading warrior bands became kings whose territories, however, were absorbed into seven somewhat larger kingdoms by the seventh century, the so-called Heptarchy: Kent, Wessex, Sussex, Essex, East Anglia, Mercia, Northumbria. These, in turn, as a complex result of internal competition and external pressure from the Scandinavian invaders, were transformed into three even larger kingdoms by the ninth century (Wessex, Mercia, Northumbria). The idea of a single kingdom of the English whose ruler could claim the title of *Bretwalda* ('overlord of Britannia') was developed in those days, although the term had been used as early as the seventh century. It was clearly envisaged by Alfred, king of Wessex (871–99), but could not be taken for granted before the reign of his great-grandson, Edgar (959–75). Similarly, the single kingdom of the Scots evolved from competitive struggles among smaller units. Reacting to a complex mixture of recurrent jostling for power within and amongst themselves, as well as to

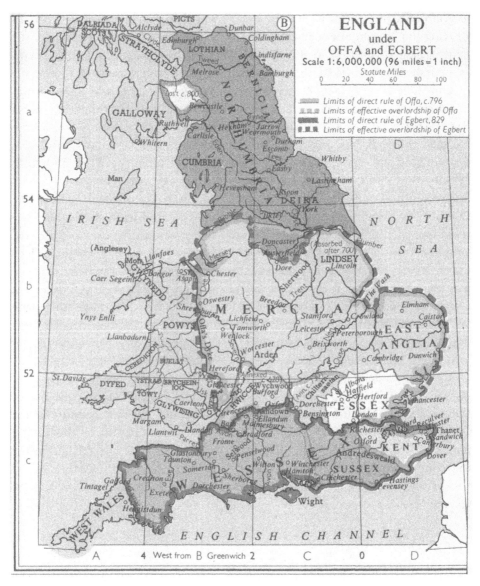

Map 8 England in 800 from R. F. Treharne and H. Fullard (eds) *Muir's Historical Atlas. Ancient Medieval and Modern* (1976), vol. II, p. 7

external pressure from the Scandinavians, who succeeded in making the Northern and Western Isles as well as the north of Scotland a part of their world, Dalriada (itself subdivided in three chief kindreds), Fortriu (i.e. Pictland) and Strathclyde were step by step transformed into the kingdom of Alba. This Gaelic word, originally applied to the larger one of the British Isles, 'Albionon', was used for Scotland in 900 for the first time. It was the overriding achievement of the mac Alpin dynasty from the middle of the ninth century onwards, not only to have its members accepted as undisputed kings, but also to ensure its continuity (if only for a century) by a power-sharing arrangement which, by rotating the kingship between the two branches of the family, kept them from fighting each other. Ireland also was a land of multiple kingdoms, with as many as a hundred before the ninth century. In fact, in Ireland, there were three types of king. The *rí* or *rí túaithe* was king of a single tribe; the *ruiri* ('great king', 'overking') was king of his own tribe as well as overlord of several other tribes and their tribal kings; the *rí ruirech* ('king of overkings') was king over a large area and above all these. By the eighth century, the lesser kingdoms were being downgraded while, over the next three centuries, the concept of the 'high king' or 'king of all Ireland' appeared. Although a number of rulers, particularly in the eleventh and twelfth centuries (such as Brian Boru, Máel Sechnaill II, Diarmit Mac Máel Mbó and Turloch O Brien), aspired to it, their status was temporary and did not lead to an ordered succession as, for example, in England or Scotland. The situation in Wales (a word of Anglo-Saxon origin, reflecting their word for 'foreigner') was roughly comparable to that in Ireland. It also had many kingdoms (the most powerful were Dyfed, Glywysing, Powys and Gwynedd), and this multiplicity survived until the eleventh and twelfth centuries, when the Normans invaded Wales. Although Wales also saw smaller kingdoms slowly coalesce into larger units, it did not really experience the rule of 'overkings'. Some kings (such as Rhodri Mawr, Hywel Dda and Llywelyn ap Gruffudd) may have enjoyed pre-eminence amongst their peers, but they did not succeed in securing it beyond their individual rule. Moreover, the rise of Wessex and its ambition to dominate all England put additional pressure on the Welsh rulers, who mostly acknowledged their subordination to their more powerful (English) neighbours. The title 'prince of Wales' was created in the thirteenth century, temporarily acknowledged by Henry III in the second half of the century, but seized by Edward I who conferred it on his son (cf. Chapter 3).

THE SCANDINAVIANS

Towards the end of the eighth century a second wave of migrants reached the British Isles. This time, they came from all sides: the Norwegians concentrated on Scotland, Ireland and north-west England, and the Danes on eastern and southern England. Once they ruled the Irish Sea, they also raided the Welsh coast. While it appeared in the beginning that their main interest was booty, which they could easily loot from unprotected monasteries (Lindisfarne was sacked in 793, Iona in 795) and ill-defended coastal settlements, later, when a Danish army had overwintered on Thanet (Kent) in 850, it became clear that they had come to stay. And stay they did, causing more of their kind to follow suit. In 865 a great raiding army invaded East Anglia, moved northward and captured York (867), turning it into one of their strongest settlements (Jorvik). On its return to East Anglia the army turned south-east, marching through

Essex and Kent into Wessex, where it was eventually stopped by Alfred, who ruled the only remaining Anglo-Saxon kingdom. In 878, Alfred, as his biographer Asser put it,

> gained the victory through God's will. He destroyed the Vikings with great slaughter, and pursued those who fled as far as the stronghold, hacking them down; he seized everything which he found outside the stronghold – men (whom he killed immediately), horses, and cattle – and boldly made camp in front of the gates of the Viking stronghold with all his army. When he had been there for fourteen days the Vikings, thoroughly terrified by hunger, cold and fear, and in the end by despair, sought peace.

Alfred (849–99), king of Wessex (871–99)

Alfred, the only 'English' monarch to be given the epithet 'the Great', became king of Wessex in 871, during a period of constant Viking attacks. When the Danes, who had already conquered Northumbria, Mercia and East Anglia, invaded Wessex, Alfred defeated them in a desperate last-stand at Edington (878). His opponent, Guthrum, king of the Vikings, had to make peace and to accept baptism. When Alfred won back London (886), all the Anglo-Saxons not subject to Danish rule submitted to him. He divided the army (*fyrd*) into two (home and away) to safeguard agriculture and defence, had ships built to establish a fleet, and, most important, established a network of some thirty *burhs* (fortified centres, such as Winchester) to protect Wessex from further invasions. Furthermore, Alfred issued a law code and sponsored learning and religious reform. He himself translated several Latin works into English (such as Pope Gregory's *Pastoral Care*, Boethius' *Consolation of Philosophy* and Augustine's *Soliloquies*) and had others translated by renowned scholars (such as Bede's *Ecclesiastical History of the English People*). As far as we know, Alfred possessed charisma and authority; and, while he undoubtedly had a genuine sense of duty and responsibility, he also reigned with a mixture of shrewdness and ruthlessness.

Although Alfred had to recognise a distinct legal and administrative system in the area settled by the Scandinavians north of the Thames (the 'Danelaw'), his successors were gradually able to re-establish their power over the Midlands and the North in the first half of the ninth century (Document 2), expelling the last Viking king of York, Eric Bloodaxe, in 954. Some twenty years later, however, another wave of widespread raids began, and this time the ultimate aim was political domination, which was eventually achieved when Cnut (or Canute) became king of England in 1016, of Denmark in 1019, and gained mastery of Norway in 1028. The House of Denmark ruled England until 1042 and gave it, at least until Cnut's death (1035), a period of substantial peace and prosperity. Thereafter the House of Wessex returned to the throne with

Edward the Confessor (*c*.1005–66), who was related to Cnut through his mother but had spent the years of Danish rule in exile in Normandy. Harold II, who succeeded Edward despite competing claims from William (i.e. Guillaume), duke of Normandy, and Edward's grandson Edgar, the Atheling (i.e. 'the prince'), repulsed the last Scandinavian bid for power in England by defeating Harold, king of Norway, at Stamford Bridge (just east of York) in 1066. Three days later, however, William of Normandy landed near Hastings. So, paradoxically, at the same time that the Scandinavian threat was eliminated, the English throne passed to a descendant of Scandinavians who had previously settled in Normandy.

The Scandinavian impact on Scotland was equally strong. As with England, where the Scandinavians indirectly contributed to its unification by destroying most of the rivals of the kings of Wessex, the Scandinavians also indirectly furthered the first stages of the evolution of Scotland. However, they also successfully colonised large parts of what today is Scotland's north and west, and controlled it for a long time: the Hebrides were held until 1266, the Orkney and Shetland islands until 1469. The first Viking raid on Ireland took place in 795, but the Scandinavian impact was largely confined to the coast, where settlements such as Dublin, Waterford, Cork and Limerick were established. As the Scandinavians were wide-ranging traders and soon dominated the Irish Sea, they gave a boost to the Irish economy. Wales remained relatively untouched, although it had its fair share of raids on coastal settlements. But, in contrast to the English and Gaelic languages, Welsh was not subject to any Scandinavian influence.

Historians still debate the causes for these migrations, which brought the Scandinavians not only to the British Isles but also as far as North America, the Mediterranean and, via the Baltic Sea and the Dnieper, the Black Sea. On the one hand, climatic and demographic changes, which made it increasingly difficult to feed a growing population, may have interacted with patterns of inheritance, which divided land to a point where the inherited land could not sustain the next generation any longer. On the other hand, technical improvements in ships and navigation as well as military strength may have encouraged the already successful Scandinavian traders to take advantage of military weakness in the British Isles and on the European continent (Francia). Undoubtedly, these invasions had far-reaching, if contradictory, consequences. By destroying most of the Anglo-Saxon and some of the Scottish kingdoms, the Scandinavians indirectly prepared their own downfall: the long and eventually successful struggle against them produced two dominant powers in Britain, the kingdoms of England and Scotland, whose degree of political centralisation clearly distinguished them from the fragmented local dynasties in Wales and Ireland. A careful look, however, at some elementary indications of statehood reveals essential differences. Scotland's development lagged behind that of England: the first English charters date from the early seventh century, while the first

Scottish charters were issued at the end of the eleventh century; coinage was issued in England during the eighth century, in Scotland four hundred years later; an episcopally organised church also developed much later in Scotland than in England (with the first name of a Scottish bishop mentioned at the beginning of the twelfth century).

The Scandinavians were not the only people on the move in Europe. The Hungarians (or Magyars, as they called themselves) arrived in the Danube basin around 900. From there, they raided Germany, Italy and southern Francia, but eventually retreated to Central Europe and settled down as farmers.

The Muslims spread with their faith – initiated by Muhammad (570–632) at the beginning of the seventh century – from Mecca and Medina eastwards and westwards: by the beginning of the eighth century, Islamic warriors could be found from Spain to India. Strikingly enough, Islam progressed seven times faster than Christianity, perhaps an apt demonstration of the fact that the Arab cultures in those days were far superior to those of Christian Europe. In 732 the Muslims were repulsed near Tours and Poitiers (in today's France), but in the ninth century they conquered Sicily and raided northern Italy as well as southern Francia. The rise of Islam had contradictory effects: the Ummayad/Abbasid empire in the Middle East (621–1258) and the Fatimids in North Africa (909–1171) virtually cut off Europe from the rest of the world, but also acted as bridges to it, across which an ever-increasing amount of goods, scientific and technological knowledge, as well as ideas, passed into Europe. Thus, while Islam turned Europe into Christianity's main base and, thereby, to a certain extent, turned Europe in on itself, the Europeans, at the same time, immensely benefited from the complex oriental network of trade and communication. Moreover, Islam gave a major stimulus to feudalism and, as a result, to European identity: by imagining themselves as 'Christendom' in contradistinction to the 'pagan infidels' of the Middle East, the Christian states developed political, administrative and ideological structures in opposition to the Islamic Other which enabled them to produce the necessary military clout, to meet its inevitable expense, and to create the religious fervour for a long struggle (see Chapter 3).

THE NORMANS

The year 1066 is easily the best remembered and, therefore, most famous date in British history. One could even say that 1066 is a metonym for British history as a whole. This requires an explanation. Was there anything particularly traumatic about the Norman Conquest and, if so, what was it? The battle near Hastings is reported to have been one of the longest in all medieval history. It was certainly bloody, and the Anglo-Saxons lost it, but it was not the first defeat the Anglo-Saxons had experienced. The greater part of the British Isles had been subjected to successive waves of invaders for a millennium, only half a century ago a Dane had occupied the Anglo-Saxon throne, and this was just another invasion – or was it? Historians have argued that for the majority of the population not much changed after the arrival of the Normans: the peasants tilled the soil, raised sheep and cattle, and paid taxes to their lords; small-scale producers followed their trades; and merchants traded within the islands and across the Channel on the European continent. Everyday life hardly changed at all. But, then, some real changes took place in the upper strata of English society (Document 3). When in 1086 the so-called Domesday Book, a quite comprehensive collection of data concerning the distribution of land and property throughout England, was put together on William's order it transpired that only four of the great landowners were of Anglo-Saxon origin, while the rest were Normans. All in all, more than 4000 thegns were dispossessed and replaced by fewer than 200 Norman barons. Those who survived were still Anglo-Saxons, but they were second-class citizens in a country which was no longer theirs. When the old families protested and, eventually, revolted against being shouldered aside by William's warrior and clerical following, William responded by 'harrying' them (i.e. sacking and pillaging their estates, villages and cities). These campaigns took him as far as Wales and lowland Scotland, and went on for six years. Much damage to the country was done by these operations, but William (i.e. Guillaume) was interested in ruling first and rebuilding second: he saw to it that his small but aggressive military Norman elite was evenly distributed throughout the country, with strong castles to defend themselves against potential aggressors. So the Norman Conquest implied the imposition of a new royal family, a new culture, a new language (Norman French) and, most important, a new ruling class.

Perhaps we have to imagine the situation in this way. After centuries of invasions, one particular group – the English (as we can now call the former Anglo-Saxons) – had succeeded in forging some kind of territorial and, at the same time, some kind of proto-national identity for themselves. First and foremost, this was the work of their social, political and cultural elites. When the English ruling stratum was replaced by the Norman elite, this had a number of decisive consequences: socially, a greater emphasis on the obligations of (English) subjects towards their (Norman) lords tightened the social hierarchy; politically, in the domestic scene the control from the centre (the king's court and government) increased, and internationally a shift away from close relations with Scandinavia towards a growing involvement in Continental affairs took place; culturally, Anglo-Saxon was replaced by Norman French as the language of the ruling class, a process which was not reversed before the fourteenth century.

Perhaps processes like these *were* quite normal in those days and not anything extraordinary. But, then, 1066 is the date of the last extensive invasion of the British Isles. Of course, people in those days could not know that and, as a consequence, for some of them (the elites) 1066 may have been important,

---

The Norman yoke

This is essentially a political term which emerged for the first time in the mid-seventeenth century. It holds that the democratic, freedom-loving Anglo-Saxon society was destroyed by the Norman Conquest. The story, according to the historian Christopher Hill, was constructed along the following lines: 'Before 1066 the Anglo-Saxon inhabitants of this country lived as free and equal citizens, governing themselves through representative institutions. The Norman Conquest deprived them of this liberty, and established the tyranny of an alien King and landlords. But the people did not forget the rights they had lost. They fought continuously to recover them, with varying success. Concessions (Magna Carta for instance) were from time to time extorted from their rulers, and always the tradition of lost Anglo-Saxon freedom was a stimulus to ever more insistent demands upon the successors of the Norman usurpers.' The importance of this narrative lies not so much in its relation to the historical truth but in the use that has been made of it over the centuries by groups of people criticising their oppressors. The most famous example is that of the Levellers in the Wars of the Three Kingdoms (see Chapter 4).

---

while for many of them (the ordinary people) it may have been of little consequence. But it may be worth reflecting that the date has also acquired its importance in later centuries through the fact that, although some invasions of the British Isles were planned (and very few attempted) by, for example, the French and the Germans, none of these was successful. In this way, 1066 may be a good example for the thesis that history is not (or, at least, not only) 'what really happened', but a reconstruction of the past in the present, and that the significance of a historical event is produced by historians of all kinds.

Lords, vassals, serfs

While Muslim and Byzantine rulers based their power on mercenaries and salaried officials, their Western counterparts ruled by ensuring personal loyalty. Society was structured like a pyramid, with the king at the top and the peasants at the bottom. On each level of this pyramid everyone had rights and obligations, although there were few obligations at the top and few rights at the bottom. Everyone was bound to perform certain duties for the man above him and in return was protected by him. The system was based on the holding of land, all of which belonged to the king. He gave it to his vassals on condition that they, in return, recognised his supremacy and, if necessary, fought for him (either personally or by supplying soldiers). In Anglo-Saxon times these vassals were called thegns; under Norman rule, they were called barons. They had to pay 'homage' to their lord, i.e. they had to declare openly to be 'his men', and they also had to promise 'fealty' (fidelity, trust, service), taking an oath on the

Bible. The period of active service depended on the amount of land the vassal held: usually it was forty days for every fief (or 'fee'). Life in this overwhelmingly rural society revolved around the manor, a self-contained and self-supporting farm. The lord of the manor received some or all of his income from the sale of farm produce, but the actual work was done by peasants – 'serfs' or 'villeins' – who were dependent on him, almost like slaves. A serf had to work on the lord's demesne. In return he was allowed to live in a cottage on the manor and to work on a portion of the common land allotted to him and, thereby, support himself and his family. In return for the use of the land and the cottage the serf had to pay certain dues and tithes ('tenths') as well as perform his labour service. Moreover, neither he nor his family was allowed to leave the manor without their lord's permission.

More generally speaking, the social, political and cultural life in Western Europe came to be dominated by – greater and lesser – landowners, who regarded themselves as regional military leaders (magnates) with a clear perception of their relative position in the social hierarchy. It was based on the belief that God had assigned three tasks to mankind: these were to pray for salvation (allotted to priests and bishops), to fight and protect (allotted to the knights and nobles), and to work in order to provide for the support of the first two groups (allotted to the peasants). These magnates shared a common lifestyle centred on their manor-houses. As the Anglo-Saxon word for 'to build' – *timbran* – indicates, most of them were built in timber. Initially, their great halls served as places not only for meeting, eating and feasting, but also for sleeping. In the course of the centuries, manor-houses became more sophisticated and followed the general trend to greater privacy (and, as a consequence, greater architectural subdivision).

In a social system based on the possession of land, the question of inheritance was of vital importance. As long as it sufficed, if the land was large enough to feed a family, it seemed proper to practise partible inheritance (i.e. give land to all children, including the daughters). When, however, the amount of land also came to imply the relative power of its owner (and his family), it seemed wiser to give the family inheritance only to one child, the oldest son ('primogeniture') or the youngest ('ultimogeniture'). More generally, the importance of the family (or, rather, the clan) grew as well. Marriages had always been political, but they became even more so as the number of kingdoms decreased while their territories increased (as we have seen in the cases of England and Scotland).

Repercussions, at home and abroad

While Norman rule did not reach Ireland before the second half of the twelfth century, and was only piecemeal and temporarily successful in Wales before the second half of the thirteenth century, Scotland (Alba) came to feel the fallout of the invasion immediately. For one thing, many Anglo-Saxon nobles found refuge at the court of the king of Scotland, Malcolm III 'Canmore' (Mael Coluim mac Donnchada, 1057–93), who in 1072 took the West Saxon princess Margaret, sister of Edgar, 'the Atheling', as his second wife. This clearly worried William, who rightly suspected that Malcolm would support the rebellious nobles in the north of England. However, William did not try to conquer Scotland but was satisfied with establishing a loose overlordship: at Abernethy in 1072, Malcolm became William's vassal and handed over his eldest son, Duncan, as a hostage. But this did not mean that peace prevailed. Seven years later, Malcolm invaded England, and William had to send troops north to re-establish and secure the frontier. When Malcolm died in 1093, William's successor in England, William II Rufus ('the Red'), intervened on behalf of Malcolm's Normanised sons Duncan (in 1094) and Edgar (in 1097) to secure his overlordship. Edgar (1097–1107), in turn, was followed by his brothers, Alexander (1107–24) and David (1124–53), who both opened Scotland to Norman political and cultural influence.

As long as the Normans ruled, they suffered from disputed successions. On William's death (1087) Normandy fell to his elder son, Robert, and England to the younger, William II, as intended by their father. However, this created a problem for magnates who possessed estates on both sides of the Channel because they found it difficult to serve two masters. This problem was temporarily solved when Rufus acquired Normandy from his brother, who went on a Crusade in 1095 but reappeared on Rufus' death, when a third brother, Henry (i.e. Henri Beauclerc), had himself made king (1100–35). When Robert eventually returned from the Crusade, he retook Normandy and invaded England in 1101. Although the two brothers eventually compromised, their agreement did not last. In 1106, Henry defeated Robert, imprisoned him and reunited Normandy and England. But Henry I also faced a succession problem: he had married the daughter of Malcolm and Margaret (of Scotland), but his only legitimate son was drowned in 1120, so that his only daughter, Matilda, was his heir. Henry's death in 1135 was followed by a prolonged civil war which saw, at times, two rival courts in England, and was only resolved when Henry's nephew, Stephen of Blois (i.e. Etienne de Blois, 1135–54), who had successfully repulsed Matilda's claim to the throne, eventually acknowledged her son, Henry of Anjou (i.e. Henri FitzEmpress Plantagenet), as his heir.

3 Late-medieval struggles: within the British Isles and on the Continent, 1154–1485

From the early twelfth century onwards, the Europeans began to flex their muscles. First, they improved their economy. In agriculture, they brought new land into cultivation by felling trees, clearing land, draining marshes and setting up dykes; they also improved working conditions by using iron ploughs drawn by heavy horses; and they raised wider varieties of crops and obtained greater yields by introducing the three-field system (Document 4). The increasing productivity of the countryside led to an improvement in people's health and fertility. Although this implied the feeding of a growing population, the surprisingly great surpluses from agriculture easily contributed to the growth of old and new urban centres. These towns (and, later, cities) developed around castles and monasteries where artisans set up shop and merchants came to trade their goods (Document 5). Second, the Europeans reorganised their Catholic church (with an emphasis on spiritual and worldly hierarchy and power) and created new forms of religious life (particularly through the creation of the new orders of mendicant friars, who did not live in secluded monasteries but preached the gospel in public). Third, they expanded their intellectual horizons (by, for example, rediscovering Roman law and Greek philosophy, and translating Arabic works on science and philosophy) as well as their geographical frontiers, waging war in the East (Prussia, Lithuania), the Near East (the Crusades to the Holy Land) and Spain (Reconquista). The reasons for this expansion of Europe were fourfold: (i) Europe's major military enemies (Vikings, Central Eurasians, Muslims and Slavs) were either in decline or appeared vulnerable, while (ii) European political policy-making was dominated by feudal aristocracies, who saw their legitimate occupation as the expansion of Christendom and the exercise of martial values. (iii) Economic success and a growing population provided the resources for military campaigns, while (iv) the Catholic faith provided their ideological impetus.

Against this background, five major political developments occurred in Western Europe which heavily involved the British Isles. The first has already been mentioned in the last chapter: William (in fact, Guillaume), duke of Normandy, conquered England in 1066, replaced its Anglo-Saxon aristocracy by a Norman elite and thereby ensured that the political and cultural ties of England ('Angleterre') to the Continent (and France in particular) became very close over the next four centuries. Second, the Angevin/Plantagenet royal dynasty (1154–1399) created an increasingly powerful monarchy which, third, quickly succeeded in exercising its hegemony within the British Isles to such an extent that in 1171 the Irish, in 1174 the Scots and in 1177 the Welsh recognised the ultimate authority of the king of England. Fourth, as dukes of Normandy and counts of Anjou, the Plantagenet kings of England were vassals of the king of France – and France was the senior kingdom in the medieval hierarchy. To counterbalance this tie of subordination, they tried to expand their sphere of influence on the Continent and to unite the crowns of France and England. Both strategies failed after centuries of costly struggle. Finally, waging wars was expensive. As the coffers of the monarchs were usually not sufficiently filled, money had to be collected to finance the wars. As a consequence, the monarchs had to persuade their subjects, high and low, to pay taxes. However, whoever paid taxes wanted to have a say in how (when, where and for what reason) the money was spent. From this conflict slowly, but distinctly, early forms of representational government developed.

POLITICAL STRUGGLES IN THE ISLES, 1154–1272

Henry II, king of England, duke of Normandy, count of Anjou and duke of Aquitaine, spent only thirteen (out of thirty-four) years in England, where he sought to consolidate what had disintegrated under his predecessor Stephen (i.e. Etienne de Blois). He not only re-established a stable government after two decades of civil war, but also improved it in such a way that it could work when the ruler was absent, by delegating authority to one or more chief justiciars (viceroys or regents). He also reformed both civil and criminal law, making the king's law truly national in scope. Finally, while he succeeded, by a mixture of carrot and stick, in winning the consent and cooperation of the greater magnates of the realm, he had a great conflict with the Church (Thomas Becket). However, although the Angevin 'empire' was held together by a capable ruler, it did not rest on any institutional unity. After Henry's death it was doomed to fall apart into its constituent elements. Moreover, Henry had very ambitious sons, who did not shy away from staging a family rebellion against their father (with the help of their mother, Eleanor of Aquitaine, and the French king, Louis VII) in 1173. Although he could put down the rebellion, the final years of his reign were less successful. He was succeeded by Richard I ('the Lionheart', 1189–99), a warrior with charisma, who spent no more than six months in Britain but kept Henry's 'empire' intact. Under his brother John, alternatively nicknamed 'Softsword' and 'Lackland' (i.e. Jean Sans Terre, 1199–1216), the

The Norman and Angevin Kings of England

Kings of France and England and the Dukes of Burgundy during the Hundred Years' War

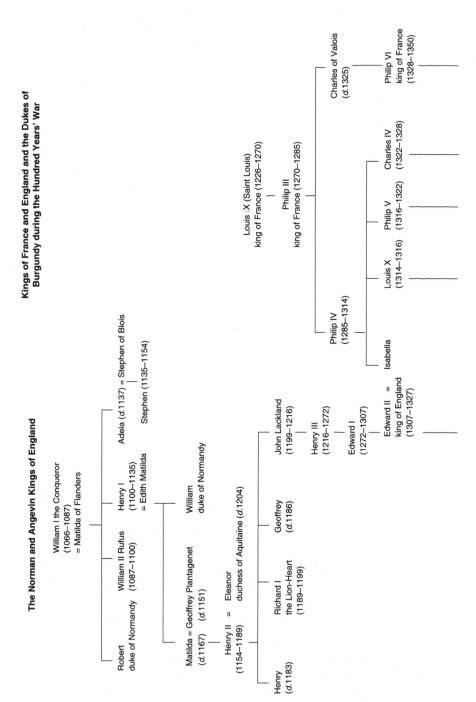

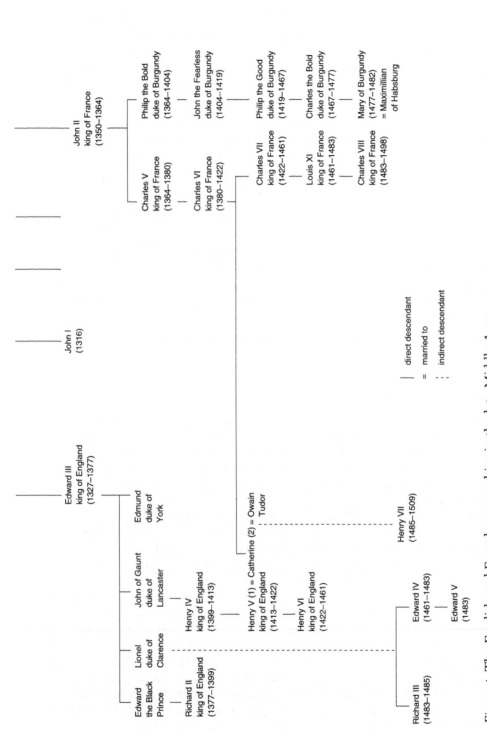

Figure 4 The English and French monarchies in the late Middle Ages

Angevin 'empire' collapsed: by the time of his death, all of the Angevins' Continental lands (except Gascony) had been lost, while England itself had been briefly invaded by the French. It has been said that John had a genius for making enemies: he trusted no one, no one trusted him, and he bled his subjects dry (Robin Hood). Eventually, the opposing magnates produced a document, Magna Carta, in which they noted specific limitations of royal rights with the implication that 'good government' depended on agreed rules observed by everyone including the king (Document 6). What may be memorable about John is that he was the first king of England since Harold II to be born and to die in England. His son, Henry III (1216–72), succeeded him at the age of nine, beginning his personal rule in 1232. Henry was a very cultured person, who loved display and ceremony and, by using them extensively, may have tried to emphasise the aura of kingship *vis-à-vis* the growth of constitutional ideas. Moreover, by becoming embroiled in high-flown, but eventually costly and unsuccessful, plans for recovering those parts of the Angevin 'empire' lost under John and expanding it into Sicily and the east Mediterranean, he alienated his barons who, in the Provisions of Oxford (1258) and of Westminster (1259), tried to limit royal authority and to make him listen to their opinions. In the ensuing civil war (of 1264–8) Simon de Montfort

---

The Angevin / Plantagenet royal dynasty

The term 'Angevin empire' has been used by historians to describe the lands held (or claimed) by the family of the counts of Anjou, most notably by Henry (i.e. Henri) II (1154–89) and his immediate successors Richard I 'the Lionheart' (i.e. 'Cœur de Lion') (1189–99) and John (Jean, 1199–1216). Henry brought together under his rule three inheritances: (i) the former Anglo-Norman realm (i.e. the duchy of Normandy and the kingdom of England) from his mother Matilda, (ii) the counties of Anjou (hence *Angevin*), Maine and Touraine from his father Geoffrey of Anjou, and (iii) Aquitaine (with its core in Poitou and Gascony) through his marriage to Eleanor (Aliénor) of Aquitaine (1152). Eleanor (c.1122–1204) was perhaps the most powerful woman of twelfth-century Europe: she married Louis VII, the king of France in 1137, went with him on the Second Crusade, and after the annulment of their marriage in 1152 married Henry. In the 1160s she turned her court at Poitiers into a model of courtly love and culture visited by the most famous troubadours of the time.

   If one includes the territories over which the counts of Anjou claimed suzerainty, the Angevin empire covered a vast territory stretching from Scotland to the Pyrenees, making the family the most powerful dynasty in Europe at the time. The (nick-)name 'Plantagenet' (derived from the *Planta genesta*, or sprig of broom, which Geoffrey of Anjou is supposed to have liked) has traditionally been attributed to the second group of Angevin kings: Henry III (1216–72), Edward I (1272–1307), Edward II (1307–27), Edward III (1327–77) and Richard II (1377–99).

St Thomas Becket (?1120–70), Archbishop of Canterbury

Born of Norman parents, Thomas Becket worked as accounts clerk to a banker before entering the service of Archbishop Theobald of Canterbury in 1145. Impressed by his wide range of talents, Theobald appointed him Archdeacon of Canterbury in 1154. In the following year he attracted Henry II's attention, was appointed Chancellor, and proved to be a competent and, more important, a loyal administrator. Because of this, Henry, on Theobald's death in 1161, decided to make Becket the latter's successor. Although the Canterbury tradition required that the archbishop should be a monk, the monks of Canterbury Cathedral Priory dutifully elected the king's favourite servant. But with the new office Thomas also seemed to have acquired a new frame of mind. His steady loyalty to the king was replaced by constant opposition. In less than a year Henry and Thomas were open enemies. The most controversial issue between them was the king's wish to end the 'benefit of clergy' (by which clergy could be tried only in ecclesiastical courts, which, for example, could not impose the death penalty) and to bring the clergy under the jurisdiction of secular courts. When Henry formulated what he regarded as his customary rights over the English church in the Constitution of Clarendon, Becket at first reluctantly accepted it but then tried to wriggle out of his commitment. In response to this, the king asked him to account for all the money he had administered during his chancellorship. Realising that the king was determined to break him, Becket fled into exile in France, where he remained for almost six years. Louis VII of France and Pope Alexander III unsuccessfully urged a reconciliation. The coronation of Henry the Young King (in 1170) broke the stalemate: Henry had asked the Archbishop of York to do the crowning, but as Becket thought that crowning the king was a Canterbury privilege he came to terms with Henry. However, after his return he excommunicated all his enemies, especially the Archbishop of York and the bishops of London and Salisbury. Their complaint to the king prompted Henry's angry reaction ('Will no one rid me of this turbulent priest?'). Four of the king's knights took this literally and murdered Becket brutally in his own cathedral. The shock in the Christian community was tremendous, and Henry did public penance at the archbishop's tomb. Only two years later Becket was canonised, and his tomb became a place of pilgrimage – famously immortalised by Geoffrey Chaucer in his *Canterbury Tales*.

(1208–65) was the leader of the baronial opposition. He won the battle of Lewes (in May 1264), capturing both the king and the heir to the throne (the future Edward I); and, because of this, became *de facto* ruler of the country. In order to legitimise his regime he summoned knights and burgesses to a parliament in January 1265. This is why, almost immediately after his death at the battle of Evesham (in August 1265), he was regarded (by his supporters) as a champion of liberty (attracting pilgrims to his grave) and why, particularly since the nineteenth century, he has been regarded as the founder of the House of

Robin Hood, Outlaw

Robin Hood, one of the archetypal heroes of modern folk-mythology, has been famous for robbing the rich and giving to the poor as well as for fighting injustice and tyranny. The facts behind the legend are uncertain. All attempts to identify him, his 'merry men' and his arch-enemy, the Sheriff of Nottingham, have been unsuccessful, but stories about his adventures have been told for over six hundred years. Robin Hood's first appearance by name was as early as 1377, in William Langland's poem *The Vision of William concerning Piers Plowman*. The oldest ballad giving a detailed history of Robin Hood dates from 1495: 'Lythe and listin, gentilmen, / That be of frebore blode; / I shall you tel of a gode yeman, / His name was Robyn Hode' (*A Lytell Geste of Robyn Hode*). By 1600, over two hundred references to Robin Hood already existed. Over time, his social status has varied. While he was a yeoman in the earliest sources, by the sixteenth century he had acquired noble status. The idea, however, that he fought with the Anglo-Saxons against the Normans was first voiced in Sir Walter Scott's *Ivanhoe* (1819).

Magna Carta ('Great Charter') (1215, 1216, 1217, 1225)

Magna Carta is one of the most important documents in British history. Its first version (of 1215) redefined many feudal practices, after King John's disastrous foreign policy and what was regarded as his arbitrary rule had produced violent opposition from his barons. As it put constitutional restraints on royal power, John tried to ignore it. For the barons, however, this document was indispensable, because they felt that the royal administration had attacked their traditional rights for too long. Consequently, they demanded that John's successor, Henry III, confirm the charter.

The most famous clauses of Magna Carta guaranteed that (i) no freeman could be taken, imprisoned, outlawed, exiled 'or any otherwise destroyed' nor could he be condemned 'save by the lawful judgement of his equals or by the law of the land'; (ii) the church of England was to have 'all her whole rights and liberties inviolable'; (iii) the power of the sheriffs was restricted; and (iv) the liberties of the boroughs were confirmed. A council of 25 barons was set up to enforce the charter.

Although in the beginning Magna Carta was no more than a document of feudal conflict between the king and his barons, its significance changed over the centuries and it came to be regarded as a milestone in British constitutional history. (Document 6)

Commons. However, his motives may have been more mixed, perhaps combining a soldier's bravery with a magnate's lust for power, wealth and influence.

The conquest of Ireland, briefly contemplated in 1155, began twelve years later, when an exiled tyrannical Irish chief, Dermot MacMurrough, asked

Henry II to help him restore his kingdom of Leinster. All he got was a letter in which Henry called on his liegemen to assist him if they so wished. A Norman baron from Wales, Richard fitzGilbert de Clare (later known as 'Strongbow'), dispossessed of his lands by royal decree, jumped at the chance to make good his loss and offered MacMurrough a deal: if he and his men helped MacMurrough to recover his kingdom, he would be given the Irish chief's daughter, Aífe, in marriage. Late in 1167, MacMurrough sailed for Ireland with a group of Norman mercenaries. They were followed in May 1169 by a larger contingent and, in May 1170, by Strongbow himself and his army. In the autumn of 1170 the Normans held Dublin. Strongbow married Aífe and, when MacMurrough died a year later, he had himself proclaimed king of Leinster (which was contrary to Irish law, but legal in English practice). Henry II, in turn, did not like Strongbow's success because (he thought) he could not allow him to carve out a kingdom for himself across the sea, which he might use as a basis for the recovery of his forfeited Welsh lands. So Henry II went to Ireland in person, stayed for six months, and saw to it that all the lesser Irish kings and bishops submitted to him. In May 1177, Henry awarded 'the lordship of Ireland' to his youngest son, John (i.e. Jean). When, against all expectations, John became king of England in 1199, the lordship of Ireland was fused with the kingdom of England.

Scotland had survived 1066 intact, but the Anglo-Norman kings had established some kind of lordship over it and had repeatedly intervened on behalf of suitably Normanised claimants to the Scottish throne (Chapter 2). This did not prevent David I (1124–53), who combined Celtic and Norman traditions to form a strong Scottish monarchy, from profiting from Stephen's turbulent reign by overrunning northern England (1141). But when his successor, Malcolm IV (1153–65), in turn became embroiled in internal Scottish conflicts, Henry II recovered Cumberland and Westmoreland (1157). William I, 'the Lion' (i.e. Guillaume le Lion, the most Anglo-Norman of the Scottish kings, 1165–1214), who had signed the first formal treaty between Scotland and France in 1168 (the beginning of what was later called 'the Auld Alliance'), tried to regain what had been lost, but he was defeated, captured and humiliated. In the Treaty of Falaise (1174) he vowed homage to Henry II 'for Scotland and for all his other lands'. Although the terms of this treaty were abrogated in 1189 by a formal quit-claim (which cost the Scots 10,000 marks – money Richard I needed for the Third Crusade), it cannot be denied that a certain (albeit shifting) overlordship was exercised by the English monarchs over the Scottish kings. (And, if it was disputed, its claim was repeated over the next four centuries: by Edward I in the 1290s, Edward III in the 1330s, Edward IV in the 1480s, and Henry VIII in both 1512–13 and the 1540s.) The nature and scope of this suzerainty, however, should not be overestimated: it was similar to that which the French kings wielded over the kings of England on the Continent.

The situation in Wales was much less clear. The Welsh princes could hold their own without much difficulty, but could not oppose the Anglo-Normans directly, which is why they worked with shifting alliances. In 1157, Henry II succeeded in obtaining the main Welsh princes' oaths of allegiance; eight years later he suffered a crushing defeat at their hands, but on his third visit, in 1177, his overlordship was again acknowledged. The most powerful Welsh prince of that age was Llewellyn the Great (i.e. Llewellyn ap Iowerth, 1194–1240), who cooperated with the Plantagenets (so that he could more easily claim lordship over the lesser Welsh princes) but joined the baronial opposition to John (in 1215) so that he could decisively influence the Welsh clauses of Magna Carta.

POLITICAL STRUGGLES ON THE CONTINENT AND IN THE HOLY LAND

As already indicated above, from the beginning of the twelfth century onwards, the Europeans extended their geographical frontiers. Aiming at the conversion of the Slavic and Baltic pagan peoples, the military-monastic order of the Swordbrothers (founded in 1204 and later a branch of the Teutonic Knights) expanded into eastern Europe (today's Poland, Lithuania and Estonia) and colonised the region with German-speaking people who brought their cultural institutions and practices (such as feudal laws, social structures and Catholic religion) with them. Furthermore, the Spanish peninsula was slowly being regained by the Christians from the Muslim invaders. This recovery eventually resulted in the creation of the kingdoms of Aragon-Catalonia and León-Castile (which together eventually formed Spain) and Portugal, and the development of a strong, militant Christian mentality which, later, was to shape ideas and attitudes of the conquistadores in the Americas, Asia and Africa.

Finally, mixing pilgrimage and holy war, in the Crusades to the Near East the Europeans followed (and sometimes combined) various aims: to recapture the Holy Land from the Muslims, who had taken Jerusalem and the shrine of the Holy Sepulchre in 638, to safeguard Christian pilgrimages, to win material gain, to look for chivalrous adventures and, it was hoped, to bring about the reunification of the Eastern (Orthodox) and Western (Roman Catholic) churches, based in Constantinople and Rome respectively, which had separated in 1054 over issues of doctrine, liturgy, and ecclesiastical administration and jurisdiction. The Crusades began when Alexius I Comnenus, emperor of Constantinople, asked the Christian West to help repel the invading Seljuk Turks and, in response, Pope Urban II proclaimed the First Crusade in 1095. The Crusades lasted for two centuries and were, at least in the beginning, real mass movements comprising not only the cream of the feudal lords of western Europe as well as their knights and soldiers, but also common men, women and children. The First Crusade (1096–9), in which, incidentally, Robert, the eldest son of William the Conqueror, took part, was the most successful, wresting the Holy Land from the Muslims and setting up Christian kingdoms

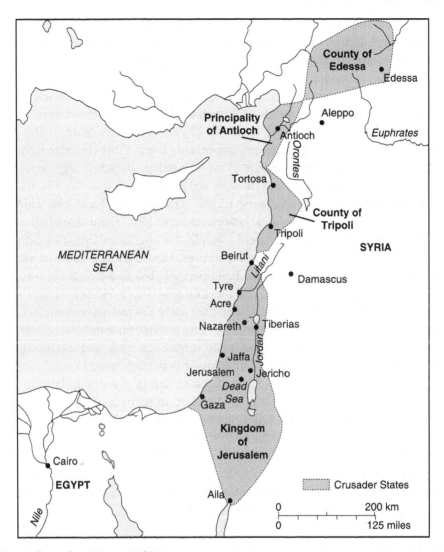

Map 9 Crusader states *c.*1100

there. However, it was also in the run-up to this crusade that anti-Jewish pogroms of hitherto unknown violence were perpetrated and nearly wiped out the
Jewish communities of Speyer (Spires), Mainz and Worms (in today's Germany). Thus, while the Crusades allegedly contributed to a more Christian
image of the knight, they certainly also demonstrated its darker features:
deadly intolerance not only of Muslims but also of *any* non-Christian people.
As was to be expected, the First Crusade provoked Muslim reconquests. These,
in turn, led to the Second Crusade (1147–9), which, however, could not regain
what had previously been lost. With their third attempt (1189–92) the
Crusaders, led by Richard I ('the Lionheart'), Frederick I Barbarossa (the Holy
Roman Emperor) and Philip II Augustus (of France), hoped to retake Jerusalem

from Saladin, sultan of Egypt and Syria. Frederick drowned before he reached the Holy Land, Philip and Richard besieged and took Acre, but failed to liberate Jerusalem. However, Richard's negotiations with Saladin ensured the survival of the crusader states for another century. Four more Crusades followed (1202–4, 1217–21, 1248–54 and 1270–5), not to speak of the Children's Crusade (1212) and Emperor Frederick II's (1228–9). Interestingly, not all of them were fought against the Muslims: some were aimed at Christian heretics (such as the Albigenses in southern France). More important, during the Fourth Crusade, Constantinople was sacked, whereby the Crusaders paradoxically weakened the most effective barrier against Islam in the East.

The results of the Crusades were mixed. Those to the Near East failed to achieve their religious and political objectives – the Holy Land remained under Muslim control into the modern era – while the Northern Crusades into the Baltic region were successful colonial ventures. Moreover, the eventual victory of the Muslims (in 1291) on the one hand partially blocked European overland trade to the East and thereby forced the Europeans to seek new routes – sea routes – to India and the Far East. When they were discovered, Britain, because of its maritime location, was excellently placed for an ever-expanding trade. On the other hand, however, the Crusades had stimulated trade and the transfer of knowledge between East and West, enabling Italian merchants from Venice (as, for example, Marco Polo [1254–1324]), Pisa and Genoa to enter and profit from the larger Muslim trading networks so that they, in turn, could take the lead in Europe's future development. Often Franciscan or Dominican friars followed or accompanied European merchants to Iran, Inner Asia and China to establish missions and preach Christianity. While the number of converts was limited, Europe benefited immensely from the philosophical, scientific and technological knowledge these missionaries conveyed in their detailed accounts of what they could not but regard as admirable civilisations.

POLITICAL STRUGGLES IN THE ISLES, 1272–1485

Most historians agree that Edward I (1272–1307) was an outstanding king. In his domestic policy he focused on three areas. First, he codified much of the legal machinery set up by Henry II by introducing statute law, a new type of law (in fact, legislation passed by the king in Parliament) which took precedence over all other laws. Second, he appreciated the necessity of an institution in which the king and a group of invited officials and influential subjects could meet to discuss matters of policy and taxation. Under Edward and his successors, in this institution which was to become the national parliament, knights from the shires and burgesses from the boroughs were increasingly invited to complement the great lords of the realm. The parliament of 1295 became the model for the ensuing centuries, requiring all forty counties and 114 chartered boroughs to send two representatives each. This representative principle above all

Parliament

Monarchs, in order to be able to rule successfully, were in need of advice, information and, most important, money. Moreover, as not all of their subjects (high or low) usually agreed with their rule, they also needed ways and means of dealing with complaints and petitions. From these needs the uses of Parliament sprang.

In England it can be traced back to the Saxon *witenagemot* (meeting of counsellors) and the Norman councils. The latter initially consisted of two bodies: the great council and the king's council. While the former was a meeting of the tenants-in-chief, the great barons and prelates, and largely advisory in nature, the latter (*curia regis*) consisted of household officers responsible for day-to-day administration. From the great council the House of Lords developed; the king's council split into more specialised bodies such as, for example, the Star Chamber (concentrating on judicial work) and the Privy Council which dealt with day-to-day business.

Money or, rather, the lack of it, was the driving force in the evolution of Parliament. While in the early Middle Ages monarchs were expected to 'live of their own', i.e. on revenues from their own (or crown) lands, in the high and late Middle Ages almost permanent warfare and its constantly rising costs made an ever-increasing taxation of the king's (or queen's) subjects unavoidable. Edward I's reign (1272–1307) is a graphic example: within the Isles Edward tried (largely successfully) to subjugate Ireland, Wales and Scotland while at the same time fighting France across the Channel. It is not surprising that out of this particular 'crisis' Edward's so-called 'Model' Parliament (1295) evolved. It included not only 2 archbishops, 18 bishops, 67 abbots, 48 lay barons and the lower clergy, but also 2 knights from each of the 40 shires as well as 2 burgesses from each of 114 boroughs – all in all more than 400 members. Its most important task was to provide funds for war against the Scots – funds which had to be exacted in such a way that, while being as high as politically desirable, they did not endanger the 'social fabric' of the kingdom.

In the course of the fourteenth century a separation into two houses evolved. The lay lords and the greater clergy met in the House of Lords, while the knights and burgesses formed the House of Commons. Under the Tudors the power of Parliament increased, as Henry VIII in particular needed it to establish the Church of England and assert his authority against the Catholic church and its representatives on the Continent (see Chapter 4). With the Glorious Revolution of 1688–9, Parliament reached its zenith: while its sovereignty was effectively affirmed, William III and Mary II had to accept great limitations on the crown's powers.

In Wales a tradition of consultation was known in the Middle Ages, but representation on a regular basis began only in 1536 when Wales was annexed by England. The Scottish parliament differed from the English one in that it assembled in one chamber. Its proceedings were first recorded in 1235. Its reputation has long been that of a willing executant of royal decisions, but this opinion misses the point that many Scottish parliaments defied their kings (particularly in the fifteenth and sixteenth centuries). In

1707 the English and Scottish parliaments were united (see Chapter 5). The Irish parliament – instituted at the same time as the English one (1295) – was in fact an English parliament, as the native Irish were excluded. Poynings's Law (see Chapters 4 and 5) determined that Irish legislation had to be confirmed by the English parliament. Real political power was wielded by the monarch's representative (the Lord Deputy) and the government in London. With the Act of Union of 1800 the Irish parliament ceased to exist (see Chapter 5).

ensured Parliament's role in uniting England into a national community. Third, Edward succeeded in negotiating a difficult compromise with the Church which, on the one hand, set limits to the further extension of its (landed) property without royal consent and which, at the same time, ensured its contributions to state finances (by obtaining the payment of a heavy income tax).

However, if we appreciate his merits, we also have to scrutinise the darker sides of Edward's reign. In 1290, England became the first country in Christian Europe to expel its Jews, who had entered the British Isles in greater numbers in the wake of the Norman Conquest. Put somewhat crudely, the situation in England did not differ much from anywhere else: since Jews were excluded from all offices and almost all trades, and since Christians were not allowed to practise money-lending, Jews earned their living by working as traders, money-lenders and financiers, and Christians, mixing religious zeal with greed and envy, hated them for doing so. Repeatedly accused of the ritual murder of innocent Christian children (because they needed blood to bake their unleavened bread for Passover), the Jews in England had severe restrictions placed upon them. At first they were confined to Jewries; from 1238 they had to wear badges; in 1285 they were forbidden to lend money but not offered any alternative means of earning their living (though they were still allowed to trade and to own property). When Edward needed money in 1290 (perhaps because of the immense costs of the Welsh wars), Parliament demanded and obtained the expulsion of the Jews in exchange for a large subsidy. Some 3000–4000 Jews had to leave the country within three months; and, although they were given safe conduct, many of them were set upon and robbed, and some of them were killed.

Ireland, Wales and Scotland had to cope with a different kind of trauma: the threat of subjugation. If Edward I envisaged a unification of the different parts of the British Isles, it undoubtedly was from an exclusively English perspective. His great-grandfather, Henry II, had successfully safeguarded his overlordship of Ireland by introducing an Anglicising administrative structure (English common law with justices and courts, and a feudalised Church). However, with the last great population rise in medieval Europe in the final decades of the twelfth and the first decades of the thirteenth centuries, the English interest in

Ireland changed from maintaining a lordship over men to colonising land. As a consequence, colonists, both high (knights, free tenants, burgesses) and low (artisans, peasant farmers, cottiers), but all of them personally free, were 'imported' from England, Wales and continental Europe (e.g. Flanders). They occupied the best parts of the land, while the native Irish either worked for them – they were termed 'betaghs' and considered as serfs – or were confined to the woods, bogs and uplands of the country. For Edward I and his son, Ireland was important as a source of men, money and maintenance (especially food) for his campaigns (abroad in France as well as in Wales and in Scotland). But when the agricultural boom levelled off in the second half of the thirteenth century, when the North European Famine struck (1315–17) and the Scottish Wars of Independence spilled over into the country, the structure of the lordship began to crack; economic and social instability followed and was increased by the effects of the Black Death; the control exercised by the Irish government in Dublin began to break down and was eventually restricted to the Pale. Although a Gaelic resurgence set in, it eventually foundered because the Irish chiefs were unable to achieve long-term cooperation and the powerful Anglo-Irish magnates, who occupied the agriculturally profitable and well-populated areas of the country, were strong enough to resist their individual attacks.

The Welsh princes had benefited from the weak rule of John and the turmoil of Henry III's reign. In the Treaty of Montgomery (1267) Henry even had to concede Llywelyn ap Gruffudd's claim to the title of Prince of Wales as well as territorial gains. Edward I set out to make good these losses and subjugated Wales in two devastating campaigns (1276–7, 1282–3). While after the first campaign Llywelyn was required to do homage and swear fealty to Edward I, surrender all the conquered lands to him, and pay his debts to the English Crown, but was allowed to retain the title of Prince of Wales, after the second

---

The Pale

The Pale is that area in Ireland in which English law and the royal administration were respected. It derives from the Latin word *palus*, an old name for a pointed stake driven into the ground. Originally this implied a fence and figuratively referred to a border. The extent of the Pale varied: in the mid-fourteenth century it comprised Dublin, Louth, Meath, Trim, Kilkenny and Kildare. Later it progressively shrank until the Tudors reasserted the English presence in the sixteenth century. When English administration reached beyond the Pale, it ceased to have defensive aspects and merely became a geographical expression. (Another Pale existed in France around Calais until 1558.)

The expression 'beyond the pale' entered the English language, designating unacceptable behaviour, which existed outside (but not inside) the bounds of the pale.

campaign (triggered by a rebellion of Llywelyn's brother David), in which Llywelyn was killed, his lands and the principality were bestowed on Edward's son. To safeguard his conquest and ensure the suppression of later revolts Edward I had a series of castles built (Conwy, Caernarfon, Criccieth, Harlech, Beaumarais, Builth, Flint, Rhuddlan and Llanbadarn [Aberystwyth]) and, in the Statute of Rhuddlan (1284), he introduced English common law. Moreover, in 1301 he made his infant son the first English Prince of Wales. (Since then the title has been reserved for the heir apparent of the English and, later, British monarch.) Shires (on the English pattern) were created to govern the conquered territories, and the Welsh church was brought more firmly under English control. Despite serious revolts (in 1287 and 1294–5), these new structures of government were to last until the mid-sixteenth century. Even Owain Glyndwr's revolt (1400–8), the success of which was largely due to the turmoil of Henry IV's reign, could not change this.

Where Ireland and Wales eventually succumbed, Scotland fought back. The three long reigns (of William I, 'the Lion', 1165–1214, Alexander II, 1214–49, and Alexander III, 1249–86) had succeeded in stabilising the country and, particularly in the thirteenth century, in producing a largely friendly relationship between England and Scotland. This was all the more welcome because many landowners possessed land on both sides of the border and, therefore, owed loyalty to both rulers. But with Alexander III's accidental death a new phase of conflict began. Moreover, it quickly spiralled into deadly warfare and lasted, on and off, for more than a century. The root of the problem was a succession crisis: Alexander's infant granddaughter Margaret, the 'Maid of Norway' (the child of Alexander's daughter, Margaret, and Erik II, king of Norway), was his sole surviving descendant. Six guardians to administer the kingdom and to arrange Margaret's coming to Scotland were elected by the Scottish governing community. They acted very circumspectly. First, they waited to see if a posthumous heir was born to Alexander (who had married again five months before his death); then they made treaties with Erik (to ensure Margaret's safe passage to Scotland) and Edward I (to ensure Scottish independence) because Edward (who was also Margaret's great-uncle) had signalled a strong interest in joining the two kingdoms by a marriage between her and his son, the future Edward II. However, these plans came to nothing when Margaret died on her arrival (in 1290). As a consequence, the descendants of previous kings had to be examined to establish the succession. As no simple solution was in sight, civil war could not be ruled out, and Edward I was asked to help keep the peace. Within a year he was not only accepted as arbitrator of the case, but had also made himself overlord of the country. Of thirteen claimants to the throne only three had a substantial case: John Balliol, Robert Bruce and John Hastings, all of them descended from David, the younger brother of William I. While the first two claimed the whole kingdom, Hastings claimed only a third share of it. A partition of the kingdom was not regarded as a viable option, so John Balliol

The Stone of Destiny

The Stone of Destiny, also known as the Stone of Scone or the Coronation Stone, is a block of sandstone weighing 152 kilograms, historically kept at the now ruined abbey in Scone, near Perth in Scotland. In Celtic mythology, it was called Lia Fail, 'the speaking stone', and was believed to possess the magic power of naming the rightful king. Since the time of Kenneth Mac Alpin (r. ?842–58) the Scottish kings had been seated on it at their coronation. In 1296 the stone was captured by Edward I during his invasion of Scotland. He took it to Westminster Abbey, where it was placed under the Coronation Chair on which English sovereigns sat in order to symbolise their domination of both England and Scotland. Although it has been suggested that monks at Scone Palace hid the real stone, thus deceiving Edward I with one of similar size and shape, this theory has not been confirmed. In 1328, as part of the peace treaty between Scotland and England, Edward III agreed to return the captured stone to Scotland, but this was never done. On Christmas Day 1950 a group of students stole the stone from Westminster Abbey in order to return it to Scotland. In the process the stone went missing. Four months later it was recovered from the altar of Arbroath Abbey. Again, the English claimed the stone back. But on St Andrew's Day, 30 November 1996, the Stone of Destiny was finally installed in Edinburgh Castle after the British government had decided that it should be returned to Scotland after all.

and Robert Bruce remained as the two main competitors. As there was no precedent for such a procedure in any law of the Isles, the Great Cause (as the case was later known) was heard by a jury of 104 men – 40 each chosen by Balliol and Bruce, and 24 appointed by Edward I. In November 1292, Balliol's claim was judged to be the stronger, and he was accordingly crowned at Scone. As King John owed his victory (at least to a certain extent) to Edward, he had to pay homage to him. Edward, in turn, let him (and the country) feel that he wanted to exercise his feudal rights. To prevent the erosion of their kingdom the Scots signed a treaty of mutual aid (1295) with England's first and foremost enemy, France, which had been at war with England since 1294. Fulfilling the treaty, in spring 1296, the Scots made raids south of the border. The English immediately retaliated, invading Scotland with a large army. The Scots were defeated at Dunbar, and John had to submit to Edward; he was stripped of his kingship and imprisoned, while Scotland was placed under direct English government. In the later summer of 1297, when Edward had returned to his war with France, Scotland erupted into revolt. Led by Andrew Murray and William Wallace, the Scots defeated English forces at Stirling Bridge, only to be defeated in turn at Falkirk nine months later. A war of attrition followed. The stalemate was broken when Robert Bruce (grandson of 'the Competitor' of John) killed another potential rival (John Comyn) and seized the throne in 1305. Lack of support amongst the Scots (for whom John Balliol was still the rightful king)

The Declaration of Arbroath (1320)

The Declaration of Arbroath, more correctly entitled 'Letter of Barons of Scotland to Pope John XXII', is one of the most famous documents in Scottish history. It is seen by many as the founding document of the Scottish nation. In Canada and America the anniversary of the Declaration of Arbroath (6 April 1320) is regarded as a day on which Canadians and North Americans of Scottish descent celebrate their Scottish roots ('Tartan Day'). The Declaration was most likely written by Abbot Bernard on behalf of the nobles and barons of Scotland. It was originally phrased in eloquent, emotional medieval Latin prose. Above the seals of eight earls and forty-five barons, it asked for both Pope John XXII's intervention in the bloody quarrel between the Scots and the English and the recognition of Scotland's independence. Not only did the creators of the Declaration want the pope to admonish the king of England to 'leave them in peace'; they also asked him to acknowledge Robert the Bruce as the country's lawful king. At the same time they emphasised their readiness to depose their king should he fail to free the Scots from the English. After having received the Declaration, the pope wrote a letter to Edward II urging him to make peace, but it was not until 1328 that Scotland's independence was acknowledged. The most striking aspect of the Declaration is the fact that it set the will of the people and their right to freedom above the king. A contemporary copy of the Declaration of Arbroath is held in Register House in Edinburgh.

---

and Edward's angry reaction threatened Robert I's downfall. However, Edward's death (in 1307) provided Robert with some breathing space, which he skilfully used to consolidate his position. His victory over Edward II at Bannockburn (June 1314) won him the support of many a wavering Scot, but he had to improve his relations with the Pope to have his kingship acknowledged. When Edward II was deposed and brutally murdered (in 1327), the unstable regency government made possible peace negotiations which resulted in the admission of Scottish independence in the Treaty of Edinburgh (1328). However, peace was not to be: Robert I died in 1329, his son David II was a minor (born in 1324), whose reign (1329–71) was immediately challenged by John Comyn's descendants and, above all, by John Balliol's son, Edward Balliol, who enjoyed the support of all who had opposed Robert I. In 1332 he was made king of Scotland after having defeated David's forces with the help of the English. In return, Edward Balliol acknowledged Edward III as his overlord and ceded southern Scotland to him. While David spent seven years (1334–41) in exile in France, Scottish leaders recovered lost ground for him. When David returned, Edward III was involved in the Hundred Years War with France. Combining his gratitude to France with the necessity of having his kingship admitted by Edward, David invaded the north of England in 1346. He was captured, however, and held as a prisoner until 1357, when Edward III eventually recognised him as king of Scotland (one year after Edward Balliol had given up his claim). While the great battles between the two countries slowly came to an end, the Borders remained a war zone for centuries to come. And the Hundred Years War (1328–1453) gave Scotland a particular (geopolitical) position in its relations with England and the Continent. There is no doubt that England, particularly in military terms, was much stronger than Scotland and would certainly have conquered it, had it not been involved in wars on so many fronts. The Scots, in turn, forged a robust national consciousness and an eventually coherent political community out of their many wars (with more defeats than victories) with their neighbours. The English failure to achieve complete victory and the Scottish failure to achieve permanent independence kept the enmity and the struggle alive beyond the formal peace of 1474. The Treaty of Perpetual Peace (1502), concluded between James IV of Scotland and Henry VII of England, and sealed by a marriage (1503) between James and Henry's daughter, Margaret Tudor, lasted barely a decade, and whether the union of the crowns (in 1603) and of the parliaments (in 1707) improved Anglo-Scottish relations is at least a matter of debate.

THE HUNDRED YEARS WAR, 1328–1453

When Charles IV of France died in 1328 (leaving no male heir), Edward III had a claim to the French throne through his mother, Charles's sister Isabella. But the French governing community, adhering to a strict interpretation of the Salic law (by which females were excluded from the succession), let Philip VI (i.e. Philippe of Valois) succeed. When in 1337 a quarrel arose concerning Edward's tenure of Aquitaine as a fief of the French crown, the feudal dispute turned into dynastic war: in 1340, Edward adopted the title of king of France and went from victory to victory (Crécy 1346, Poitiers 1356). In the Treaty of Brétigny (1360), however, he agreed to a lucrative territorial settlement instead of enforcing his claim to the throne. Hereafter, the French succeeded in recovering lost ground until the beginning of the fifteenth century. The victory at Agincourt (1415) started a new series of English successes which was sealed by the Treaty of Troyes (May 1420) and Henry V's subsequent marriage to Catherine of Valois, whereby he became both heir and regent to (the insane) Charles VI. However, Henry died two years later; and, although the English controlled most of northern France between 1420 and 1435, the impact of Joan of Arc on French morale (1429), and the defection of the Burgundians (1435), weakened the English position. After a truce in 1444, the loss of Normandy (1450) and of Gascony (1453), the Hundred Years War was at an end, although Calais remained English until 1558 and the kings of England continued to call themselves kings of France until 1802. At first sight, the war achieved nothing: it had begun as a feudal dispute, had then turned into a dynastic war, and had finally become a conflict between two 'nations' in the making. In the course of these

---

St Joan of Arc ('La Pucelle' or 'The Maid of Orleans') (1412–31)

Joan was born into a peasant family at Domrémy in the Champagne. At the age of thirteen she began to have visions, which she described as voices accompanied by bright light. She identified these voices as those of St Catherine, St Michael and St Margaret, who were telling her that she was destined to free France from English domination. She left home and managed to gain an audience with Charles VII, the Dauphin. We do not know exactly how, but Joan managed to convince him of her genuine divine mission and consequently led the army to free Orleans in 1429. After she had won the battle, she took the Dauphin to Reims (the ancient French coronation place) to be crowned Charles VII. In April 1430 she set out to relieve Compiègne, but she was captured by the Burgundians, who acknowledged Henry V's right to the French throne. They handed Joan over to the English, who put her on trial in Rouen in 1431. Abandoned by the king, she was accused of witchcraft and heresy, of which the court found her guilty and sentenced her to be burned alive. Twenty-four years later, in 1456, a papal court reversed the judgement of the Rouen court by a *procès de réhabilitation*. The sentence was annulled, and in 1920 Joan of Arc was canonised.

---

years, the English and the French may have become more conscious of their different identities, but they paid dearly for it by exhausting their human and financial resources.

MEDIEVAL CHANGES IN AGRICULTURE

The most important development was the replacement of the simple wooden 'scratch-plough' by the heavy iron plough. The latter consisted of three pieces – a vertical sod-cutter (or coulter), a horizontal ploughshare and a tilted mould-board – and ran on wheels. The main problem with such a plough, which could turn the heaviest soils, was how to pull it. Up to the early Middle Ages teams of oxen were the norm. (Land was measured in ox-hides, i.e. in units of land which could be served by one ox-team.)

Five developments had to occur before the plough could be more widely used. While the horses of warriors had to be fast and agile, farmers needed strong horses which could pull heavy loads. However, breeding a particular kind of horse was not enough: a horse-collar, which enabled the horse to pull the plough without being throttled by putting the weight on its shoulders, and the iron horse-shoe, which protected the horse's hoofs against injury, had to be developed as well. The origins of the heavy mouldboard plough are obscure. The horse-shoe was used by the Huns as early as the fifth century (and may have entered eastern Europe via Byzantium in the late ninth century), while the collar harness was pioneered by the Chinese in the third century.

Watermills, which emerged in China in the first century BC, were already widespread in England in 1086 (recorded in Domesday Book); while windmills, which were first mentioned in Persia in the seventh century AD, were adopted towards the end of the twelfth century, most probably as a result of the transfer of knowledge facilitated by the Islamic 'bridge' between Europe and Asia.

The cultivation of oats provided the staple food of the workhorse, and the introduction of the three-field system of crop rotation greatly improved crop yields. Instead of dividing the arable land into two fields, of which one was tilled while the other was allowed to lie fallow, i.e. uncultivated, it was now divided into three fields, one of which was allowed to lie fallow, one was seeded in autumn, and one was seeded in spring. This increased the productivity by reducing the risk (if the winter crop failed, the summer crop could still be good, and vice versa) and by redistributing the farmer's workload. By the twelfth century these improvements had begun to be implemented by most European farmers, but they were not completed until the fifteenth century.

The increase in cultivated area and in agricultural productivity allowed the English population to increase to over 5 million (and that of the British Isles as a whole to some 7–8 million) people until 1300. However, the income from the land differed greatly between England, Scotland, Wales and Ireland: on average per square mile, Wales produced twice as much wealth as Ireland, while Scotland produced 50 per cent more wealth than Wales, and England, in turn, produced three times as much wealth as Scotland.

THE BLACK DEATH

The disease which was later called the Black Death was an epidemic of catastrophic proportions: a bubonic plague (and its variant, pneumonic plague), caused by the bacillus *Yersinia pestis*, and transmitted from its hosts (rats) to human beings by flea bites. It spread from Central Asia along trade routes to the east and to the west, reaching Italy in 1347 and the south coast of England (Melcombe Regis, Dorset) in June 1348. People died within days of being infected: in the first eighteen months of the plague's activity, a little less than half of England's population died. The progress of the plague was unpredictable, and it cut across all sections of the population; the general rule was: the bigger (i.e. the more densely populated) the city or region, the greater the impact. This was a trauma of hitherto unknown proportions; the old, sick and weak were left to die, families were split up, children shunned their parents, and the survivors could barely bury the dead. As one contemporary wrote: 'Alas this mortality devoured such a multitude of both sexes that no one could be found to carry the bodies of the dead to burial, but men and women carried the bodies of their own little ones to church on their shoulders and threw them into mass graves from which arose such a stench that it was barely possible for anyone to go past the church yard.' Although recovery seems to have been quick after the first attack, further outbreaks in the course of the century (1361, 1369, 1375 and almost every decade thereafter) resulted in a decline of the population to somewhere between a third and a half in the British Isles as a whole.

SOCIETY AND CULTURE

The Black Death contributed to a decisive transformation of the societies in the British Isles. The decreasing demand for food (and other commodities) brought an end to the preceding decades of economic expansion and led to a reorienta-tion in agriculture (most notably, the return to subsistence production and the transformation of much arable land into pasture) as well as to a decline in trade and industry which, in turn, resulted in the contraction of the towns. More-over, the sharp decline in population caused an acute labour shortage and, concomitantly, an inflationary rise in wages. Although the government attempted to secure a cheap labour supply and fix wages by passing the Ordin-ances (1349) and the Statutes of Labourers (1351), it was difficult to enforce this legislation when landlords competed for labour. Villeins and wage-labourers seriously resented the government's attempts to deprive them of their bene-fits from the post-pandemic labour shortage: they rioted and revolted (1381). In the long run, these developments tilted the economic relationship between employers and employees in favour of the latter. The feudal structure cracked. Serfdom (or villeinage, cf. Chapter 2) – which in the beginning had meant either labour rent (i.e. work on the lord's demesne) or rent in kind (i.e. delivery of a share of the harvest to the lord) and which, in the decades of economic expansion, had already been transformed into money rent (i.e. payment of fixed dues to the lord) – came to an end. From now on the lords had to accept that the peasants were no longer 'theirs' but came and went in relation to the wages they were offered. And the general standard of living rose.

If this combination of demographic and economic factors strained the sinews of the feudal structures in the British Isles on the one hand, the struggles (which sometimes turned into civil wars) between monarchs (such as John, Henry III, Edward II, Richard II and the Lancastrians) and their ambitious aristocracies contributed to the disintegration of the feudal system on the other. Conflicting loyalties, in particular, resulting from the fact that a lord could hold fiefs from more than one monarch, added to the strain on this system of mutual rights and obligations. For example, many English (and some Scottish) lords held fiefs on both sides of the Scottish border, while many lords on the Continent, who held fiefs from the Plantagenet kings, could (and did) also hold some from the king of France at the same time. In a case of conflict between the monarchs, the lords had to decide whom they wanted to back. Schematically speaking, if they backed the one, it usually implied the forfeiture of their fiefs with the other. If they backed the winner, they could, perhaps, get their forfeited fiefs back after the conflict was over. If they backed the loser, they could lose all their fiefs (because the winner could – and most probably would – punish their disloyalty). If they decided not to back either of the two, they could also lose everything because they could be accused of disloyalty by either. These two factors together – the increasingly weak position of the (land-)lords *vis-à-vis* their hitherto dependent labourers because of the labour shortage and the inability of the European aristocracies to determine the results of their competitive struggles other than in terms of costly warfare, which finally destroyed these aristocracies themselves – eventually led to the erosion of the feudal system. Slowly but distinctly, this system based on personal loyalty was replaced by one in which, on the one hand, loyalty was owed to a country and its monarch. In this process the representative principle of parliament was to play a distinctive role in uniting the English nation in the making. On the other hand, personal loyalty came to be replaced by contracts between employers who bought and employees who sold (their) labour power for wages (with the additional advantage that free peasants could be taxed).

The period under consideration witnessed the construction not only of great castles (to secure Anglo-Norman rule) but also of great cathedrals and abbeys throughout the British Isles (such as at Lincoln, Salisbury and Westminster). These buildings demonstrated the combined effort of the Catholic church, the monarchy and the richer lords of the realm to sustain the pyramidal structure of society. The worldly rulers invested in these buildings because their splendour and spirit added to their lustre and authority. Stylistically, English architecture was largely French in inspiration, but towards the end of our period (with the growing alienation between the English and the French) different ideas came to the fore: in particular the austere geometry of the Perpendicular style.

The growing complexities of government and administration, the demands made on the clergy, the necessity to collect and transmit knowledge required the foundation of adequate educational institutions. The Church not only provided a body of educated and disciplined clergy who, by conveying an orthodox creed which mirrored and underpinned the status quo, made itself an irreplaceable part of medieval society, but also controlled all forms of worldly education. In the humblest schools elementary reading, psalms and prayers were taught, often coupled with singing (which is why they were called 'song schools'), while the greater churches and monasteries could offer higher learning (including grammar and writing). The language of instruction was Latin. From the eleventh century onwards, more 'advanced' schools emerged which offered the seven liberal arts consisting of the *trivium* (grammar, rhetoric, dialectic) and the *quadrivium* (arithmetic, geometry, astronomy, music). Winchester College (1382) and Eton College (1440) were the most renowned of these grammar schools (which later became public schools). They prepared scholars for the higher education reserved for the universities. (The term 'university', then as now, referred to 'the whole body' of masters and students.) Oxford was founded in about 1185, Cambridge in 1209; the Scottish universities at St Andrews (1410), Glasgow (1451) and Aberdeen (1494) were papal foundations which, after the Reformation, could be attended by dissenters while the English universities remained closed to them. The idea of two Welsh universities, which would train an independent Welsh clergy, came to nothing when Owain Glyndwr's rebellion at the beginning of the fifteenth century was crushed.

From the Norman Conquest onwards, six languages were used in the British Isles: Latin, Anglo-Norman French, English, Gaelic, Welsh and Cornish. The last three were marginal in politics, but survived in everyday use, folklore, poetry and song. Latin was the language of the highest cultural authority, used by the Church and in the academic sphere. Anglo-Norman French was the language of the royal court, the governing elite and the courts (while the rolls and records were kept in Latin). Since 1066, English had been the language of an oppressed people. But it survived in its many variants and re-emerged (albeit in a new form) in the thirteenth century. On the one hand, the demographic and economic effects of the Black Death lent greater weight to the English-speaking lower classes. On the other, the prolonged wars with France produced not only a growing alienation between the two cultures but also – because of the loss of their Continental possessions – a ruling elite without the constituent parts of its material base and cultural context. Although the royal court would continue to speak French, and educated English society would remain trilingual for some time to come, the balance between these languages began to tilt in favour of English. The oldest surviving legal document in English dates from 1376. Thirteen years previously, the Lord Chancellor had reportedly opened a parliamentary session in English for the first time – a session which passed the so-called Statue of Pleading: 'The King has ordained . . . that all pleas which shall be pleaded in any court whatsoever . . . shall be pleaded, shown, defended, answered, debated and judged in the English tongue, and that they shall be entered and enrolled in Latin.'

Moreover, this rise of English was accompanied, encouraged and under-pinned by the growth of a vernacular literature. With insular French in decline and Latin without a popular base, the different varieties of English underwent processes of expansion, standardisation and legitimisation. As there were two sovereign kingdoms, two distinct standards developed: Scots English (spoken in Lowland Scotland) and the English of England (based on the dialect spoken in and around London). Literary examples of the former are the works of John Barbour (c.1320–95; *The Bruce*, 1376) and William Dunbar (?1456–?1513), while the latter can be found in the works of John Gower (?1330–1408) and, above all, Geoffrey Chaucer (c.1343/4–1400; *The Canterbury Tales*, 1387). The use of English expanded geographically (through political and commercial contacts) and socially through the growth of educational institutions (schools and universities), giving an ever-increasing community access to written texts. When, furthermore, printing presses were set up (in 1476 by William Caxton in Westminster and in 1507 by Walter Chapman and Andrew Myllar in Edinburgh), the monopoly on the reading and writing of texts (held for centuries by the clergy and associated scholars) was finally broken. Both factors were to play a decisive role in the Reformation in the sixteenth century.

4 Renaissance – reconnaissance – reformation – revolution, 1485–1688/9

The four terms in this chapter's heading are loan words from Latin. Their common prefix, 're-', signals 'again' to indicate repetition. However, as time moves on, every repetition implies a new departure.

Renaissance (literally 're-birth') refers to the time (and spirit) of the great revival of art, literature and learning in Europe beginning in the fourteenth century and extending to the seventeenth century. This revival entailed the rediscovery of the Greek and Latin classical texts which had been forgotten in Western Europe but had survived – partly in their original forms, partly in translation – in the Byzantine (Constantinople, Mount Athos) as well as Arab (Alexandria, Cairo) empires. From the beginning of the twelfth century onwards a period of intense translating activity from both Arabic and Greek into Latin occurred in Spain and Italy, in the course of which, to name just one example, Adelard of Bath (possibly 'the first English scientist', c.1080–c.1150) translated Euclid's *Elements*, the standard teaching text on geometry in the West for the next eight centuries, as well as the most up-to-date astronomical reference book then available (the *Zijj*, written and updated by Islamic scholars in the ninth and tenth centuries). Moreover, he wrote original books on the abacus and the astrolabe. This transfusion of cultural knowledge, in which Greek, Muslim, Jewish and Christian scholars cooperated, also included items of material culture such as paper and the pointed arch as well as the procedures of Greco-Arab medicine. Finally, it has been convincingly argued that the idea of the university in the modern sense is of Islamic origin. It certainly was no coincidence that the first universities developed in Christian Europe were founded in cities bordering the Islamic world as, for example, Salerno (with its famous medical school from the ninth century onwards), Bologna (specialising in canon and civil law from the late eleventh century onwards), Salamanca (founded in 1218) and Montpellier (1220). The diverse ways of knowledge transfer sketched above were complemented by activities of scholars like Francesco Petrarch (1304–74), Peter Paul Vergerio (1370–1444), Desiderius

Erasmus (*c*.1466–1536) and Sir Thomas More (1478–1535), who came to be called humanists because they believed that the study of classical poetry, rhetoric and philosophy (i.e. the humanities) could infuse daily life with ethical values. What they studied they called *artes liberales* ('liberal arts') because, as one humanist wrote, 'they make man free', 'they perfect man' (Document 7). By this view, the individual (regarded as stained by original sin for centuries by church theologians) came to gain a new sense of self: from now on the lay person could claim to be able to understand morality through the ancient texts themselves (i.e. without the guidance of the clergy). In fact, this gain was, once more, a re-gaining because this idea had been present in ancient Greek culture but had been largely forgotten since then.

Reconnaissance refers to the processes of discovery, exploration, colonisation and settlement which – from the European perspective – started with the activities of the Portuguese prince Henry 'the Navigator', who not only captured Ceuta (on the North African coast), but also initiated and supported voyages which led to the discovery of the Madeira Islands (1418), the Azores and the Cape Verde Islands as well as parts of the West African coast as far as today's Sierra Leone. Christopher Columbus' discovery of the North American continent in 1492 (which had, however, most probably been visited by Viking seafarers earlier), Vasco da Gama's rounding of the Cape of Good Hope and voyage to India (1497–9), and Ferdinand Magellan's attempt at circumnavigating the globe (1519–22) (completed by Sebastian del Cano) were the early achievements of what has traditionally been regarded as the rise of Europe and its expansion, first, to the West (across the Atlantic) and, then, to the East (around Africa to the Indian Ocean and beyond or around South America to the Pacific). What has, however, been neglected until quite recently is that, in fact, the Europeans were latecomers to a global trading network which had been established by the Arabs, Persians, Indians and Chinese. That is to say, the European ventures, on the one hand, relied on navigational technologies which had been developed in China and the Islamic world and then diffused across Europe. Two examples. (i) The regular crossing of the Atlantic would have been impossible without the combination of different shipbuilding traditions which resulted from the combination of the best features of ships from the Baltic Sea and the Mediterranean. Rigging and steering were perfected, and the sternpost rudder (a Chinese invention) came in, together with combined square-rigged sails (from northern Europe) and lateen-rigged sails (from the Indian Ocean via the Mediterranean) which enabled the Europeans to sail not only with but also into the wind. (ii) The mariner's compass was first used in the European context towards the end of the twelfth century, but had been deployed in Chinese ships about a century earlier. On the other hand, many of the initial feats of discovery would have been impossible to achieve if the Europeans had not had skilful non-European helpers such as Ibn Majid, the Indian pilot, who led da Gama from Malindi (East Africa) to Calicut (India).

Reformation refers to the very diverse religious movements of the sixteenth century which aimed at reforming the Roman Catholic church but resulted in establishing the Protestant churches. Three related crises of papal authority lay at the root of the Reformation. (i) While in principle the pope governed the Church in all Western Christendom, the monarchs of Europe's strongest states (France, England and Spain) claimed greater authority in the religious affairs of their countries: they wanted to appoint the higher clergy (bishops and arch-bishops) and to impose taxation (cf. Henry II's quarrel with Thomas Becket: Chapter 3). These conflicts – summarily labelled as 'investiture contest' – lasted for centuries and eventually led to the 'great schism' (1378–1417) in the course of which, first, the popes were installed in Avignon so that the French mon-archs could influence them more easily; second, competing popes governing from Avignon (supported, amongst others, by France and Scotland) and Rome (supported, amongst others, by Portugal and England) were elected; finally, a third pope was elected (in 1409) to resolve the conflict, but when the other two did not want to resign it took the Council of Constance (1414–18) to put an end to the conflict and initiate church reform. (ii) However, paradoxically, this very Council of Constance strengthened *and* weakened the authority of the papal office. It strengthened it by re-establishing its singularity (*one* pope) and by punishing heretics and their movements. People like the English monk William of Occam (*c.*1290–1349), for whom individual piety was at the centre of religious life, the English cleric and scholar John Wyclif (*c.*1328–1384), who de-emphasised the role of rituals in favour of faith in obtaining eternal salvation, and the Bohemian theologian Jan Hus (*c.*1369–1415), who had learned of and propagated Wyclif's teachings, had all challenged the authority of the pope and the Catholic church and were condemned as a consequence; Hus was burned at the stake at Constance. At the same time, the Council weakened the office by simply enhancing the status of the Council, so that some participants even held the 'conciliar' view that it could override papal authority. (iii) While the Church tried to protect its authority, it appeared increasingly venal to a growing num-ber of its members. In particular, clerical abuses such as immunity from civil justice and exemption from taxes, as well as the sale of offices and, most important, of indulgences, were attacked. By granting indulgences, the Church claimed to be able to reduce the time a soul had to spend in Purgatory to atone for its sins: 'The moment the money tinkles in the collecting box, a soul flies out of Purgatory.' Thus, people who did not sufficiently engage in good deeds and pious acts could 'improve' their 'balances' by buying indulgences (Docu-ment 8) which, by the early sixteenth century, were 'abused' for secular pur-poses, such as adding to the pomp of the Church and its representatives. These abuses provoked the German monk Martin Luther to deny a special status to the clergy, to insist on the 'priesthood of all believers' and to contend that faith, not good works, was the key to salvation (Documents 9 and 10). After that there was no turning back. Luther's ideas spread within the German states and

---

Lollards

Lollards (from Middle Dutch *lollaerd* = 'mumbler') were members of a religious movement in late medieval England which mostly consisted of artisans and yeomen farmers. (The initial backing of some influential landowners soon waned when the Lollards became associated with sedition.) They were critical of clerical celibacy, wealth and privilege, denied the need of a priest as mediator between God and man or woman, and rejected the pope. They emphasised the role of individual piety and the authority of the scriptures. They also translated the Bible into English (1390), stressing the importance of the vernacular as a vehicle of religious reform. Parliament was alarmed by Lollardy and responded by enacting the statute *De heretico comburende* (1401), which threatened the Lollards with prosecution and burning at the stake. The statute was repealed in 1559.

---

beyond, following trade routes. They were particularly successful in northern Europe (Denmark, Sweden and, later, England and Scotland), while the majority of southern Europe stayed Catholic. These religious divisions had political repercussions: arguments, conflicts, wars. A series of attempts at reconciliation of the two camps proved as unsuccessful as compromises such as the Peace of Augsburg (1555), which stipulated princely control over religion (*cuius regio, eius religio*). Wars of religion and religious persecution have been a feature of European politics ever since – not least between Britain and Ireland (see Chapters 5 and 7). In France, within three days following St Bartholomew's Day (24 August 1572), more than 20,000 Huguenots (after Besançon Hugues) were butchered, sparking a civil war of religion which lasted a quarter of a century and was only ended when Henri IV granted religious freedom to the Huguenots in the Edict of Nantes (13 April 1598). (Three generations later, in 1685, the Edict was repealed by Louis XIV – a fact that caused many Huguenots to emigrate to Britain and Prussia.) At the same time the northern provinces in the Netherlands fought for their independence from Spain (obtained in 1609). Finally, the Thirty Years War (1618–48) in the Holy Roman Empire, the most devastating of these conflicts, involved virtually all major European countries.

Revolution refers to what today we describe as a complete (and perhaps forcible) overthrow of an established government or political system. However, for people in the fifteenth and sixteenth centuries, the word 'revolution' first and foremost indicated a revolving movement in space or time, as in 'the earth completes one revolution each day'. The most general word for resistance against a lawful authority was 'rebellion', although there was a third word, 'revolt', which was used in a political sense. With the political developments of the sixteenth and, in particular, the seventeenth centuries, the original meaning of the term 'revolution' was affected by its closeness to the word 'revolt'.

However, even more interestingly, 'rebellion' and 'revolution' carried different connotations: while Oliver Cromwell's revolution was called, by its enemies, the 'great rebellion', the allegedly bloodless transformation of 1688 was called, by its supporters, the 'great' and, eventually, the 'glorious revolution'. It is in this context that we have to understand (i) the achievement of the Tudor monarchs, who succeeded in establishing a centralised national English monarchy (with Wales and Ireland annexed in 1536 and 1541 respectively) in which the great territorial magnates of the realm were forced to cede their feudal prerogatives and, thus, were eventually brought under control; (ii) the difficulties of the Stuart monarchs (and, between 1649 and 1660, of their republican opponents) in dealing with three causes of instability, which also troubled other European monarchies: the problems of multiple kingdoms, of religious division, and of how to finance a political system in the face of inflation and the rising cost of war; and (iii) the final settlement (1688–1701) which established a framework of government by which the monarchical power could be checked by the social groups represented in Parliament. In this context, the Restoration of the Crown (1660) is to a certain extent a misnomer: while it certainly re-established the English and Scottish monarchies with the same rights that they had held before the wars of the three kingdoms, the fact that this process was brought about not by the institution which was to be restored – the monarchy itself – but by social forces outside it – the army and a convention parliament – demonstrates the limits of what could be restored. In these long and often tortuous developments, the humanist and reformatory seeds first sown in the sphere of religion bore further fruit in politics, thought (the 'new philosophy of science') and culture.

THE PROTESTANT REFORMATIONS

In contrast to most other European states, in England the Reformation resulted not primarily from a popular movement (although there was a strong anti-clerical sentiment among all English classes) but from an act of state which was intended to resolve a complex political situation. Although the English monarchs could look back on a long history of maintaining their rights against the papacy, when Luther's ideas spread to England and apparently fell on fertile ground, Henry VIII (b. 1491, r. 1509–47), urged by his ministers, rushed to the pope's defence, declaring his Catholic convictions in a treatise justifying the seven sacraments. While Luther's response was contemptuous, the grateful Pope Leo X (1513–21) granted Henry the title *Fidei Defensor* ('Defender of the Faith'), a title that, paradoxically, British monarchs have held to this day. (Charles, the present Prince of Wales, let it be known some time ago that, should he succeed to the throne, he would wish to change the title to 'Defender of Faith' to make it more inclusive.)

Clearly, Henry had no problem with Catholicism. But he had a political

---

Sacraments

The term 'sacrament' is derived from the Latin word *sacramentum*, which means 'oath' or 'sacred act'. Primarily, it is a visible sign of inward grace. Every sacrament consists of the following elements: the outward sign, the inward grace and the divine institution. That is to say that, first, there is a material aspect to every sacrament (objects with symbolical connotations, such as wine symbolising blood); second, a specific form has to be followed (for example, words have to be uttered in a specific way); third, a minister is needed, who is authorised to administer the sacrament. Today the Roman Catholic and the Greek Orthodox churches distinguish seven sacraments. (i) Baptism is considered to be the gate to spiritual life. Through this ceremony, people become members of Christ and of the body of the Church. (ii) Penance means confession and repentance of sins, and, thus, absolution from them. (iii) The Eucharist symbolises the 'reception' and 'consumption' of the body (bread) and blood (wine) of Christ. (iv) Confirmation 'confirms' the believer's loyalty to Christ and demonstrates his/her formal acceptance into the Church. (v) The Anointing of the Sick, or Extreme Unction, is performed on a dying person as a preparation for heaven. (vi) Holy Orders, or Ordination, stands for the process by which men are ordained to the clergy. And, finally, to (vii) Matrimony, three qualities are ascribed: the begetting of children and their bringing up in the worship of God; the fidelity of husband and wife; and the indissoluble character of marriage. The Roman Catholic church believes that all of their seven sacraments were instituted by Christ himself, as to define 'divine' living in the service of God. The sacraments of Protestant churches, in contrast, are baptism and the Eucharist.

---

problem: with the memory of the Wars of the Roses still fresh, he wanted to secure a smooth succession which would guarantee peace and order for the Tudor dynasty, and for such a succession a male heir was preferable to a female one. However, his wife, Catherine of Aragon, daughter of Ferdinand and Isabella of Spain, had had numerous miscarriages and stillbirths; and, by 1527, their union had produced only a daughter, Mary (b. 1516). Henry also had a private problem: he was in love with one of his wife's ladies-in-waiting, Anne Boleyn, and wanted to marry her. But he could only do so – divorce being out of the question because, in the Catholic faith, marriage is a sacrament – if Pope Clement VII granted him an annulment of his marriage to Catherine. For such an annulment, specific and detailed reasons had to be given. Henry engaged his Lord Chancellor, Cardinal Wolsey, to secure this annulment. He was to argue that Henry should not have been allowed to marry Catherine in the first place (arranged as early as 1503, but not effected before 1509) because she was the widow of his elder brother, Arthur, and their union had been sinful because it violated God's judgement against incest. But, back in 1503, Henry's father (Henry VII, b. 1457, r. 1485–1509) had regarded his younger son's marriage to his deceased brother's widow as a good political move to ensure England's alliance with Spain. On his accession in 1509, Henry VIII hastened to fulfil the agreement. But, as he had already known then that this marriage would be at least dubious (if not downright unlawful) in the eyes of the Church, he had obtained a special papal dispensation by Pope Julius II (1503–13), arguing that the marriage in 1501 between fifteen-year-old Arthur (who died of consumption five months after the wedding) and sixteen-year-old Catherine had, as the latter corroborated, never been consummated.

Confronted with this past history in 1527, Pope Clement VII faced two problems. The first was theological in nature. How could he justify the annulment of a marriage that had been approved by a dispensation of one of his predecessors? Did such a decision not undermine the (already weakened) authority of the papal office? The other problem was political in nature. The soldiers of the Holy Roman Empire had just sacked Rome, and Clement VII was a prisoner of Charles V, the Holy Roman Emperor and, perhaps more important, Catherine's nephew. In this situation the pope simply decided to do nothing. As a consequence, Wolsey's diplomatic efforts failed, and Henry dismissed him in disgrace after two years. His new advisers, Thomas Cranmer and Thomas Cromwell, suggested a change of perspective: if the king were declared supreme in England's spiritual (as he was in temporal) affairs, no papal permission would be needed for a new marriage. Between 1529 and 1536, Parliament – by then the most authoritative institution to bring about the necessary changes – established the king's authority over the clergy by (i) giving him jurisdiction over the clergy and canon law (1532), (ii) ending all payments of the English clergy to Rome (1534), (iii) giving the king the sole right to fill high ecclesiastical positions (1534), (iv) proclaiming Henry 'the only supreme head on earth of the Church of England' (1534) (Document 11), and (v) dissolving, first, the smaller and, then, the larger monasteries (1536) whose endowments were confiscated by the king. By the end of the 1550s roughly a quarter of the land in England had been transferred from ecclesiastical to lay hands.

After Thomas Cranmer had secretly married Henry to the pregnant Anne Boleyn in January 1533, he became Archbishop of Canterbury in March of the same year. In May he declared that the king's marriage to Catherine had never been valid, and in September 1533 Anne gave birth to a daughter (Elizabeth). Henry's disappointment was tempered by his expectation of having more children with Anne. However, in 1536, he had her executed for alleged adultery and treason. It was only Henry's third wife, Jane Seymour, who bore him the long-desired male heir, the later Edward VI, in 1537.

Henry's boldness in politics was not matched by any radicalism in piety. While he broke with Rome, established the Church of England and approved the use of English Bibles, his (or his advisers') theological reforms were only mildly Protestant. It was in the reign of his son, Edward VI (b. 1537, r. 1547–53), that England became a genuinely Protestant country. Cranmer's Book of

---

Henry VIII (1491–1547) and His Six Wives

Henry Tudor, born 28 June 1491, was the second son of Henry VII and Elizabeth of York. He became heir to the throne on the death of his elder brother, Arthur, in 1502 and succeeded in 1509. Significant events during his reign (1509–47) included the Protestant Reformation, by which the Church of England was formed of which he became 'the only supreme head', and the annexations of Wales and Ireland.

Henry VIII was known to be a passionate gambler and dice player, an enthusiastic sportsman, a gifted musician, author and poet, and a great lover of women. He was married six times, and certainly one important motive in his many marriages was to produce a male heir and thereby ensure the Tudor succession. His first wife, Catherine of Aragon, bore him a daughter, Mary. Their marriage was annulled in 1533. His second wife, Anne Boleyn, also bore him a daughter, Elizabeth. Anne was executed for infidelity in 1536. Henry's third wife, Jane Seymour, gave birth to his only male heir, Edward, but died of childbed fever only two weeks later. Four years later, Henry married Anne of Cleves, a German princess. This marriage was immediately annulled because Henry regarded Anne, whom he had agreed to marry after having seen a portrait of her, as too ugly. Henry married his fifth wife, Catherine Howard, in the same year. However, she was executed for infidelity only two years later. Henry eventually married his sixth and last wife, Catherine Parr, in 1543. Catherine, who had been married before, outlived Henry – he died on 28 January 1547 – and married a third time. After all his concern over establishing a dynasty, Henry's six marriages had only produced one son and two daughters – none of whom were to have children.

Common Prayer and a forty-two-article confession of faith (1552) became the theological cornerstones of the Church. However, when Edward died in 1553 and was followed by his sister, Mary (b. 1516, r. 1553–8) made it her mission to bring England back into the Catholic fold. Although Mary tried to heal the breach with Rome, married Philip of Spain, son of the Holy Roman Emperor, to procure a Catholic heir, and engineered a bloody persecution of Protestants, she failed to undo the work of her father and brother. (Her rigorous anti-Protestant stance earned her the nickname 'Bloody Mary', which seems not altogether fair because under her predecessors and successors religious non-conformists were equally persecuted.) Mary's sister, Elizabeth I (b. 1533, r. 1558–1603), inherited the throne and succeeded in forging a religious compromise which formed the basis of a moderate but firmly Protestant national church. The Elizabethan settlement defined the sovereign as the supreme governor of the Church and imposed a revised form of the Edwardian prayer book (1559) as well as the Thirty-nine (instead of Forty-two) Articles (1563).

The Tudor rulers and their governments wanted to impose the religious changes of the English Reformation upon Ireland and Wales. While the Irish local lords were inextricably linked to the Catholic church and successfully resisted, so that the reformative impact was negligible, resistance in Wales was scant because the lords and gentry quickly realised their profit from the dissolution of the monasteries, and for the majority of the population the changes in their daily religious lives were initially small and slow to come. This changed with the reign of Edward, whose determined Protestantism caused such a deep resentment that Mary's succession was greeted with genuine rejoicing. The Elizabethan settlement was regarded as alien at first, but it contained an element that was to give a boost to Welsh Protestantism: the government in London accepted Welsh as the official language of worship throughout Wales (1563). A group of Welsh ecclesiastics had persuasively argued that Protestantism, as a form of belief which privileged the individual believer, had to be preached in the vernacular. Thus, while in Ireland (and the Scottish Highlands) Gaelic was associated with Catholicism, in Wales Welsh became the official voice of Protestantism. In 1588 the first complete version of the Welsh Bible was published. The price the English government paid for religious unity was linguistic diversity (which, in effect, ensured the survival of Welsh into the twenty-first century).

The course of the Scottish Reformation differed markedly from that of the English. Lutheran ideas began to spread in the 1520s, and a decade later the political pattern that was to dominate the religious debates in Scotland began to emerge: Catholicism became identified with Scotland's alliance with France, while Protestantism became identified with friendship with England. To understand this pattern some brief background is required. In 1502, Henry VII (of England) and James IV (of Scotland, b. 1473, r. 1488–1513) concluded the so-called Treaty of Perpetual Peace between the two countries and tried to cement it with James's marriage to Henry's daughter, Margaret Tudor (1503). However, tensions grew when Henry VIII wanted to restart the Hundred Years War (against France), so that James renewed the Franco-Scottish ('Auld') alliance. When Henry's plan foundered, James invaded Northumberland but was defeated (and killed) at Flodden (1513). He was succeeded by his son, James V (b. 1512, r. 1513–42), who was a pawn of different regents (and their factions) until he took control of his kingdom at the age of sixteen (1528). Although his authority was readily accepted, his reign was not without turbulence, including war with England. Moreover, James V also died young, leaving his seven-day-old daughter, Mary, the sixth minor in a row, to inherit the throne. Henry VIII at once planned to have her (his niece) married to his son Edward, and thereby to unite the crowns of England and Scotland. However, Henry's 'rough wooing' found no favour with the Scots, who, at the time, rather wanted to maintain their alliance with France. Because of this, from 1548 onwards Mary lived at the French court, and in 1558 she married the dauphin, François II (b. 1543, r. 1559–60). Meanwhile, in Scotland, Lutheran ideas were being replaced by the more radical teachings of John (i.e. Jean) Calvin (1509–64), and under the governorship from 1554 of Mary's mother, Marie de Guise, the religious

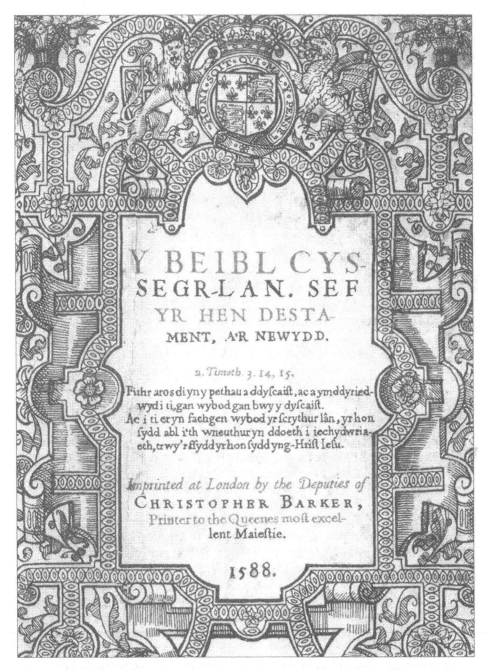

Figure 5 Y Beibl Cys-segr-Lan/The Welsh Bible (1588). By permission of llyfrgell Genedlaethol Cymru/The National Library of Wales

grievances of Protestants combined with increasing political fears that Scotland was becoming a satellite of France. When, in 1559, Marie de Guise attempted to suppress Protestant preachers, they and their powerful lay supporters, the Lords of the Congregation, rose in arms against Catholicism and France. Military deadlock between the two sides followed but was broken by English intervention in 1560. With the withdrawal of both French and English troops power was in the hands of the Congregation, and the Reformation Parliament of 1560, acting in the name of the 'commonalty of Scotland', banned the saying of mass, rejected papal authority, and accepted a reformed (basically Calvinist) confession of faith. Carried out in the name of the 'commonweal', the Scottish Reformation was not only rapid but also primarily from below. When Mary's French husband died in December 1560, she returned to Scotland in August 1561. Although she was allowed to remain Catholic, she could not undo the Reformation, which, as it had been carried out in defiance of the Crown, represented a major threat to royal authority. However, this threat was no threat to all authority: although there were many demands for reform which came from below, the Reformation was also carefully controlled from above, principally by the landed classes and the new groups in urban society.

John Knox (*c.*1514–1572)

Born in Haddington and educated at St Andrews University, Knox became the key figure of the Scottish Reformation. In 1546–7 he was influenced by the heretical Protestant ideas of George Wishart and John Winram. In the late 1540s he went to England, where he served as a minister in Newcastle and Berwick. When Mary Tudor acceded to the throne, he left for the Continent, where he became minister to exiled congregations (Frankfurt, Geneva). When Mary died, Knox wanted to return to England, but Elizabeth, infuriated by Knox's criticism of female rule – *First Blast of the Trumpet against the monstrous regiment of women* (1558) – denied him entry. So he sailed for Scotland, arriving when the conflict between the Protestants and Mary de Guise was reaching its height. Knox became one of the chief propagandists of the Lords of the Congregation, who established the Protestant regime in 1560. When Mary Stuart returned to Scotland in 1561, Knox feared that the Reformation could be endangered by the monarch's Catholicism. Knox met Mary three times during her reign, and he frankly and outspokenly criticised her beliefs and way of life. When she abdicated in 1567, he supported her baby son and the regent, Moray.

Knox regarded himself as being called by God to be his prophet. In his eyes, idolatry (i.e. the worship of idols) was the worst sin. He enjoyed a huge reputation because of his inspiring sermons and captivating language, but the consolidation of the Reformation and the Scottish Kirk was largely the work of his lesser-known contemporaries.

One could argue that, while the Reformation in England was initiated from above (as an act of state), in Scotland it was initiated from below but carefully controlled from above. And while the (Anglican) Church of England eventually adhered to Protestant dogma, but rather Catholic rituals and a hierarchical Episcopalian structure, the Church of Scotland had a (more egalitarian) Presbyterian structure and adhered to Protestant (Calvinist) dogma and rituals.

STATE AND SOCIETY UNDER THE TUDORS

The Tudor monarchs

When Henry VII succeeded to the throne in 1485 his foremost interest was in how to consolidate and, if possible, extend his royal authority. He did so, first, by putting his finances in order, reducing expenses and filling the royal coffers by selling monopolies (the exclusive right to import and sell goods); second, by marrying Elizabeth of York and thereby uniting the rival branches of the royal family; and, third, by winning the loyalty of most surviving nobles as well as assuming control over the rest by letting Parliament grant jurisdiction over cases involving the nobility to the Court of Star Chamber (which was staffed by his key advisers). Moreover, he put many administrative duties (such as dispensing justice, collecting taxes and maintaining local order) into the hands of some 600 unpaid justices of the peace (JPs), mostly drawn from the gentry (i.e. that part of the nobility which was socially inferior to the peerage: knights, esquires, gentlemen and, from 1611, baronets). The latter measure not only saved a lot of money – France had at least forty times as many officials as England – but also encouraged the self-confidence of the gentry whose support counterbalanced the titled nobility's dominance and tendency towards factionalism, and it eventually made the laity the main agency of government enforcement. In the 1530s the gentry supported Henry VIII's separation from the Roman Catholic church and, in turn, benefited from the sale of the dissolved monasteries. Under the later Tudors, however, problems of defence led to the introduction of lord-lieutenants (in 1549), which again strengthened the influence of the great magnates, as it was they who filled most of the posts.

The Tudor monarchy was personal (centred on the king and his court) and patrimonial (financed by the revenue from the crown lands). Like other Renaissance monarchs the Tudors claimed to govern 'by the grace of God' and to rule by 'divine right', i.e. being accountable to God alone: disobedience to the monarch was ultimately regarded as disobedience to God. As of old, the kings and queens were obliged to defend the realm, uphold the Church and administer justice impartially. If they did so, they were regarded as virtuous executants of 'good government'. Their worldly objectives, however, were to augment their regal power so that they could secure their territorial sovereignty as well as dynastic succession, which, as a consequence, made it necessary to subordinate the nobility, control feudal privileges and, above all, increase revenues (to finance the necessary military forces). Monarchical authority was also enhanced by symbolic politics: royal buildings – Henry VIII possessed over sixty houses, Elizabeth I still had almost forty – heraldry, elaborate rituals (public processions) and ceremonial displays such as royal progresses (the monarch touring the country) significantly added to the prestige of the monarchy.

The only limitation to the monarch's power was that he could not, as one fifteenth-century jurist had written, 'at his pleasure change the laws of the kingdom'. That is to say, in the long run the Tudor monarchs, unlike the kings of France, could not govern without the consent of Parliament. Although Parliament was still an instrument in the monarch's hands, Henry VIII needed it to establish the Church of England and himself as its 'supreme head'. When Mary I wanted to divest herself of that title, she could not legally do so without Parliament, and the latter only consented after terms had been included in the statute which safeguarded the validity of the land sales of the dissolved monasteries. Again, Mary's marriage to Philip of Spain was approved, while her plans to have him crowned king of England were thwarted by Parliament. More important, during Elizabeth's reign it became possible to think of the 'state' as separate from the monarch and as an impersonal form of political authority. This separation of the state and the monarch made it conceivable that to *serve* the former's 'weal and advancement' could (and was to) be regarded as the latter's obligation. From here, the idea of a 'mixed' or constitutional monarchy was just a step away.

The periphery

In many parts of the Isles, however, consolidating Tudor authority meant *establishing* it in the first place. In particular this applied to what from an English perspective appeared as the periphery (or 'borderlands'), which comprised three regions: Wales with the marcher lordships (established in the eleventh century) and the principality (annexed to the English crown as its direct possession in 1284), the far north (a mountainous buffer zone between England and Scotland) and, in Ireland, the land beyond the Pale around Dublin. While all of these borderlands were remote from the centre of power, predominantly pastoral in character (with relatively poor soil), with harsh(er) climates, sparse populations and traditionally strong landlord–tenant ties, they differed fundamentally in other aspects. Wales and Ireland had their fragmented political landscapes and Celtic cultural backgrounds in common, but Ireland was geographically separate from England, while Wales was not; in terms of government Ireland had its separate central administration in Dublin, while Wales had the marcher lordships, and, in the north, wardens of the marches tried to counter internal disorder as well as the military threat from Scotland. English–Scottish relations were particularly difficult: there was no formal peace between the two kingdoms between 1333 and 1474. Mostly, these regions were war zones in which semi-independent ('reiving', i.e. raiding) clans preyed on their neighbours beyond the border. As the English administrative system was at best partially in force, power very often rested not with the JPs but with the local lords. Moreover, these administrative difficulties nurtured the centre's negative views of the people of the periphery. The English regarded the Scots, the Welsh and the Irish as rude, uncouth, savage, wild and lawless, who needed to be taught law and order first so that they could be civilised later and, perhaps, eventually integrated. While the Scots were subjects of the Scottish monarch and, because of this, subject to Scottish jurisdiction, the Welsh and the Irish were disabled at law under English jurisdiction: Poynings' Law (1494), by which Irish parliamentarian sessions and proposed legislation had to be previously approved in England, was just the most blatant example. From today's perspective such conditions clearly suggest a devolution of power, but bad political experience then favoured its increased centralisation.

From the perspective of the Tudors, the administrative reorganisation of Wales was the most successful. In 1536 and 1543 two Acts of Union were carried which (i) reduced the powers of the marcher lords, (ii) created seven new shires, which were added to the already existing ones of the principality, (iii) introduced the whole apparatus of English county government (sheriffs, JPs, Members of Parliament [MPs]), (iv) replaced Welsh by English laws, and (v) made English the language of judicial and administrative business, but retained Welsh as the language of religion and worship. Although under this union the Welsh came to enjoy the same rights and privileges as the English, the imposition of English laws and customs had a traumatic effect.

Fifteenth-century Ireland was divided into the 'Englishry' where Anglo-Irish lords held land from the English crown (but were relatively independent of it) and the 'Irishry' where Gaelic chiefs ruled according to Irish custom. As in the far north of England, Henry VII tried to rule in Ireland through a local family (the earls of Kildare). But Henry VIII attempted a more assimilative stance: his aim was integration. In 1541 he had himself proclaimed king (not just lord) of Ireland by the Irish parliament and offered the Gaelic nobles English law and charters for their lands if they submitted peacefully: the motto of this policy was 'surrender and re-grant'. However, what had worked in Wales did not work in Ireland: the latter was much larger and politically even more fragmented than the former. In Wales, Henry's personal ties to the people (his family was partly Welsh), the rise of the gentry and the acceptance of Welsh as the language of religion had acted as catalysts of unity, while in Ireland progress was slow and died with Henry. When Edward VI's government tried to force the issue, Anglo-Irish relations broke down again. In Mary's reign, however, the Irish parliament passed laws allowing English settlers to take land in Ireland (1557). Under her successor, Elizabeth I, English colonists were introduced to monitor and control strategic trouble spots. This measure added to the already

Shires and Boroughs

Shires (or counties) are administrative areas in Britain, still used today for local government purposes. Some counties still have 'shire' in their names, e.g. Hampshire, Cambridgeshire, North Yorkshire. Shires are the oldest divisions of the country in England and Scotland. Some of them (such as Kent) may have their origins in ancient kingdoms, and many of them already existed before the Norman Conquest: in England they date from the seventh or eighth century, in Scotland from the tenth or eleventh. They were controlled by a royal official, the so-called 'shire-reeve', or sheriff, who was responsible for keeping order and collecting revenues. Eventually, each shire had its court, which was an important forum for justice governing all aspects of everyday life in Anglo-Saxon and Norman England. In 1295 all forty shires were required to send two representatives each (knights) to Edward I's 'Model' Parliament. The later justices of the peace (JP) were also organised on a shire basis. The 'shiring' of Wales and Ireland came later. In Wales, it was carried through in two steps: in 1282, following Edward I's conquest, and in 1536, when in the process of annexation the Marcher lordships were converted into counties. In Ireland, the introduction of shires occurred in more piecemeal fashion, beginning in the thirteenth century and ending in 1606.

The term 'borough' ('burgh' in Scotland) is derived from the Latin *burgus* and denotes a fortified settlement with urban characteristics. Its inhabitants were known as *burgenses*, or burgesses, who, because they held a certain amount of property ('burgage'), enjoyed local political privileges. From the twelfth century onwards these settlements grew into towns (and some of them, later, into cities) which, because of their economic importance, succeeded in acquiring different kinds of privileges from the crown or from their lords, such as administering justice (juridical boroughs), being exempt from certain forms of taxes (taxation boroughs), or sending representatives to Parliament (parliamentary boroughs). In 1295, 114 chartered towns were instructed to send two representatives each to Edward I's 'Model' Parliament.

While the government usually responded (albeit very slowly) to economic and demographic developments by creating new boroughs where necessary, it rarely disfranchised those which became unimportant. This problem was not tackled until the first Reform Act in 1832 (see Chapter 6).

existing 'colonial' conflicts between the Gaelic chiefs and Old English land-owners the crucial aspect of religious difference: while the latter were both Catholics, the New English settlers were Protestants. As many Gaelic chiefs felt threatened by the influx of English (and Scottish) settlers, Elizabeth's govern-ments had to deal with numerous revolts (1568–73, 1579–83). In 1594, Hugh O'Neill, earl of Tyrone, began a rebellion which grew into a Nine Years War (1594–1603); and, although at one time it had the support of Spanish troops (1601), it ended in defeat: O'Neill submitted to royal authority.

While the English Reformation exacerbated the problems of the borderlands in Ireland and, at least for some time, in Wales, it influenced the north of England in a different way. The English Reformation, for various reasons, was established by a strong monarch, his government and his allies in Parliament, but in Scotland the Reformation came about largely because of the absence of a monarch capable of rule. Mary Queen of Scots was still in France when her mother, Marie de Guise, regent for her daughter from 1554, died in 1560. When, with a little help from Elizabeth I, the French troops were expelled from Scotland, the Reformation Parliament was free to act. Needless to say, the ideological affinities between the two Protestant churches improved Anglo-Scottish relations for some time and thereby eased both governments' difficulties in defending their frontier. The wardens of the marches ('the northern earls'), who had already rebelled against Henry VIII in the Pilgrimage of Grace (1536), sensed one more chance to reinforce their position, when Mary was forced to abdicate in Scotland (1567) and fled to England (1568) where she was imprisoned: they planned to rescue her, to help her restore Catholicism and thereby to regain and strengthen their traditional influence. However, their rising (in 1569) collapsed, and Elizabeth appointed a southern noble as president of the Council of the North.

The social order

While the Middle Ages had viewed the world as being compounded of three complementary estates – knights to defend the realm, priests to pray for it, and peasants to provide the upkeep of the first two (cf. Chapter 2) – by the mid-sixteenth century English 'society' had become more stratified (Table 1). For the ruling elite the central concept of such an ordered society was hierarchy: the idea of an ordered series of gradations of rank ascending from the lowest to the highest member. The peerage and the gentry comprised no more than 5 per cent of the population but owned roughly 60 per cent of the land. The titular nobility (peerage) consisted of some fifty families in 1600 and well under 200 a hundred years later. Despite the fine gradations between them, what united the aristocracy was a powerful sense of common interest – as landowners they had a stake in the country – and of collective identity as 'men of rank' and 'persons of honour'. In contradistinction to the 'middling' and 'poorer sorts' they were the 'better sort' whose status was primarily conferred by the nobility of blood (lineage). But a gentleman also was a gentleman because his peers considered him as such. Such a way of life consisted in living without physical labour off one's landed income (rent), knightly service and, later, acceptance of administrative duties (such as acting as a JP), shared social values, learning, manners and deportment. A family's house was the visible sign of its wealth, position of authority and dynastic continuity. The two meanings attached to the word 'house' – a family as a dynastic succession (as in 'the house of Marlborough') and a place of residence – demonstrated that connection.

Table 1 The social order in sixteenth-century England

(Titled) Nobility/Peerage	c.55 peers (families) owned c.15 per cent of the land.
[Lords Temporal]	[Lords Spiritual] archbishops
dukes marquesses earls viscounts	
	bishops
barons [Country]	[City]
Gentry	c.10,000 persons owned c.45 per cent of the land.
baronets (from 1611) knights (e)squires gentlemen	great merchants
The Middling Sort (Later: Middle classes) yeomen (c.160,000) well-to-do tenant farmers clerics	merchants/tradesmen artisans/craftsmen professional men
The Poorer Sort (Later: Labouring/Working Classes) husbandmen smallholders cottagers living-in servants outworkers	small artisans wage labourers
vagrants, vagabonds	

The view that not only every person but also every creature had its allotted place in the 'great chain of being' was shared by the common people. Such a view of a hierarchical universe beginning with God and the angels and stretching down through human beings and animals to the vegetative and mineral worlds not only possessed oppressive features (as we may imagine today) but also provided physical protection and mental security. The Church played a central role in inculcating the values of such a universe (Document 12). The commonwealth was imagined as a family (with the 'godly prince' as the paterfamilias) and vice versa: relationships between men, women and children were formulated in terms of authority and subordination. Inequality between the sexes was considered as natural as social differences between men of different ranks.

Figure 6 The Great Chain of Being © Copyright the Trustees of The British Museum

The economy

Early Tudor England shared the general prosperity of contemporary Europe. Its unfinished broadcloth, in particular, taken to Antwerp to be dressed and dyed, was sold all over the Continent: English cloth exports doubled in quantity between the 1470s and the 1550s. With the growing trade adequate shipping had to be provided: England's tonnage doubled between 1570 and 1630. Slowly but distinctly English merchants drove out their competitors: the Venetians ceased their regular visits to London after 1533 – they were last seen at Southampton in 1587; the North German Hanseatic merchants were ousted in 1598, and thirteen years later English merchants for their part were given privileges at Hamburg. Although the crown in general welcomed the economic efforts of its subjects (and very often invested in them), it only reluctantly and tardily took responsibility for distant trades and colonies. In general, royal support took the form of granting a monopoly to a merchant (or trading) company and passing laws which privileged English merchants.

Chartered Companies

Chartered companies were associations of merchants specialising in overseas trade. The aims of these companies were twofold. On the one hand, they made it easier for merchants to build, man and equip ships for long-distance trade as they 'pooled' money from different sources (joint-stock companies, including so-called 'sleeping partners') and shared the risk from potential losses. (In the sixteenth century, only one out of three ships in long-distance trade returned to port.) On the other hand, they received charters, grants of privilege, from the government which allowed them (and only them) to trade in specific goods in certain parts of the world. Because of these privileged trading concessions (monopolies), these companies made great fortunes and also contributed decisively to the state's revenue. One of the greatest English trading companies was the Merchant Venturers of London. In 1505 they were granted their charter by Henry VII recognising the company's monopoly on cloth export. Even though supporters of free trade and others protested against it, the Merchant Venturers defended their monopoly until 1689. When they were deprived of their exclusive trading rights, the export of cloth was open to all merchants and companies.

Chartered companies and their monopoly trading power also played an important role in the history of colonisation. The East India Company was granted a royal charter in 1600 by Elizabeth I; it gave the company exclusive permission to trade in the East Indies. The company established itself as a commercial and military power in India, gaining substantial administrative and governmental control of the country. Another important trading company was the Royal Africa Company (established in 1672), which supplied slaves for the West Indies and traded gold and ivory with West Africa.

However, the economically relatively stable fifteenth century gave way to an increasingly unstable sixteenth century. The rich got richer because they profited from the redistribution of the monastic lands and a growth in population (from 2.5 million in 1520 to 4.5 million in 1620), which led to a rise in grain prices. The poor got poorer because, between 1510 and 1625, the cost of living rose fivefold. Most probably, the main cause of this unprecedented inflation (with a rate of 2 per cent per year) was the quantity of gold and silver bullion which flowed from Spain's South American colonies into Europe and, as a consequence, vastly increased the amount of money in circulation. At the same time, the purchasing power of wages was cut by 60 per cent. These developments went hand in hand with the growth of wage labour (mostly in agriculture) which resulted from the gradual dissolution of feudal relations from the second half of the fourteenth century (cf. Chapter 3). The traditional English peasants (the moderately prosperous farmers) disappeared: some moved up to yeoman status, but most of them joined the ranks of the labourers. With the loosening of feudal ties the extent of poverty became more obvious as nobody felt inclined to accept responsibility for the poor. Consecutive Tudor governments passed laws (in 1531, 1536, 1572, 1598 and 1601) which tried to gain control of the problem.

Poor Laws

In the Middle Ages canon (i.e. church) law required that every member of a parish had to pay a tithe (i.e. one-tenth) of their income to the Church. One-third of this amount was set aside for poor relief. When this system ceased to function properly because, for example, tithe revenues were spent on other things, the state had to step in. Various parliamentary Acts (1388, 1391, 1536, 1601) tried to come to grips with the problem. From the early seventeenth century onwards, each parish was responsible for its own poor. To contribute to the parish collection had become a legal requirement. Justices of the peace set up a framework for the administration of the law – who had to pay how much and who was to receive how much and when or under what circumstances.

From the second half of the eighteenth century onwards, the administration of the law became more difficult as people began to migrate to the places where they could find work. The law, however, stipulated that they could get poor relief only in the village of their birth. In 1834 a new poor law Act was passed which imposed a strict regime (including workhouses) on those who received funds. This system remained in place until 1929.

INTERNATIONAL RELATIONS, 1485–1603

After the Wars of the Roses, international relations had to be restored as well because the contending parties had found different allies on the Continent (the French, for example, supporting the Lancastrians, and the Burgundians York). Henry VII not only tried to secure and maintain peace but also to win recognition by the neighbouring dynasties: the marriage of his son Arthur to Catherine of Aragon (1501) and of his daughter Margaret to James IV of Scotland (1503) have to be understood in this light. In those days, England was not a global player but a second-rate power whose main role in European politics was (for understandable historical reasons, cf. Chapter 3) to be opposed to France, while France was allied to England's northern neighbour, Scotland. Henry VIII's war with both (1512–14) had the appearance of victory (Flodden, Tournai) but resulted in financial exhaustion. After the Habsburg Charles of Spain had been elected as the Holy Roman Emperor Charles V, European diplomacy was dominated by the struggle between the houses of Valois (France) and Habsburg for some forty years. Henry VIII's policy was generally pro-Habsburg, but his breach with Rome complicated the situation as much as the growing influence of Protestantism under his son, Edward VI. Catholic Mary I adhered to the Habsburg alliance but paid for it dearly: her husband, Philip, forced England into a war with France which resulted in the loss of England's last Continental foothold, Calais (1558). But, between 1559 and 1572, England's position *vis-à-vis* France improved because Scotland became detached from the latter by its Protestant reformation (1560) and France sank into the turmoil of a religious civil war (1572–98). Elizabeth I, who had been declared excommunicate and deposed by Pope Pius V in 1570, made the most of France's weakness and concluded a mutual defence alliance with the French in 1572. In the same year, Dutch Calvinist resistance against Spanish oppression and the Catholic inquisition, which had been smouldering since the early 1560s, became a fully-fledged rebellion. While the elite of the southern Catholic provinces had second thoughts, the northern Calvinist provinces detached themselves in 1579 and declared their independence from Spain as the Dutch United Provinces. When this insurrection nearly collapsed, Elizabeth I, who had succeeded in giving her country twenty-five years of peace, agreed to give minimum help to them (1584). To put an end to Elizabeth's support and to reimpose Catholicism in England, Philip of Spain sent his Armada in 1588. A combination of luck, good tactics and winds favouring the English navy but putting the Armada at a disadvantage ensured England's victory, while the war with Spain dragged on until 1604.

English overseas expansion began at Bristol, when John Cabot (originally Giovanni Caboto from Venice) claimed in 1497 to have crossed the Atlantic to North America and to have reached Newfoundland. Further voyages in the northern hemisphere (by Martin Frobisher and John Davis) and in the southern hemisphere (by Richard Grenville, Francis Drake and Thomas Cavendish) expanded the knowledge of the Atlantic and beyond, and thereby discovered new fishing grounds and, more important, prepared the way for new trade routes to the West and the East. For this reason, many chartered trading companies were instrumental in these ventures. And, although the expansion of trade was their main interest, some of these companies were also involved in settlement projects. Finally, these voyages enabled the English to loot Spanish ships (of the 'silver fleet'), and to attack and destroy Spanish forts and trading posts. This was what Elizabeth's 'sea dogs' revelled in: Francis Drake (c.1540–96) was not only the first Englishman to circumnavigate the globe (1577–80); he also harried the Spanish wherever he could find them. John Hawkins (1532–95) was not only Drake's kinsman but also his comrade-in-arms against Spain. Moreover, he became the first Englishman to traffic in slaves, carrying Africans to the Spanish West Indies on three occasions between 1562 and 1567. Walter Ralegh (1552–1618) combined acts of piracy with settlement projects (Roanoke Island in the 1580s) and fighting the Spanish (1590s) with attempts at discovering a mythic 'El Dorado' (in today's Guyana) in 1595. All three of them were knighted for their services to the country.

While the Spaniards and the Portuguese concentrated their activities in Central and South America (causing the death of roughly 90 per cent of the indigenous population in half a century), the English had to make do with what was left: North America. Attempts at early settlement were made at Roanoke Island (today's North Carolina) in 1585 and 1587. Both failed because the settlers could not (yet) manage without regular supplies from England. The first settlements that could be maintained were founded in the next century.

STATE AND SOCIETY, 1603–89

An unstable union

When James VI of Scotland (b. 1566, r. 1567–1625) also became king of England as James I (r. 1603–25), the problems of how to rule such a composite realm became even more acute. The Stuart monarchs and, between 1649 and 1660, their republican opponents, although in different form, had to deal with three long-term causes of instability: the problems of (i) multiple kingdoms (such as an absentee monarch, different traditions of ministerial and parliamentarian advice, as well as jealousies and antagonisms of the component territories which resulted from their respective domestic and foreign interests), of (ii) religious divisions (within and between the different kingdoms), and of (iii) how to keep a financial and political system intact in the face of inflation, the rising cost of war and different traditions of financial exaction. These causes of instability were 'overdetermined' by (iv) other, even more long-term developments in the economic vitality, political power and cultural prestige of different groups in the societies of the Isles, such as the decline of the aristocracy (cf. Chapter 3), the rise of the gentry and the middle classes, and the slow but distinct shift from a feudal to a capitalist economy.

While, under the Tudors, Wales had been integrated (with Welsh MPs in London) and Ireland annexed (with its separate, but subordinate, parliament in Dublin and the Lord Deputy representing the king of England), Scotland had been an independent kingdom. However, from 1603 onwards, Scotland suffered from an absentee monarchy: James, who had promised to return every three years, came back only once (in 1617). Charles I (b. 1600, r. 1625–49) came twice: in 1633, eight years after his accession to the throne, to have himself crowned in a provocatively Anglicised coronation ceremony, and in 1641, after he had made war on Scotland twice, to have his powers curtailed by a furious Scottish parliament. More important, in the light of the Irish example, the Scots refused to accept any royal deputy or viceroy. On the other hand, while the English parliament constantly legislated for England, Wales and Ireland (e.g., abolishing the monarchy in 1649, restoring it in 1660, declaring the throne vacant in 1689), it never tried to do so for Scotland. With one exception, though: when the (English) Rump Parliament abolished the Stuart monarchy in England, Wales and Ireland in 1649, it did not do so in Scotland. Only when the Scots crowned Charles II as king of Britain and Ireland in 1651 did the army of the Commonwealth invade, conquer and incorporate Scotland, abolishing the Scottish monarchy, parliament and executive. Thus, a union of sorts was achieved by military force. The Restoration (1660) put the clock back twenty years. It restored the traditional powers of the Crown in England, Wales and Ireland as well as in Scotland. James I and Charles I had regarded themselves as ruling by divine right (Document 13), and so did Charles II and James II, although the Restoration had been engineered by Parliament. The idea of a monarch's God-given mandate to rule lingered on until the eighteenth century, but a decisive change towards what came to be called constitutional monarchy was achieved by the Glorious Revolution (1688), the ensuing legislation (particularly by the Act of Succession, 1701) and political practice. Finally, in the union of 1707 a single British state was created: the United Kingdom of Great Britain.

The War(s) of the Three Kingdoms

While James I had mostly chosen a 'softly softly' approach to the problems outlined above, suggesting compromises where possible and assenting to them where necessary, his son preferred confrontation (Document 14). Immediately after his accession Charles attempted to fill the royal coffers by renegotiating the terms of land tenure in Scotland (Act of Revocation). Needless to say, he offended many of the nobility, and particularly those who had benefited from having former church lands conferred upon them by the Crown. The result was

---

National Covenant and Solemn League and Covenant

In the Christian Bible the term 'covenant' refers to conditional promises made to man by God. More specifically, it points to the agreement between God and the ancient Israelites, in which he promised to protect them if they were faithful and kept his laws. In Scottish history, the National Covenant is an agreement (1638) among Scottish Presbyterians ('covenanters') to uphold their faith. Although this document is dull and drily legalistic, it successfully combined a direct defiance of the king's will with a declaration of loyalty to Charles I.

While the National Covenant was a document of Scottish self-assertion, the Solemn League and Covenant (1643) was an agreement between the Scots and Charles I's parliamentary opponents in England which intended the promotion of Presbyterianism in Scotland and England. However, once Charles was defeated, the English parliamentarians would have nothing to do with religious conformity on the Scottish model.

---

non-compliance and non-cooperation. Later, when Charles tried to impose English religious forms on the Church of Scotland (a new book of canons [church laws] and a new prayer book) without reference to a general assembly (responsible for matters of the Church) or parliament, the deeply offended Scottish people reacted with a massive act of passive disobedience, the National Covenant (1638). Although the nature of this 'protest movement' was initially peaceful, Charles decided to react with military force, involving the English army, Protestant forces from Ireland and also (if necessary) loyal Catholic forces from Ireland and the Scottish Highlands. The king did not seek the support of the English parliament for this war but financed it by loans and non-parliamentarian exactions. This was unusual but understandable: when he had summoned his third parliament ten years earlier (1628), it had condemned non-parliamentarian taxation and other royal policies in its Petition of Right, and, as a consequence, Charles had dissolved it in the following year and ruled without Parliament since then. (This period [1629–40] has been called Personal Rule or, more abusively, 'Eleven Years Tyranny'.) However, the First Scots' War came to a swift end in June 1639, when Charles's money dwindled, the envisaged Irish assistance failed to materialise, and the Scots seemed prepared to fight. In the autumn, the Scottish general assembly and parliament, dominated by coven-anters, began a legislative programme which continued until 1640 and resulted in a constitutional revolution. The most important elements were that Parlia-ment was to meet (with or without royal summons) at least once every three years (Triennial Act) and legislation no longer required the royal assent. In May 1640, Charles, bent on subduing the Scots at all costs, was forced to summon his (fourth) English parliament (thereby ending his Personal Rule) to find finan-cial support for such a war. However, the parliament which met on 13 April

1640 was hostile not only to Charles's outstanding military bill but also to his plans for renewed war. Moreover, it claimed redress of grievances which had accumulated over the past decade. And, perhaps most important, the king's opponents suspected that a monarch who had employed Irish troops against the Scots might also abuse any army at his disposal to crush opposition in England. Charles angrily dissolved Parliament on 5 May 1640 (which is why it has been called the Short Parliament) and prepared for war without its backing. However, English mobilisation was slow, so that when the Scottish covenanter army took the initiative, towards the end of August 1640, Charles lost the Second Scots' War in a single engagement. A truce was concluded at Ripon in October 1640, but the final peace settlement was a different and lengthier matter. Charles's attempt at crushing one of his kingdoms with the help of the other two caused the Scots to demand a durable religious and political settlement which was to embrace not only Scotland, but England and Ireland as well. The Scots envisaged a federal-type union with the English, with close cooperation in commerce and politics. In terms of religion they strove for uniformity and wanted to replace the English Episcopalian church by the Scottish Presbyterian type. However, neither Charles nor his (fifth) English parliament, which he was forced to summon in November 1640, reciprocated these Scottish overtures. While the English parliament clearly benefited from the Scottish example, passing its own Triennial Act in February and an Act against dissolution without its own consent in May 1641, it baulked at a closer union of the two nations. In the summer of the same year Charles I visited Scotland to ratify the treaty and witness the massive reduction of his monarchical powers. While he was there the Irish rebellion began.

When the Nine Years War (1594–1603) had ended with O'Neill's submission to royal authority, to the great resentment of the English soldiers and officials who had fought him for many years, O'Neill was allowed to retain possession of his lands in Ulster. But, realising that he would no longer be master in his own house in anything but name, the Earl of Tyrone and his ally, the Earl of Tyrconnell, left Ireland on 4 September 1607 for exile on the Continent ('the flight of the earls'). Their fertile lands (of over 2 million acres) were declared forfeit to the Crown and given to settlers: half of them English, half of them Scottish and all of them Protestant. This was the Plantation proper; although exact figures are notoriously hard to come by, it is a fair estimate that a generation later some 40,000 people had settled in Donegal, Tyrone, Derry and Armagh (the earls' territories) as well as in Cavan and Fermanagh. It was a truly colonial situation with two separate societies: the Gaelic Catholic Irish (natives) deeply resented the dispossession of their land, and the Protestant British (settlers) felt surrounded by enemies in their new homes.

Charles' defeat in the Scots' Wars politically weakened the monarchy in England and Scotland, nourishing hopes in Ireland that, as a consequence, some of the dispossessed land as well as lost political and religious rights might successfully be reclaimed. While the Catholic social elite, notably the Anglo-Irish, tried to negotiate with the king, their social inferiors quickly lost patience and staged a rebellion against the settlers (October 1641), in which bitterness over the loss of property and status was transformed into hatred of the persons who had apparently benefited from it. Between 2000 and 4000 Protestant settlers were brutally killed, some ten thousand fled from their homes, many of them dying of hunger. By the late spring of 1642, most of Ireland was in the hands of the rebels, who made plans to consolidate their position politically and religiously. In May a Catholic Confederation of Ireland (also known as the Confederation of Kilkenny) was agreed, by which the Irish Catholics (like the Scottish covenanters) bound themselves to defend their church, crown and liberty.

The Irish rebellion had a profound impact in England and Scotland. Most important, English and Scottish settlers had been its victims, a fact which demanded an Anglo-Scottish response and thereby associated the two nations more closely than the recently concluded peace treaty had envisaged. Moreover, Charles, who may have toyed with the idea of returning to Personal Rule in England, could not even attempt to do so because he needed Parliament to finance the war against the rebels. However, rumours that Charles had been involved in (and had perhaps authorised) the rebellion intensified doubts whether he could be trusted with control over an army. What occurred in the winter of 1641–2 can only be called a breakdown of trust within the English government. A 'Grand Remonstrance' which listed what Parliament regarded as royal abuses was debated in November and presented to Charles on 1 December. When he tried unsuccessfully to seize and arrest his leading opponents in Parliament in early January 1642, further acts curbing his powers were passed, and in the summer Parliament demanded full control of the army (in the 'Militia Ordinance') and the executive. (This particular incident has influenced political protocol to this very day: the monarch is not allowed to enter the House of Commons and, as a consequence, the state opening of Parliament takes place in the House of Lords.) Charles insisted in his answer *nolumus leges Angliae mutari* ('we do not wish the laws of England to be changed'), but had to quit London shortly afterwards. In June both king and Parliament began raising armies. When Charles eventually raised his standard in Nottingham in August, the war (in England) formally began.

In the spring of 1642, a first wave of 2500 Scottish soldiers and men was despatched to Ireland to support the Protestant settlers. By the end of that year, this army, commanded by Robert Munro and paid by England, consisted of some 11,000 men who succeeded in restoring order in much of Ulster. Dublin and the greater part of the Pale remained in the hands of English commanders loyal to the king. With the beginning of hostilities in England a stalemate developed in Ireland: the poorly equipped and poorly organised rebels could not make further inroads into Protestant territory, nor could the royalist English or the Scots covenanters mount a successful counter-offensive.

Between 1642 and 1646, England endured an intense conflict between two large and largely equal parties: the royalists ('Cavaliers') and the parliamentarians ('Roundheads'). During the first phase the royalists, who by the autumn of 1643 held about two-thirds of England and Wales, appeared to be winning the war. The tide turned during late 1642 and early 1643 as a result of both sides seeking support from the other two kingdoms and thereby giving the English civil war a more distinctly British character. In June 1642, Charles began negotiations with the rebel confederation of Kilkenny, offering religious concessions in exchange for troops he needed in England – his own English troops and not (yet) Irish Catholic troops as the parliamentarians alleged – which became available when a one-year ceasefire was agreed in September. This development brought back into the picture the Scots who, so far, had stayed neutral in the internal English conflict. As they regarded the prospect of a victory for Charles in England as a threat to Scottish Presbyterianism (and also feared pro-royalist uprisings), the Scots allied with the English parliamentarians. While the latter were interested in a military alliance only, the Scots wanted more: the final deal, the Solemn League and Covenant (ratified by both sides in the autumn of 1643), also included English financial support and naval protection of Scotland, an understanding that a truce or peace with Charles could only be concluded with the consent of the Scots, and the prospect of Presbyterianism being established throughout the British archipelago. Early in 1644 the Scottish covenanter army crossed the Tweed, secured northern England, linked forces with English parliamentarian forces, besieged York (in the spring) and defeated the royalist army at Marston Moor (in July).

However, early in 1644, Charles had authorised the Marquis of Antrim to raise 2000 Catholic Irish troops to invade western Scotland and join the forces of the royalist Marquis of Montrose. Between September 1643 and September 1644 these troops wreaked havoc on the Scottish mainland, tying down large parts of the covenanter army which unsuccessfully tried to control them. But, by the time Montrose attempted to leave the Highlands in the summer of 1645, it had become clear that Charles was losing the war in England. The royalists were defeated at Naseby in June; Montrose was crushed by the covenanters at Philiphaugh in September; Charles eventually surrendered to the Scots at Newark in May 1646. While it was clear that the decision of the latter to intervene in support of the parliamentarian forces had changed the tide of the war, the amount of economic and material resources available to the respective parties certainly also had its impact: while the royalists generally held the less populous and less developed parts of the country, Parliament held the most densely populated and the richest areas and the port cities.

The wars were bloody, and their costs were immense. While levels of violence and destruction differed widely, there were some twenty battles involving more than 10,000 men, and probably another forty involving more than 5000. According to one estimate, there was a higher proportion of fighting and dying in these wars than in the First World War (1914–18). But neither these sacrifices nor Charles's surrender brought any solution to the issues which had started the wars. Despite the Scots' decisive contribution to the defeat of the royalists, divisions between the Scottish and English representatives on the committee of both kingdoms (particularly with regard to a closer Anglo-Scottish political union and to religious uniformity) had already begun to grow before the war was over. On the basis of the recent successes of the reformed 'new model' army, the English parliamentarian side acted as if it was the real (and only) winner of the war. And when the king tried to play off one side against the other the Scots withdrew early in 1647 and left Charles as prisoner of the English parliament. The latter, in turn, roughly consisted of three parties: those who favoured a compromise deal with the king (the 'peace group', also known as Presbyterians), those who wanted a complete victory with a radical political and religious settlement (the 'war group', also known as Independents), and a large 'middle group' floating in between. During the uneasy peace of 1646–7 the Presbyterians came to dominate the House of Commons and made preparations for a settlement with Charles. At the same time the army demanded from Parliament remedy for a number of grievances (such as payment of arrears, provision for maimed soldiers and surviving dependants) as well as religious toleration. The majority in Parliament regarded these demands as a threat to its own type of settlement and tried to break the power of the military by disbanding parts of the army and sending other parts to Ireland. In reaction to these moves army unrest grew, perhaps influenced by the radical ideas of the Levellers. In the summer of 1647 the army staged a coup, seized the political initiative from Parliament, and took custody of the king. However, with its own position improved, divisions within the army itself opened up. While a moderate group wanted to reach a swift agreement with the king which left the

---

Putney Debates

From 28 October to 1 November 1647, the general council of the New Model Army discussed the reconstruction of postwar England at Putney Bridge and Whitehall. On the council, two officers and two soldiers each represented their regiments. The central question they had to deal with was whether or not to go on seeking a negotiated settlement with the king. Although the outcome of the debates must be regarded as inconclusive, the Agreement of the People (put forward by the Levellers) aimed at a substantial widening of the parliamentary franchise and openly advocated manhood suffrage.

judicial and executive powers to him, but demanded biennial parliaments and broad religious toleration (as laid down in the 'Heads of the Proposals'), a more radical group asserted that power lay with the people and their representatives and that people had certain 'inalienable' rights, such as equality before the law and religious liberty ('Agreement of the People').

Meanwhile Charles, who may have been rubbing his hands at the spectacle of his opponents falling out among themselves, escaped from his captivity only to be caught again immediately. However, in December 1647 he made an agreement with the Scots ('the engagement') in which he pledged not only to accept the 1641 constitutional settlement and improve economic, political and diplomatic relations between England and Scotland, but also – paradoxically – to enforce Presbyterianism in England and Wales (if only for a trial period of three years). Although many covenanters held aloof from the engagement, it was supported by the Scottish parliament. An army of some 20,000 men was raised, only to be shattered by the English parliamentarian army, which had duly reunited to face the threat, at Preston in August 1648. After Marston Moor (July 1644) and Naseby (June 1645), this was the third decisive victory the parliamentarians owed to their powerful commander, Oliver Cromwell. The power of the 'engagers' collapsed, and the covenanters, supported by Cromwell, took over again. In early December, the parliamentarian forces entered London and purged from the House of Commons all Members of Parliament (MPs) who were believed to be either hostile to the army or inclined

---

Oliver Cromwell (1599–1658)

Oliver Cromwell, English soldier and statesman, is one of the country's most controversial public figures. He rose from the middle ranks of English society to be Lord Protector of England, Scotland and Ireland. Born on 25 April 1599 in Huntingdon, Cromwell was educated at Cambridge and in London. As a student, he converted to a radical version of Puritan faith, although his precise religious orientation is still disputed. Cromwell served in both the Short Parliament (1640) and the Long Parliament (1640–60). He was commissioned into the army and – as a result of his military career – actively contributed to the brutal military conquest of the English over their neighbours. Given his lack of previous experience, Cromwell's military rise was exceptional. He succeeded not by innovative strategies but rather by instilling an extraordinary self-belief into his men. Cromwell formed the unconquerable 'Ironsides', combining rigid discipline with strict morality. In 1649, Cromwell played a leading role in the trial and execution of Charles I. Cromwell ruthlessly suppressed his opponents, subdued the Irish (1649–50) and the Scots (1650–1) and, for the first time in history, unified the British Isles under one central government. On his death (3 September 1658), this centralised authority collapsed.

to negotiate with Charles ('Pride's purge'). The 'rump' of fewer than eighty MPs set up a high court which tried the king for treason, formally abolished the monarchy (and the House of Lords) in England, Wales and Ireland (March 1649), and established England and Wales as a 'Commonwealth and Free State' (May 1649) with a republican government.

On 30 January 1649, Charles I was executed (Document 15). The regicide horrified royalists and moderates within the three kingdoms as well as foreign powers. Moreover, it changed the direction of Scottish politics yet again. Whatever their allegiances over the past decade, the fact that their king was killed by the English without Scottish consultation deeply shocked many Scots. When, in addition, the English parliament abolished the monarchy in all parts of the Isles except Scotland, the Scots could not but realise that instead of winning a closer Anglo-Scottish union they had had their regal union severed. Promptly (in February) the Scottish covenanter government reacted by proclaiming the eldest son of Charles I – later Charles II (b. 1630) – as king of Great Britain (England and Scotland) and Ireland. Charles II, however, took his time because, on the one hand, he knew that the Scottish political nation was divided on the matter of his succession and, on the other, he regarded Ireland as a better stepping stone to the recovery of England. In the end, both options came to nothing. Between the autumn of 1649 and the spring of 1650, Cromwell re-established English military control over much of Ireland. When he left to deal with Scotland, his son-in-law, Henry Ireton, took over to do the rest. In July, Cromwell invaded Scotland and defeated the Scottish royalist army at Dunbar. The Scots disintegrated into parties, but fighting did not stop. In January 1651, Charles II was crowned at Scone. Although Cromwell won a number of battles in Scotland during the following summer, the Scottish-royalist army circumvented his forces, moved into England, reached Worcester, but was pursued there, surrounded, and finally defeated on 3 September by the parliamentarian army.

When the Wars of the Three Kingdoms ended, unity was achieved, but at a certain price: Scotland was placed under English rule, its parliament and general assembly were abolished, English administration and military control were established. Instead of the desired Anglo-Scottish federal union the Scots had to stomach an enforced union on English terms. The lot of the Irish was even worse. On top of an enforced union with England (with a military and civilian administration in Dublin) they had their rights and liberties drastically curbed, many people were transplanted from Ulster, Leinster and Munster to Connacht (a measure which amounted to what we would now call ethnic cleansing), and huge tracts of land were confiscated and redistributed, so that by the end of the 1650s perhaps some 20 per cent of Irish land was left in Catholic hands. Would there be peace now? If so, what kind of peace would it be? Would it bring regeneration? The economic resources of the Isles were massively depleted, large parts of their ruling elites were destroyed, and their people

---

Political Ideas

The study of political ideas focuses on fundamental questions concerning government, politics, law, property, etc. What makes a good government? Which form should it take? Can it be overthrown in case of misuse of power and authority? How? Who should be in power? What is the law like? How is it enforced? Which rights and duties should citizens have and why? Can individuals own property, or what should property rights look like?

Two of the most influential political philosophers who published their work in English and dealt with questions like these were Thomas Hobbes (1588–1679) and John Locke (1632–1704). Hobbes is renowned for his book *Leviathan* (1651), in which he defends the principle of sovereign rule. To him, the 'state of nature' – characterised by competitiveness, fear and war among the people – is the greatest threat to human security. In order to avoid this miserable condition, and to guarantee peace and safety, men must relinquish their (individual share of) power to establish an absolute sovereign who maintains law and order. The absolute ruler, for his part, contracts to protect the governed in exchange for power and their obedience. Contrary to Hobbes, John Locke challenges the theory of absolute power in his *Two Treatises of Government* (1690). Those who govern are accountable for their actions and can lose their authority if they abuse their power. If a ruler turns into a tyrant – as Charles II and James II did – people can resist his authority and find a new one. In this form of government, people give their consent to be governed but retain their sovereignty as well as their property. Locke's *Treatises* had an enormous influence on liberal thinking in America and France as well as in Britain.

---

were physically and psychologically exhausted. In truly Hobbesian fashion, the settlement and its nature were determined by the question of who was militarily and politically strong enough to offer protection in exchange for obedience. At the end of the wars only one person appeared to be able to do this: Oliver Cromwell.

Interregnum? Commonwealth? Republic? Protectorate?

The period from the declaration of the Commonwealth (1649) to the Restoration of the monarchy (1660) has been given different labels. 'Interregnum' signifies a 'period between reigns'. As such the term covers the whole eleven-year period. Sometimes its use implies a royalist perspective in which 'interregna' do not count; at other times its use implies a view of the period informed by the benefit of hindsight: only when the monarchy was restored was it clear that the previous eleven years had constituted an 'interregnum'. The period itself consisted of Commonwealth, Protectorate and, again, Commonwealth. The Commonwealth was a republic, ruled by a single-chamber parliament (the 'Rump' of 1648) and a council of state (with Cromwell as its chairman). When the Rump was too slow to follow Cromwell's Puritan vision of a 'godly government' for a 'godly nation', he ejected it and, together with his council of officers, nominated an assembly of 144 handpicked members (from all parts of the republic). This assembly soon voted to call itself parliament (later nicknamed 'Barebone's parliament' after one of its members), but resigned its authority back into Cromwell's hands after only six months. In December 1653 the army proposed the 'Instrument of Government' (designed to create a balance between the army and Parliament), the first and (until the constitution of the Irish Free State in 1922) only written constitution in the British Isles which divided political power between a single-chamber parliament, an elected council and the executive, with Oliver Cromwell as Lord Protector – hence the term 'Protectorate'. When Cromwell's first parliament (1654) – 400 members from England and Wales and thirty each from Ireland and Scotland – did not ratify the 'Instrument', he first purged and then dissolved it. The second Protectorate parliament (1656–8) formulated a second written constitution, the 'Humble Petition and Advice' (1657), the main purpose of which, besides strengthening its own powers and proposing a second chamber, was – paradoxically – to make Cromwell king. This probably was as much an expression of Cromwell's absolute political power as an attempt to curtail it by obliging him to respect the ancient laws of kingship. Cromwell did not want the crown, but he accepted the constitution and the right to name his successor.

Cromwell's deeds, for good or ill, were without historical precedent in the British archipelago. By bloody conquest he incorporated the four nations into a single political unit for the first time in history. He coolly engineered the trial and execution of Charles I and, perhaps more important, he systematically transformed the established frame of government (resting on custom, precedent and common law) by imposing a written constitution. Whatever he did rested on his use and control of military power. To him, government was 'for the people's good, not what pleases them'. Strangely enough, this dictatorial view of political power was counterbalanced by an equally strong insistence on freedom of conscience, which applied to any sect or confession (other than Catholic) and included the Jews, who were re-admitted to England in 1655, 365 years after their expulsion by Edward I.

When Cromwell died in September 1658, immediately squabbles between different factions in the army and in Parliament broke out which his successor, his son Richard, could not contain. His fall in May 1659 led to the re-establishment of the Commonwealth and a re-introduction of the Rump. When an army junta dispersed the Rump in October, but failed to gain support, another army group restored it, and General George Monck, the commander of the army of occupation in Scotland, invaded England, reached London, complemented the Rump by restoring those MPs who had been excluded in

1648 ('Pride's purge'), on condition that they dissolved Parliament to make way for new elections. When this had duly taken place and the 'Long Parliament' (1640–60) had ceased to exist, the army supervised the election of a Convention Parliament (so called because it met without royal summons) which invited Charles II to return from his exile on the Continent and established the terms of the Restoration.

The Restoration

Charles II, who had promised in his Declaration of Breda (4 April 1660) to dress and heal 'those wounds which have so many years together been kept bleeding . . . by extending our mercy where it is wanted and deserved', was greeted with almost universal enthusiasm when he entered London on his thirtieth birthday (29 May 1660). However, although the Restoration settlement was magnanimous, granting full indemnity to all but the regicides and satisfactorily settling the disputes over the land confiscated in the wars and the Interregnum, peace and stability would not come. In terms of legislation and government, in England, Wales and Ireland the monarchy was returned to its status before 1641 (with separate legislatures in London and Dublin), and in Scotland it was returned to its status before 1633 (with the Scottish legislature in Edinburgh). Throughout the Isles, a pervasive spirit of religious intolerance (nourished from all sides) came into being: on the one hand, in Scotland, the re-imposition of bishops on a largely Presbyterian population was deeply resented, while in England the Clarendon Code re-established the Anglican church and ended the former toleration of independent sects and congregations. On the other hand, anti-Catholic feelings increased when it became known that Charles II had secretly agreed (in 1670), in exchange for a pension from Louis XIV of France, to convert to Catholicism at some time in the future and to improve the lot of English Catholics. As a consequence, Parliament passed two Test Acts which required office-holders to receive Anglican communion, swear allegiance to the monarch and repudiate Catholic doctrine. The first Act (1673) excluded Catholics from military and civil office; its most prominent victim was the king's brother, James, duke of York, who had converted to Catholicism on his (second) marriage to Mary of Modena (1672). The second Act (of 1678) excluded all Catholics (with the sole exception of James) from Parliament. In the later 1670s, anti-Catholic feelings were amplified by scares of an alleged Popish Plot (1678) to replace Charles II by his brother, James. These scares triggered the so-called Exclusion Crisis (1678–81) in which a group of 'Whig' parliamentarians tried to have the king's Catholic brother, James, duke of York, excluded from the succession in favour of Charles' Protestant, but illegitimate, son James, duke of Monmouth. Three successive parliaments debated and passed appropriate bills, but were dissolved by the monarch. After 1681, Charles reigned without parliament

---

Court and Country – Whigs and Tories

The court and country parties were names used for the government and opposition in the late seventeenth and early eighteenth centuries. 'Court' suggested a clique which supported and, at the same time, was dependent on the monarch (patronage), while 'country' was associated with the interest of the country as a whole (with a distinct patriotic inflection). From 1689 and, in particular, from 1714 onwards, 'court' was associated with the Whig party, which had been instrumental in securing and supporting the Hanoverian succession, while 'country' was associated with the Tory opposition. During the reign of George III, when power alternated between these two parties, these names were no longer used, and the parties were simply called Whigs and Tories. These were nicknames earned by opposing factions in the 'Exclusion crisis'. 'Tory' was derived from *toraighe* (Irish for 'bandit' or 'bog-trotter') and 'Whig' was derived from 'whiggamore', a derogatory epithet of the Scots covenanters.

---

until he died (proclaiming his conversion to Catholicism on his deathbed) in February 1685.

The crisis of 1688 and its solution

Although James II (and James VII of Scotland) inherited a strong position, he quickly squandered it. The fact, for instance, that he did not denounce Louis XIV's revocation of the Edict of Nantes (which ended toleration for the Huguenots in 1685) caused his Protestant subjects much anxiety. Moreover, as he expected to be succeeded by Mary, his Protestant daughter from his first marriage, who was married to the Dutch ruler William of Orange (who was also James's nephew), he determined to obtain religious freedom and civil equality for Catholics in the expectation of massive conversions which, in turn, would make future religious persecution impossible. However, his measures went far beyond the lifting of sanctions against Catholics: they included positive discrimination for them (particularly in the appointment to offices). When, in addition to this, a Catholic heir (James Francis Edward) was born to him in June 1688, five Whig and two Tory politicians, who were later dubbed the 'Immortal Seven', invited William of Orange to protect Protestant religion and ancient liberties. Different participants in this move had different objectives. The Whigs wanted to depose James and limit the powers of the Crown; a number of Tories and the Anglican clergy wanted to stop him undermining the Church of England; many ordinary people detested his Catholicism. William himself wanted England as an ally in his war on France. When William landed at Torbay in November, James could not fight because most of his officers had defected. Demoralised, he fled the country. In February 1689 yet another

Convention Parliament declared the English and Irish thrones 'vacant' and offered them to William and Mary as joint sovereigns. They were duly crowned in April. In May they also accepted the Scottish crown after the parliament in Edinburgh had chosen the more radical measure of deposing James.

The Bill of Rights, the crowning piece of legislation of what has been termed the Glorious Revolution, was passed in December 1689 (Document 16). It had originally been presented as the Declaration of Rights by the Convention Parliament to William of Orange and Mary together with the offer of the crown in February 1689. It condemned as illegal various acts of Charles II and James II and, to prevent such abuses of power in the future, stated that (i) parliaments had to be held frequently, (ii) elections had to be free, (iii) freedom of speech, and debates and proceedings in Parliament should not be questioned other than in Parliament, and (iv) parliamentary consent was necessary to suspend statutes, levy taxation and maintain a peacetime standing army. Although this represented a substantial shift in the balance of power between monarchy and Parliament, it is important to note that this was less a statement of rights of the people than a bill of limitations upon the authority of the new monarchs. The 'revolution' of 1689 established Britain as a constitutional monarchy, not as a democracy. According to the Bill of Rights, the authority of the state originates not in the people but in Parliament. The latter creates and controls the constitutional framework and is not bound (or limited) by any written constitution.

The adjective 'glorious' has often been attached to the events of 1688–9 because they allegedly occurred without bloodshed. This, however, depends on the perspective from which one views the transformations. While opposition was negligible in England and Wales, in Scotland, Jacobite (from Jacobus, the Latin form of James) supporters held out against William until 1692, when they were brutally suppressed. In Ireland, James II put up the fight against William which he had nervously evaded in England two years before. On 1 July 1690 one of the biggest battles on Irish soil was fought at the river Boyne, where William's 36,000 men defeated James's 30,000 (which also included some French troops). (The yearly demonstrations commemorating this victory, and thereby causing renewed grief and hatred, take place on 12 July because a calendar reform eliminated eleven days in September 1752.) A further victory at Aughrim led to the Treaty of Limerick (1691) which sealed yet another confiscation of Catholic property, laid down a rigid penal code against Catholics and thereby became the reason for the exodus of another group of Catholic leaders to Europe ('the flight of the wild geese'). In 1688 the Catholic Irish held 22 per cent of the land; in 1700 they held a mere 14 per cent. Understandably, the adjective 'glorious' has not rung too well in many Scottish and Irish ears.

INTERNATIONAL RELATIONS, 1603–89

Across the Channel, England faced three states: France, Spain and the Dutch Republic, which had obtained its independence in 1609. France and Spain were Catholic, politically strong, and potentially hostile. The Dutch Republic was Protestant, a potential ally in politics but a rival in commerce. In the first half of the seventeenth century many European states were involved in the Thirty Years War (1618–48), which was a continuation, on the one hand, of the religious wars of the preceding century and, on the other, of the confrontation between the houses of Habsburg and Bourbon (France). Accordingly, the war originated in a conflict between German Protestants and Catholics and German princes and the Holy Roman Emperor. When Ferdinand, Habsburg archduke of Styria, acceded to the throne of Bohemia (1618), true to his motto 'One church, one king', he revoked the religious freedoms of the Bohemian Protestants. The latter rebelled and, on Ferdinand's election as Holy Roman Emperor as Ferdinand II (1619), refused to recognise his jurisdiction, declaring their allegiance to the Elector Palatine Frederick V, leader of the Evangelical Union. Frederick had been married to Elizabeth Stuart, the daughter of James I, since 1613. Against James's advice Frederick accepted the Bohemian crown. With the help of Spain, Ferdinand crushed Frederick's army (1620), suppressed the Bohemian nobility, and systematically catholicised the population. Frederick fled into exile (in the Dutch Republic), and his lands in the Palatinate were invaded by Spanish and Bavarian troops, and passed into the possession of his Catholic cousin, Maximilian, Elector of Bavaria and leader of the Catholic League. James' attempts at mediating in this conflict and having Frederick and Elizabeth restored came to nothing; his offer to have his son Charles married to the Infanta, the daughter of the Spanish king, ended in a fiasco. When Charles I succeeded his father he tried to force the issue – and found himself at war with Spain and France at the same time. Needless to say, this lunatic policy resulted in a double failure.

Interregnum foreign policy, however, was no less aggressive. While under Elizabeth and the early Stuarts international trade had been conducted by individual merchants and/or privileged merchant companies, the passing of navigation laws represented the establishment of a national trading interest by closing England and its colonies to foreign shipping. It was a cornerstone of what became known as 'mercantilist' economic policy. The minimum objectives of such a policy were even balances of trade and political power. But in fact every state sought more than an even balance, trying to achieve superiority and, thus, be able to 'give the law' to other countries. In particular, the Navigation Act of 1651 attacked the prominent role of the Dutch in European and colonial trade and almost 'naturally' resulted in the First Anglo-Dutch War (1652–4). Further wars followed during the Restoration (1665–7, 1672–4). They cost a lot

The Navigation Acts or British Acts of Trade

In English history, the Navigation Acts or British Acts of Trade were a series of laws designed to expand the English carrying trade, provide England with materials it could not produce, and establish colonial markets for English manufacturers. The laws were a product of mercantilism and corresponded with the principles laid down by Tudor and early Stuart trade regulations. The Navigation Acts soon became a powerful form of trade protection. However, they had a rather destructive effect on the Channel Islands, Scotland and Ireland, as they were excluded from favoured positions within the system until 1707 (Scotland) and 1779 (Ireland).

Moreover, the British Acts of Trade influenced international relations in general. When, for instance, English trade was threatened by Dutch competition, a law was enacted in 1651 to restrict the Dutch carrying trade. This was one major cause of the First Dutch War (1652–4). The Acts of Trade also played an important part in the relations between England and its colonies: all goods to and from English colonies had to be carried in English or colonial ships manned by English or colonial crews and go through English ports. In return for these regulations, colonial merchandise was given a monopoly in the English market and privileged tariff treatment. However, this legislation impeded the manufacturing of goods in the colonies and thereby made (and kept) them dependent on the mother country. Although the revolt of the American colonies demonstrated that the Acts of Trade could no longer be enforced throughout the Empire, they were repealed only in 1849, when free trade proved to be more profitable for Britain than protected trade.

Mercantilism

Mercantilism constitutes somewhat of a paradox. While trade – i.e. the exchange of commodities – is in itself without bounds, mercantilist economic policy frames it in strictly nationalistic terms. Every nation is required to achieve a balance of trade 'in favour' of its own country, so that the national stock of precious metals (money) is optimally maximised. The following principles roughly reflect the mercantilist philosophy. (i) Accumulate as much money as possible. (ii) Don't export (cheap) raw materials but import them. (iii) Don't import (expensive) finished products but export them. (iv) Put protective duties on foreign goods (to make them dear and your own cheap). (v) Build new industries. (vi) Improve the country's infrastructure (roads, canals, etc.). (vii) Unify the systems of weights and measures. (viii) Acquire colonies (suppliers of raw materials). (ix) Build a national merchant fleet.

of money and inflicted mutual defeats but did not cripple the contending parties.

Colonial expansion in the East was effected by the widening network of the East India Company (granted its charter in 1600) which established a number of trading posts, primarily in India (Surat [1618], Madras [1639], Bombay [1661], Calcutta [1690]). In the West it resulted mainly from migration. Europe's religious problems (such as the Thirty Years War, the wars of the kingdoms of the British Isles and the revocation of the Edict of Nantes) and the custom of deporting criminals ('transportation') contributed to the growth of settler colonies in the temperate zones of North America (such as New England). New York was a case in point: named after James, Duke of York and brother of Charles II, it was annexed from the Dutch in 1664, triggering the Second Anglo-Dutch War (1665–7) at the conclusion of which the Dutch received Surinam as compensation. Other places of interest were plantations in the tropical regions of the Caribbean. People with economic means purchased land and grew certain crops (such as tobacco, sugar, cocoa, indigo and cotton) which came to be increasingly in demand in Europe. The land was worked by either 'indentured servants' who mortgaged their labour power (usually for seven years) in return for payment of their passage, or African slaves whose purchase on the African coast and sale in the Americas was organised by big trading companies such as the Royal African Company (granted its charter in 1662) as well as small individual slave traders.

Jamaica, the third largest of the Caribbean islands, was seized by the English from Spain in 1655. In the short run, its strategic position at the heart of the Spanish Indies was all-important. It was ideally placed for trade in times of peace, while in wartime it became the meeting point of smugglers and privateers (i.e. privately owned vessels with a licence by the state to wage war on enemy shipping; the term being a contraction of 'private' and 'volunteer'). In the later seventeenth and early eighteenth centuries, many of the privateers operating in the West Indies and the Indian Ocean degenerated into pirates; Port Royal in Jamaica was one of their central haunts in this classic age of piracy. In the long run, because of the amount of sugar and the wide range of minor staples produced in the island, Jamaica became one of the brightest jewels in Britain's imperial crown in the eighteenth century.

THOUGHT AND CULTURE IN THE SIXTEENTH AND SEVENTEENTH CENTURIES

The development of the humanities (briefly sketched at the beginning of this chapter) was not without parallels in other areas. Traditionally, learning in the Middle Ages was conceived of as a process of recovery of what had been revealed in the Bible and to the founders of the Christian church, on the one hand, and of what had already been discovered by ancient philosophers (such as

Aristotle [384–322 BC] and Ptolemy [AD c.85–165]), on the other. Renaissance scholars, however, assumed that learning also involved creating new knowledge. While medieval scientific inquiry was regarded as serving theological ends, the representatives of the new philosophy of science, which came into being in the sixteenth and seventeenth centuries, envisaged the possibility that mankind could understand and, by understanding, master nature. In contrast to the Catholic church, which regarded new knowledge as a threat to its traditional world view, the 'natural philosophers' did not see any contradiction between their Christian belief and their discoveries, arguing like Galileo Galilei (1564–1642) in a letter to Christina of Tuscany in 1615: 'I do not feel obliged to believe that that same God who has endowed us with senses, reason, and intellect has intended to forgo their use and by some other means to give us knowledge which we can attain by them.' The ensuing intellectual transformations contained the following key elements. (i) The view of a stable, fixed and finite universe, with the earth at its centre, was gradually replaced by that of a moving and infinite universe, with the earth as merely one of countless bodies, which were all subject to the laws of nature. (ii) Instead of scholastic methods of ascertaining the truth dependent on reference to traditional authorities, the new methods emphasised exact reasoning based on observed facts and mathematical laws. (iii) Theological questions gave way to secular ones. Slowly but distinctly, scientific inquiry came to occupy a position of cultural supremacy over other forms of intellectual achievement, a position that it still enjoys today.

Astronomy, philosophy, institutions of learning

The first field of inquiry was astronomy. Nicolaus Copernicus (1473–1543), whose name was later used to name the intellectual 'revolution' derived from his perspective, rejected the view of an earth-centred universe. Tycho Brahe (1546–1601) tried to collect as many astronomical data as accurately as possible to determine the movement of the heavenly bodies (paradoxically while he wanted to defend the traditional Ptolemaic system against Copernicus' refinements). After Brahe's death, Johannes Kepler (1571–1630) continued his work. Galileo Galilei followed the hypothesis that the universe was governed by rational laws which could be stated in mathematical formulae. This regularity could be found in heaven but also everywhere else in nature. It was just a question of discovering these formulae. Isaac Newton (1642–1727), an English mathematician and professor at Cambridge, synthesised many strands of the above and other discoveries together in his book *The Mathematical Principals of Natural Philosophy* (in Latin 1687; trans. 1729), in which he presented his theory of universal gravitation (i.e. the existence of forces of attraction and repulsion that operate between objects). It was Newton's conviction that mathematics was the key to understanding nature. However, he was equally certain that a theory had to stand the test of explaining empirical data and observation (Document 17).

These ideas had a profound influence on the field of philosophy. While philosophers had previously assumed that an understanding of the universe might eventually reveal divine mysteries, they now concluded that the knowledge of nature might reveal nature, but nothing beyond. The universe was thought of as a gigantic machine or clock with God as, perhaps, the original clockmaker who, however, was no longer needed and, consequently, was reduced to the position of observer once the clock was finished. Francis Bacon (1561–1626) championed empirical observations and induction, while René Descartes (1596–1650) relied more on deduction. Thomas Hobbes (1588–1679), who was acquainted with Bacon, Galileo, Descartes and others, used this materialistic, mechanistic way of thinking to explain human behaviour. John Locke (1632–1704) regarded the mind of a newborn child as a blank tablet on which knowledge was inscribed through sensory experience: knowledge was not innate but produced by the impact of the environment on the human mind.

As the universities were slow in reacting to the new ways of thinking, new institutions came into being. Most prominent among these were the Académie Française (founded in 1635) and the Royal Society of London. The latter's origins lie in an 'invisible college' of natural philosophers who began meeting around 1645 to acquire 'knowledge by experimental investigation'. It was officially founded on 28 November 1660 when twelve philosophers (including men like Christopher Wren, Robert Boyle and Robert Moray) met at Gresham College and decided to found 'a college for the promoting of physico-mathematical experimental learning'. In 1662 the society was granted its charter, and in the second royal charter of 1663 it was named as the Royal Society of London for Improving Natural Knowledge. Further institutions, such as the Royal Observatory at Greenwich (1675), the Royal Society of Edinburgh (1783) and the Royal Irish Academy in Dublin (1785), followed.

Witch hunts

The slow but distinct transformation of the traditional view of the world not only had the positive ('progressive') aspects sketched above but also caused a lot of fear and suspicion. While religious difference (mainly Catholics vs. Protestants) was one fault line along which these anxieties were acted out, both religious communities also had a common scapegoat whom they could blame for their 'panics': people practising magic and witchcraft. It has been estimated that in Europe between 1400 and 1700 somewhere between 70,000 and 100,000 people were condemned to death for this offence.

While Ireland and Wales were hardly affected by witch hunts, the pattern in England and Scotland was different. In both countries legislation against witchcraft was passed in 1563. But while England saw few real 'panics' (1590s, 1645–7), with an increasing number of trials and executions, in Scotland the 'panic' periods were more numerous (1590–1, 1597, 1628–30, 1649 and 1661–2 in particular). From the mid-sixteenth to the end of the seventeenth century, in England, with a population roughly five times that of Scotland, some 500 persons were put to death, while in Scotland between 1000 and 1500 persons were executed. One reason for this difference can be seen in the different legal traditions: in England it was not permissible to torture suspects, in Scotland it was – and torture eventually makes the victim say whatever the torturer suggests. A more persuasive interpretation is the aggressive Calvinism of the Scottish Kirk which regarded witchcraft not so much as a product of ignorance and superstition but as a heretical, diabolical conspiracy against God (and the God-ordained government). Of the victims, 85 per cent were women, most of them single and between forty and sixty years of age. Even if Calvinism's strong misogynist elements are taken into account, the reasons for this are not entirely clear. On the one hand, these women, who were neither 'supported' nor 'controlled' by a spouse, may have been regarded as a burden on or a threat to a male-dominated society and so could be easily victimised. On the other hand, certain female professions (such as nurses and midwives) may have associated them with mysterious deaths and thereby may have made them vulnerable to suspicion and persecution.

The reasons for the decline of the witch hunts in the last quarter of the seventeenth century are not clear, either. It has been suggested that educated people, even if it was impossible for them to deny the theoretical possibility of witchcraft, found it increasingly difficult to collect empirical evidence of it in individual cases. The last executions took place in 1685 (in England) and in 1727 (in Scotland); the statutes against witchcraft were repealed in both countries in 1736.

Literature

The humanists had encouraged the individual lay person to read texts (ancient and modern) without the mediating (and meddling) help of the clergy. In due course, more and more writers turned to producing texts in the vernacular for a growing audience. The number of new books published in England per year rose more than tenfold between 1500 and 1630 (from 45 to 460 respectively). This was not yet sufficient for writers to live on; they still needed patrons who supported them financially. Support, however, was not enough; protection was needed as well because of, at times, drastic censorship. Moreover, with the increase of titles, a rising number of books in the vernacular, and a (consequent) growth of the reading public, debates on the nature and function of 'literature' (a concept used in a much wider sense then) became the order of the day. Philip Sidney's *Apology for Poetry* (published posthumously in 1595) is

Figure 7 Sir Walter Ralegh, *The History of the World*. Permission The British Library (fJ/ 249 DSC)

just the best known. Although not very original, its views of imaginative literature have endured, in particular its claim that literature offers 'a speaking picture – with this end, to teach and delight'. Such a claim from an ardent Protestant was all the more important, as the more radical Protestants distinguished themselves by their fervid (and iconoclastic) criticism of everything delightful. Most crucially, literature became a central means of depicting, disseminating and discussing the material and intellectual transformations of the age.

Elizabeth's reign saw a real flowering of letters. In prose, there were treatises on education and court etiquette (Roger Ascham, John Lyly), historical chronicles and histories (Ralph Holinshed, Sir Walter Ralegh), geographical descriptions (Richard Hakluyt) and philosophical essays (Francis Bacon). In poetry the sonnet (in its Petrarchan or English version) provided a new form of self-expression, and in drama Christopher Marlowe, Thomas Kyd and Ben Jonson provided popular entertainment.

The Elizabethan age found its most sublime expression in the works of William Shakespeare (1564–1616). His thirty-four plays (comedies, tragedies and histories) brilliantly met the needs of his audience *and* transcended them in their acute analyses of human motivation and emotion clad in breathtaking poetry. The complex developments of an individual human being – instigated by the secularising tendencies of the Renaissance, the humanist interest in a person's inner self as well as his or her social relationships, and the liberating (but also alarming) experience of an unmediated communication with one's personal God – were represented on the stage and thereby made all the more accessible for close perception, deep reflection and intense debate.

Plays were first given in courtyards of inns, but in 1576 the first theatre was built in London, soon to be followed by others. Many plays were also staged at court. During the Interregnum the Puritans closed the theatres, but with the Restoration the theatres were reopened to popular acclaim. Moreover, many actors who had spent some years in exile on the Continent on their return brought new ideas with them, such as having female roles played by women.

The metaphysical poets (such as John Donne [1573–1631] and Andrew Marvell [1621–78]) incorporated the emerging world view in amazing conceits, unconventional paradoxes and strange imagery. John Milton (1608–74), in his biblical epic *Paradise Lost* (1667), presented the story of the fall (i.e. Adam and Eve's expulsion from paradise) as, in the last resort, an example of God's saving grace. In its ending 'The world was all before them' there is a kind of secular optimism which understands the loss of paradise as a chance 'to till the ground from whence he [Adam] was taken' (Genesis 3.24), i.e. to subdue the earth and, by putting into effect God's plan, to fulfil himself. John Bunyan's (1628–88) book *The Pilgrim's Progress from This World to That Which Is to Come* (1678/1684) combined biblical allegory with moral instruction. It told the story of Christian's conversion and his life (conceived as a pilgrimage) in which he has to face and overcome despair, terror and derision until he and his family reach their final destination. The book's great popularity was second only to the King James Version of the Bible (1611), and it was translated into more than a hundred languages.

5 Towards internal stability and external expansion, 1689–1789

The settlement of 1688–9, peacefully acknowledged in England and Wales and enforced by war in Scotland and Ireland, was just the beginning of a much longer process of political consolidation and, at least partial, integration which occupied the four nations in the following century. At its beginning, the Act of Union (1707) transformed the two kingdoms of England (including Wales) and Scotland into the 'United Kingdom of Great Britain'; and, at its very end, another Act of Union (1800) created the 'United Kingdom of Great Britain and Ireland'. Controversial as these processes of incorporation were within the British Isles, internationally they were enviously and critically watched, first and foremost by Britain's chief enemy, France. During the century under discussion, these two countries went to war against each other on at least five major occasions: when France would not allow the leader of its Continental opponents, William of Orange, to expand his power base by ousting the Stuarts from the Isles (1689–97); during two European succession crises in Spain (1702–13) and Austria (1740–8); in the Seven Years War (1756–63), triggered by imperial competition in India and North America; and, finally, when France entered the American War of Independence on the side of the British colonies (1778–81). If we add the wars caused by the French Revolution and Napoleon (1793–1815), we could be tempted to speak of another Hundred Years War.

In the long run, however, neither intense international warfare nor internal strife and dispute prevented Great Britain from becoming economically more prosperous (with the largest free-trade area in the world, a booming agricultural sector that produced higher yields every year, and an international trade that grew by leaps and bounds), politically more influential (in its interventions on the Continent and in its ever-enlarging empire), and culturally more coherent (in the use of English) as well as more versatile with its immense creativity in the arts, philosophy and scientific inquiry. On the contrary, the processes of national consolidation, international self-assertion and imperial expansion helped create a particular sense of British identity and nationalism which was expressed in various ways. John Bull, the personification of the (dominant) English nation, first appeared in a pamphlet by John Arbuthnot (1667–1735) in 1712; 'Rule Britannia', Britain's almost secular national anthem, was a song from the masque *Alfred* (1740) by the Scottish poets James Thomson and David Mallet, set to music by the London composer Thomas Arne.

FROM UNION TO UNION

When William III and Mary II were made joint rulers of England, Scotland and Ireland, Louis XIV of France (b. 1638, r. 1643–1715) continued to support the Stuarts. After nine years of war, which brought no real advantage for either side, France was financially exhausted. In the Treaty of Ryswick (1697), William was eventually recognised as king of England, Scotland and Ireland. When, however, four years later, the king of Spain (Charles II) died childless and willed his kingdom to a grandson of Louis XIV of France (Philip V), an alliance of European countries led by William regarded this as a threat to the balance of power on the Continent and the war against France was resumed (the War of the Spanish Succession, 1702–13). As a countermove, France recognised the son of James II (who had died in 1701), James Francis Edward Stuart (1688–1766, 'the Old Pretender' [claimant to the throne]) as 'James III' and king of England, thereby violating the terms of the Treaty of Ryswick.

Meanwhile, the English parliament had passed the Act of Settlement (1701), which was designed to end anxieties over the royal succession. It provided that the crown should next descend to Anne (daughter of James II and sister of Mary II) and then, if none of her children survived her, to Princess Sophia of Hanover. The latter was a granddaughter of James I, a daughter of the Protestant Elizabeth and Elector Palatine Frederick V (cf. Chapter 4) and married to Ernest Augustus, Elector of Hanover. By overruling the hereditary rights of the Stuarts and ignoring the legitimate rights of fifty-seven living claimants to the throne, Parliament confirmed what could have been suspected in 1660, when a convention parliament restored the monarchy, and what had become clear in 1688, when another convention parliament offered the crown to William and Mary: in the last resort the monarchy had become secondary to Parliament. Moreover, the Act (amongst others) provided that future monarchs had to support the Church of England and were allowed neither to leave the country nor to involve England in war without Parliament's consent (Document 18).

The Union of 1707

Mary II died in 1694, leaving William III sole ruler until his death in 1702. When he was followed by Anne, whose sixteen children had all died in infancy, the problem of the succession, although anticipated in the Act of Settlement, reached yet another level of complexity. In the 1630s and 1640s (cf. Chapter 4), Scottish governments had tried to achieve a closer union with England only to be met by the latter's indifference. At the beginning of the eighteenth century the roles were reversed: William's and Anne's initiatives to form a closer union between England and Scotland (triggered by reasons of national security, first and foremost the wars against France) were rebuffed by the Scottish parliament, which had profited from the transformations of 1688–9 by an increase in its authority. Thus, while the Act of Settlement provided for the succession in England, Wales and Ireland, the Scots passed their own Act of Security (1703) insisting on their independent right to choose their own monarch, who might even be a Stuart. Since 1688–9, Jacobite sentiments had been fostered by the preachings of hundreds of Episcopal clergymen who refused to accept the Presbyterian settlement of the Kirk. If the Scots were to agree to the same monarch, their government thought, they could demand something in return, and demand they did 'free communication of trade' with England and her colonies. Furiously, the English House of Commons passed the Alien Act (1705), which stipulated that if the Scots did not agree to discuss a union between the two countries, and if negotiations were not advanced by Christmas 1705, all Scots (except those living in England) would be treated as aliens and there would be an embargo on all major exports from Scotland to England (cattle, linen, coal). Although this straightforward piece of blackmail caused an outcry, it brought the Scots to the negotiating table. Once the independence of the Scottish Kirk and the continued use of Scottish law were assured, it was but a matter of money. Besides 'inducements' for individual parliamentarians (such as places, peerages and financial compensation), Scotland was offered the 'Equivalent', a sum of £398,085.10s. (= almost £26 million in today's values), to pay for losses private persons might have by the change of coinage, to repay the capital of the Darien venture, and to pay all other public debts. Scotland also gained the eagerly desired freedom of trade with England and her colonies. The Treaty of Union, which the English and Scottish commissioners had agreed in London, consisted of twenty-five articles which were debated in Edinburgh for ten weeks. In the voting for the final agreement there was a majority of 110 to 69. Its most important political terms were that 'the two kingdoms of England and Scotland shall for ever after be united into one kingdom' and that 'the succession to the monarchy of the united kingdom of Great Britain be to the most excellent Princess Sophia of Hanover, and the heirs of her body being Protestant'.

On 1 May 1707, Great Britain came into being; a new British parliament replaced the former legislatures of England and Scotland. In reality it was an enlarged English parliament (which continued to sit at Westminster): in the House of Commons, 513 English and Welsh members were joined by 45 Scottish representatives; 16 Scottish peers joined 190 already sitting in the House of Lords. If we count the heads of the respective populations, this appears to be

Darien

William Paterson (1658–1719), a keen supporter of the Glorious Revolution and one of the founders of the Bank of England (1694), was the first who thought of establishing a trading colony in the Isthmus of Panama. When the Company of Scotland Trading to Africa and the Indies was founded in 1695, Paterson and Andrew Fletcher tried to interest its merchants and to secure English as well as Scottish investment. The East India Company, however, protested and lobbied English MPs to such an extent that the London parliament forced English investors to withdraw their money. Paterson tried to find investors in Holland and in Hamburg, but it was to no avail, as William III's diplomatic interests were averse to the project. The Darien, New Caledonia, lay within the sphere of influence of the Spanish monarch, Charles II. As he would die childless, the greater European powers wanted to divide his realm without bloodshed. They made two treaties (1698, 1700). While these treaties were being negotiated, William did not want any English or Scottish interference in Spanish territories. So the Scots had to go it alone.

The idea was that such a trading station would link the Caribbean with the Pacific by carrying the goods overland from coast to coast. Although this was a brilliant scheme, the Company had not paid sufficient attention to the potential difficulties, first and foremost the intractable terrain and the deathly climate. Three expeditions went to the Darien; all failed (or had to accept defeat by the Spanish). By the summer of 1700 the experiment, which had cost a lot of money, was over. When Charles died in 1702, Louis XIV, one of the signatories of the partition treaties, simply ignored them, and the War of the Spanish Succession (1702–13) began.

unfair (with England's 5 million and Scotland's 1 million). But it was property (not people) that was the basis for allocating political power: the ratio of crown revenues (taxes) between the two countries was estimated at forty to one, and this was indeed generous to Scotland. There is no use denying the fact that Scotland was a much poorer country than England, as poor harvests and a dramatic slump in trade around the turn of the century had amply demonstrated. Federation instead of incorporation would have left the weaker state permanently at the mercy of the stronger. In that sense, Scotland did not give up her sovereignty, because this had been for some time illusory. Although the amount of corruption was not extraordinary (compared to other political manoeuvres of those days), it caused distress and, following from that, widespread popular opposition. But what would have been the alternative? As England, in terms of international strategy, could not have countenanced the possibility of a Stuart restoration in Scotland, it would most probably have resorted to invasion and conquest.

The first Jacobite reaction to the union occurred in the following year. Louis XIV sent a naval expedition (with the 'Old Pretender' on board), which retreated when the promised Scottish army did not appear. Queen Anne died in 1714 and, as Princess Sophia had died a few weeks before her, the crown devolved on her son who became George I (b. 1660, r. 1714–27), king of Great Britain and Ireland. The Hanoverian succession was peaceful, but unpopular in Britain – the king could not speak a word of English and relied heavily on Whig politicians, who had been instrumental in bringing about the Hanoverian succession and, thus, were not prone to the lure of Jacobitism. So James Francis Edward Stuart tried again to win what he regarded as his throne. This time France could not help him because by the previous year's Treaty of Utrecht, which ended the War of the Spanish Succession, the Act of Settlement had won international recognition. James Stuart had to find supporters in Britain. These were not too hard to come by, as the union had been tried for seven years – and found wanting. In particular, contemporaries complained about the 'singular insensitivity and clumsiness with which the English political establishment treated Scotland after 1707'. In 1713 a proposal to dissolve the union was put to the House of Lords and defeated by only four votes.

The rebellion started in Scotland and got as far south as Preston. But when James arrived in late 1715 the Jacobite troops were already in retreat. In early February 1716, James sailed for France where, however, he could not stay as George I's government had succeeded in negotiating an alliance (1716–31) with the regency government that followed Louis XIV's death in 1715. The 'Old Pretender' found refuge in Rome. Another Jacobite raid (in 1719) was engineered by James's new ally, the king of Spain, and ended in a fiasco. Prudently, James Stuart had not even bothered to show up. The '15 ended Jacobitism in England; its termination in Scotland came thirty years later. From 1740 to 1748 the War of the Austrian Succession was fought on the Continent and in many colonies all over the world. James Stuart's eldest son, Charles Edward (1720–88, the 'Young Pretender' or 'Bonnie Prince Charlie'), utilised the fact that British troops were tied down in a number of battle theatres, overran most of Scotland and crossed into England, reaching Derby (some 120 miles from London). But when the promised English and French support did not materialise, after a crisis of confidence in the prince, the Jacobite army retreated. On Culloden Moor near Inverness it was mercilessly crushed by the superior British forces (including a substantial Scottish contingent).

While the reaction of the Hanoverian government to the '15 had been lenient (and had to be so, because of the recent Hanoverian succession), after the '45 they aimed at Jacobitism's total destruction. In what can only be called a reign of terror, the military under the Duke of Cumberland broke up the highland clans (which had traditionally manned the Jacobite armies to a great extent), plundered and laid waste numerous settlements, and confiscated cattle as well as other domestic animals on a massive scale. The military attack was followed by a legislative onslaught. The Gaelic language and the kilt were proscribed, the carrying of weapons of war (which included the playing of

> ## Culloden
>
> The battle of Culloden took place on Wednesday, 16 April 1746, about five miles south-east of Inverness near the village of Culloden in the area of Drumoisse Moor (often called Culloden Moor). The Jacobites were led by Prince Charles Edward Stuart, while Prince William Augustus, the 3rd Duke of Cumberland (the second son of George II) led the British army. With a superior force of 9000 men against 5000, the British army defeated the Jacobites. Cumberland's merciless pursuit of the defeated and killing of the wounded earned him the nickname 'The Butcher'. The battle of Culloden marked the effective end of the Jacobite cause and, incidentally, it was also the last land battle fought on British soil.

bagpipes) was prohibited, estates of rebel landowners were forfeited to the crown, and Episcopalian meeting houses were suppressed. While the people concerned suffered these brutalities with a stubborn defiance, the destruction of Jacobitism was greeted with relief and celebration in those parts of Scotland which had been hostile to it from its very beginning: the Presbyterian Lowlands.

The Union of 1800

The new British parliament of 1707 was purely Protestant – as was the Irish. However, while the population in Britain was nine-tenths Protestant, the Irish population was three-quarters Catholic. Moreover, the Irish parliament had been held in a (sometimes more, sometimes less) clearly subordinate position to that of the English one since Poynings' Law (1494; cf. Chapter 4). Although the transformations of 1688 had enhanced the status of the Irish parliament, the Declaratory Act (1720), 'an act for the better securing of the dependency of the kingdom of Ireland upon the Crown of Great Britain', once more asserted the right of the British parliament to pass legislation binding on Ireland. In practice, the British and Irish administrations preferred to proceed by cooperation and mutual accommodation, but a real improvement did not occur before the last quarter of the century. By that time a new awareness and self-confidence had emerged among the Protestant Irish, who had come to see themselves not only as English or Scottish colonisers of Ireland (wary of Catholic resistance) but also as Anglo-Irish Protestant 'patriots', giving expression to what could be called 'colonial nationalism'. They argued that Ireland, although it was a possession of the British crown, was a separate kingdom which should be governed according to its own laws and through its own institutions. Henry Grattan, one of the patriots, argued in 1780 that 'as long as [Britain] exercises a power to bind this country, so long are the nations in a state of war', demanding that 'a country enlightened as Ireland, chartered as Ireland, armed as

Ireland, and injured as Ireland, will be satisfied with nothing less than liberty'. The wider political context – such as the debate preceding and following the American Declaration of Independence – clearly influenced these processes.

In 1778 the most serious restrictions on Catholic land ownership (whose proportion had fallen to an all-time low of 5 per cent) were removed; in 1779 free trade with Britain and her colonies was granted. In June 1782 the British Declaratory Act was repealed; in July 1782, Yelverton's Act substantially amended Poynings' Law, and a Catholic Relief Act abolished the worst restrictions on the clergy and constraints on lay people. This was not (yet) 'legislative independence' as some enthusiastically rejoiced, but it was an important step towards it. A step, however, that was overtaken by much more radical events, first outside and then inside Ireland.

The revolutions in the American colonies (1776) and in France (1789) did not fail to have their effects on Ireland. Fifteen years after *Common Sense* (1776), the most influential pamphlet in the struggle for American independence, Tom Paine published *Rights of Man* (1791–2), a bold vision of an egalitarian society founded on natural rights, which was hugely successful and quickly went into seven editions in Ireland. The most important group, taking up these ideas and combining them with older Whig and 'patriot' traditions, was the Society of United Irishmen, which was established in Belfast and Dublin in the autumn of 1791. The membership in both cities was mainly middle class, in religious terms, the Belfast members were Presbyterians, while the Dublin members were equally Protestants and Catholics. The group was committed, first, to parliamentary reform and, second, to Irish control of Irish affairs. Somewhat later it also embraced universal male suffrage. Its most important commitment, however, was to a union of Irishmen of all denominations. When members of the group were arrested and the Dublin society was suppressed (as happened to other groups throughout Great Britain, when the government was afraid of the French Revolution spreading to the Isles; cf. Chapter 6), it reorganised itself as a secret movement geared to armed insurrection. Wolfe Tone, one of its founding members, who had been arrested and exiled to America as early as 1795, went to France to seek military support. When this was granted, recruitment and morale were boosted, and by February 1798 the society claimed to have over 280,000 active members. Further repression through government forces resulted in the arrest of the main leaders in the spring of 1798, so that the insurrection, which began in May, was almost leaderless and soon collapsed. Tone, who was captured in a French uniform, was convicted of treason but committed suicide before he could be hanged.

The British government regarded the events of 1798 as confirming the need for direct control of Ireland because its instability posed a double threat: nationally, the established conventions of 1782 had proved to be unreliable in times of crisis (as, for example, in the regency crisis of 1789); internationally, the insurrection of 1798 had been supported by French troops and thereby had

---

Wolfe Tone (1763–98)

Theobald Wolfe Tone (often called Wolfe Tone) was born in June 1763 in Dublin where he grew up in a middle-class Protestant family. After studying at Trinity College, Dublin, he became a lawyer in 1789. In October 1791 he was involved in the foundation of the Society of United Irishmen. When the politics of the Society became increasingly militant and radical, Tone and other leaders were forced to flee Ireland in 1795. Tone lived in exile in America from August to December 1795. He returned to Europe and stayed in France where he tried to convince the French government to invade Ireland. After two unsuccessful attempts Wolfe Tone was captured in Ireland in October 1798. He was convicted of treason and sentenced to death. Before his public hanging he committed suicide. Wolfe Tone is generally regarded as the father of militant Irish republicanism.

---

been instrumental in enabling the enemy to enter the country. A union was negotiated between the two parliaments. It was achieved by an exchange of patronage for support which (as historians attest) remained 'within the limits of eighteenth-century convention'. As a result, 4 bishops and 28 peers entered the House of Lords, and 100 MPs entered the House of Commons. If based on the principle of universal suffrage, this was a considerable underestimate; if property qualifications were reckoned, it was a fair assessment. Interestingly, many Protestants were not too happy about the union because they feared that London would not continue to support their supremacy. Catholics, in contrast, very often supported the union because they expected their political emancipation (i.e. their right to hold senior government offices, to be judges or sheriffs, or to sit in Parliament) but, because of the hostility of the House of Lords and of George III and George IV, they had to wait until 1829.

The union of 1800 came into effect from 1 January 1801, but it did not really make Ireland part of a British unitary state. Although the two exchequers were united in 1817 and the systems of taxation were gradually brought into line after that, Ireland's physical separateness and size made it necessary to conduct day-to-day government from Dublin. The decades immediately following the union, similar to the union of 1707, meant economic hardship for the 'newcomer', while the 1850s and 1860s witnessed a better incorporation of Ireland in the politics of the United Kingdom.

EIGHTEENTH-CENTURY SOCIETY

The social order of early modern Europe (1500 to 1800) was determined by a hierarchical class structure which had been inherited from the Middle Ages. The nobility and the clergy were orders (or estates) whose numbers and privileges varied from country to country. While in most states the nobility numbered no more than 2–3 per cent of the population, in others such as Spain (10 per cent) and Poland (15 per cent) the proportion was much higher. In France there were somewhere between 25,000 and 55,000 noble families with about 125,000 to 300,000 people claiming a noble title. All of these (plus the clergy) were exempt from taxes.

In England, in contrast, in 1700, fewer than 200 noble families (the peerage or aristocracy) owned about 15–20 per cent of the landed wealth (in 1800 they owned 20–25 per cent), and some 4000 gentry families owned about half the land in the country, with some 80–100 of them owning 10,000 acres (c.40 square kilometres) or more. The landowners had to pay property taxes, but they could well afford them: land values almost doubled in the period under discussion, as more land was cultivated and agriculture became more productive (cf. Chapter 6). Still, as only the eldest son inherited the title and the land (primogeniture), younger sons had to find other sources of income (offices in the Church, commissions in the Army or the Navy or, increasingly, positions in trade and commerce). Young gentlemen were either tutored at home or sent to boarding schools. Afterwards they often attended university and went on the 'Grand Tour' of the Continent to encounter foreign cultures, learn their languages, and acquaint themselves with fine art and good manners. Young women were instructed at home in their future responsibilities as members of a family with a particular social status linked to specific socio-cultural codes.

While the landed aristocracy strongly influenced the court and national politics, the country gentry exercised local authority (mainly as justices of the peace). From 1707 to 1801 the membership of the House of Commons remained at 558, while its relative power *vis-à-vis* the House of Lords steadily grew. But this did not cause much friction because the political interests of the two houses were very similar. As they predominantly represented the same class (i.e. landowners), and as the peers could manipulate the selection of candidates to the lower house, in most elections the outcome was hardly ever in doubt (cf. Chapter 6). The House of Commons, in short, was neither a democratic nor a representative body, but it provided Great Britain with a kind of unity, which met with more general approval than that of most absolutist monarchies on the Continent.

The class owning the land, however, controlled the class of its tillers. The peasants formed the majority of the population: about 75 per cent. In Western Europe, almost all peasants were free. From the eleventh year of Elizabeth I's reign (1568–9) we have a legal document which states that 'one Cartwright brought a Slave from Russia, and would scourge him, for which he was questioned: and it was resolved, That England was too pure an Air for Slaves to breathe in'. However, the peasants' status depended on the amount of land they either owned or controlled through leases (whose terms could differ widely). The nobles, the Church and the State exacted taxes, tithes and other obligations in labour, kind or cash. The peasant population was by no means

Figure 8 *Mr and Mrs Robert Andrews*, c.1748–9 (oil on canvas), Thomas Gainsborough (1727–88). National Gallery, London, UK/The Bridgeman Art Library

unified: there were those (small in number) who could work their fields and make a profit, remaining unscathed by wars and famines, but there were also those (more numerous) who were constantly in debt, afraid of the next bad harvest and very often living in utter destitution. Many of these were driven off their small plots of land when the commons were enclosed to be more intensively and profitably farmed by large landowners. In the latter half of the eighteenth century, roughly a quarter of the farmland of England (some 7 million acres) was subject to parliamentary acts of enclosure.

If the landowners and the peasants were concentrated on the land, the social group in the middle, the 'middling sort' (and, later, middle classes), primarily lived in the towns and cities. Most of them were engaged in commerce and manufacture. Again, the middling sort was very diverse: there were the great merchants and entrepreneurs (whose wealth matched or surpassed that of many landowners), but there were also small traders, struggling craftsmen and the proverbial shopkeepers. In between them, there were those engaged in the steadily expanding liberal professions (such as barristers and physicians).

Although Daniel Defoe, the author of *Robinson Crusoe*, claimed that 'men are every day starting up from obscurity to wealth', social mobility was rare in Britain (but not as rare as on the Continent). Of course, wealthy merchants and bankers aspired to live like the nobility, and an increasing number succeeded in becoming 'country gentlemen' by purchasing landed estates or marrying into the gentry. There were no legal or cultural barriers to prevent such an ascent, but only very few rose from commoner to nobleman. Downward social mobility, on the other hand, was much more frequent. For many people the line between employment and begging, having enough to eat and starvation was very thin indeed. Towards the end of our period about 30 per cent of the population depended on some kind of poor relief. And, while the rural poor could sometimes find solidarity in the 'moral economy' of their villages (based on the tradition of mutual support), the urban poor were left to their own devices. No wonder that many of those who did not know how to make ends meet resorted to crime. To this, the ruling classes reacted with harsh measures of social control. Between 1688 and 1810, the number of offences punishable by death rose to over 220. For example, hunting, a domesticated form of warfare, was the exclusive privilege of the nobility and the gentry. Poaching in its various forms – killing game and fish, but also chopping down trees and collecting wood – was relentlessly punished. Even if death sentences were often commuted, some 200 criminals were executed every year in England. Other forms of punishment included transportation (first to the American colonies, later to Australia), flogging, branding, or being exhibited in stocks.

Social mobility is an indication of individuals moving between different levels of the social hierarchy. It became historically significant when feudal relations, in which everyone was born into (and was supposed to stay in) a particular social group situated on a specific rung of the social ladder, were eventually eroded (cf. Chapter 3), to be replaced by market relations, in which supply, demand and the cash nexus dominated all social spheres. To ensure that this transformation occurred without loss of property and power may have induced the British ruling classes of the eighteenth and early nineteenth centuries to implement draconian measures in order to discipline, subordinate and control the lower classes. But, then, and equally important, British people enjoyed greater political freedom than most people on the Continent: no standing army intimidated the population, free speech and freedom of association were possible, and the press and public debate flourished when, in 1695, the Licensing Act was allowed to lapse. Given the freedom to write, print and sell, newspapers and other publications quickly flourished. London had several newspapers before 1700; by 1780 there were fifty provincial dailies and fourteen in London.

More generally speaking, slowly but distinctly, a 'public sphere' came into being which enabled individuals of the middle classes (merchants, artisans, independent scholars) to congregate, debate and constructively influence society's norms, values and institutions so that they became ever more effective in the accumulation of knowledge, power and money. By creating and running clubs dedicated to various interests (such as trade, education, sport and many different kinds of sociability) these classes formed what has been called 'civil society', which not only increased Britain's supply of expertise but also helped create a decidedly patriotic sense of cultural identity. The former served as a motor for Britain's growth as a world political and industrial power, the latter became indispensable when the country's internal cohesion was questioned or when external aggression became necessary.

THE ENLIGHTENMENT

In its simplest sense the Enlightenment was the creation of a new framework of ideas about nature, society and the place of human beings in them. The ideas themselves continued and developed the philosophical debates of the preceding century. They were accompanied by, and in turn influenced, many innovations in culture (writing, painting, printing, music, sculpture, architecture, gardening and the other arts) as well as in technology (agriculture and manufactures). A somewhat more complex (but still simplified) formula could describe the Enlightenment as a communicating network of intellectuals subscribing to a characteristic cluster of ideas, which grew into an intellectual movement, created an international community of *philosophes* (i.e. men of letters who were also freethinkers) and irreversibly influenced the world view of generations to come.

Despite their different origins, intellectual developments and fields of work, most *philosophes* would have agreed that the following cluster of ideas was important for them. (i) Reason and rationality (tempered by experience and experiment) are the ideal ways of organising knowledge. (ii) Reason is the prime faculty of human beings. It can produce secular knowledge which is free of religious dogma. It is from the metaphor of the 'light of reason', shining brightly into all the dark recesses of ignorance and superstition, that the age eventually received its name. (iii) All knowledge about the natural and social world is based upon empirical facts which human beings can apprehend through their sense organs. (iv) Scientific knowledge, based upon the experimental method as developed in the preceding century, is the key to expanding all human knowledge. (v) As the concept of reason can be applied to any and every problem, and as its principles are the same in every situation, scientific discovery produces general laws which govern the entire universe, without exception. (vi) The individual is the starting point for all knowledge; it cannot (and must not) be subjected to any higher authority. Society is the sum of the individuals living in it. (vii) The principal characteristics of human nature are always and everywhere the same. Because of this, cultural differences should not be the cause of discrimination but should be tolerated. (viii) By the application of reason, the natural and social conditions of human beings can be improved and can result in ever-increasing happiness and well-being, although the extension of freedom to the lower classes and to women may prove problematic.

The *philosophes* and their ideas

Although *philosophe* is a French term, there were, in fact, three overlapping and closely linked 'generations' of enlightened thinkers whose names testify to the European character of their enterprise. The first, typified by Charles Louis de Secondat, baron de Montesquieu (1689–1755) and François Marie Arouet, known as Voltaire (1694–1778), were born in the last quarter of the seventeenth century, and their ideas were strongly influenced by the writings of John Locke and Isaac Newton. The second generation includes men like Jean-Jacques Rousseau (1712–78), Denis Diderot (1713–84), Jean le Rond d'Alembert (1717–83) and David Hume (1757–1838), who combined a scathing critique of clerical institutions with an interest in the scientific method(s) of their predecessors to form a coherent modern view of the world. Representatives of the third generation, such as Adam Smith (1723–90), Adam Ferguson (1723–1816), Immanuel Kant (1724–1804), Anne Robert Jacques Turgot (1727–81), Moses Mendelsohn (1729–86), Cesare, marchese de Beccaria (1738–94), Marie Jean Antoine Nicolas de Caritat, marquis de Condorcet (1743–94) and Mary Wollstonecraft (1759–97), developed from the Enlightenment world view a series of more specialised perspectives (which later became academic disciplines): economics, sociology, political economy, legal reform, and epistemology.

It is to Kant that we owe not only the slogan of the Enlightenment but also one of its most trenchant definitions:

Enlightenment is man's leaving his self-caused immaturity. Immaturity is the incapacity to use one's intelligence without the guidance of another. Such immaturity is self-caused if it is not caused by lack of intelligence, but by lack of determination and courage to use one's intelligence without being guided by another. *Sapere aude!* Have the courage to use your own intelligence! is therefore the motto of the enlightenment. ('What Is Enlightenment?' [1784])

In this spirit, the *philosophes* followed their common desire to reform intellectual attitudes, social relations and governmental practices by asking pointed critical questions. They met informally in coffee-houses, clubs and taverns, and more formally in fashionable salons of aristocratic ladies or women of the upper 'middle classes', in country houses of like-minded nobles or even at the court of their 'enlightened monarch' to 'make *public* use of their own reason and to submit *publicly* their thoughts' (Kant). In doing so, they formed the nucleus of a public sphere (or, as it was called then, a 'republic of letters') which represented a new and increasingly influential cultural force: public opinion.

Their foremost objects of criticism were the teachings of the Christian churches, be they Catholic or Protestant, which were associated with unthinking, irrational and dogmatic attitudes. (Voltaire's battle cry was: 'Ecrasez l'infâme!' ['Crush the horrible thing!']) Both churches adhered to the concept of original sin according to which human nature was basically flawed and could not be improved. In contrast, the *philosophes* argued that, by diverting the attention of human beings from the fact that they could better themselves, the teachings of the churches stressed the importance of God's grace and the world to come to the detriment of the possibilities of reforming the present world. Moreover, the *philosophes* alleged that by these teachings the churches intended to divert attention from their material privileges. But this criticism did not mean that all *philosophes* were agnostics (people who think that an ultimate cause [God] and the nature of things are unknown and unknowable) or atheists (people who deny or disbelieve in the existence of God or gods). Many of them wanted a religion based not on revelation but on reason. Such a religion, which was called Deism (from the Latin *deus* = 'God'), conceived of God as the rational creator of an ordered universe who would also want human beings to think and behave rationally. Essentially, such rational behaviour implied a commitment to religious tolerance. (Locke's *Letter Concerning Toleration* [1689], Voltaire's *Treatise on Toleration* [1763] and Gotthold Ephraim Lessing's drama *Nathan the Wise* [1779] were just three examples of the importance of this idea.)

From the critique of religion the *philosophes* proceeded to the critique of society. Beccaria, for example, suggested in his work *On Crimes and Punishments* (1764) that an accused should be regarded as innocent until proved guilty and instead of regarding crime as a transgression of God's will it should be seen as a transgression of the laws of nature. From such a perspective, punishment ought to be understood not as a (secular) enactment of God's wrath but, rather, as a (utilitarian) means to prevent future crime(s) by deterrence. In the economic sphere, mercantilist principles came under fire. In France, the *physiocrats* wanted to limit government intervention to the protection of property. Adam Smith, in his *Inquiry into the Nature and Causes of the Wealth of Nations* (1776), went even further. While the mercantilists had assumed that the resources of the earth were limited (with the implication that one nation's profits were another's losses), Smith claimed that they were boundless. If individuals could pursue their self-interest without being hindered by monopolies, tariffs and other laws regulating the economy, on the one hand, and if they could meet the needs and demands of the market, on the other, they would prosper individually and thereby create an ever-expanding economy which would benefit everyone.

In Britain, Adam Smith was regarded as the central political economist. But Smith built many of his arguments on François Quesnay, the French *physiocrat* who, crucially, was indebted to Chinese ideas of political economy. The concept of *wu-wei*, translated into French as *laissez-faire*, was of particular importance to him. It implied, first, that agriculture was an all-important source of wealth and, second, that it could only be fully exploited if the laws of supply and demand were allowed to rule without government intervention. This is just one small example of the way in which many ideas of the Scientific Revolution and the Enlightenment were indebted to the transfer of knowledge from China to Europe. Paradoxically, in the second half of the seventeenth century and the first two-thirds of the eighteenth century, China was regarded as *the* example of rational thought and technological advance – Voltaire and Leibniz, for example, paid extensive tributes to it in their works – but towards the end of the eighteenth century, as if the teacher's example had become an embarrassment to the pupils, the European image of China changed, and it became a backward barbarian land ruled by despots.

Political thought and practice

Viewed from the Continent, the British political experience appeared enviable: the power of the monarch was limited, political sovereignty resided in Parliament, British subjects were protected from arbitrary actions of the government (Document 19), and the press was freer than anywhere else. Moreover, as these liberal policies had produced neither chaos nor disorder they stimulated imitation. Both Voltaire and Montesquieu had spent some time in Britain (in 1726–8 and 1729–31 respectively) and returned full of praise.

> The *English* are the only people upon earth who have been able to prescribe limits to the power of Kings by resisting them; and who, by a series of struggles, have at last establish'd that wise Government, where the Prince is

all powerful to do good, and at the same time is restrain'd from committing evil; where the Nobles are great without insolence, tho' there are no Vassals; and where the People share in the government without confusion. (Voltaire, *Letters Concerning the English Nation*)

Debatable as this view may appear (and may have appeared even then) to a critical eye, there can be no doubt that to Voltaire (and other Anglophiles) the British political system demonstrated opportunities for reform which were badly needed in France and other Continental countries. Montesquieu, in his book *De l'esprit des lois* (*The Spirit of Laws*) (1748), reviewed the political institutions of ancient and modern nations. He also described and analysed the different forms of government and eventually opted for a limited monarchy – the system he had closely studied in Britain. The idea, however, which most influenced later democratic developments was that power should be divided among different branches of government. According to the (partly unwritten) British constitution (with its common law as well as its collections of statute laws and of conventions), legislative power was vested in Parliament, executive power in the monarch and his or her government, and judicial power in the courts. Again, a critical appreciation of these ideas could point out that this was not (yet) a real division of powers, as patronage and corruption allowed a handful of nobles to control the Houses of Parliament, on the one hand, and the judicial power of the courts could be overruled by the final court of appeal, the House of Lords. However, the powerful appeal of the principle of the division of power can be seen in the fact that it became a constitutive element of the constitution of the United States in 1787.

Very few *philosophes* were feminists. Although many women, particularly from the aristocracy, were instrumental in providing spaces for discussion in their fashionable salons, social equality was denied to them. They liberated the social discourse between the sexes, but it hardly earned them more than a nickname: bluestockings. (English *salonières* prided themselves on their elegant casualness: their blue stockings contrasted with the white or black ones of men's formal dress.) And although some of them made original contributions to the ongoing debates – Emilie, marquise de Châtelet (1704–49) and Voltaire, for example, during their fifteen-year relationship, cooperated on a number of projects and co-authored books – the sexual double standard was never questioned. Indeed, many *philosophes* advocated more education for women, but no one before Mary Wollstonecraft in her *Vindication of the Rights of Woman* (1792) demanded the same liberty for women (Document 20) which the *philosophes* had claimed for men for more than a century.

Some absolutist rulers such as Frederick II of Prussia (r. 1740–86), Joseph II of Austria (r. 1765–90) and Catherine II of Russia (r. 1762–96) liked to consider themselves as 'enlightened monarchs'. Leopold II of Tuscany (r. 1747–92) declared that 'the sovereign, even if hereditary, is only the delegate of his

---

Mary Wollstonecraft (1759–97)

Mary Wollstonecraft published several children's books, novels and essays but she is also remembered for being an early feminist. Her most famous work, *A Vindication of the Rights of Woman* (1792), in which she argued for an egalitarian society, was one of the first influential feminist statements. According to her, the principles of the French Revolution, liberty and equality, applied equally to men and to women. She argued that what seemed to be women's natural characteristics were actually the result of their (lack of) education. She herself was an educated woman who received some school instruction but like most women of her time she was largely self-taught. In 1797, shortly before her death, she married William Godwin, a British philosopher. She gave birth to her daughter, Mary, the future Mary Shelley, author of *Frankenstein* (1818), but died of childbed fever a few days later.

---

people', and Frederick II called himself the 'first servant' of his state. This is an interesting example of self-fashioning: none of the rulers resigned any of their monarchical prerogatives. Instead, they harnessed Enlightenment rationality to the actions of the State in order to strengthen their own (and not their subjects') power and interest.

The British experience

Why did eighteenth-century England not produce such a great number of daring intellectuals as did France? One reason may have been that England, before the eighteenth century opened, was already undergoing those trans-formations in politics, religious and personal freedom for which the French *philosophes* unsuccessfully clamoured throughout the century. In the so-called Glorious Revolution, England had produced a system of parliamentary representation and constitutional government which included individual lib-erty, substantial religious toleration, and freedom of speech and publishing. The problem which English intellectuals faced in the eighteenth century was not how to criticise an old regime or design a new one but, rather, how to make the existing reformed polity work. Would the checking and balancing mechan-isms of a mixed constitution prevent anarchy and despotism? Would a large measure of individual liberty be compatible with socio-political stability? Would individual prosperity be compatible with social cohesion? Would the pursuit of private gain prove disruptive, or would it produce a consumer soci-ety which bound people to each other by the chains of commerce? Would individual wealth enhance the wealth of the nation, or would it subvert liberty and corrupt the constitution? In short, would capitalism be the solvent of society or its very cement?

The Scottish experience is a partial answer to these questions. As we have seen, early eighteenth-century Scotland was relatively backward in economic terms. Moreover, it lost its political independence in the Act of Union (1707), and the ensuing failure of Jacobitism may have further divided and weakened the nation. But Scotland's losses were more than compensated by its gains. The access to a wider and more prosperous economy (England and its colonies) gave a boost to the Scottish economy. In this context, the pioneering analyses of the laws of a commercial economy by Scottish thinkers such as David Hume and Adam Smith were of vital importance well beyond Scotland and the British Isles. The balanced process of Anglicisation – sticking to Scottish traditions in matters of religion, law and education, but following the English model in other spheres – opened up Scotland to a host of influences which broadened and deepened its cultural life and vitality. To have understood and realistically thought through that Scotland's future lay not in a return to past glories, but in rapid (though balanced) social and cultural modernisation, constitutes the great achievement of the practical genius of the Scottish Enlightenment, which peaked between the 1740s and 1790s and justly earned Edinburgh the epithet 'the Athens of the North'.

Literary culture

Since its introduction in the fifteenth century, print had been an important factor of intellectual life in Europe which, for example, had substantially contributed to the success of the Reformation. But it was not until the eighteenth century that a real print culture emerged. With culture moving from the closed world of the court or the country house into the public domain, print became the chief vehicle for communicating ideas. Private (household) and public libraries were founded. Reading, which had largely been a group activity because of the scarcity of books, became a private undertaking, while discussing books (in coffee houses [Document 21], clubs or salons) became the new group activity. But as books were still expensive it also became necessary to provide for people who could not buy (but might share) them by establishing lending libraries. Periodicals such as Daniel Defoe's *Review* (1704–13) and Joseph Addison's *Spectator* (founded in 1711–12, 1714) were of increasing importance because they communicated information and opinions, and thereby provided food for thought and discussion. With an increasing supply of reading material, literacy grew: it has been estimated that by the end of the eighteenth century about half of the men and between a third and a half of the women in north-western Europe were literate. (The percentages in southern and eastern Europe were much smaller.) Thus, national reading publics came into existence whose rapid growth was also owed to the fact that the vernacular languages took an irreversible lead over Latin. The most astonishing fact is perhaps the relative rise of prose fiction; its share of literary production as a whole was about 7 per cent in 1700, about 20 per cent after 1740, and almost 40 per cent towards the end of the century.

Although sermons and tracts formed the largest part of all print products until well into the nineteenth century, other genres came to the fore in the eighteenth century. As always in times of rapid development, reference books (encyclopedias, dictionaries) enjoyed great popularity as they provided their readers with comprehensive up-to-date articles on the most relevant spheres of knowledge. The most famous was, of course, the *Encyclopédie* edited by Diderot and d'Alembert; its seventeen volumes of text and eleven volumes of illustration appeared between 1751 and 1772. The much more modest *Encyclopedia Britannica* was first published in Edinburgh between 1768 and 1771. It was put together in three volumes by a 'Society of Gentlemen', consisting of its editor William Smellie (who wrote all the articles), its printer Colin Macfarquhar, and its engraver Andrew Bell. But already, in 1728, Ephraim Chambers had published his *Cyclopedia*, and in 1755 Dr Johnson's *English Dictionary* appeared. The countless volumes devoted to all spheres of knowledge and behaviour were tributes to the overwhelming optimism of the period, which seriously believed in the perfectibility of human knowledge.

The single most important literary innovation of the eighteenth century was the novel. Miguel de Cervantes' *Don Quixote de la Mancha* (1605) can be credited with announcing the arrival of the novel in European culture, and Madame de La Fayette's *La Princesse de Clèves* (1678) provides the first landmark in France, but Daniel Defoe (1660–1731) is usually regarded as the founder of the English novel, particularly with his *Robinson Crusoe* (1719) and *Moll Flanders* (1722), closely followed by Samuel Richardson (1689–1761), Henry Fielding (1707–54) and Laurence Sterne (1713–68). A novel may be defined as a long work of prose fiction which contains characters and action organised around a plot. Usually a novel aims to represent a picture of 'real life' in the historical period and social context in which it is set. As such, it has become one of the most enduring empirical, sceptical and critical instruments for intellectually and emotionally probing the vagaries of human life. This is particularly owing to the fact that its form has proved to be adaptable to various uses. Defoe's novels combine spiritual autobiography and adventure, Richardson's *Pamela* (1740) and *Clarissa* (1747–8) were epistolary novels (as was about a fifth of all eighteenth-century literature) which wanted 'to cultivate the principles of virtue and religion', while Fielding's *History of Tom Jones, a Foundling* (1749) is distinguished by its non-idealised hero and its complex narrative structure. Sterne's *Tristram Shandy* (1760–7) is different from the novels mentioned before in that it dismantles accepted narrative conventions, introduces baffling changes of perspective, and avoids a reliable narrator with a clear storyline. These models of narration have been imitated, improved on and transformed until the present day without becoming exhausted.

Daniel Defoe's *Robinson Crusoe* was an immediate success and has become a literary archetype. Like Sir Thomas More's *Utopia* it has also named a genre: the German speak of a *Robinsonade*, the French of *robinsonnade* while, paradoxically, English-speaking literary criticism has to make do with the formula 'Robinson Crusoe story'. The novel has invited many different readings. On the one hand, it can be read as the success story of 'economic man' whose initiative, stamina and perseverance enable him not only to survive a shipwreck but also to prosper and succeed in his 'projects' of reproducing his particular way of life on an island. On the other, it has been understood as the spiritual autobiography of 'religious man' who has to go a long, stony and tortuous way to 'find' his god and a way of communicating with him. Furthermore, it has been read as the foundational myth for European plantations or colonies and the related clashes of cultures between Europeans and indigenous people. In Crusoe's description of Friday we recognise the gaze of the slave trader; in his interactions with him we recognise the treatment of a servant, a slave, or any 'other' by his European master. More generally speaking, one could say that Defoe's story primarily represented the adventurous and entrepreneurial (capitalist) ethos of the rising middle classes, first in Britain and later in the whole of Europe.

THE TRANSATLANTIC ECONOMY

Europe's expansion across the world, which began in the final years of the fifteenth century, occurred in four stages. A first phase of exploration and conquest was followed by a second during which either settlements or trading relations (or both) were established. The latter usually led to rivalries among the great colonial powers (Spain, France and Great Britain) as every power wanted to acquire as many trading partners as possible and, thus, to oust any potential or real competitor. In the western hemisphere the Atlantic commercial system reached its climax in the eighteenth century. During a third phase, from the late eighteenth to the early twentieth century, European nations occupied large parts of Australia, Asia and Africa, building and administering empires there. The fourth phase features the complex processes of decolonisation in the twentieth century.

Table 2 notes the main colonial possessions of the major European powers after the Treaty of Utrecht (1713).

The goals of the colonial powers were initially determined by the mercantilist idea that the world's resources were limited and every nation did well if it tried to obtain as much of them as possible. Consequently they aimed at exploiting their colonies by (i) extracting precious minerals (gold, silver and, later, diamonds), (ii) growing raw materials (sugar, tobacco, cotton, coffee, cocoa, etc.) which could be refined in the mother country and re-exported, and (iii) excluding other nations from trading with these colonies. Because of this dependence of the colony on the mother country, the latter would be sure to

Table 2 The main colonial possessions of the major European powers after the Treaty of Utrecht (1713)

Portugal	Brazil
Spain	All of mainland South America (except for Brazil); Cuba, Puerto Rico and half of Hispaniola (Haiti); Florida, Mexico, California
Britain	North Atlantic Seaboard (thirteen colonies), Nova Scotia, Newfoundland; Jamaica, Barbados; trading stations in India (such as Bombay, Madras, Calcutta)
France	The valleys of the Saint Lawrence, the Ohio, and the Mississippi rivers, the islands Martinique, Guadeloupe and the other half of Hispaniola in the West Indies; trading stations in India (such as Pondicherry, Chandernagore)
United Dutch Provinces	Surinam (Dutch Guiana, South America), trading posts in Ceylon, Bengal and Java

acquire the colony's raw materials cheaply and to sell goods produced at home at a favourable price in the colony. In this context trade expanded roughly fivefold in the eighteenth century. The main axis on which this expansion turned was the so-called triangular trade, which rested on a simple triangle of trading relations which in the course of time grew more and more complex and intensive. From Europe manufactured goods (such as cloth, iron, rum and guns) were exported to Africa in order to be profitably exchanged against slaves who could be sold in the Americas. The empty ships were then loaded with raw materials (such as sugar, cotton and tobacco) which were processed and consumed in Britain or re-exported to the European continent. On all three voyages profits were made which flowed into the European commercial centres (Document 22).

The slave trade

In his book *De l'esprit des lois*, Montesquieu answered the question why it was necessary to transport African slaves to the Americas: 'The Europeans, having extirpated the [native] Americans, were obliged to make slaves of the Africans for clearing such vast tracts of land.' It is not entirely clear how many people lived in the Americas before the Europeans arrived, but the latest estimates give figures of 80 million to 100 million people. Roughly a hundred years later about 8 million to 10 million people were left; the others had died through diseases, wars and exploitation. The consequent lack of manpower impeded the production of agricultural raw materials and the extraction of mineral resources. The Amerindian labourers were succeeded by the poor whites who came as indentured servants, 'redemptioners' or convicts. But white servitude had serious disadvantages. White labourers might wish to rival the mother country in manufacturing; they could escape quite easily; their supply could dry up; they had a right to a piece of land at the end of their contract. All these disadvantages pointed to the African slave as a viable alternative, which had the additional benefit of being cheaper: the money to be paid for a white man's services for ten years could buy an African for life.

African slaves were sold and bought almost anywhere on the West African coast between Senegambia and Angola. In the early days of the slave trade most of them lived on the coast; later, however, when the demand increased, the 'middlemen' (white agents and cooperating Africans) had to resort to the hinterland. But, wherever they came from, they were mainly acquired through warfare, kidnapping and tribute. Basically there were two modes of buying slaves for a European slaver: he could either sail from area to area collecting a few slaves at a time until he had a full cargo ('ship trade'), or he could make use of European agents who secured slaves from African traders so that they were ready when the ships arrived ('factory trade'). While the factory trade was usually more expensive – the trading posts had to be maintained and protected – it saved a lot of time (and thereby money): the slaver could quickly leave the African coast, which was, at least in terms of health and hygiene, beneficial for the survival of the slaves that were kept in the ship's hold.

It has been reckoned that all in all some 12 million to 15 million Africans were taken across the Atlantic, but only 80–90 per cent reached their destination; the others died on the 'Middle Passage'. The average mortality rate before 1700 was 20–25 per cent, in the eighteenth century it was 15 per cent, and in the nineteenth century 10 per cent. In the second half of the seventeenth century a male slave cost £3–4 on the African coast, around 1700 a slaver had to pay £10 for him, and thirty years later £18. The self-same slave in Jamaica in the middle of the eighteenth century cost about £50. With this sum of money a single person could comfortably live in Britain for a year.

On the African coast the slaves were, first of all, examined; those who were not completely healthy, strong and young were not bought. The barter was a very complex affair: slaves were paid for in 'bars', but of what different goods and of how much a bar consisted was different from place to place and from time to time. As soon as the slaves were bought they were branded, their heads were shaved and they had to take off all their clothes. On board ship, the men were shackled and put into the hold, the women and children were kept separately (sometimes on deck). The space allotted to them was exceedingly small: every man was allowed 6 feet by 1 foot 4 inches, every woman 5 feet by 1 foot 3 inches, and every child 4 feet 6 inches by 1 foot (Document 23). When the slave ship arrived in the Americas, the slaves were sold either to somebody who had bought them in advance, or by public auction, or in a 'scramble' (in which the slaves up for sale were kept in a corral, their prospective buyers being allowed to rush in and simply grab whoever they wanted to buy). The journey across the Atlantic could be somewhere between 3200 and 6000 miles long, depending on where it started and ended; under average circumstances it lasted for about 40–70 days. When it lasted longer (because of the weather, a rebellion or a mutiny), the lives of the slaves were immediately in danger.

In the eighteenth century, particularly after the Treaty of Utrecht (1713), by which Britain obtained the right to provide the Spanish colonies in the Americas with African slaves (the so-called *asiento*), Britain was the leading slave-trading nation (Document 24). Its share was 41.3 per cent, while Portugal carried 29.3 per cent, Denmark 1.2 per cent, and Sweden and Brandenburg together 0.1 per cent. Early estimates of the profits (16–30 per cent) were most probably too high: a more recent estimate ended up with a profit of 9.5 per cent. This was definitely more than could be made in agriculture at home – where 3.5 per cent was regarded as normal – but only slightly more than could be achieved in other spheres of commerce.

BRITAIN, EUROPE AND THE WORLD

Foreigners praised the British model of constitutional monarchy; but the English, faced with what they regarded as excesses of patronage and corruption of incompetent governments, doubted whether it would work. The colonies on the Atlantic seaboard were treated with what Edmund Burke later called 'wise and salutary neglect' and allowed to develop a tradition of self-government, but they rose up against British rule. What kind of connection is there between these different states of affairs, their evaluation and their eventual outcomes?

European and global rivalries

At any time before, probably, the second half of the twentieth century, warfare was a universally accepted means of building and extending nations and their spheres of influence. This was also true for the eighteenth century, in which a mixture of disputed royal successions and colonial rivalries led to a number of global conflicts. These wars were fought in as many theatres as the contenders could man. Every party aimed at becoming stronger while weakening its opponents. Paradoxically, this led to a system in which every nation was interested in producing a 'balance of power' as the ideal state of affairs.

The War of the Spanish Succession (1702–13) had strengthened Bourbon France and weakened Habsburg Austria. The rulers of both countries had claimed the Spanish throne for a grandson, but Philip of Anjou, the grandson of Louis XIV, eventually became king of Spain. Austria's position became further imperilled by the fact that Emperor Charles VI (r. 1711–40) had no male heir and feared that after his death some of the European powers would intervene in Austria as they (including himself) had in Spain – and right he was. Although he tried to have his daughter Maria Theresa (r. 1740–80) accepted as his rightful heir by a document (the 'Pragmatic Sanction') signed by Europe's chief nations, as soon as Charles VI was dead Frederick II, the new ruler of Prussia (r. 1740–86), invaded (and later annexed) Silesia. France, traditionally opposed to Austria, joined Prussia, hoping to take the Low Countries from Austria. To prevent this, Britain entered the war allied to Austria. In 1744, France began to back Spain in the Americas (where the latter had been fighting Britain since 1739), and the war spread beyond Europe. Four years later all parties were exhausted and made peace in Europe, while the fighting between French and English settlers in North America escalated into the French and Indian War.

In 1756, after a dramatic reversal of alliances (euphemistically called 'diplomatic revolution'), the war in Europe resumed. As Frederick feared an invasion from Russia, he negotiated an alliance with Britain. After the first shock, the Austrian government realised the potential of the fact that Austria's long-standing ally had joined Austria's chief enemy: to allay its fear of being caught between Britain and Prussia, the French government was prepared to conclude an alliance with Austria. Again, Frederick II opened the hostilities, this time invading Saxony. Although Sweden, Russia and a considerable number of small German states joined the French–Austrian alliance, the war ended with no significant losses of land on either side in Europe. This was different in the colonies. France ceased to be a great colonial power, and the Spanish empire became prey to British infiltration. The British were singularly successful: in North America, they took all of Canada, the eastern half of the Mississippi river valley, and the Ohio river valley; in the West Indies, although they returned Martinique and Guadeloupe to the French, they became the dominant power; in India, after the defeat of the French at Plassey (1757), Britain's East India Company imposed its authority on a steadily growing number of small indigenous states, thereby stabilising its increasing influence. But the success had a price. The financial burden of the war was preposterous: the British national debt doubled.

Political corruption

The first two Hanoverian kings, George I (r. 1714–27) and George II (r. 1727–60), depended very much on the advice of a group of Whig politicians who had supported the Hanoverian succession, and in particular on the abilities of a man who has traditionally become known as Britain's first prime minister: Robert Walpole (1676–1745). Walpole came from Norfolk gentry and was a Whig MP almost uninterruptedly from 1701 to 1742. From the early 1720s to the early 1740s he conducted the affairs of the country. When George III (r. 1760–1820), the first English-born-and-bred Hanoverian, succeeded to the throne, he believed that his predecessors had been too much dominated by those few powerful Whigs. He decided to choose his own ministers and enhance his monarchical powers. Using a lot of royal patronage (i.e. money and offices), George tried to buy influence in Parliament. But the latter resisted and did not back the politicians of George's choosing. In 1763 the forces in opposition to the king found a spokesperson, John Wilkes (1725–97), a London political radical and MP. Wilkes used his newspaper, *The North Briton*, to criticise the government. He was accused of libel, found guilty and expelled from Parliament. He fled the country, but many regarded him as a victim of political persecution. On his return to Britain in 1768, when he was re-elected to Parliament, the House of Commons bowed to George's wish and refused to let him take his seat. Subsequently, he won another three elections, but was not allowed to take his seat. People from the middle classes demonstrated for him, aristocrats who were critical of the monarch supported him. Wilkes identified himself with English liberty; the government's opponents created the slogan 'Wilkes and Liberty'. Finally, in 1774, Wilkes was allowed to take his seat. Is it any wonder that these events let many people in Britain and its colonies think that the monarch had reverted to an increasingly arbitrary use of power, Parliament was corruptible, and both held the voters (and the public in general) in contempt?

Colonial rebellion: the thirteen colonies

The Seven Years War left Britain not only with a huge amount of war debts but also with a much larger territory in North America which had to be protected and administered. As the separate colonies could hardly be relied on to supply troops if a neighbouring colony was under threat from either the indigenous population or a colonial competitor, some kind of imperial defence organised from London became necessary. And, because the colonists benefited from this, it seemed natural to let them contribute one-third to the cost of a standing army, while the British taxpayer would pay the rest (including the cost of the Navy). This idea appeared reasonable as the population of the colonies had grown from 250,000 in 1700 to 2.5 million in 1775 (as compared to 6.4 million in England) and the colonies received about 20 per cent of the exports and supplied 30 per cent of the imports of Britain. While there was no doubt that Parliament in London had the right to legislate for the colonies to raise revenue, exercising this right appeared arbitrary to the colonists, who had been used to practical independence for a long time. Their battle cry, 'No taxation without representation', popular as it may have been, made little sense to the British because all of them were taxed but only one in ten adult males had the vote.

As it had become clear during the Seven Years War that the mercantilist laws were hardly observed by the American colonies, the government decided to collect taxes more rigorously while, at the same time, lowering them. In 1764 the Sugar Act was passed, followed in 1765 by the Stamp Act (a tax on legal documents, newspapers etc.). When the colonists reacted by threatening to boycott British imports, the Stamp Act was repealed, but Parliament passed the Declaratory Act (1766) insisting

That the said colonies and plantations in America have been, are, and of right ought to be, subordinate unto, and dependent upon the imperial crown and parliament of *Great Britain*; and that the King's majesty, by and with the advice and consent of the lords spiritual and temporal, and commons of *Great Britain*, in parliament assembled, had, hath, and of right ought to have, full power and authority to make laws and statutes of sufficient force and validity to bind the colonies and people of *America*, subjects of the crown of *Great Britain*, in all cases whatsoever.

When, a year later, taxes were imposed on various goods, the pattern was repeated. The colonists resisted, the government tried to enforce its measures by stationing troops in Boston to protect its customs agents. Tensions grew, the soldiers fired into a group of demonstrators, and five people were killed ('Boston Massacre'). Later in the year, Parliament repealed all duties except those on tea. Yet, another three years later, a new law was passed in London which permitted tea to be directly imported into the American colonies (making it thereby cheaper) but which also included a tax imposed without the colonists' consent. When, in 1773, a group of colonists (thinly disguised as Native Americans) threw the cargo of a ship into Boston harbour, Parliament passed the Coercive Acts (dubbed the 'Intolerable Acts' by the American colonists), closing the port of Boston, quartering more British troops in America, and strengthening the authority of the administration. While the pressure from Britain achieved some sort of unity among the formerly anything but united colonies, British public opinion and governmental action were divided. While experienced politicians like William Pitt, earl of Chatham (1708–78) and Edmund Burke (1729–97) advocated conciliation (Document 25) and suggested self-governing dominion roles for the colonies, George III adamantly opposed any change in the relationship between Britain and its colonies (Document 26).

In September 1774 the First Continental Congress tried to persuade Parliament to leave colonial affairs in the hands of the colonists. By April 1775 the first shots 'heard round the world' had been fired (at Lexington and Concord) so that the attempts at conciliation of the Second Continental Congress in May came to nothing. By August, George III had declared the colonies in rebellion, and in the following winter Thomas Paine's pamphlet *Common Sense* made a most persuasive case for separation (Document 27). In the spring of 1776 the Americans opened their ports to trade with all nations, and on 4 July 1776 the Declaration of Independence was adopted. Its central passage avowed its authors' secular belief in natural rights, government by consent and the right to revolution.

We hold these truths to be self-evident, that all men are created equal, that they are endowed by their Creator with certain unalienable Rights, that among these are Life, Liberty and the pursuit of Happiness. – That to secure these rights, Governments are instituted among Men, deriving their just powers from the consent of the governed, – That whenever any Form of Government becomes destructive of these ends, it is the Right of the People to alter or to abolish it, and to institute new Government, laying its foundation on such principles and organizing its powers in such form, as to them shall seem most likely to effect their Safety and Happiness.

In the beginning, the conflict was essentially a civil war within the British empire because about a quarter of the colonists ('loyalists') supported the British side while the 'patriots' advocating separation were in a minority. Although George III insisted on a determined war policy, he was but reluctantly supported by his irritable prime minister, Lord North. The naval war was correspondingly half-hearted, while the army overextended its capacity in the attempt to contain the vast colonial territory. (The British had to establish and maintain supply lines across the Atlantic, while the colonial army was virtually self-sufficient.)

After two years, the nature of the conflict changed. Unlike in previous wars, Britain had no ally, and this isolation encouraged its competitors to 'meddle' in and (as they hoped) to profit from the conflict. When Benjamin Franklin persuaded the French to support the colonies in 1778, the conflict became a world war. This alliance not only furnished the colonists with additional troops, weapons and money, but also revived the spectre of a French invasion of the British Isles. Spain joined the war on the American side in 1779, Holland in 1780, while Russia, Sweden, Prussia, Denmark and Portugal continued to trade with and thereby support the colonies. In 1781 the British had to surrender at Yorktown, and in the Treaty of Paris (1783) the independence of the former colonies as the United States of America was recognised.

Prudently the British offered generous terms to the Americans which eased future economic and political relations. However, the independence of the United States had wider repercussions. With it, a political system became reality which hitherto had only been an idea beyond the existing framework: a polity based on the consent of the governed. Admittedly, the franchise remained limited to white male citizens. The rights of Native Americans and of women were not addressed; slaves were not emancipated. But a society more free than any seen before was created – a fact which encouraged reform movements in many other places. The experience of losing the thirteen colonies also helped reshape British attitudes towards its empire, at least to its colonies of settlement. Even if colonies were regarded as 'children', a responsible 'mother' would allow them to mature and then release them into independence. Canada (1867), Australia (1900) and New Zealand (1907) were to benefit from this insight.

Traditionally, the loss of the American colonies has been regarded as marking the end of Britain's first empire, the empire in the west. Although there is something to this perspective, it is not completely true. The sugar islands in the Caribbean remained important until well into the nineteenth century, and it was not without reason that the abolition of the slave trade (1807) and the abolition of slavery in the empire (1833) were hotly contested issues. However, it can hardly be denied that there was a certain 'swing to the east' in British imperial interests which, in fact, antedates the loss of the American colonies but was subsequently strengthened by it. From the mid-eighteenth century onwards, the East India Company's activities in India gathered momentum: between 1744 and 1805, the Company fought at least nine wars, bringing some 30 million people under Company rule by 1800. Another highly profitable trading triangle was created with manufactured goods being exported from Britain to India, opium from India to China, and tea, silk and chinaware from China to Britain. Finally, James Cook's explorations of the Pacific (1768–78) prepared the settlements in Van Diemen's Land (Tasmania) and Australia, the latter replacing Georgia as a penal colony.

6 Political reforms, Industrial Revolution, imperial rule, 1789–1914

Arguing from a primarily European perspective, historians tend to speak of the 'long' nineteenth century. They date it from 1789 to 1914 and frame it by two cataclysms: the French Revolution of 1789, which led to a series of wars in Europe and beyond (1792–1815), and the First World War (1914–18), which, in its course, produced the Russian Revolution of 1917. Internationally speaking, the years in between were relatively peaceful and permitted sustained economic, social and political development in many parts of Europe. Looking for the main actors of the nineteenth century, it could be argued that, from a Continental perspective, it was Germany's century because of its irresistible (economic and political) rise under Prussian dominance after the mid-century, while, from an international perspective, it certainly was Britain's century because of the expansion of the Empire: by 1900 the United Kingdom of Great Britain and Ireland controlled over a fifth of the world's land surface and ruled a quarter of the world's population.

EUROPEAN PERSPECTIVES

In this period, most European nations had to confront similar and (inter-) related problems, although, perhaps, not necessarily at the same time and of the same intensity: the French Revolution and its aftermath; Europe's political order, faced by pressures from within (popular demands for liberal reforms transforming many of these absolutist monarchies into constitutional ones or republics) and from without (by international and colonial rivalry); the various phases of the Industrial Revolution and their economic, technological and social repercussions; the integration of those parts of their populations into the body politic that hitherto had not participated in political decisions; the loss of traditional world views and their replacement.

The revolution in France and the reconstruction of Europe's political order

The European nations had to deal with the fact that one of their kind (France) had experienced such a degree of revolutionary change that its effect involved the whole of Europe. What began as a middle-class attempt to limit the powers of an absolutist monarchy in 1789 soon – with strong support of the lower classes – grew into a widespread popular revolt. It resulted in the abolition of feudalism, the 'Declaration of the Rights of Man and Citizen', which owed much to American precedent and listed mankind's 'natural, inalienable and sacred rights' (Document 28), and the passing of a constitution that made Louis XVI a constitutional monarch, no longer above the laws, but bound by and required to enforce them. So far the middle class had succeeded in retaining control of the political scene, but when counter-revolutionary forces inside France found support outside the country the struggle acquired a new dimension. France declared war on Austria in April 1792 and, as a consequence, Prussia and Austria prepared a joint invasion. Early defeats produced panic reactions, including the massacre of political suspects and the deposition and subsequent execution of Louis XVI. The latter event served as a pretext for a group of European states including Britain (the First Coalition) to declare war on France, but Danton and the Girondins succeeded in unifying the country against the external threat. However, they were displaced by the Jacobins, a more radical group, who gained support by placing government on a more democratic basis and by terrorist measures against dissidents. Carnot's 'citizen armies' not only expelled the foreign invaders but also attacked and annexed territories to secure France's frontiers. At home the Jacobins were less successful: their extreme radicalism produced a revulsion, and France once more reverted to a middle-class government. A new constitution provided in 1795 for a bicameral government on a limited franchise and an executive 'Directory' of five elected leaders. Although initially successful, the Directory proved too weak and corrupt to consolidate the achievements of the revolution and to prevent economic, political and military decline. These tasks fell to Napoleon Bonaparte, who seized power in 1799 and, in the ensuing fifteen years as first consul (1799–1804) and as emperor (1804–14), not only re-established revolutionary institutions in France (albeit in a modified form) but also exported them by military conquest to many parts of Europe.

The impact of the French Revolution cannot be overestimated: the destruction of the strongest and most centralised absolutist state of the *ancien régime* in the space of a few months sent shockwaves around the world. In France, the political supremacy of the middle class in the towns was established, and the bulk of landed property was transferred to the peasantry in the countryside. For Europe, despite the excesses of the Jacobins, which made the revolution a byword for fear among the aristocracies and property owners, the revolutionaries represented the ideals of liberty, equality, fraternity as well as popular sovereignty while, for the first time, identifying the whole people with the nation. Two cardinal features of nineteenth-century Europe – liberalism and nationalism – were derived from it.

In most European countries the French Revolution either politicised already existing popular discontent or inspired debates on citizens' rights, parliamentary reform and the nature of government. In these respects, Britain was no exception (Documents 29 and 30). For the British government, links between French revolutionaries and members of the Society for Constitutional Information, the London Corresponding Society (Document 31), independent radicals and the enthusiasm of many intellectuals were a source of concern. When these people debated plans for summoning a British (National) Convention, the government suspended Habeas Corpus (1794) and introduced additional repressive measures such as the Two ('Gagging') Acts (of 1795), which limited the freedom to hold public meetings or lectures on political subjects. A French-backed rebellion by the United Irishmen (1797–8) was violently suppressed (cf. Chapter 5), as were naval mutinies at Spithead and the Nore (1797), which had put most of the fleet in home waters out of action. The British war efforts were concentrated in three fields: to 'rule the waves' of the world in compensation for the dominance of the French army on the European continent; to defeat French attacks on imperial outposts; and to provide financial support for various allies. In the final resort, these measures were successful: the victory in Egypt (1798) established Britain's mastery of the Mediterranean; in the same year the French were ousted from India, and the victory at Trafalgar (1805) destroyed the combined French and Spanish fleets and thereby ended any possibility of a French invasion of Britain, which had been in preparation. Napoleon attempted to close the whole of Europe to British goods, but British naval power in the Baltic and the Mediterranean constantly subverted these efforts, and eventually the combined efforts of the British navy and the Prussian, Russian and Austrian armies made Napoleon's defeat possible. The loss of life caused by the wars was very high; and the financial costs of these war years were unprecedented. In the short term, the latter may have slowed down the Industrial Revolution; in the long term, however, Britain gained very much from the extension of trade at the expense of France.

After the end of the Revolutionary and Napoleonic Wars (1792–1815) the European nations had to (re-)construct a viable international political order and to make it work in a long-term perspective. Attended by 15 kings, 200 princes and 126 European diplomats, the Congress of Vienna (1814–15) met to establish the post-Napoleonic order of Europe. It succeeded in finding a moderate territorial settlement which satisfied the main requirements of the victors (Russia, Austria, Prussia, Britain and their minor allies) without humiliating France. Moreover, the four main allies set up a congress system to safeguard the peace settlements, which proved to be effective, while conservative attempts to use it as a means of holding back liberal ideas, economic and social change, as well as constitutionalism, lost ground throughout Western Europe in the – once again revolutionary – 1830s and 1840s. And, while Britain and France jointly resisted Russian ambitions to expand westward and southward in the Crimean War (1853–6), the unification of Italy (1861, 1870) and Prussia-dominated Germany – facilitated by three wars against Denmark (1864), Austria (1866) and France (1870–1) – gave a new pattern to European politics with Prussia (at the head of a newly created German empire) as the Continent's leading power. These developments resulted in a system of balanced antagonism ('armed peace') which failed to produce war in Europe simply because a new phase of imperialism – an acceleration of the well-known pattern of European penetration, domination and conquest of the non-European world – 'exported' the conflicts particularly to Africa, to east and south-east Asia as well as to the Pacific, and thereby acted as a safety valve.

Industrialisation

The Industrial Revolution confronted Europeans with various challenges which had to be turned into a coordinated process of economic growth, technological expertise and social progress. While industrialisation shared common features throughout the Continent, every region developed in its own way. The English midlands saw the birth of the Industrial Revolution, but other regions such as southern Wales, north-eastern France, Belgium, the Ruhr, Silesia and the Donets basin soon followed. Despite all differences, these developments were basically characterised by the way in which labour power (increasing numbers of workers) could be mobilised and effectively combined with new sources of power (as well as power-driven machines and engines) to work in particular places of production (mills, factories) under certain conditions (contractual wage labour), which differed in many respects from traditional modes of production (increasing division of labour, longer hours, labour contracts) (Document 32). Until the mid-century, Britain certainly benefited from having been the first industrialising nation and proudly demonstrated this in the Great Exhibition (1851). Thereafter, however, particularly from the 1870s onwards, Britain's competitors (France, Germany and the United States in particular) profited from the fact that they had *not* been the first: they could avoid mistakes, detours, dead ends, which beginners are bound to make; moreover, they could import technical knowhow (inventions), expertise (engineers) and capital necessary for rapid industrial development.

Europeans also had to construct and eventually make profitable use of traditional and newly invented means of communication under an increasingly global perspective. What began as part of the necessary infrastructural improvements of industrialising regions – consolidating natural and constructing artificial waterways – ended in two great feats of engineering which parted four continents and facilitated a much quicker global exchange of goods: the canals of Suez (1869) and Panama (1914). The newly invented railways grew spectacularly: in 1835 the United Kingdom had 338 miles of railway track, while France had 88 and Germany 4. Twenty years later, the figures were 7298, 3130 and 4863 miles respectively, rising another twenty years later to 14,519, 12,028 and 17,381 miles. The time required to travel overland from Paris to St Petersburg was cut from twenty days in 1800 to thirty hours in 1900. When steamships replaced sailing ships, not only was the time of the voyage cut, but timetables also became more reliable. But not only were more and more people on the move; there was also a huge increase in the movement of information. Postal systems were established throughout Europe from the 1840s; the telegraph was invented in 1832, a cross-Channel service was in operation from 1850, a transatlantic cable from 1865. The telephone (1876) added a new dimension; moreover, the nineteenth century saw the birth of photography (1827, 1839), sound recording (1876), the wireless radio and the moving picture (both 1895).

Colonialism – imperialism

Competition for colonies – profitable as suppliers of raw materials, as buyers of goods (or both) or as strategic places in the global geopolitical struggle – compelled the European nations to try to maximise their share of the non-European world while minimising their risks in the conflicts with their rivals. The Revolutionary and Napoleonic Wars were fought not only in Europe but worldwide; they resulted in huge losses for France and considerable gains for Britain (with, amongst others, the Cape of Good Hope, Ceylon, Mauritius, Trinidad and Tobago, Malta and Heligoland). Although it has often been thought that, from the perspective of continental Europe, the postwar years were years of imperial retreat, this is only partially true: while Spain and Portugal lost their colonies in Central and South America, France tried to re-establish itself as an imperial power by taking Algiers (1830) and annexing a number of islands in the Indian and Pacific oceans. Britain followed a dual strategy: if possible, it contented itself with penetrating foreign countries economically ('trade without rule where possible'), but very often the 'need' to anticipate some competitor 'forced' the British formally to occupy a region they were interested in ('trade with rule where necessary', as, e.g., in the case of New Zealand). When, after 1870, the world, with the exception of Africa, appeared to be shared out among the colonial powers, rivalry grew fiercer as demonstrated by the ignoble 'scramble' for Africa, beginning in the 1880s.

Theories explaining the 'nature' of 'imperialism' abound. Three strands in particular may be distinguished: all of them may have some application somewhere, but none of them can stand alone in so complex a process. *Economic* explanations concentrate on the needs of the imperial powers in terms of resources (raw materials) and outlets for trade (mass-produced goods) and investment (export of capital). *Political* explanations embrace all manner of expressions of nationalism (including a state's disposition to unlimited frontier expansion and to reactions to threats on its periphery). *Sociological* explanations focus on the idea of spreading 'civilisation', analysing associated notions of racial superiority, social organisation, culture and religion.

The right to vote

All the processes sketched above by necessity involved a constantly growing number of people – first the middle classes, then the working classes – to an ever increasing extent in the making of the economic well-being of society, without giving them a say in the political fashioning of its nature. Those (major) parts of the populations that hitherto had not participated in political decisions had to be integrated into the body politic (preferably without endangering its established power structure). With the example of the American constitution and the (French) 'Declaration of the Rights of Man and Citizen', the right to vote was on the agenda for the whole of Europe. And, step by step, however limited by property, literacy and gender qualifications, the proportion of the population with the vote grew, so that, by 1890, 27.1 per cent had the vote in France, 23.2 per cent in Greece, 21.7 per cent in Germany, 16.3 per cent in Britain, 13.9 per cent in Denmark, 9.7 per cent in Italy, and 9.1 per cent in Norway. With the exception of Finland (1906) and Norway (1907), women obtained the vote (in national elections) only after the end of the First World War. It was in this context that political parties as we know them today (as 'representative' of certain groups of the population with specified interests) were developed by such groups. However, political participation, as well as being involved in increasingly complex processes of production and exchange, demanded an educational system which could provide a measure of general education for the whole population. The figures for adult male literacy may be a possible indicator of these efforts, particularly after the mid-century: in England and Wales, illiteracy fell from 33 per cent in 1840 to 3 per cent in 1900 (in Scotland from 11 per cent in 1855 to 2 per cent in 1900). In France it fell from 32 per cent in 1855 to 3 per cent in 1905, in Prussia from 16 per cent in 1825 to zero by 1910. By contrast, in Ireland it was still 34 per cent in 1900 (in Italy *c.*38 per cent, in Spain *c.*50 per cent, in Russia *c.*60 per cent in 1910).

Culture and ideology

Without any doubt, these economic, social and political developments went hand in hand with (i.e depended on and, at the same time, facilitated) changes in the mental outlook of their protagonists: nineteenth-century Europeans had to 'handle' (i.e. perceive, formulate and discuss) the dissolution and eventual loss of traditional world views (as embodied in the absolutist monarchies and certain dogmas of the Christian religion) and find new ways of making sense of the world as it was. The Enlightenment bequeathed an ambiguous legacy to the nineteenth century which consisted of both self-confident continuity and disruptive self-doubt. While the former found expression in an almost unshakeable belief in and documentation of (e.g. in museums, galleries and exhibitions) what individuals might achieve in the spheres of productive labour or intellectual and artistic creativity to further the progress of humanity, the latter pointed to the social and intellectual 'costs' (such as alienation and loss of religious faith) of these achievements. And, while the former welcomed the emergence of science, invested in the creation of systems of thought and knowledge (many academic disciplines were established in the second half of our period) and gave particular prominence to historical thinking (thereby, understandably enough, marking their own historical 'moment'), the latter demonstrated the limits of the natural sciences as well as the waning capacity of literature and the arts to capture and criticise social reality as a whole.

THE UNITED KINGDOM OF GREAT BRITAIN AND IRELAND

The Industrial Revolution

While political revolutions were on the agenda of nearly all European states and societies between 1789 and 1848, the United Kingdom of Great Britain – which initially reacted to this threat within the British Isles by, among other things, repressing sympathising movements within, joining anti-revolutionary alliances abroad and forcing unification on Ireland (1801) – had to deal with another 'revolutionary' development, which would occupy the European continent (and North America) but only after a certain time-lag: the Industrial Revolution, its origins, development and effects. In most history books the idea of the Industrial Revolution has been associated with, first, those economic, technological, political, social as well as cultural processes that transform an agrarian society into an industrial one, and, second, with Britain, because that is where these processes took place for the first time. More specifically, it has been associated, third, with a number of technical inventions and innovations that changed the processes of production (and, as a consequence, of exchange as well as consumption), and, last, with a related process of general social change. While it is understandable that contemporaries experienced many of these processes as taking place relatively quickly, and many later historians located them within a clearly defined time-span (say, between 1770 and 1830), many factors seem to indicate that what has been regarded as a 'great leap forward' was perhaps no more than the final stage of a much longer process of growth (say, between the beginning of the eighteenth and the middle of the nineteenth century) which, when it reached its climax, gave new directions to the economic and social sectors of Britain. Perhaps it was an even longer process which Britain and Europe did not initiate but, rather, joined as latecomers.

No change happens without announcing itself (or being announced) in many ways. The Industrial Revolution in Britain was preceded by 'improvements' in the *agricultural sector*, which resulted in higher yields. These higher yields were due, first, to an increase in the amount of arable land through enclosures (which had begun in the fifteenth century and had led to a redistribution of the land in favour of the better-off landowners and the emergence of an ever-growing agricultural proletariat); second, to improved seed, increased and improved fertilisation, and more extensive use of manpower, which contributed to better harvests; third, to technological innovations such as the change from the three-field system to the four-course rotation system (which included the introduction of new crops) on the one hand, and improvements of the soil (by embanking, drainage, irrigation) as well as tools (e.g. the replacement of the sickle by the scythe) on the other; and last, but not least, to local and regional specialisations.

These increasing yields, which dated from the beginning of the eighteenth century, also contributed to the sum of money available in every household for *consumption*. This, in turn, created a growing demand for consumer goods, which were either imported from the colonies (like sugar, tobacco, coffee, tea, rum, but also luxury goods for the better-off) or were produced at home by the expanding sectors of skilled manual workers and the domestic industry.

Moreover, through the union with Scotland, Ireland and the conquest of numerous colonies in the Americas and elsewhere, Britain had acquired 'a common market of sorts' that constituted a large, quickly expanding area of *trade* (including the former American colonies) for British merchants. World trade and the world market initiated the modern history of capital, first, by making possible the accumulation of profits, which could be used as investments in the first phase of industrialisation; second, by opening up markets that would later absorb mass products from the mother country; and, third (and most important), by creating a complex network of relations of exchange with a flexible infrastructure (banks, insurance companies, etc.) that facilitated the circulation of goods.

The developments in agriculture, trade and commerce changed the people involved in them. From the middle of the eighteenth century onwards, the *population* in Britain grew dramatically: from 7 million in 1750 to 10 million in 1801 to more than 20 million in 1851. The reasons for this population growth have to be seen in the combination of a falling death rate and a rising birth rate. The former was due to better nourishment/food, hygiene and healthcare; the latter resulted from the fact that women tended to marry earlier – a fact that itself indicated a general improvement in living conditions. The rapidly increasing population moved to the towns, in particular to those which, because of the onset of industrialisation, offered work. These towns grew into cities: in 1801,

London, Dublin, Edinburgh, Liverpool, Glasgow, Manchester and Birmingham were the biggest cities; sixty years later London was followed by Liverpool, Glasgow, Dublin, Manchester, Birmingham and Leeds.

Taking a closer look at the developments in agriculture, trade and population, one can see how they interacted and triggered further developments: the rising yields in agriculture provided improved nourishment for the population; consequently, the population increased, thereby contributing to the expansion of trade and commerce. This in turn resulted in greater profits and a general improvement in the standard of living. The expansion of trade led to the creation of better ways and means of transport and communication (canals, roads, later railways; ships, coaches, engines). These could only be produced by a growing labour force. The wages of this growing labour force bought goods in the home market. The growing demand for domestic and foreign products, which was a perpetual incentive for producers and merchants, could only be met by more and more labourers working with and within the framework of new methods of work: as, for example, in manufacture, the putting-out system and, later, factories. In addition to that, the growing demand for colonial goods necessitated the expansion of the merchant fleet, the strengthening of the merchant companies and last, but not least, the administration and financing of a political and military state apparatus that could protect the colonial markets.

Once these developments could be complemented by technological *innovations and inventions*, which made it possible to replace natural sources of energy (wind, water, human and animal power) by artificial ones (steam and, later, gas and electricity) and to build machines that were capable of surpassing human and animal power many times over, the Industrial Revolution was irreversible.

In the beginning the Industrial Revolution embraced neither all spheres of production nor all regions of the country. On the contrary, in the beginning only three branches of production were of particular importance: the cotton, coal and iron industries. The importance of the *cotton industry* for the industrial development of Britain cannot be overestimated. It not only produced exceptionally high rates of growth and export, but also functioned as a pacemaker for other sectors of industry. Many *inventions* that influenced the tempo of technological development in general were made in this industry: the flying shuttle, various spinning machines and the mechanical loom. The production of these machines increased demand in the iron industry, which could only satisfy its own need for iron ore and coal if adequate ways and means of *transport* were constructed. Another important factor was that, from very early on, the cotton industry was organised in *factories*, and in the early phase of industrialisation the cotton workers represented the majority of all factory workers. Moreover, most of the cotton workers were *female workers and children*. The particular reasons for this were that they were more productive (because they were nimbler, more dextrous and more disciplined) than men, and they allowed the factory owners to reap a higher rate of profit because they received lower wages: some 35–50 per cent of men's wages. In addition, they were more adaptable to new forms of production.

The Industrial Revolution is unthinkable without *coal* because it was the main source of energy for the whole process of industrialisation. Without coal no steam could be produced, no iron ore smelted. As a consequence, the amount of mined coal rose from 0.5 million tons in 1700 to 4 million tons in 1750, to 10 million tons in 1800 and to 50 million tons in 1850. Originally the steam engine (improved by James Watt in 1769) had been used in coal and copper mines because their pits were often flooded and adequate pumps had not yet been developed. Steam engines, driven by coal, helped pump the water out of the pits so that more coal could be mined. In turn, increasing amounts of coal had to be moved to the places where they could be used for other purposes. The steam engine in the form of the locomotive was used (from 1812 onwards) to transport coal from the mines to the nearest river or canal. This was the beginning of the railways. In 1825 the first public railway (from Stockton to Darlington) was opened; five years later the first public railway for passengers and goods (from Manchester to Liverpool) followed; and twenty years later Britain already had some 6215 miles of railways.

The third important industrial sector was the *iron* industry. Iron became the building material of choice in the Industrial Revolution, largely replacing wood and stone. The machines for the production of goods, as well as the ways and means of their transport, were made either in great part or totally of iron; in the second half of the nineteenth century *steel* could be produced profitably and tended to replace iron. Of course, there were also other industries – potteries, breweries, printing shops and paper factories – but they were less relevant than the three mentioned above.

Within the British Isles, these processes of industrialisation proceeded unevenly. In the same way in which particular regions of the Midlands and the north of England had become centres of industry, other distinctive parts of the British Isles were transformed. Lowland Scotland, for example, was a powerhouse of innovation and entrepreneurs: shipbuilding was responsible for Glasgow's growth, Dundee almost monopolised the processing of jute. Wales possessed coal in abundance (particularly in the south) as well as deposits of copper, iron and other ores. In Ireland, by comparison, industrialisation occurred only belatedly and almost exclusively in the north around Belfast.

It does not diminish Britain's achievement if one keeps in mind that many elements of its industrial revolution were of foreign origin. They were transmitted in the usual ways: merchants who often complemented their cargoes from abroad with useful tools and inventions; explorers and their soldiery who looted not only the riches and raw materials but also the material culture of the occupied and colonised communities; missionaries (in the case of China, particularly Jesuits) who realised that their task was twofold: to carry the gospel to the heathens and to organise 'knowledge transfer' from them to Europe, its scientists and engineers. In agriculture, for example, the iron mouldboard plough, the rotary winnowing machine (which separated the husks and stalks from the grain), the seed-drill and, most important, the new crop-rotation system had been used and practised in China for about a millennium. Many of the technological inventions were pioneered by the Chinese as well. The essentials of the steam engine, for example, were first described in print in a fourteenth-century Chinese treatise. Inventions in the cotton industry stemmed from either Chinese silk or Indian cotton technologies which were superior to their British counterparts until well into the nineteenth century. Moreover, the Chinese and the Indians had produced iron and steel much earlier and on a much larger scale. By 1842, Indian iron and steel were still not only superior to British products but could also be produced more cheaply. The first iron bridge was built in Britain in 1779, in China thousands of them had existed a millennium earlier. Street gas-lamps, which appeared in Britain shortly before 1800, had been in use in China for two millennia. The British built some 6000 kilometres of canal between the 1750s and 1850s, but the Chinese had constructed some 50,000 kilometres during the Song period some seven hundred years earlier (960–1279).

Taking this much longer and more global view, some historians have argued that it might make sense to regard Britain, Europe and North America not so much as path-breaking innovators but, rather, as latecomers to a development that had been going on for two millennia. Its particular form and impetus, however, was achieved by the way in which the British (and, later, other Europeans and North Americans) succeeded in combining the following four factors. (i) They assimilated and refined foreign technological discoveries and, in that particular context, invented some (such as the crankshaft) themselves – a process made possible by a singularly dense structure of civil institutions (social clubs and scientific societies). (ii) They harnessed their advanced technology to an economic system bent on growth (capitalism) – a process also facilitated by the development of specific institutions (such as banks, stock exchanges, insurance, etc.). (iii) They created medium-sized states (with their sophisticated administrations) which grew out of a history of fiercely competing with each other and, thereby, constantly learning to improve their ways and means of warfare. They used the latter not only to hold each other in check but also to acquire colonies and rule empires abroad which could be exploited as suppliers of raw materials and privileged markets for finished products from the mother countries. (iv) Once the British had successfully employed the advantages drawn from the above three factors, they combined them with yet another adapted idea – *wu-wei* or *laissez-faire* (cf. Chapter 5) – which eventually, and paradoxically, compelled the rest of world, at least for some time, to fashion itself in Britain's image.

Political reform

Developments like those outlined above occur neither without debates on their nature and effects nor without struggles over the social, political and cultural gains and losses they engender (Documents 33 and 34). In Britain these transformative processes were accompanied by recurrent protests, riots and revolts of the labouring population. These reactions wrung some concessions from the dominant social classes, but also led to the construction of a relatively centralised bureaucratic state exercising a high degree of social control (through, for example, newly created police forces, a harsh poor law and repressive moral codes).

Basically, there were three *social classes*: the landowners, the trading and manufacturing bourgeoisie as well as the rural middle classes (tenant farmers), and the labouring classes. There is no consent among historians as to whether and to what extent the landowners and the bourgeoisie formed a kind of 'coalition of common interests'. But what is clear is that the industrialised world of the working classes was totally different from the world of labour a hundred years previously. Machines and factories demanded that the labouring people adapted to hitherto unknown processes of work; moreover, the relations of production and living conditions changed fundamentally: the invention and introduction of new technologies – then as now – made workers redundant. Production made high demands on the discipline of the workers. The 'natural' rhythms of seasonal work had to give way to the artificial rhythms of the machines, which had no natural limits: machines do not know the difference between day and night. A moral consensus as to the rights and duties of the lords and their dependants, which had not been compulsory but nevertheless existed, was replaced by the more abstract relations of the market and the cash nexus: the ideas of supply and demand, profit and competition became more and more dominant. The labouring classes reacted to these developments in two ways: on the one hand, with protests, demonstrations, riots, attacks on factories, and – sometimes, although not very often – with armed uprisings; on the other, by forming political and cultural organisations through which they agitated and petitioned for an improvement in their situation. Trade unions, friendly societies, cooperatives and Workers' (Educational) Institutes, not to mention newspapers, played a particularly important role.

The politically dominant classes, for their part, with the experience of the French Revolution in mind, reacted harshly wherever possible, but proved to be able to compromise whenever necessary. (i) They passed factory laws (1833, 1844, 1847 and 1850) that reduced the working hours of women and children but also gave them a lower status. (ii) They reformed the penal code in such a way that the convicted criminal would not be 'lost', either through his or her death or through transportation, but could be 'corrected' and reintroduced into the workforce. (iii) They passed a Poor Law Amendment

Trade Unions, Friendly Societies and Cooperatives

With the advent of industrialisation new forms of work and its organisation increased the conflicts between the employers (capital) and employees (labour). Trade unions were attempts by the latter to combine in order to ensure minimal requirements with regard to wages, working hours and working conditions. Fear of revolution led to their suppression between 1800 and 1825, but from then on trade unions became increasingly effective. At first only skilled workers could becomes members, but in the second half of the nineteenth century new unions for the semi-skilled and the unskilled were established. Overall membership rose from 750,000 in 1888 to over 4 million just before the First World War. As many of these trade unions were small and local, their number was huge: some 1300 in 1900. The development of collective bargaining in industrial relations and the provision of death, sickness and unemployment benefits for their members were the central tasks the trade unions set themselves. To coordinate actions better, the Trade Union Congress was founded in 1868. (The Scottish TUC followed in 1897.)

Friendly societies were local workers' associations with distinct socio-economic and cultural functions. On the one hand, they provided sickness and funeral benefits in return for a small weekly or monthly payment into a common fund. On the other, in order to stress the common lot of the common male (and, increasingly, female) worker, they 'invented' ceremonies and rituals, held open-air processions and organised festivities. It has been reckoned that towards the end of the nineteenth century some 80 per cent of the male industrial workers (of some 7 million) were members of friendly societies. The reaction of the ruling classes towards these societies was ambivalent. On the one hand, they welcomed the emphasis on thrift and self-help embodied in them; on the other, they feared that they, like the trade unions, might become means of socio-political agitation.

Like friendly societies, the cooperative movement originated in the need to find new ways of community-building ('civil society') in the context of industrial society. The stress was on mutual assistance instead of on competitive individualism. The main idea was to provide a shop which sold unadulterated foodstuffs at reasonable prices. (Previously, many workers had depended on shops set up by the factory owners.) Moreover, these shops tried to attract customers who wanted to save as they spent, i.e. they worked with discounts. This discount was not given immediately but when it had been allowed to accumulate (for example, by collecting trading stamps). In this way, these shops tied customers to them; once these shops could rely on a certain number of customers, they could buy goods in bulk, get bulk discount and hand it on to their individual customers.

Act (1834) that was intended to prevent the starvation of the poor. When its implementation implied such a high degree of social degradation (in particular through the workhouse), many of the poor preferred to starve rather than claim their rights. (iv) Most important, they passed three Reform Acts – in

1832, 1867 and 1884 – to extend the franchise and reorganise the constituencies.

The unreformed House of Commons consisted of 489 MPs for England, 24 MPs for Wales and, from 1707 onwards, 45 MPs for Scotland. In 1800 another 100 MPs for Ireland were added. These MPs represented either counties or boroughs. In the counties a person owning freehold property valued for the land tax at 40 shillings per year had the vote. In the boroughs, various and very complex qualifications applied. This system, which had basically remained unreformed for at least three centuries (the '40-shilling-freeholder' qualification had been enacted in 1430), had a number of deficiencies. First, the number of electors per constituency varied greatly. In 1790, for example, 149 English boroughs had fewer than 500 electors, while 32 had 500 to 1000 electors, and 22 boroughs had over 1000 electors. Constituencies with very few electors – Malmesbury had thirteen, Gatton two, and Old Sarum none – were known as 'rotten boroughs'. Second, the system worked very unevenly in the three parts of the kingdom. In 1831 the electorate in the United Kingdom consisted of 516,000 adult males (in a population of 24 million people); of these England and Wales had 435,000 electors, but Scotland a mere 4500. Third, the system was totally corrupt. In many cases, the return of an MP for a constituency was controlled by the dominant landowner who himself, of course, sat in the House of Lords. At least one case is known in which one family controlled two seats between 1688 and 1832 unopposed. Boroughs such as these earned the name 'pocket boroughs' as they were regarded as being in the pocket of a patron. It has been reckoned that by the 1760s the number of seats under patronage had risen to more than 250 (out of 558).

The *first Reform Act* (1832) increased the Scottish electorate from 4500 to 65,000, the Irish from 49,000 to 90,000, and the English and Welsh from 435,000 to 653,000. As most of the new voters were from the middle classes, and many of the working classes correctly perceived themselves as excluded, a large section of the labouring population reacted to these developments by forming part of the greatest political movement Britain had ever seen: *Chartism*. The Chartists demanded equal constituencies, universal male suffrage, vote by (secret) ballot, payment for MPs, abolition of the property qualification for MPs, and annual elections. They submitted their charter to Parliament three times: in 1839, 1842 and 1848. Each time it was rejected. But how important these demands were can be judged from the fact that all of them, with the exception of annual elections, were met by the 1920s. Agitation for an extension of the franchise, however, did not abate, and in the *second Reform Act* (1867) the vote was extended to working-class electors (in the boroughs) on the basis of household suffrage. This Act added some 938,000 voters to the existing electorate, which, through natural increase, had risen to over 1 million. By 1884 the electorate had grown to some 3 million, and Gladstone's *third Reform Act* added another 5 million, extending the vote to working-class voters in the

Table 3 Numbers of adult males able to vote after the various Reform Acts

	England & Wales	*Scotland*	*Ireland*
1833	1 in 5	1 in 8	1 in 20
1869	1 in 3	1 in 3	1 in 6
1885	2 in 3	3 in 5	1 in 2

Chris Cook and John Stevenson, *The Longman Handbook of Modern British History, 1714–2001*, Harlow/London: Longman, 4th edn, 2001, p. 81.

countryside. All these acts were accompanied by no less important *redistribution measures*, which reorganised the size and principles of representation for the constituencies. Although opponents to the extension of the franchise usually expressed fears that the new voters would prove fickle and irresponsible – the Act of 1884 was tellingly called 'a leap in the dark' – their fears were unfounded: the new voters did not principally differ in their behaviour from the older ones. Table 3 summarises how many adult males were able to vote after the various Reform Acts. Perhaps the most astonishing fact may be that only with the third Reform Act was a more or less uniform franchise established for the whole of the United Kingdom.

The monarchy

While most of the Tudor and the Stuart monarchs (such as Henry VII, Henry VIII, Elizabeth I, James I and Charles II), despite their recurrent political clashes with either the titled aristocracy or the increasingly influential House of Commons, had succeeded not only in maintaining but also in enhancing royal authority as well as adding lustre to the institution itself, under their Hanoverian successors the prestige of the British monarchy waned. There were several reasons for this development. The first two Hanoverians had not been raised in Britain and had difficulties in adapting to its culture. George I (b. 1660, r. 1714–27) did not speak a word of English. George II (b. 1683, r. 1727–60) was not much better. George III (b. 1738, r. 1760–1820), the first Hanoverian to be born and raised in Britain, had to be relieved of his official duties, which were taken on by the Prince Regent (later George IV), in 1811 because of madness. George IV (b. 1762, r. 1820–30), an 'inveterate voluptuary', was despised by almost every section of British society so that *The Times* could write on his death that 'there never was an individual less regretted by his fellow-creatures than this deceased King'. His brother, William IV (b. 1765, r. 1830–7), who had no fewer than fifteen illegitimate children, was described in the press as 'a weak, ignorant, commonplace sort of person' endowed with 'feebleness of purpose and littleness of mind'. These negative judgements of personal traits were complemented by severe criticism of their politics. George I and George II were dependent on the Whig faction which had 'engineered' the Hanoverian succession. When George III tried to gain greater influence through patronage (awarding pensions and offices) to MPs, this soon earned the age the nickname 'old corruption'. Moreover, George III, instead of listening to advisers who sought to mediate in the conflict with the American colonies, added fuel to the fire by acting boldly but rashly (cf. Chapter 5). Both George III and George IV were against Catholic emancipation and parliamentary reform. George IV eventually agreed to the former, but left the latter to his brother, William IV.

In the first decades of the nineteenth century, therefore, the monarchy was in low repute, regarded as either incompetent or corrupt or decadent (mostly all three), a laughing-stock rather than a symbol of (or an example to) the nation (Document 35). When parliamentary reform became unavoidable and an almost permanent item on the political agenda, questions were also repeatedly raised and hotly debated whether it made sense to have a monarchy at all. Would the abolition of the monarchy not save the taxpayers a lot of money, and might it not make further (and more democratic) reforms much easier?

So, when Victoria (b. 1819, r. 1837–1901) acceded to the throne in 1837, the monarchy was extremely unpopular, although many people thought that she made a change from her 'wicked uncles'. But when she chose the German

Victoria (b. 1819, r. 1837–1901)

Victoria, queen of the United Kingdom of Great Britain and Ireland (1837–1901) and empress of India (1876–1901), came to the throne because George IV had no heir, and his brother, William IV, had only illegitimate children. On her accession she was barely eighteen years of age but approached her task with great verve. 'I do regular, hard, but to me delightful work,' she wrote to her uncle, King Leopold of Belgium. When she died sixty-four years later, she had seen and worked with ten prime ministers – and with some of them more than once. She had also become the 'matriarch of Europe', having borne nine children whose forty children and forty grandchildren peopled the courts and thrones of the Continent. And she had given her name to an age: the 'Victorian Age' became, for good or ill, labelled as 'prudish', 'repressed' and perhaps 'old-fashioned'. Although Victoria can be held responsible neither for this term nor for its connotations, her black clothes (worn in mourning for Albert) may have contributed to the image post-Victorians developed of the Victorians. One should not forget, however, that Victoria was a very lively and spontaneous person who enjoyed the pleasures of the body (eating, drinking and sex). When her doctor told her after her ninth child that it might be better for her not to have any more children, she is reported to have said: 'Oh, Doctor, can I have no more fun in bed?' Moreover, her long and perhaps excessive mourning for Albert did not prevent her from having a decade-long relationship with her personal servant, John Brown.

prince Albert of Saxe-Coburg-Gotha as her spouse and had a total of nine children with him, many complaints were voiced: politicians feared she might be unduly influenced by her (foreign) husband, aristocrats regretted what they regarded as the 'dull respectability' of a 'bourgeois family on the throne', in the population monarchical overspending and the queen's too frequent invisibility – owed, at least in part, to her numerous pregnancies – were criticised. But Victoria took her office seriously from the start, and Albert earned a lot of respect as a good administrator and an intelligent patron of the arts. His role in the Great Exhibition (1851), an impressive demonstration of Britain's industrial position in the world, endeared him to entrepreneurs and politicians. His early death (of typhoid fever) in 1861, however, indirectly added to the still prevalent unpopularity of the monarchy, as Queen Victoria went into deep mourning and chose to withdraw even further from the public. With the agitation for the Second Reform Bill in the mid-1860s republican ideas achieved greater prominence. Although the second Reform Act (1867) almost doubled the number of voters, it left many desires unsatisfied. As a consequence, republicanism grew, boosted by developments elsewhere (as, for example, in France where the Third Republic was proclaimed in 1870). Anti-monarchical demonstrations took place in London in the same year, and in 1871 some fifty republican clubs were founded in Britain. Parliament discussed whether the allowances for the royal children should be abolished or reduced. But then, within a decade, the monarchy was 'reinvented', despite the third Reform Act (1884–5) and a remarkable strengthening of the labour movement. The recovery of the Prince of Wales, who almost died of the same illness as his father, caused a tremendous wave of enthusiasm for the monarchy. Victoria had herself made 'Empress of India' (1876), which transformed the British monarchy into an imperial institution and gave its monarch the same status as the emperors of Germany, Austria-Hungary and Russia. Her children and grandchildren were married to many royal and imperial houses across the Continent, making Victoria the 'matriarch of Europe'. Royal rituals (which had fallen into neglect in the Georgian age) were greatly improved and, with the support of suitable pieces of music (composed, for example, by Charles Parry and Edward Elgar), became national spectacles (Document 36). They triumphed in the monarch's Golden and Diamond Jubilees in 1887 and 1897. Increasingly, Victoria came to be regarded as the symbol of the nation and its greatness and, at the same time, as the novelist Henry James wrote on her death, as 'the safe and motherly middle-class queen, who held the nation warm under the fold of her big, hideous Scotch-plaid shawl'.

Reigning for sixty-four years, Victoria remains to this day Britain's longest-reigning monarch. Her name has come to characterise a whole epoch, although what in fact is associated with it varies from writer to writer: some point to morality and hypocrisy, values (e.g. self-help), heavy furniture and massive architecture; others stress high-mindedness, domesticity and amateurism (in

The Labour party

The Labour party is the principal party of the left. Although it became an effective political party only in the twentieth century, its roots were to be found in the working-class movements of the nineteenth century. In 1900 the Labour Representation Committee was established by a group of socialists and trade unionists. It won two seats in the general election of that year, but already by 1906 Labour's tally had risen to thirty MPs – although this was partly the result of a secret electoral pact with the Liberal party. (This pact was made in 1903. It stipulated that, in order to prevent a split of the vote and a Conservative win as a consequence, the two parties would not run candidates against each other.) Labour benefited from the extension of the vote in 1918 and became the official opposition in 1922, when it won more seats (142) than the Liberal Party (116). In 1924 it formed its first government. Although the government did not outlast the year, Labour had proved its ability to govern. Labour returned to power in 1929, became part of the National Government in 1931 and also joined Churchill's coalition government in 1940. After the war, Labour's 'finest hour' came, when it introduced those innovative social policies which became collectively known as the welfare state. Moreover, Labour began a radical programme of nationalisation (the Bank of England, coal mining, iron and steel, road transport, railways, etc.) which resulted in about 20 per cent of the economy being in the public sector by 1950. Finally, Labour initiated the process of decolonisation (India in 1947, Burma [Myanmar] and Ceylon [Sri Lanka] in 1948).

After thirteen years in opposition, Labour regained office in 1964, beginning another period of social reform (abolition of censorship, legalisation of abortion, abolition of capital punishment, reform of the laws concerning homosexuality, expansion and reform of the education system, introduction of equal pay for men and women, etc.). However, Labour failed in modernising the economy and curtailing trade union power.

Interestingly, the Labour party was often divided over central political issues. Neither did it have a unified standpoint on whether or not to support the government in the First World War, nor was it united on nuclear armament/disarmament or entry into the European Economic Community. More often than not, this was a question of left/socialist or right/social-democrat values or alignments, but sometimes it also signalled a conflict between traditionalists and modernisers.

contrast to professionalism). Perhaps the length of her reign also contributed to the fact that the British monarchy could be reinvented in the way sketched above – relinquishing some real political power while acquiring new symbolic influence (Document 37) – and could survive into the twentieth century. It could provide a particular sense of national continuity, while increasingly representative government was slowly achieved, the power of the House of

Commons slowly waxed at the expense of that of the House of Lords (which, from 1911, could delay but no longer prevent the legislation of the House of Commons), the Empire permanently grew and inter-imperial rivalries multiplied.

Gender relations

The pre-industrial household was structured patriarchically: men were the masters in their homes, which were the places where people worked and lived. They had to organise the processes of production (from the acquisition of raw material to the selling of the final product) and discipline the producers. Women and children contributed to the work as a matter of course; even if their work was regarded as inferior and/or supplementary, it had an irreplaceable function in the household. When production was shifted to the factories, the concomitant reorganisation of working practices not only separated the places of work from the places of living, thereby tearing apart a whole way of life, but also made necessary a new – although no less patriarchal – definition of the social roles of men and women.

The middle-class family was a strictly hierarchically structured social group with the husband's absolute authority as its apex: he was responsible for the economic prosperity, the legal security and social contact of the family with the outside world. His wife had to be 'the angel in the house' (after Coventry Patmore's four-volume poetic treatment of married love, 1854); she had to run the household without friction, bring up the children and create a sphere of warmth and harmony, which contrasted amiably with the rougher and tougher world in which the men conducted their business (Document 38 and 39). Such a division of roles – desirable or not – was impossible for the families of the working class because the majority of its men and women were forced to work for their living. Nevertheless, we can detect clear and eventually successful attempts by men to regain and fortify their formerly dominant position. On the one hand, we can observe (e.g. in the textile industry) how technological transformations of certain sectors of production were tried out with the help of women workers and how then, once the new method of production had proved to be successful, the female workers were replaced by male ones because technologically advanced work was regarded as more valuable and thus worthy of men. On the other hand, the idea of a *family wage* – as propagated by trade unionists and bourgeois reformers at the beginning of the nineteenth century – was nothing but the acceptance of the idea of the bourgeois ideal family, in which the father was responsible for the livelihood of his wife and children. Although it was clear that a working-class family needed both wages to feed its members, this discussion led to a practice in which men received higher wages than women because they were believed to be responsible for the whole family, while women only had to look after themselves. In this way male workers fortified their patriarchal position *vis-à-vis* female workers, and the factory owners succeeded in creating a workforce divided along gender lines.

Famines

While the Act of Union terminated Ireland's formal status as a dependent kingdom, the Union was almost universally interpreted as an annexation in response to the revolutionary conflicts of 1798 because it was accompanied by hardly any economic and administrative integration. On the contrary, the Irish administration remained distinctively colonial in both form and function, and economic non-development (particularly of the agrarian sector) left a growing population dangerously dependent on decreasing means of subsistence: by the mid-1840s, the potato was the staple diet of a third of the population (8.5 million). Although Irish people were better nourished – Irishmen were on average taller than Englishmen – their food was not sufficiently diversified to be safe in times of bad or failing harvests.

When the blight (*Phytophthora infestans*) struck in 1845, with crops failing entirely in 1846 and 1848 and poor yields in 1847, the population fell by more than 2 million people between 1845 and 1851; just under 1 million people died of starvation or malnutrition-induced diseases, the rest emigrated, first and foremost to Britain, the United States and Australia. The responses of the government in London varied: while Peel's Tory government bought and distributed Indian corn from America and established a programme of public works (so that everybody claiming relief was compelled to work for it), Russell's Whig government, which had been elected in 1846 because of its strong *laissez-faire* programme, refused to tamper with market forces by buying and distributing food. However, in early 1847 kitchens had to be opened throughout the country to provide for the starving, at one time serving 3 million meals a day. But seven months later these kitchens were wound

---

Corn Laws

When Britain's population grew from the 1750s onwards, the country became a food importer instead of a food exporter. The Napoleonic Wars led to a rise in domestic prices, and when the wars ended the government was afraid of a postwar collapse. A Corn Law was passed which prohibited the importation of wheat (or any other cereal) until the domestic price reached a certain level. Although this system was frequently modified, it was rightly regarded as a symbol of aristocratic privilege. It was only after the Irish potato famine that it would be totally repealed. In the years that followed it came to be regarded as the vanguard of liberalism and free trade.

up and relief was provided through the expanded (but wholly inadequate) workhouses (Document 40). More people died of diseases than of starvation: typhus and relapsing fever (both transmitted by the body louse) were the most common diseases, particularly afflicting the old and the very young.

Incidentally, the Scottish Highlands were struck by a simultaneous potato famine in which, however, for a number of reasons, the catastrophic results of the Irish experience would be avoided. First, there was a difference in scale. While in Ireland some 3 million people were affected, in the Highlands around 200,000 were at risk. Second, 'potato dependency' was less decisive in the Highlands because of a greater diversity of food (grain, fish) and occupations as well as a better ratio of land to population. Third, while in Ireland the state was the principal source of relief, in Scotland three great charities – the Free Church of Scotland and the Edinburgh and Glasgow Relief Committees – bore the burden of the effort. And, although a hated 'destitution test' caused a lot of distress in the afflicted regions, the threat of starvation was successfully averted. Fourth, in contrast to Ireland, where many landowners were not only indifferent to the sufferings of the people living and working on their estates but, in fact, abused the famine to hasten evictions in order to get rid of what they regarded as useless surplus population, many Scottish landowners (who, admittedly, had better financial resources than their Irish counterparts) actively supported the inhabitants of their estates in the time of crisis. Finally, while the Highland famine occurred the – industrialising – Scottish Lowlands experienced an economic boom so that people from the stricken parts of the country could migrate (temporarily or permanently) to regions where they could earn their living.

Horrible as these famines and their repercussions were, one should not forget that in the last quarter of the nineteenth century, for example, large parts of India were repeatedly devastated by famines in which at least 10 million people lost their lives, while India's annual grain exports increased from 3 million to 10 million tons in the same period. As in Ireland, it was the political will not to interfere with market forces which determined the course (and effect) of these famines. It has even been argued that they were used to control resistive populations (in India) or to get rid of useless surplus populations (in Ireland).

Catholic emancipation – repeal – Home Rule – migration

Irish politics after the Act of Union (1800) had first of all been determined by continued agitation for Catholic emancipation. While the political argument had apparently been won by 1821 when an emancipation bill passed the Commons, the House of Lords and George IV remained hostile. In 1824 the Catholic Association was founded and quickly grew into a mass movement. Suppressed under the Unlawful Societies Act in March 1825, it was relaunched as the New Catholic Association in July confining its formal proceedings to religious issues and public welfare while dealing with political matters in separate meetings. In 1828, Daniel O'Connell (1775–1847), a popular Catholic champion since the beginning of the century, stood against Vesey FitzGerald in the County Clare by-election, won the seat with an overwhelming majority and thereby demonstrated that the Protestant proprietors could no longer control their Catholic voters. (The paradoxical situation was that he could be a candidate for Parliament but, as a Catholic, could not sit in it.) The Catholic Relief Act became law in April 1829. As it applied to the whole of the United Kingdom it shattered the unity of church and state enshrined in the 1689 settlement by allowing both Protestant and Catholic dissenters to enter Parliament.

After the election of 1832, O'Connell became the leader of a party of 39 Irish MPs who wanted to repeal the Act of Union. A first attempt (in 1834) was crushingly defeated in Parliament (by 523 votes to 38); a second and more sustained attempt, growing out of a combination of agitation and 'monster meetings', collapsed when O'Connell and other leaders were arrested on charges of conspiracy in 1843. While O'Connell had always been prepared to negotiate reform measures which were short of a restoration of the status quo of Ireland before 1800, other groups such as the nationalist Young Ireland (1844–8) rejected such pragmatic concessions. Their rebellion of 1848 (triggered by the Paris revolution of February 1848) was infiltrated by government informers and quickly collapsed. Its leaders were transported or fled to America. Some of the latter (such as James Stephens and T. C. Luby) later founded the Fenian movement (the Irish Republican Brotherhood) in 1858, dedicated to Irish independence. Different insurrections in the second half of the 1860s collapsed but provided the basis for two further developments: the disestablishment of the (Protestant) Church of Ireland (which became law in July 1869) and the launching of the – constitutional – Home Rule movement.

The famine had put the land question at the top of the political agenda, as the great number of smallholdings had failed to provide for the population dependent on them. As a consequence, in post-famine Ireland, the number of smallholdings declined (with the dispersal of the cottier class by death and emigration), the number of holdings between fifteen and thirty acres doubled, that of over thirty acres trebled. From this process of redistribution and consolidation many Irish profited as more than three-quarters of the purchasers were locals. However, this did not ease the situation of their dependants: often the opposite was the case. When the liberal W. E. Gladstone (1809–98) became prime minister in 1868, he reportedly vowed: 'My mission is to pacify Ireland'. After disestablishing and disendowing the Church of Ireland he saw a land act through Parliament (in 1870) which gave the force of law to customary tenant right (the right of a departing tenant to sell his saleable interest to the highest bidder) and provided for compensation in the case of eviction. In his second term in office, Gladstone had a more comprehensive land act passed (1881) which granted the 'three Fs': fair rents – of importance for poor tenants; fixity of tenure; and free sale (another name for tenant right) – demanded by larger tenant farmers. In his third (very short) term in office Gladstone finally responded to the agitation for Home Rule which had been going on since the early 1870s. Its first representative was Isaac Butt (1813–79) (Document 41), who envisaged a kind of devolutionary compromise which was to give Ireland the right to handle its domestic affairs while national and international politics would be in the hands of the government in London. Charles Stewart Parnell (1846–91) followed a more nationalist (i.e. separatist) course which, however, remained within the constitutional framework. Gladstone used Butt's ideas and colonial precedents as the basis for his bill. But his initiative did not get the unanimous support of his party (which split over the issue) and was defeated in the House of Commons. Another attempt in his fourth (and last) period in office passed the House of Commons (1893, with the decisive help of the majority of the Irish MPs) but was defeated in the House of Lords. Only when a Liberal government (which depended on Irish nationalist support) had reduced the power of the House of Lords (in 1911) did the passage of a Home Rule Bill become possible. It was enacted in 1914, but its implementation was suspended until after the First World War.

Ireland's position within the United Kingdom also informed its relationship to the Empire. For the republicans and separatists, Ireland suffered from subjection to a foreign force which had to be expelled as soon as possible. For the loyalist unionists, the existence and survival of the Union and the Empire were one and the same thing. For 'devolutionists' (arguing for Home Rule), the Union was to become part of an imperial federation embracing the whole Empire. But perhaps this is only part of the story as many Irish knew (and a growing number of them came to know in the course of the century) what it implied to be *both* a colonial and a colonialist: the Empire offered opportunities of employment (principally in the colonial and armed services) and of emigration (mainly to Canada and Australasia). As a result, many Irish people became a significant element of the settler colonies. Whether the fact that they knew the position of the colonial made them 'better' colonialists is an unsettling question which has not yet been answered.

While the Irish emigrated from the mother country to many different parts of the British Empire, a distinctly smaller wave of immigrants arrived from Tsarist Russia after a series of pogroms (1881–4), which let the Jewish population in Britain of some 60,000 in 1880 grow to 265,000 by 1914. Some 200,000 more lived in the Empire (mainly in Canada, South Africa, Egypt, India and Australia); and another half million may have stayed in Britain for a year or two before they continued their migration. In the mid-eighteenth century an attempt to naturalise Jewish immigrants had been met with strong resistance, and Lionel Rothschild, elected as MP for London in 1847, was not allowed to take his seat, but at the end of the 1850s Jews were eventually granted full parliamentary rights.

Cultures and ideologies

While the 'high' culture of the later eighteenth century had been predominantly aristocratic and cosmopolitan, finding its inspiration in the art and literature of ancient Greece and Rome, this European 'Classicism' was disrupted by
the French Revolution. The ensuing wars against Revolutionary France and
Napoleon encouraged nationalist loyalties, which, in turn, stimulated curiosity
about national traditions, myths, histories and literatures. An intense interest in
the past (particularly the Middle Ages), a sincere concern for the lives of ordinary people, and a deliberate preference for the vernacular (replacing stilted
classical conventions by a certain plainness of expression) combined to form a
new mood, giving voice to both revolutionary ideas and their critique, which
later came to be called *Romanticism*. And, while until the end of the eighteenth
century aristocratic patronage had been the social basis of 'high' cultural productivity, in the course of the nineteenth century writers and other artists came
to depend on the growing 'bourgeois' public. Writers, for example, no longer
created 'works of art' for their patrons (who supported them), but sold them to
one of the growing number of publishers (of books, periodicals or newspapers). Parallel to this development, new institutions were created which
allowed better access to works of art, such as galleries, museums, opera houses,
public libraries. When the spectre of revolution gave way to the practice of
reform in the 1830s, the historical 'moment' of the 'realist' novel had arrived.
Writers like Dickens, the Brontës, Disraeli, Gaskell, Thackeray, Eliot, Hardy,
James and Conrad perceived, understood and, critically and creatively,
responded to the great variety of political, cultural and moral issues at work in
a rapidly changing society. Their increasingly plural perspectives and complex
narrative constructions were testimonies to both their confidence in and their
doubts about society's ability to reform.

Moreover, the social, political and technological transformations of the
period under discussion were inextricably linked to mental transformations in
at least three different fields. First, a strong interdenominational evangelicalism
developed in many parts of the British Isles. Its representatives regarded faith
not only as a matter of the heart rather than of the mind but also as a gift from
God revealed in a process of conversion. In Scotland it eventually split the
Church of Scotland over patronage in 1843. In Ireland it strengthened the
religious resolve of Catholics as well as of Protestants, although it came to play
a greater role in the anti-Catholic agitation in the north of the country. In
Wales, which had been traditionally Anglican Protestant until the middle of the
eighteenth century, after 1800 dissenting chapels were opening at the rate of
one every fortnight, sometimes one every week. This applied to the whole of
the country and not only to the newly industrialised districts in the south.
These evangelical revivals commonly advocated a literalist reading of the Bible;
they practised conversion-preaching, sabbatarianism and temperance to achieve

self-control, a reform of the heart and personal salvation. Second, a strong interest in the cultural traditions developed in the 'Gaelic' nations of the British Isles. In Scotland, a pride in national lore and national heroes (who originally represented anti-English sentiments) came to underpin a sense of identity which enabled the Scots to see themselves appreciated as equal partners in the United Kingdom and the British Empire. The works of Robert Burns (1759–96) and Walter Scott (1771–1832) played a powerful role in this process. In Ireland, associations such as the Gaelic Athletic Association (founded in 1884) and the Gaelic League (founded in 1893) aimed at the restitution of a Gaelic Ireland which they regarded as being swamped by a process of Anglicisation. Academic research in Gaelic language and literature as well as archaeological discoveries supported the Irish claims to an impressive ancient culture. In Wales, although the great mass of the people spoke Welsh, things Welsh were in bad repute (as in the paradigmatic nursery rhyme 'Taffy was a Welshman, Taffy was a thief'). In the second half of the eighteenth century, a Welsh sense of history was slowly being recovered, Wales's rich literary and musical traditions became more widely known, and cultural practices such as the eisteddfod (a competition held for poets, singers and musicians), which had ceased to exist in the mid-sixteenth century, were revived by the end of the eighteenth century. Third, while in Wales and Scotland these revivals remained mainly cultural in nature – the Welsh and the Scots, for the time being, regarded themselves as integral parts of the United Kingdom – in Ireland the 'Irish Renaissance' was decidedly linked to nationalist ideas and planning which resulted in Home Rule and, in the twentieth century, the partition of the country.

All of these developments, be they religious, cultural or political, testify to the great social upheavals of the nineteenth century. There can be no doubt that the interrelated processes of industrialisation, urbanisation and demographic change produced social fragmentation, intellectual doubt and need of orientation which, in turn, resulted in a greater diversity of religious, cultural and political perspectives trying to make sense of these developments. One important ferment was added to these debates by the ideas of Charles Darwin (1809–82). Observing that animals and plants produced more young than could possibly survive, he hit on his theory of evolution by natural selection: those young that were better adapted to their environment would be 'selected' by nature, survive and bring forth new young plants and animals. What revolted Darwin's Christian opponents was perhaps not so much that human beings could be conceived of as being descended from apes but, rather, that this theory described the process of creation as open-ended, without any plan or law and without any intelligent design behind it. However, while the evangelical movements (and their effects on society at large) suggest that religion was a central force in nineteenth-century Britain, it is worth remembering that a religious census of church and Sunday-school attendance in England, Wales and Scotland in 1851 estimated that nearly half the population had *not* attended any place of worship on that particular Sunday (30 March); but, then, nearly half of those who had attended were Nonconformists. In place of their increasing religious doubt the Victorians developed a critical agnostic spirit with an intense interest in the systematic collection, classification and dissemination of knowledge. The universities were liberated from religious restrictions, and Education Acts in England and Wales (1870), Scotland (1872) and Ireland (1892) made elementary education compulsory for all.

THE BRITISH EMPIRE

The history of the British Empire before 1914 can be divided into three periods. First, from the sixteenth century to the 1780s the Empire was concentrated in the American colonies and the West Indies; this was sometimes called the Old Colonial System or the First Empire (cf. Chapters 4 and 5). The next hundred years, roughly from the acquisition of Quebec (1763) and the loss of the American colonies (1783) to the creation of the Dominion of Canada (1867) and the opening of the Suez Canal (1869), formed the Second Empire. In the period between 1870 and 1914, which is also sometimes referred to as the 'new imperialism', the most dramatic expansion took place: in area, the Empire more than doubled from 4.5 million square miles to 11.1 million square miles, implying a population growth from 202 million to 372 million people.

In the first period the mercantilist philosophy of wealth being increased through protected trade prevailed. But how far can this practice account for the evolution of the British Empire in the following 150 years? (i) The 1651 Navigation Act (and others which followed) laid the foundation for a very lucrative trade with the West Indies. (ii) The end of the War of the Spanish Succession (1713) not only resulted in British control of the seas but also secured for Britain monopoly control over the supply of black slaves to the Spanish-American Empire and thereby made it the leading slave-trading nation of the eighteenth century (cf. Chapter 5). (iii) English foreign trade in general almost doubled between 1700 and 1780, and then trebled over the next twenty years (before Napoleon's continental system took effect). The capital accumulated from these profits fed the early Industrial Revolution, which had Britain at its hub, and conversely the Industrial Revolution would not have occurred if Britain had not possessed a colonial empire which provided outlets far in excess of anything the home market could absorb. This position, at least in its initial stages, was secured by the conquest of overseas territories in North America and India during the eighteenth century. After the end of the Revolutionary and Napoleonic Wars (1815), Britain indeed ruled the waves and was becoming the world's workshop.

In these circumstances, a twofold strategy appeared to make sense: on the one hand, it was advisable to consolidate those territories (mostly white-settler colonies) that would later become the dominions (Canada, Australia, New

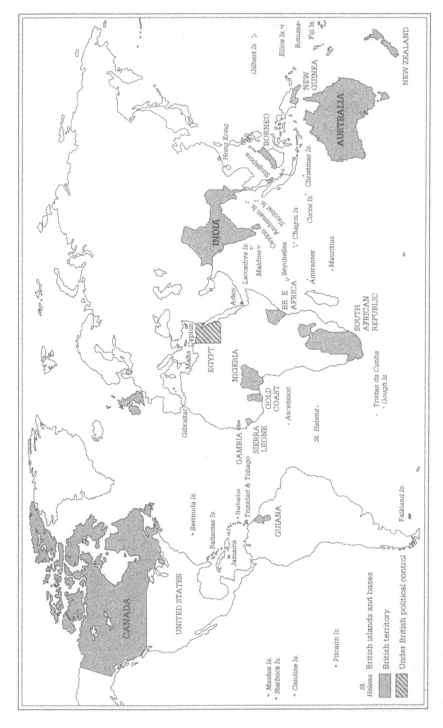

Map 10 The British Empire by the 1890s, from K. T. Hoppen, *Mid Victorian Generation, 1846–1886* (Oxford University Press, 1998), map 11. By permission of Oxford University Press

Zealand and the Cape Colony); on the other hand, further major direct (or formal) annexations became unnecessary: economic penetration (e.g. in Central as well as South America and the Near East) could take the place of military conquest. A country with industries that were able to undersell those of its competitors was well placed to preach free trade to the world – which Britain did. Moreover, it established itself at the centre of an international network resting upon privileged relations with Europe, North and South America, and small industrial regions in other continents. The peak of this development was reached in the third quarter of the nineteenth century when an 'imperialism of free trade' enabled the leading manufacturing nation, Britain, to use free trade to open up the world to further influence and control.

The subsequent grab for Africa, beginning in the early 1880s, was a sign that this form of 'liberal imperialism' was on the wane. Britain's competitors were fast catching up, and it became necessary once more to lean on the 'formal' Empire – India above all, but Egypt and Africa as well, in so far as they could be controlled. India was the key to Britain's imperial structure: politically (because of the size of the Indian army) and economically (because the country financed two-fifths of Britain's payment deficits). In one way or another, this enormous country became the keystone of the imperial arch before 1914.

Colonial relationships, modes of imperial control, 'race', and colonial resistance

Although they overlap in time and in some of their characteristics, the colonial countries fall very roughly into three main categories. First, there are areas such as North America (Canada and the United States), Australia and New Zealand. These were conquered and settled by Europeans who had either exterminated or shoved aside the indigenous peoples, whose way of life was based either on hunting and gathering or on settled agriculture. Since then, power has been firmly in the hands of the white majority in these areas, although the indigenous populations in Canada and New Zealand (and, to a lesser degree, in Australia and the United States) have recently succeeded in obtaining equal citizens' rights, reclaiming parts of their land, and re-establishing their cultural identities. Second, in areas such as South Africa and Zimbabwe (formerly Rhodesia) the indigenous populations, which were relatively large in number, and mostly living in settled agricultural communities, were defeated and dispossessed. Their lands were transformed into white settlements, while the original inhabitants were used as cheap labour. In these areas, a white minority maintained its privileged position by force (in Rhodesia until 1980 and in South Africa until 1994). Third, the largest category consists of countries such as India, other parts of Asia and of Africa which were not settled by Europeans, but were governed by them as overseas colonial possessions. The British West Indies are also part of this group: although their indigenous populations were largely exterminated, they were not settled by white people alone but repopulated with slaves from Africa and, later, with indentured labourers from India and China.

These countries were subjected to different modes of imperial control, which clearly depended on the nature of the colonial relationship. Most of the white-settler colonies evolved through the stages of 'representative government' (formally allowing colonial opinion to influence a colony's administration) and 'responsible government' (entailing colonial internal self-rule) to the status of self-governing dominions (Australia, Canada, New Zealand and, though not without difficulties, the Union of South Africa), while crown colonies were directly ruled from London (some with an elected house of assembly, some with a partly legislative council, some with a legislative council nominated by the Crown and some without any such provision). An additional number of dependencies were, directly or indirectly, controlled by various bodies, such as the Colonial Office, which was established as late as 1854, the India Office, the Foreign Office, the Admiralty and the Home Office.

Imperial control cannot be imagined without racial stereotyping. While colonised people had already been negatively described and categorised in the eighteenth century, in the nineteenth century 'racial' differences became the objects of scientific research: the developing disciplines of Biology, Medicine and Anthropology contributed to their description, codification and propagation. In the explanation of cultural differences two approaches were dominant: 'degenerationism' and 'progressive social evolution'. According to the former, God had initially graced humankind with one civilisation but had later punished human hubris (graphically captured in the narrative of the tower of Babel) by differentiating this one civilisation into more advanced and more 'degenerated' ones. Social evolutionary thought, in contrast, stressed not the descent of some cultures, but rather the ascent of others. All human life had been 'primitive' in the beginning, but some cultures had developed better and more quickly. Human history could be divided into three major 'ethnic periods': savagery, barbarism, civilisation. These were conceived of as stages of technological development through which all societies were believed to evolve, eventually progressing towards civilisation. Victorian society represented the latter in its highest currently extant form, while other contemporary 'primitive' cultures were thought of as 'living fossils' (or earlier stages) of human development. Needless to say, if 'more advanced' and 'less advanced' cultures came into contact, the former were regarded as destined to dominate, to civilise or, should this be impossible, to destroy the latter. The related idea of the 'survival of the fittest' (coined by Herbert Spencer) was a convenient element in any imperial philosophy in that it not only justified such a domination of one culture by another but, in fact, demanded it as if required by natural law. Thus, by this 'dialectic of inclusion and exclusion', economic exploitation, political

Anti-colonial resistance

There is a pattern which repeats itself endlessly in colonial relations. In the beginning, communicative acts of getting to know and understand each other are complemented by simple exchange processes and, perhaps, negotiations about further exchanges of goods. Usually the indigenous people regard these additional trading relations as positive as long as they do not disturb other, already existing, trading relations with neighbouring tribes and other people. If these trading relations are then complemented by expeditions carried out with the intention of opening up further markets and/or developing raw materials (e.g. mineral resources, etc.), serious conflicts are to be expected – in particular, if these colonial acquisitions imply the loss of the indigenous people's trading partners and raw materials. Usually the colonisers try to defuse these conflicts by proposing treaties which, however, are most often in their favour. Persuasion, deception and coercion are decisive in this context. Very often the consent of the colonised is obtained because they hope to profit from their cooperation or are protected from internal or external enemies. Once the imbalance of the treaties becomes clear (or the treaty is broken by the colonisers), the colonised people tend to stage rebellions which, in turn, are suppressed by the colonisers. The colonisers conduct military (punitive) expeditions, the colonised retaliate with guerrilla warfare. Usually, not big battles but small wars are fought. If (as nearly always) the colonisers defeat the colonised (if only temporarily), they replace the indigenous systems of (self-)rule by colonial regimes which employ collaborating individuals or elites willing to do the work of the colonisers (indirect rule): collecting taxes and – if necessary – the implementation of forced labour. The consequences are political unrest, poverty and angry rebellion. Repeated and, perhaps, intensified resistance on the part of the colonised (petitions, strikes, boycotts) leads to longer and more extensive military fighting. If the colonisers win, they continue to exploit the colony. This eventually leads to the destruction of the social and political structure of the colonised people. Military superiority enables the colonisers to kill or deport opponents, while the feeling of inferiority amongst the colonised fosters millenarianism as well as other religious phenomena and leaders who propagate a final war ('that settles the matter once and for all') against the colonisers.

domination and cultural proselytisation appeared to be in the interests of the colonised.

Needless to say, all colonial powers met with some measure of resistance: the Haitian Black Jacobins, who modelled their revolution (1791) on that in France and achieved independence (1804), became the model for innumerable uprisings in the Caribbean and beyond. In the British Empire, the most notorious revolts and their invariably brutal suppression occurred in British North America (1837), New Zealand (1845–7, 1860–72), Afghanistan (1838–42,

1878–80), India (1857–8), Jamaica (1865), China (1839–42, 1856–60, 1899–1901) and different parts of Africa (1879, 1881–6, 1898, 1898–1901). The obverse of the highly praised *Pax Britannica* was a series of 'small wars' which kept Victoria's soldiers busy in all parts of the Empire.

7 The twentieth century: devastation and decline, reconstruction and reorientation, 1914–99

If the nineteenth century has often been dubbed 'long', the twentieth century has sometimes earned the epithet 'short'. Historians have framed it by the cataclysmic events of the First World War (1914–18) and the Russian Revolution (1917), on the one hand, and the implosion of the Soviet Union and its allies 1989–91, graphically demonstrated by the fall of the Berlin Wall in 1989, on the other. Alternatively, and from a distinctly European perspective, the century began and ended with bloody ethnic conflicts on Europe's periphery: the Balkans. More generally and most crucially, however, the last century witnessed social, political and cultural change that was without precedent in its scope and rapidity. A better understanding of what follows may benefit from an – obviously highly selective – bird's-eye view of the period.

While at the beginning of the twentieth century the world was dominated by the European nation states, many of which (such as Britain, France and Russia) directly controlled large areas as their colonial empires, by 2000 Europe no longer dominated the world, and its formal empires were reduced to a few negligible remnants. The first half of the century saw the apogee of nationalist ideology and politics and their catastrophes in two world wars, but the second half witnessed the growth and development of supranational as well as international ideas, institutions and forms of cooperation (as, for example, the United Nations and the European Union) which so far may have helped prevent further conflict. Moreover, within pacified Europe many formerly unified nation states have 'broken up': regions such as Brittany in France, Catalonia in Spain, and Scotland, Wales (and, at times, Northern Ireland) in Britain have succeeded in reconstructing their distinct cultural and political identities and in achieving various forms of 'home rule' (devolution).

In 1914, Britain was the greatest power in the world; in the 1990s it was a second-class power, endlessly dithering whether it wanted to be in a 'special relationship' (Winston Churchill) with the United States or 'at the very heart of Europe' (John Major). After the First World War the British Empire reached its zenith through its acquisition of mandates over former German and Turkish possessions, effectively controlling over a fifth of the world's land surface and ruling a quarter of its population, but when Hong Kong was handed over to the People's Republic of China in 1997 all but very few and small territories had achieved their independence.

In the course of the century, the franchise was widened and the voting age was lowered: in 1918, for the first time, the vote was granted to all men at age twenty-one (as well as to those under twenty-one who had served in the First World War) and to women aged thirty or above who were either independent householders, wives of householders or university graduates. (The electorate grew from 6,730,935 in 1900 to 21,392,322 in 1918.) Ten years later legislation, for the first time, gave women the vote on exactly the same terms as men. (The electorate grew from 21,731,320 in 1924 to 28,850,870 in 1928.) Finally, in 1969, the voting age was lowered from twenty-one to eighteen. (The electorate grew from 35,964,684 in 1966 to 39,342,013 in 1970.) Moreover, while at the beginning of the century the Conservative party and the Liberal party were the major political forces, the latter split irrevocably in the war period and was replaced by the Labour party in the 1920s. Amidst much change there was some continuity as well: while many European states changed their constitutional framework in the course of the twentieth century – as, for example, Germany from constitutional monarchy (until 1918) to democracy (1918–33) to fascist dictatorship (1933–45) to democracy (from 1949 in the West and from 1990 in the whole of the country) – Britain's political system as a whole remained intact. The one major shift which occurred was the curtailing of the power of the House of Lords: this began with the Parliament Act (of 1911) which allowed the Lords to delay but not ultimately reject decisions of the Commons and temporarily ended, for the time being, with the reduction of the House to ninety-two hereditary peers (from some 600) elected by their fellow peers (in 1999).

The population of the British Isles rose from some 41 million people in 1901 to some 61 million in 1991 (including almost always modest gains and losses due to immigration and emigration). In the same period, life expectancy at birth rose from fifty-one years for men and fifty-eight for women to seventy-six and eighty-one respectively. This was mainly due to improved standards of living: at the end of the century the average British citizen was four times better off than at its beginning. For instance, the population was increasingly better housed, although considerable housing shortages had to be overcome after both wars. Before the First World War somewhere between 10 and 20 per cent of the population of England and Wales owned their homes, before the Second World War the proportion had risen to 32 per cent and by 1996 to 67 per cent, while council housing accounted for about 10 per cent of the housing stock in England and Wales before the Second World War, for 32 per cent in 1980 and – owing to the Thatcherite policy of minimising public ownership of housing – 18 per cent in 1996. (Scotland's proportion of owner-occupiers was consistently lower.) While, in 1951, 28 per cent of households had no bath, in 1971 this figure had decreased to 16.7 per cent and in 1981 to 6.3 per cent. Then, advances in medical research and healthcare also contributed to this development. The capacity of medicine to diagnose and cure sickness expanded massively. Infectious diseases such as diphtheria, tuberculosis, measles, whooping cough and scarlet fever declined; other diseases such as rickets (caused primarily by malnutrition) almost disappeared. Preventive measures such as inoculation have been as important as antibiotic drugs (such as penicillin, which helped cure pneumonia and puerperal fever). A better understanding of the immune system facilitated the transplant of organs; advances in surgical techniques enabled the development of 'keyhole surgery', which puts less strain on the patient than normal surgery. Finally, the people in the United Kingdom were increasingly better educated. The 1870 Education Act had ensured elementary education from the age of five, although the school-leaving age was set at ten. Attendance was made compulsory in 1880, and state education was provided free of charge in 1891. The school-leaving age was raised to twelve in 1899, to fourteen in 1918, to fifteen in 1944, and to sixteen in 1973. More important, the 1944 Education Act ensured free, compulsory secondary education for all children.

Throughout the century, there were distinct shifts in social and cultural values. For example, at the beginning of the century, birth control was socially not acceptable; when the century closed, access to means of safe and reliable birth control was taken for granted. In the first five years of the century, an average of some 800 divorce petitions a year were filed in England and Wales, slightly more by husbands than by wives. Once women could obtain a divorce on the same grounds as men (from 1923), the number of wives seeking divorce constantly outstripped the number of men. The number of divorces rose to an average of some 32,000 in 1951–5 and some 122,000 in 1971–5. In 1994 slightly fewer than 160,000 divorces were granted in England and Wales. Around 1900 it was generally accepted that the United Kingdom (Ireland excepted) was a Protestant nation. By 2000, however, Britain's religious complexion had changed dramatically. In terms of attendance figures the Catholic church (1.9 million) had outstripped the Anglican church (1.3 million), while what has been called 'active Christian church membership' declined from about 30 per cent of the adult population in 1900 to 12 per cent ninety years later. Moreover, non-Christian religions have become more important. From 1970 to 1990 the number of Buddhists rose from 6000 to 28,000, that of Hindus from 300,000 to 500,000, that of Sikhs from 75,000 to 600,000, and that of Muslims from 300,000 to 1.4 million. Finally, while gambling was denounced as sinful and a curse of modern society at the beginning of the twentieth century, it was legalised in the 1960s, became socially accepted in the 1970s and officially sanctioned in 1994 when the government introduced the National Lottery.

At the beginning of the century the postal letter was the most frequently used means of personal communication while the printed press disseminated information to the greater part of the population. Wartime technological developments facilitated the broadcast of a single sound message to a mass audience (radio) in the 1920s, shortly to be followed by the broadcast of moving pictures (television) in the 1930s. These developments were complemented by the proliferation of telephones, especially the rapid spread of the mobile phone since the early 1990s, as well as the widespread access to the Internet and electronic mail, which have transformed (inter-)personal communication in ways which would have been regarded as utopian in 1900.

WARTIME DEVASTATIONS AND PEACETIME DIFFICULTIES

In a timespan of little more than thirty years two wars that originated in Europe but involved the whole world took place: in the first (1914–18) 15 million people were killed (including 6 million civilians) and 20 million wounded, in the second (1939–45) some 60 million people were killed (including 6 million Jews in the Holocaust) and 10 million refugees transformed the demographic landscape of the world. Primarily, these wars were the fatal outcome of an endless competition among the participant nation states for resources and raw materials, which grew out of their preceding inter-imperial rivalry. When the First World War did not 'solve' but rather deferred the conflict, social and political developments within and among the adversarial nations added other dimensions to the conflict. The traumatic experiences of the war shattered not only national economies but also deeply rooted convictions. Norms and values – such as, for example, the belief in the inevitability of progress – were questioned and transformed. New, antagonistic political systems emerged: while a capitalist economy could apparently be 'ruled' by either a liberal or a constitutional democracy (as in the United States or Britain) or a fascist dictatorship (as in Germany or Italy), socialism (as represented by Russia from 1917) required the dictatorship of the proletariat or, rather, of its self-appointed representatives. Sooner or later, all of these powers indiscriminately strove to expand their political sphere of influence and enforce their economic interests. The fight against fascism required the joint effort of socio-economically antagonistic 'systems', though after its successful defeat the world was quickly divided between the victors, the (communist) East, represented by the Soviet Union, and the (capitalist) West, represented by the United States of America and its allies. The irreconcilable differences between these two 'systems', in turn, soon led to a kind of 'cold' war (i. e. one without real fighting or only by proxy as, for example, in Korea, Indonesia, Malaysia, Vietnam) which – although, now and then, it was in danger of turning 'hot' (as, for example, in the Cuban missile crisis of 1962) – was successfully contained by the 'superpowers' (the United States, the Soviet Union) and the support of international cooperation until it ended with the implosion of the Soviet Union in the late 1980s.

The Great War

At the beginning of the century, the 'armed peace' of the European imperial rivals was cross-cut by their various alliances (as in the Triple Alliance between Germany, Austria-Hungary and Italy [1882, renewed 1912], the Entente Cordiale between Britain and France [1904] and the subsequent Triple Entente that included Russia [1907]), confounded by regional conflicts (as in the Balkans in 1908 and 1912–13), and overdetermined by Britain's fear of German (or any other) hegemony on the Continent. The various crises came to a head in the summer of 1914 when the heir to the Austro-Hungarian Empire was assassinated. The ensuing war pitted two coalitions against each other, with Britain, France, Russia and, from 1917, the United States on the one side, and Germany, Austria-Hungary, Bulgaria and Turkey on the other (Documents 42 and 43). While all parties expected a short (and glorious) war, it became long and very grim. The war on the Western Front very soon became a war of attrition with the lines of trenches extending from the Channel to the Swiss frontier. For the next three and a half years, despite the deployment of devastating weapons and enormous losses of men, neither side could advance more than a few kilometres along this line. While the German colonies were overrun, the Dardanelles expedition (in 1915) against Turkey ended in disaster. The Royal Navy was expected to eliminate the threat of the German High Seas Fleet, but the two engagements between the two fleets were indecisive. However, when German submarines caused heavy losses of British merchant ships, the armed ships of the Navy were successfully used to guard convoys. Moreover, Germany's 'unrestricted submarine warfare' (by which it hoped to starve Britain into submission) eventually brought the United States into the war in April 1917. With the assistance of huge American forces, in 1918 the Allies succeeded in repelling the German offensive on the Western Front and breaking the 'Hindenburg line' in August. Germany surrendered before the Allied armies reached German territory.

The losses of men (cf. Table 4) and the financial costs of the war were immense: while the British government spent £77 million on defence in 1913, the amount had risen to £2238 million in 1918; the national debt rose from £650 million in 1914 to £7434 million in 1919. About 15 per cent of the country's wealth was wiped out. The war effectively put an end to Britain's central position within the international economy.

At home the war brought fundamental changes: a much higher proportion of the population and far more resources were involved in it than in previous wars. Perhaps more crucially, the government's control over the economy,

Table 4 Military effort of the Empire/Commonwealth in the First World War

	Total mobilised	Killed or died of wounds	Wounded	Missing POWs[a]
Australia	412,953	58,460	152,100	164
Canada	628,964	56,119	149,733	306
India	1,440,437	47,746	65,126	871
New Zealand	128,525	16,132	40,749	5
South Africa	228,907	7,241	11,444	33
United Kingdom	5,704,416	662,083	1,644,786	140,312
Others	42,000	3,336	3,504	366
Total	8,586,202	851,117	2,067,442	142,057

[a] Prisoners repatriated not shown.
Chris Cook and John P. Paxton, *Commonwealth Political Facts* (London: Macmillan, 1979), p. 207. Reproduced by permission of Palgrave Macmillan.

labour, industry and society as a whole was extended to unprecedented levels: direct taxation was increased (and never returned to prewar rates), and employers and trade unions collaborated (and avoided making use of strikes or lockouts). Although 2 million men volunteered to fight in the first two years, the length of the war and its horrendous losses made it necessary for the British government to introduce conscription for the first time in 1916. An unintended side-effect of this measure was that the relative health of the male population had to be officially acknowledged: in 1917–18, for example, some 2.5 million men (conscripts and volunteers) were examined, and 1 million were found to be medically unfit for service – an indisputable indicator of malnutrition (and its cause: prewar poverty). (If we take into account the fact that Britain desperately needed soldiers, we may even assume that this was an overestimation of the men's fitness.) In the course of the war, however, because of almost full employment and relatively successful 'management', civilian living standards improved. Women gained access to a wider range of occupations than before, and many of them experienced high levels of economic (and personal) independence which, however, rarely outlasted the end of the war (and the return of the men who reclaimed their previous jobs).

The interwar years

The two decades between the two world wars were determined by attempts at re-establishing and stabilising the national economy, searching for international security, coping with the trauma of the war and conceiving of what Britain stood for after it. According to some historians, the war cost Britain £9 billion, of which £1 billion remained as debt (to be repaid mainly to the United States). In the long run, however, it was the ruin of foreign trade – markets, previously dominated by British exports, had been penetrated by, for example, Japan and the United States – and the necessity to convert a wartime industry to peace-time production which made up the chief costs of the war. Moreover, Britain's 'invisible income' (earnings derived from services) was seriously curtailed as it had lost some 40 per cent of its merchant fleet in the war. Although the immediate postwar boom allowed the re-absorption of over 4 million troops into the economy, the following recession (in late 1920 and early 1921) quickly threw 1.5 million people out of work. Unemployment figures fluctuated between 1 million and 2 million throughout the decade and peaked at 3 million during the severe slump between 1929 (triggered by the Wall Street Crash of October) and 1934. In both decades those who had work bargained to improve their working conditions, while those who had no work joined the National Unemployed Workers Movement which organised 'hunger marches' to draw attention to the situation. At one time, 80 per cent of the men in Jarrow (near Newcastle) were out of work. As the established parties (including the new Labour party) appeared unable to offer any remedies, for a short time more radical voices made themselves heard: the Communist Party of Great Britain and the British Union of Fascists. Neither of them, however, succeeded in winning great influence. On the other hand, the high unemployment figures have to be contrasted with rising living standards for the majority of the population. The latter were the result of nascent welfare-state legislation, but these measures proved to be insufficient.

Although Britain was technically one of the victors of the First World War and, because of League of Nations mandates, added to its sphere of influence, its position as a world power became increasingly questionable. First, although the war effort of the colonies had been remarkable, each of the dominions insisted on signing the peace treaty and joining the League of Nations as an individual state: 'continuous consultation and concerted action' (envisaged in the Imperial War Conference of 1917) was being replaced by what has been called 'dominion nationalism'. Second, the problem of Ireland – from the post-ponement of Home Rule (1914) to the Easter Rising (1916) to the undeclared war, the partition and settlement (1919–22) – was a festering sore in the British political body. Third, and perhaps most important, the victors of the First World War were unable to agree on and enforce a peaceful political order in Europe. The main losers of the First World War turned fascist – Italy in 1922 and Germany in 1933 – which might have been quickly understood as their preparations to 'correct' by aggressive force what they regarded as 'unfair treatment'. But, whenever one of these nations broke a treaty or ignored its obligations, Britain and France (and sometimes the League of Nations) com-plained about or even condemned this – but did not act. Italy invaded Ethiopia in 1935; Germany took Austria in 1938. Six months later, Hitler, with a mixture of promises and threats, cajoled the French (Daladier) and the British (Chamberlain) into accepting the German occupation of Czecho-slovakia's Sudeten-German districts as fact (without ever asking any Czech

---

Appeasement

Appeasement was a particular foreign policy in the late 1930s by which the British government tried to deal with the expansionist aims of fascist Italy (mainly in Ethiopia) and Germany (in Czechoslovakia). It was believed that Hitler's and Mussolini's aims were limited, and if their desires were yielded to, it would be possible to maintain peace. This belief turned out to be wrong. However, it is not clear whether Neville Chamberlain, Britain's prime minister at the time, really had any other option. Strong public anti-war sentiment combined with a distinct lack of military and fiscal preparedness for war formed a most unpropitious context for any other – possibly more antagonistic and belligerent – position. Although appeasement was sharply criticised (by, for example, Winston Churchill), it may have bought Britain the time necessary to rearm and prepare for war when it became imminent in 1939.

---

representative) in return for his declaration that now he was 'satisfied'. Chamberlain believed that he had secured 'peace in our time'. He could not have been more wrong. Six months later, Germany seized the rest of Czechoslovakia, and another six months later Europe was at war again.

The interwar years also witnessed a difficult process of readjustment in Britain. For one, the horrendous destruction and, even more and longer visible, mutilation of human lives produced a mood in which the war appeared to the majority of the population as essentially senseless and futile. This was all the more so because there had been a number of cases (as, for example, in the trench warfare in France and the Dardanelles expedition) in which the terrible death rate appeared to be caused (at least in part) by poor military leadership: to some it was a war of 'lions led by donkeys'. Then, the British government was unable to meet its obligations as one of the war's victors: it could neither pay its war debts, nor finance the protection of its enlarged sphere of influence (a clear case of 'imperial overstretch'), nor keep its promise (made by the prime minister, Lloyd George, in 1918) 'to make Britain a fit country for heroes to live in'. Finally, and perhaps most crucially, the three prime ministers who dominated the interwar decades (Stanley Baldwin, Ramsay MacDonald, Neville Chamberlain) may have sought (and sometimes provided) stability and normality, but they neither possessed nor encouraged in others leadership qualities which might have provided Britain with an appropriately transformed sense of itself as a political power 'in transformation'. Instead, the spirit of the years leading up to the Second World War was characterised by inertia and drift. This domestic perspective was complemented in foreign affairs by a policy of appeasement.

National Government

The National or coalition government was formed in 1931 (in the wake of the 'great crash' and the ensuing economic crisis) and lasted until 1940. Its main aims were to solve Britain's economic problems, reduce unemployment and create better living conditions (slum clearance and house-building). Most of the government's measures were only moderately successful. Moreover, both the Liberal party and the Labour party suffered splits caused by the formation of the coalition government. The Labour party even expelled those of its members who joined it.

The Second World War

In March 1939, Britain had pledged to defend Poland. So, when Germany invaded that country on 1 September, Britain had to end its policy of appeasement and declare war (3 September). But, as Britain could not save Poland, it tried to blockade Germany. Not much else happened until 10 May 1940 (the 'Phoney War') when Germany invaded the Low Countries, Belgium and France. On the same day, Churchill replaced Chamberlain as prime minister of an all-party coalition. His policy, he told the British people, would be 'victory at all costs, victory in spite of all terror, victory, however long and hard the road may be; for without victory, there is no survival'; he had (he said) 'nothing to offer but blood, toil, tears and sweat'. His first task was to have the Allied armed forces that had been encircled by the Germans in the north of France (near Dunkirk) evacuated. Between 27 May and 4 June 1940, a total of 693 ships (military, merchant, and a variety of other small craft) brought 338,226 people to Britain. Of these 140,000 were members of the French army. Four days after the fall of Paris (14 June), Churchill sent out his most famous call to arms:

> I expect that the Battle of Britain is about to begin. Upon this battle depends the survival of Christian civilization. Upon it depends our own British life, and the long continuity of our institutions and our Empire. The whole fury and might of the enemy must very soon be turned on us. Hitler knows that he will have to break us in this Island or lose the war. If we can stand up to him, all Europe may be free and the life of the world may move forward into broad, sunlit uplands. But if we fail, then the whole world, including the United States, including all that we have known and cared for, will sink into the abyss of a new Dark Age made more sinister, and perhaps more protracted, by the lights of perverted science. Let us therefore brace ourselves to our duties, and so bear ourselves that, if the British Empire and its Commonwealth last for a thousand years, men will still say, 'This was their finest hour.'

Churchill refused to negotiate with Hitler, and the Germans started to attack Britain by air. In the ensuing Battle of Britain, which lasted from July to September 1940, the British succeeded not only in repelling the individual attacks but also in foiling German invasion plans. By October the Germans had chosen a new strategy: the bombing of civilian and military targets (the Blitz, derived from the German *Blitzkrieg*, i.e. 'lightning war'). London and many other towns which were important for the war effort suffered, although casualties were not as high as had been feared. The Germans abandoned this strategy in May 1941, when Hitler prepared for an attack on the Soviet Union (in June). While the Battle of Britain has become a symbol of British courage and defiance (in the sense of the few gaining a victory over many), the Blitz has become an emblem of stoicism and the will to survive, both of which sustained British resistance. With regard to the symbolic quality the Battle of Britain and the Blitz have attained in British cultural memory, we should not forget that, between June 1940 and June 1941, Britain was on its own in the war against Germany (although the United States provided finance and supplies). This changed drastically when Hitler attacked the Soviet Union in June 1941 (an effort which drained German forces from the West European and North African fronts) and when the Japanese attacked Pearl Harbor (in December 1941) and the British Empire in Eastern Asia, where they quickly captured Hong Kong, Burma, Malaya and the British naval base at Singapore. The attack on Pearl Harbor, moreover, brought the Americans into the war. Their contribution was to be decisive for the eventual victory of the Allies. By late 1942 and early 1943 the tide of war had turned: the Soviet Union halted the Germans at Stalingrad and drove them back; the British checked the Germans in North Africa; the Americans invaded Sicily. While the British and American air forces conducted a strategic bombing of enemy-occupied Europe, a cross-Channel attack was prepared which eventually took place on 6 June 1944 (D-Day). In February 1945 the Allied forces crossed the prewar German frontier in the west and linked up with the army of the Soviet Union on the river Elbe on 28 April. Germany capitulated on 7 May, and Japan, after the first two atom bombs had been dropped on Hiroshima (6 August) and Nagasaki (9 August), on 2 September.

Again, the losses of men (cf. Table 5) and the financial costs of the war were immense: while the British government spent £254 million on defence in 1938, the amount had risen to £5125 million in 1944, the national debt rose from £7130 million in 1939 to £23,636 million in 1946. About 28 per cent of the country's wealth was wiped out, and Britain shouldered the largest external debt in its history (about £10,000 million).

At home, as in the First World War, the government exercised a greater control over economic and social activities than it had in peacetime. Children were evacuated from the cities to the countryside, conscription was introduced immediately. This time, the levels of physical fitness were higher owing to the interwar decline in poverty. The whole economy was geared to the support of

Table 5 Military effort of the Commonwealth in the Second World War

	Total mobilised	Killed	Wounded	Missing	Prisoners of war
Australia	992,545	31,395	65,000	2,475	22,885
Canada	1,086,343	42,042	54,414	2,866	9,051
India	2,394,000	24,338	64,354	11,754	79,489
New Zealand	214,700	11,625	15,749	2,129	7,218
South Africa	410,056	12,080	14,363	–	15,044
United Kingdom	6,515,000	357,116	369,267	46,079	178,332
Others	504,250	7,716	7,386	14,393	8,265
Total	12,116,894	486,312	590,533	79,696	320,284

See Table 4.

the war. Agricultural output was increased to make Britain independent of imports; certain industries (such as, for example, the motor car and aircraft industries) were converted to wartime production; price control as well as rationing of food and essential goods was introduced to prevent inflation and maintain civilian morale. As more civilians than in the First World War had direct experience of the war (because of the bombing), this was of the utmost importance. More than 7 million women were drawn into the workforce, although they were expected to return to their homes after the war.

The postwar years

In the Second World War as in the First World War, in terms of international relations it proved easier to unite against a common foe than to find a common postwar perspective. After the defeat of the fascist axis powers the Allies soon split into two camps – the capitalist West and the communist East – which were to be locked in a 'cold war' for forty years. Both camps created complex effective military alliances: the North Atlantic Treaty Organisation (NATO) was set up in 1949, while the Eastern European Mutual Assistance Pact (or Warsaw Pact for short) was established in 1955 as a response to West German remilitarisation and admission to NATO. In these developments Britain's role became increasingly that of a junior partner of the United States. In 1948, when Churchill developed the idea of Britain being 'at the very point of junction' of 'three interlinked circles' – 'the British Commonwealth and Empire', 'the English-speaking world' including the United States, and 'United Europe' – he still envisaged a 'special relationship' on equal terms. During the following decade it became clear that not only was Britain economically dependent on loans from the United States, but would also have to consult them in important foreign affairs (or risk humiliation, as in the Suez crisis of 1956). Moreover, it would depend on the United States for access to nuclear weaponry. At the same time, successive British governments alienated and sometimes angered their

---

Postwar Germany and Austria

After the Second World War, Germany (and Berlin) as well as Austria (and Vienna) were each divided into four zones (British, French, American and Soviet). While Austria was eventually reunited and given independence in 1955, the British, French and American zones of Germany formed the Federal Republic of Germany in 1949, while the zone occupied by the Soviet Union formed the German Democratic Republic in the same year. Both countries were reunited in 1990.

European partners by their indifference to the process of European cooperation and integration.

At home in Britain, the war had not only put an end to unemployment but also created a sense of service and, perhaps, sacrifice which, already during the war but particularly after it, produced a desire for a better, socially and economically reconstructed society. A return to the 'devil's decade' (the 1930s) became unthinkable. The Beveridge Report (1942) in particular recommended protection against poverty, sickness and unemployment (Document 44). When the Labour party offered better housing, full employment and social security in their 1945 election manifesto, they won a landslide victory. Convinced of the merits of planning, the Labour party began to implement a planned economy (including a programme of nationalisation and social services). However, putting these plans into practice cost money. But the economic situation was desperate: Britain had lost its export markets; its 'invisible income' was severely reduced as it had lost half of its merchant fleet, not to speak of the liquidation of overseas assets; many industries had to be re-equipped and converted to peacetime demands. Although Britain was loaned money and granted a fair share of the European Recovery (Marshall) Plan by the United States, wartime deprivations continued for almost a decade. Many goods were rationed, people had to wait in queues to buy them, meagre diets and inadequate housing were common: this truly was an 'age of austerity'. Despite this unfavourable context, the government accepted responsibility for the material well-being of the population and introduced what has earned the name of welfare state. The new legislation protected against unemployment, old age and sickness; it ended the Poor Laws and made the government responsible for the poor; it provided free healthcare for the whole population; and it provided for the construction of some 800,000 new homes and for the repair of some 330,000 by 1950. When the Conservatives returned to power in 1951, they halted the programme of nationalisation but did not question or dismantle the welfare state.

RECONSTRUCTION AND ITS LIMITS

The economy

Britain received $2.7 billion Marshall Aid to kick-start her economy; but, although the first postwar decade experienced rapid growth, full employment and low inflation, the war had bankrupted the British economy. The pound had to be devalued in 1947 (which, however, gave a boost to Britain's exports as they were now cheaper to buy), and a massive rearmament programme (which was regarded as necessary when Britain supported the United States in the Korean War) led to cuts in the welfare state. Moreover, it slowed down economic recovery because scarce resources were redirected from the export-orientated industries to the armaments industry and, as a consequence, Britain lost further important export markets. Still, despite these adversarial developments, between 1951 and 1973 the British economy grew – but the economies of Britain's rivals grew faster. While in terms of Gross Domestic Product (GDP) the British economy grew by 2.5 per cent, those of France, Germany and Japan grew by 4.0, 4.9 and 8.0 per cent respectively. In the same timespan, Britain's share of world trade shrank from 25 to 10 per cent. And certain industries in which Britain had traditionally been strong declined or collapsed. In 1950, Britain's share of the shipbuilding market (measured in tonnage launched) stood at 37 per cent; twenty-four years later it had shrunk to 3.7 per cent. Although the car industry quickly expanded after 1945, by 1956 West Germany produced more cars than Britain. When the reputation of the quality of British cars went from bad to worse, the number of foreign cars registered in Britain rapidly increased: 5 per cent in 1964, 31 per cent in 1973, and 62 per cent in 1979. A number of reasons have been advanced to explain this general economic decline – poor labour relations, bad management, contradictory government policies towards industry (such as the 'stop–go cycle' of the 1950s and 1960s) which may have discouraged higher levels of investment – but historians tend to agree that no single answer is capable of explaining Britain's decline, relative as it may be.

Developments in the last quarter of the twentieth century were mixed, with two major depressions and several short periods of growth in between. In 1967 the pound had to be devalued again. The oil crisis of 1973 (when prices quadrupled) contributed to the already existing stagnation in industrial production; unemployment figures reached 1 million in 1978 for the first time since the interwar years. A modest recovery occurred in the second half of the 1970s, supported by the arrival of North Sea oil. When Margaret Thatcher came to power in 1979 she tried to introduce a radically different agenda. Intent on 'reversing Britain's decline' she was against government ownership, trade union power and welfare services, and for less government and more individual accountability. Accordingly, she cut public spending, provided incentives for the private sector, privatised many industries which had been nationalised in the 1940s (handing much of the money to the electorate in the form of tax cuts) and emasculated the trade unions. However, although 'Thatcherism' has come to stand for this particular combination of a free-market policy with that of an authoritarian state – Thatcher regarded herself as a 'conviction politician' – her record in economic policy was rather mixed. She succeeded in combating inflation, in turning unprofitable branches of industry into profitable ones by ruthless rationalisation, and in cutting government services. At the end of her

---

Margaret Thatcher (1925–)

However highly controversial her personality and policies were, the significance of Margaret Thatcher's government is undisputed. Born in 1925 in Grantham, Lincolnshire, a grocer's daughter, her political ascent was as much a product of determination as an 'awesome testimony to the importance of sheer chance in history' (Paul Johnson). Conservative MP in 1959 and Education Minister in 1970, she unexpectedly won the Tory leadership from Edward Heath in 1975. Although many senior party members never followed her, she effectively moved the Conservatives to the right. After the 'winter of discontent' she led her party to an election victory against Labour in 1979 (repeated in 1983 and 1987).

As Europe's first female prime minister she pioneered more market-orientated policies which were to be adopted around the world. Turning away from the postwar political consensus including Keynesian deficit-spending and a large welfare state, she pursued monetarist inflation control. Her creed was 'personal responsibility, responsibility for one's own family and responsibility towards others', which she translated into policy by cutting both taxes and welfare benefits, by reducing the role of government through deregulation (e.g. in the education and health sectors) and privatisation (of nationalised industries and of council houses), by promoting competition and by reducing the power of trade unions. The policy became known as 'supply-side' economics because it strengthened incentives for producers instead of stimulating demand.

In the realm of international politics, Thatcher made herself known as a resolute leader of Britain, called the 'Iron Lady' by the Soviet Union. In 1982 she ordered the invasion of the Falklands, British territory which had been captured by Argentina; and she staunchly advocated a strong defence within NATO to maintain pressure on the Soviet Union which contributed to its dissolution in 1991.

By not compromising on her sceptical attitude on European integration she upset close political friends, thus in the end lacking the support she bitterly needed. The introduction of the hugely unpopular 'poll tax' further contributed to her downfall. In November 1990 she was forced to step down. John Major took over as party leader and prime minister.

time in office, the majority of Britons (some 70 per cent) were prospering, but unemployment stood at over 3 million for five years and 20 per cent of the population lived below the poverty line.

Society

The 'age of austerity' was followed by an 'age of affluence': in the early 1950s a growing economy allowed rising wages (while the number of working hours fell slightly). As a result, the sale of consumer goods rose dramatically (Table 6).

This unprecedented prosperity led Harold Macmillan, who became prime minister when Anthony Eden resigned after the Suez crisis in January 1957, to assert: 'Let's be frank about it; most of our people have never had it so good. Go around the country, go to the industrial towns, go to the farms, and you will see a state of prosperity such as we have never had in my life time – nor indeed ever in the history of this country.' Now, while economic growth had long been regarded as politically beneficial, in the postwar period politicians began to believe that they could shape public policy to produce such growth – and the public willingly believed them. Hardly anybody considered what would happen if growth could not be sustained.

Ten years later, children born after the war were teenagers who had not only more disposable income (to spend on clothes, records, etc.) but also more leisure time in which they could enjoy their new affluence. This postwar affluence improved the way of life of almost all social groups, and in its near-universality it also had a crucial impact on the way in which people made sense of their lives, of the rules which regulated them, and of the norms and values which they adhered to. The 1960s were not only about the teenage (and student) rebellion, 'Swinging London' and 'the Pill', but also about the reform of

Table 6 Consumer durables: availability in households (%) (n/a = not available)

	1955	*1975*	*1995*
Vacuum cleaner	51	90	96
Washing machine	18	70	91
Refrigerator	8	85	98
Freezer	n/a	15	79
Television	35	96	98
Telephone	19	52	92
Central heating	5	47	85
Dishwasher	1	2	12
Microwave oven	n/a	n/a	47
Video recorder	n/a	n/a	70
CD-player	n/a	n/a	63
Home computer	n/a	n/a	20

(Derrick Murphy (ed.), *Britain, 1914–2000*, London: HarperCollins, 2000, p. 350)

Youth cultures

Evidence of 'youth culture' can found in many periods of British history. But youth cultures in all social classes have become increasingly visible since the end of the Second World War. This may have to do with the sharp increase in the number of young people ('baby boom'), their extended stay in the sphere of adolescence (the school leaving age was raised to fifteen in 1947 and to sixteen in 1973), the increasing prosperity coupled with full employment ('age of affluence') of, first, their parents and, then, the young people themselves. Moreover, decreasing hours of work expanded the time and opportunities for leisure. Personal and, more important, group identity ('Teds', 'Mods', 'Rockers') became available through consumption, particularly consumption of clothes and entertainment. The latter was largely influenced by the mass media: radio, records and films. The American film *Rock around the Clock* (1956) epitomised this tendency. In the 1960s, on the one hand, more hedonistic components ('sex, drugs and rock 'n' roll') became prominent; while, on the other, the political component achieved a more critically radical dimension (Vietnam). When the economic conditions became more fragile in the 1970s, the youth cultures took on a grittier look (skinheads, punks). Since the 1970s many of these primarily generational forms of identity have also been recognised as being criss-crossed by factors of race and gender.

---

censorship (1959 [books], 1968 [theatre, film]), the abolition of capital punishment (1965, 1969), the legalisation of family planning clinics, abortion and homosexuality (1967). The Divorce Reform Act (1969) made divorce easier: as a consequence, decrees made absolute rose from 26,000 (1960) to 62,000 (1970). A new 'structure of feeling' (Raymond Williams) was about to emerge.

While many of these cultural tendencies continued down to the end of the twentieth century – women's role in society improved, moral values concerning people's sexual orientation and lifestyles were transformed, marriage as an institution declined and was in part replaced by cohabiting – there was a drastic change in the economic sphere. After the near-universal rise in prosperity, from the mid-1970s onwards the gap between rich and poor increased dramatically (Table 7). Again, the reasons for this change cannot be attributed to one cause. Government policy (tax cuts for the affluent, benefit cuts for the poor), structural unemployment, which resulted from continuous processes of rationalisation and Britain's transformation from a society with a large manufacturing sector into one concentrating on services, as well as demographic change, which put greater strain on the social services, all contributed to the gradual erosion of what, at least for some time, appeared to be a model welfare state. Moreover, the premise of economic growth became increasingly shaky: it was first and foremost connected to a sense of the economy in terms of the British nation, but how much could British politicians influence (let alone control)

Table 7 Share of income by household group, 1977–92

	Bottom 20%	Bottom 40%	Top 40%	Top 20%
1977	4	14	69	43
1979	2	12	70	43
1985	3	10	74	47
1992	2	8	76	50

(Derrick Murphy (ed.), *Britain, 1914–2000*, London: HarperCollins, 2000, p. 352)

international capital and trade flows with their (nationally) restricted tools of economic policy?

Perhaps a fourth factor – the trade unions – also played a role. After the end of the Second World War trade unions had become powerful partners of the employers and the government in the management of the economy. In particular, they enjoyed traditionally very close relations with the Labour party. Usually, the trade unions promised to help prevent inflation by demanding only modest pay rises. In return, the government seriously considered their concerns (with regard to nationalisation, benefits, etc.). By the 1970s, however, the trade unions had become so strong – membership peaked in 1979 with some 13.5 million, which was about 50 per cent of the workforce – that, as early as 1974, the then Conservative prime minister, Edward Heath, called an election on the question 'Who governs Britain?' As it was, a Labour minority government was returned. Eventually, the trade unions were instrumental in its downfall after the 'winter of discontent' (1979) without realising how fragile was the premise of growth on which they had built their demands. Margaret Thatcher's governments, step by step, introduced legislation which eventually removed most of the rights the unions had gained throughout the century. Most important, they were now liable for damages resulting from illegal industrial action, and the definition of legal industrial action became progressively limited. For example, they were no longer immune from legal action if they called a strike without holding a secret ballot, the 'closed shop' (which required union membership if a worker wanted to work in a certain factory) was abolished, and picketing was severely limited. The concomitant decline of the manufacturing sector and growing unemployment also weakened the unions. By 1997 membership had fallen to 6.7 million (where it had been in 1940). Thatcher's policy limited the power of one factor in the race for economic growth, but it did not tackle the root of the problem.

The Second World War was also the crucially important catalyst for postwar immigration because it brought colonial servicemen from Honduras and the West Indies to Britain, of whom a substantial number preferred to remain there after the war ended. These people were easily absorbed by the labour-hungry centres of British manufacture which, at that time, swung from wartime to peacetime production, leading into the boom of the mid-1950s. The ex-servicemen were followed by people from regions in which migration for work was an established tradition. Again, the West Indies took the lead. Other so-called New Commonwealth immigrants, particularly from India, Pakistan and Bangladesh, followed. They all came to Britain in search of work, a higher standard of living and better prospects for their children. In particular, they found work in those sectors of the economy which – because of low pay, long hours and shift work – were unattractive for British workers. These immigrants were a 'replacement labour force' which became an extra labour reserve as soon as the boom was over.

The history of immigration has been punctuated by discussions of how to let 'desirable' people (of 'good human stock') in and keep others out. The legal right of the vast majority of British subjects in the colonies and dominions to enter and settle in Britain was retained by the British Nationality Act of 1948. The period of initial settlement was characterised by 'a muted optimism' (Stuart Hall): the black immigrants maintained a low profile, strove to adjust to unfamiliar conditions and were hardly regarded as serious competitors demanding access to economically, socially and culturally vital resources. It has been estimated that by 1953 about 40,000 non-white people were living in Britain. By that time, however, an intense debate was already taking place about their effects on British society as a whole. The race riots of 1958, which were triggered by racially motivated attacks of white people on black people, were to become the watershed: the moment for the state to curb black immigration had come. Three successive immigration acts (1962, 1968, 1971) steadily restricted the immigration of black people into Britain, while a racially charged public debate raged in the country. In the general election of 1964, the Conservative candidate Peter Griffith captured the seat of Smethwick by condoning the slogan 'If you want a nigger neighbour, vote Labour.' In 1968, Enoch Powell, who, paradoxically, as a member of the Conservative government in the 1950s had recruited immigrant labourers, stoked the flames by saying: 'As I look ahead I am filled with foreboding. Like the Roman, I seem to see "the River Tiber foaming with much blood!"' That tragic and intractable phenomenon which we watch with horror on the other side of the Atlantic but which there is interwoven with the history and existence of the States itself, is coming upon us here by our own volition and our own neglect.' Later in the same year, he even advocated repatriation: 'The West Indian or Indian does not, by being born in England, become an Englishman. In law he becomes a United Kingdom citizen by birth; in fact he is a West Indian or Asian still.' During the 1970s the National Front, a right-wing and racist political party, could attract some 12,000 members. In the general election of 1979, it fielded some 300 candidates but did not win a single seat. Despite three Race Relations Acts (1965, 1968, 1976), which aimed at curbing racial discrimination, and the establishing of a Commission for Racial Equality as an enforcement agency (with powers to assist individual complainants and mount formal investigations), the Scarman report (1981) into the race riots in 1980 and 1981 demonstrated the alienation of the black community from the British mainstream, and the MacPherson report (1999) concluded that the police investigation into the death of eighteen-year-old Stephen Lawrence (which occurred in 1993) 'was marred by a combination of professional incompetence, institutional racism and a failure of leadership by senior officers'.

Despite the fact that, since they arrived, the majority of Britain's non-white population have been discriminated against in all spheres of life (income, employment, housing, education, health, social services and the law), despite the fact that, at the end of the 1990s, 10 per cent of London's non-white households suffered racial harassment, and despite the fact that 33 per cent of them felt threatened by racism, they have succeeded not only in constructing their particular identity as, first, Black British and, later, Black and Asian British, but also in slowly but distinctly transforming British society, which had been predominantly white and mono-cultural, into a society which now is 'beyond black and white' and distinctly multi-cultural.

Culture

Around 1900, with the arrival of near-complete literacy of the British population (cf. Chapter 6), the age of mass communication began. While hitherto newspapers had been the daily fare of educated people, around the turn of the century three cheap daily papers, which specifically aimed at a mass readership, were launched: the *Daily Mail* (1896), the *Daily Express* (1900) and the *Daily Mirror* (1904). In the eyes of the political elite, these papers were suitable means of influencing or, perhaps more amicably expressed, 'educating' the recently (and, in future, to be) enfranchised masses in the art of politics. Most of these papers followed a conservative – and in wartime a strictly patriotic – line. Some 10 million newspapers were sold daily in 1937. Since 1945 newspapers have changed beyond recognition. Expanded coverage of ever more diverse subjects, steadily increasing numbers of pages, more sophisticated layouts (including colour photography) and, most recently, different sizes of the same paper have all played their part in maintaining the presence of national (as well as local) newspapers, which have had to face severe competitive pressure from the radio (or wireless) since the 1920s, television since the 1950s and new means of information such as the Internet since the 1990s.

In 1922 the British Broadcasting Company was created; four years later the government assumed responsibility for the British Broadcasting Corporation (BBC). Its first director-general, John Reith, regarded the radio as a force for good. Instead of giving the people what they thought they wanted he intended to counter the influence of American mass culture and, more generally, to encourage cultural self-improvement. Although this message had its critics, by

1935 98 per cent of the population enjoyed access to radio. Three years previously broadcasting to the Empire had begun. With the impending threat of war, foreign-language broadcasting started in 1938; six years later, the BBC broadcast in 44 languages. The BBC's radio monopoly continued until the 1960s, when a number of pirate radio stations began to provide alternative programmes (mainly broadcasting popular music). This led, first, to a reorganisation (1968) which created BBC 1, 2, 3 and 4 catering for a wider range of tastes and, second, to an end of the BBC's monopoly and the introduction of commercial radio stations.

Undoubtedly, television has had the greatest impact of all mass media on British society. Although television broadcasts began as early as 1936, their real influence could be felt from the 1950s onward. In order to be allowed to watch 'the box', one had (as one still has) to pay a licence fee which was used to finance the programmes, the personnel and the technology. In 1947, 15,000 television licences were granted; in 1960, the figure was some 10.5 million; in 1985, 18.7 million. The BBC's television monopoly was ended in 1954; and, in 1955, Independent Television (ITV), the first commercial channel (i.e. funded by advertising), was launched. Further terrestrial channels were created in 1964 (BBC 2), 1982 (Channel 4) and 1997 (Channel 5), the last two also being commercial channels. The big challenge to public service broadcasting (BBC) and to the commercial terrestrial channels came with the introduction of satellite and cable television. By the end of the millennium the British could watch more than a hundred television channels – which questions not only the financing (and, implicitly, the survival) of public service broadcasting, but also the quality of broadcasting as a whole.

From the 1920s to the 1950s going to the cinema was one of the best-liked leisure activities of the British. During the Second World War cinema attendance rose steadily from 19 million in 1939 to 30 million in 1945. It peaked in 1955 with 1.2 billion admissions, then – owing to the spread of television – it fell to 510 million in 1960, 190 million in 1970, and 67 million in 1987. By the end of the century, however, cinema audiences were rising again.

Media historians and critics have pointed out that, until the 1970s, the media constituted a socially, culturally and intellectually unifying force. The limited number of channels ensured that people watched or listened to more or less the same programmes. Nowadays the programmes are more diversified, the element of choice is much stronger, and the audience is more divided. While this is certainly advantageous for the individual customer, whose demands are met, and the institution (private enterprise or public service), which supplies (and profits from) the goods, it remains to be seen what it does to the cultural processes by which we make sense of our lives.

EMPIRE, COMMONWEALTH AND DECOLONISATION

The dominions

In the administration of the Empire, Britain tried to avoid a repetition of the North American experience of 1776–83. In particular, the white settler colonies, which earned the epithet 'white' because they were occupied by white European settlers (cf. Chapter 6), were soon turned into self-governing colonies with an elected legislature whose way of parliamentary accountability imitated the Westminster model. In a next step, these self-governing colonies were transformed into dominions, i.e. wholly self-governing states within the British Empire and, later, the British Commonwealth. The first to achieve dominion status was Canada (1867). (One reason to choose the term 'dominion' was to pacify American critics who railed against the possibility of a 'kingdom' on the North American continent.) Canada was followed by Australia (1900), New Zealand (1907), South Africa (1910) and the Irish Free State (1922). Furthermore, beginning in 1887, on the occasion of Queen Victoria's golden jubilee, the British and colonial prime ministers of these colonies or, later, dominions began holding so-called 'colonial conferences' in which matters of mutual interest (as, for example, defence and trade) were discussed. They met again in 1894, 1897, 1902 and 1907. One of their most enduring topics was 'imperial preference', i.e. the idea of how to transform Britain and the dominions into a 'common market', protected from foreign competition by high tariffs. But neither the British nor the colonial governments were of one mind on this question, as there were also many advocates of free trade. From 1911 onwards, these conferences were termed 'imperial conferences' (1921, 1923, 1926, 1930 and 1937). In 1926 the dominions' desire for greater self-determination (particularly in foreign affairs), which had already become plain during and after the First World War, was intensely discussed and eventually led to the following definition of the relationship between Great Britain and the dominions: 'They are autonomous communities within the British Empire, equal in status, in no way subordinate one to another in any aspect of their domestic or external affairs, though united by a common allegiance to the Crown, and freely associated as members of the British Commonwealth of Nations.' This definition, formulated by the former prime minister A. J. Balfour, was anything but revolutionary; it simply recognised current political realities. While phrases such as 'autonomous' and 'in no way subordinate' could satisfy the republican sentiments of South Africa and the Irish Free State, the 'common allegiance to the Crown' reassured loyalist minds. In the Statute of Westminster (1931), which granted legislative independence to the dominion parliaments, the definition was legally recognised (Document 45). Henceforth, a law passed by a dominion parliament would not become invalid because it contradicted British law, nor could the British parliament legislate on behalf of a dominion. Moreover, it should be noted that the definition used the formula 'British Commonwealth of Nations' instead of British Empire. Clearly, the idea of the 'commonwealth', first floated in the imperial context by A. J. Balfour in 1882, indicated a political shift from conquest and occupation to cooperation and common purpose. Equally clearly, it was aimed at the white settler colonies only.

After the 1929 Wall Street Crash and the onset of the Depression the British government finally abandoned free trade and adopted imperial preference; in the following year this was extended to the dominions. Economically, these measures were an unqualified success; Britain's trade with the colonies increased substantially during the 1930s. However, during the Second World War, Britain lost many of its overseas markets, and when it negotiated for membership of the European Economic Community in the 1960s the system of imperial preference became an acute hindrance. India, although it had not achieved self-government, was allowed to join the British Commonwealth in 1935. In 1944 the conferences were renamed 'Commonwealth conferences'; in 1949 the 'British Commonwealth of Nations' became simply the 'Commonwealth of Nations'. At the same time, the term 'dominion' was tacitly phased out. Perhaps it had all along – despite Britain's disavowals – implied a certain subordination which was no longer acceptable. Today the Commonwealth consists of fifty-three member states, all of which – with the exception of Mozambique – were once British colonies. All members recognise the British monarch as head of the Commonwealth, but only sixteen recognise the monarch as head of their state. Moreover, the majority of member states are republics. This loose federation does not wield much political power (although it suspended member states which grossly violated human rights such as South Africa, Nigeria and, most recently, Zimbabwe), but its cultural rather than political links have proved to be sustainable.

India

While Great Britain was content to accept the white dominions as (almost) equal partners in trade and the defence of the Empire, the relationship between the mother country and its non-white colonies followed a different kind of logic. Formal empire rested on the premise that British or British-led troops kept an enforced peace, colonial agents administered the colony, and local collaborators mobilised and directed the required goods (raw materials, cash crops, mineral resources) towards the imperial merchants and traders. Needless to say, these attempts at exploitation were very often resisted by the indigenous people(s), who formed nationalist movements which aimed at liberating the countries. The first non-white colony to fight successfully for its independence was Britain's 'jewel in the crown': India. The conflict was correspondingly long, intense and brutal. After the uprising (1857–8) India was administered from London by the secretary of state for India through the India Office, but control was predominantly exercised by the viceroy (i.e. the monarch's representative) and the Indian civil service. In 1885 the Indian National Congress was founded, but it was split between a majority of moderates, who wanted to work within the system of British rule, and a minority of more radical forces, who wanted to oust the British by any means possible. This split alienated a second minority, the Muslims, who formed the Muslim League in 1906. Both organisations demanded, first, participation in the governing of the country and, then, from the 1910s onwards, complete independence. Two acts in 1909 (Morley–Minto

---

Mohandas Karamchand 'Mahatma' Gandhi (1869–1948)

Mohandas Karamchand Gandhi was born into a Hindu family in Porbandar, Gujarat, India, in 1869. He studied at the University of Bombay from 1887, and went to University College (London) to train as a barrister in 1888. After having been admitted to the Bar (i.e. the legal profession), he returned to Bombay to practise as a lawyer. As the legal profession in India was overcrowded, he accepted a post with a firm in Natal, South Africa (1893). Although his contract was for one year only, he stayed until 1914. Through personal experiences and his contacts with fellow Indians he was alerted to the racial discrimination and political suppression of Indians (and Africans) in the country. He founded the Natal Indian Congress in 1894 and continued fighting against Indian grievances and evidence of British discrimination. On his return to India he became involved in India's fight for independence, becoming one of the most enterprising leaders of Congress after the First World War.

Three ideas (or concepts) are indelibly connected with Gandhi's politics: *satyagraha*, *swaraj* and *swadeshi*. With *satyagraha* (translated as 'devotion to truth' or 'truth force') Gandhi invented a technique of resisting the adversary and redressing wrongs by civil disobedience or non-violent non-cooperation. If the world followed the motto of 'an eye for an eye', Gandhi contended, it would become blind. If, however, it empowered 'truth', it would be stronger than if it possessed weapons of mass destruction. By these means *swaraj* (i.e. 'self-rule' or 'self-government') was to be attained. *Swadeshi* (translated as 'self-reliance') was Gandhi's form of insisting on economic and spiritual autonomy. Gandhi urged the Indians to boycott imported goods (and ideas) and develop indigenous products.

Gandhi had great influence among the Hindu and Muslim communities of India. When independence implied partition of the country, Gandhi deeply deplored (but could not prevent) it. On 30 January 1948, on his way to a prayer meeting, he was assassinated by a Hindu radical.

Often 'Mahatma' is mistaken for Gandhi's given name. However, the meaning of *mahatma* is 'great soul'. This deferential name was accorded to Gandhi in 1915 by his admirer Rabindranath Tagore (the first Indian writer to win the Nobel Prize for Literature). Gandhi is reported never to have accepted this honour because he found himself unworthy of it.

reforms) and 1919 (Montagu–Chelmsford reforms) gave Indians a majority on the provincial councils and created Indian ministers (in public health, education, agriculture) in the all-Indian government, but these reforms were regarded as inadequate by nationalists. The terrible Amritsar massacre of unarmed civilian demonstrators (1919) hardened feelings between the Indians and their colonisers.

The British found themselves in a quandary: in order to profit from their colony (by extracting resources) they had to establish a kind of centralised rule which, however, had to be, at least in part, devolved to the colonised in order to ensure collaboration. The more the British wanted to profit from their rule, the more they had to hand over their power. And the more power the collaborators gained, the harder it became for the British to secure their profit. After a long struggle, famously inspired by Gandhi's ideas, the 1935 Government of India Act gave control of the eleven autonomous provinces to the Indians, while the viceroy retained control of defence and foreign affairs. The Second World War evoked a divided response from India: while regular Indian troops fought with the Allies, some radicals tried to form a pro-Japanese army. In 1942, in order to ensure Indian support of the war effort, Britain offered India full dominion status. This was derided as too little, too late. Although the ensuing 'Quit India' movement led to mass arrests of Gandhi and other nationalist leaders, it was eventually successful. Britain's position in India, which had been built up over 300 years, was abandoned within months (Documents 46 and 47). But the irreconcilable differences between Hindus and Muslims made a partition of the country (into Hinduist India and Muslim West and East Pakistan, later Pakistan and Bangladesh) inevitable. When independence came on 14 August 1947 it was greeted with mass celebrations and mass rioting. Hindus fleeing from Pakistan to India and Muslims fleeing from India to Pakistan were massacred by their fellow Indians; between 250,000 and 600,000 people died in the tumult.

The Middle East and the Suez crisis

The First World War dealt the deathblow to the Ottoman Empire. Britain, which had taken large areas in the Middle East during the war, was mandated by the League of Nations to administer Palestine, Trans-Jordan and Iraq (1920). In 1917, perhaps in order to secure Jewish support in the United States for America's entry into the war, the then British foreign minister, A. J. Balfour, wrote a letter to Lord Rothschild, a leading figure among British Jews, in which he declared:

> His Majesty's Government view with favour the establishment in Palestine of a national home for the Jewish people, and will use their best endeavours to facilitate the achievement of this object, it being clearly understood that nothing shall be done which may prejudice the civil and religious rights of

existing non-Jewish communities in Palestine, or the rights and political status enjoyed by Jews in any other country.

The terms of this declaration were incorporated into the mandate. But the British had made similar promises to Arabs about an independent homeland. When Jewish immigration increased in the interwar years (comprising a third of Palestine's population in the late 1930s), initial Arab hostility turned into open rebellion. Suggestions to partition Palestine into separate Jewish and Arab states (made by the British in 1937 and the United Nations in 1947) were regarded as unacceptable. When the conflict escalated after the Second World War, British authority collapsed and the British government returned the mandate to the UN (1947). On 14 May 1948 the state of Israel was established. The conflict between Israelis and Palestinians has continued to the present time. As the British foreign secretary, Jack Straw, said in an interview with the *New Statesman* in November 2002, 'there's a lot wrong with imperialism. A lot of the problems . . . I have to deal with now, are a consequence of our colonial past. . . . The odd lines for Iraq's borders were drawn by Brits. The Balfour declaration and the contradictory assurances which were being given to Palestinians in private at the same time as they were being given to the Israelis . . . an interesting history for us but not an entirely honourable one.'

In 1922, Egypt's independence was recognised, but Britain kept military forces there until the mid-1930s and in the Suez Canal zone until June 1956. In 1930, Iraq attained full independence on condition that it agreed to a twenty-five-year military alliance. In this way, Britain hoped to secure its access to the Suez Canal and, through it, to the Arab oilfields and, beyond, to India and South-East Asia. The Suez Canal Convention, signed in 1888, stated that the Canal Company (largely controlled by its biggest single shareholder, the British government) was to enjoy financial privileges in the use of the Canal until 1968. However, in July 1956, President Nasser of Egypt nationalised the Canal Company, claiming that he wanted to collect tolls from passing ships to finance the Aswan High Dam. (Historians believe that he previously tried to obtain financial backing for this project from Britain and the United States which, however, was denied because Egypt had made an arms deal with the Soviet Union.) Britain and France thought of immediate retaliation, but were obliged by international pressure to negotiate. When these talks came to nothing, in October 1956, Britain, France and Israel hatched a secret plan to bring down the Egyptian government by force. Israel was to attack Egypt, and Britain and France would then come to 'mediate' in the conflict, thereby regaining control of the Canal. Israel invaded Egypt on 29 October, the Anglo-French force landed on 5 November. The next day, an international uproar occurred. The Commonwealth did not support Britain; India supported Egypt; the United Nations condemned the invasion and demanded an immediate ceasefire by 64 votes to 5. Most important, the United States, which had not been consulted, severely opposed the operation. This combined opposition had repercussions in the economic sphere: the value of sterling collapsed, and Britain was denied a loan from the International Monetary Fund. By midnight of the very same day, Britain and France had to halt their operations, to accept an unconditional withdrawal (on 30 November) and agree to be replaced by an international UN force in the region.

The outcome of the Suez crisis was humiliating for the British government and its prime minister, Anthony Eden, who resigned in January 1957. But, most crucially, the crisis forced Britain to accept that there was an end to independent action in foreign affairs. From now on it would have to seek the approval and support of its major ally, the United States. In the postwar world the United States and the Soviet Union were the two superpowers, and Britain had clearly been relegated to a second-power status. Wider repercussions in the Empire, i.e. a strengthening of nationalist movements and further demands for independence, were to be expected.

Africa, the Caribbean, the Falklands and Hong Kong

In 1910 the Cape Colony, Natal, the Orange River Colony and the Transvaal had formed the Union of South Africa and been given dominion status. When Eden's successor, Harold Macmillan, attended the celebrations on the occasion of the 'golden wedding of the Union' (in 1960) he gave a speech that did not please his hosts.

> In the twentieth century, and especially since the end of the war, the processes which gave birth to the nation states of Europe have been repeated all over the world. We have seen the awakening of national consciousness in peoples who have for centuries lived in dependence upon some other power. Fifteen years ago this movement spread through Asia. Many countries there, of different races and civilisations, pressed their claim to an independent national life.
>
> Today the same thing is happening in Africa, and the most striking of all the impressions I have formed since I left London a month ago is of the strength of this African national consciousness. In different places it takes different forms, but it is happening everywhere.
>
> The wind of change is blowing through this continent and, whether you like it or not, this growth of national consciousness is a political fact. We must all accept it as a fact, and our national policies must take account of it.

The South African government did not take heed but introduced strict racial segregation (apartheid). Six weeks after Macmillan's speech, sixty-nine unarmed protesters were killed and many more wounded in the 'Sharpeville massacre'. In the following year South Africa became a republic and left the

Commonwealth. It needed the struggle of a whole generation to establish South Africa's first freely elected black president, Nelson Mandela, in office (1994). But Macmillan's words had signalled the British government's intention to grant independence to its African colonies if they so wished. Of course, there was more to it than pure goodwill. The government's endeavours were speeded up by the domestic situation: racism and pressure for restrictions on immigration in Britain devalued Empire citizenship and Commonwealth membership. A new attitude towards the colonies was needed. Most of those in Africa became independent between 1959 and 1964 (Ghana had achieved independence already in 1957), and they all joined the Commonwealth. The white government of Southern Rhodesia (which had become a self-governing colony in 1922 but had not been given dominion status) issued a unilateral declaration of independence (1965). The British government did not accept it and imposed sanctions against Rhodesia which, however, were ineffective. Meanwhile the Africans had formed two political organisations which fought to liberate the country. Eventually, in 1979, a peace could be negotiated which led to multiparty democratic elections (1980) in Zimbabwe, as the now independent state was named.

In the 1960s and 1970s, most of Britain's colonies in the Caribbean also became independent. In 1982 a dispute over the Falkland Islands, a British colony in the south Atlantic, made the British government go to war against Argentina. So far this has been Britain's last colonial war, which strengthened Margaret Thatcher's flagging government and remained unopposed by the opposition, while it was greeted with nostalgia by the public and jingoism by the tabloids. These reactions surprised many contemporary observers (including myself), but perhaps they – once more – demonstrated the truth in Dean Acheson's statement of 1962: 'Great Britain has lost an empire and has not yet found a role.' There was (and still is) more to this statement than that Britain has had to find its place as a second-rate power in contemporary world politics. It also implies (although Acheson did not elaborate this point) that the process of decolonisation concerns not only the colonies but also the metropolis: the coloniser needs to be decolonised as well, and this process goes deeper and is more complex than the severing of political ties. Perhaps the reaction can, at least in part, be explained by the fact that the British could regard themselves as the victims of an act of aggression, which usually and easily suggests retaliation. The handing over of Hong Kong (1997) may not have been easy, either, because it meant, in effect, to hand over a capitalist colony to a communist country, but this transfer had been on the cards since the ninety-nine-year lease had been signed in 1898 and was arrived at by negotiation.

There are still a few remnants of the Empire: (i) overseas territories possessing substantial self-government (Anguilla, Bermuda, British Virgin Islands, Cayman Islands, Gibraltar, Montserrat and Turks and Caicos Islands – all of which, except Gibraltar, are in the Caribbean, and some of them provide services as tax oases); (ii) other overseas territories, most of which have been important for geopolitical reasons (British Antarctic Territory, British Indian Ocean Territory [leased to the United States as a military base], Falkland Islands, Pitcairn Island, St Helena, including Ascension and Tristan da Cunha, South Georgia and the South Sandwich Islands as well as the sovereign base areas of Akrotiri and Dhekelia [Cyprus]); and (iii) the Crown Dependencies Guernsey, Jersey and the Isle of Man.

DEVOLUTION

Ireland

British–Irish or Irish–British relations have, most probably, been the most dominant and most serious political problem within the British Isles in the twentieth century, in particular between 1914 and 1922 and since 1969. Home Rule was enacted in 1914, but its implementation was suspended until after the First World War. Moreover, while the Home Rule Bill was being debated in Parliament, a crisis occurred over Ulster because in the north-east of Ireland a Protestant majority opposed Home Rule. In 1912 some 100,000 Unionists formed the Ulster Volunteer Force (UVF) to fight against Home Rule if necessary. A year later, some 200,000 Nationalists formed the Irish Volunteers to defend Home Rule. At the beginning of the First World War, Ireland was on the brink of civil war. Although contingents of both groups joined the British Army in the First World War, the UVF were privileged over the Irish Volunteers. More important, when the Home Rule Act was passed, the prime minister, H. H. Asquith, promised to find ways and means to exclude the six north-eastern counties from the operation (at least for some time). Finally, in 1915 a coalition government was formed and Edward Carson, a leading Irish Unionist opponent of Home Rule, joined the Cabinet. Many Irish were frustrated about the delay and the clear attempts of the government not to stand by its word. In April 1916 a combination of various nationalist groups (Irish Republican Brotherhood, Irish Citizen Army and Irish Volunteers) staged a rising in Dublin ('Easter Rising') which, however, was badly prepared and was easily crushed by the British garrison. Sixteen leaders were executed and became martyrs for the nationalist cause. Lloyd George, prime minister since 1916, tried to find a solution by calling an Irish Convention to which all political groups were invited. It met in 1917 and 1918, but the Republicans boycotted it and the Unionists opposed any form of Home Rule. The 1918 election was to become a turning point in British–Irish relations. Sinn Fein won 73 out of 106 seats in Ireland. Moreover, instead of going to Westminster, they set up their own parliament – Dáil Eireann – in Dublin and attempted to create an independent state.

The British government responded by repression; the Republicans fought a

Political parties in the Republic of Ireland (Eire)

- **Fianna Fail**
  Founded in 1926 by Eamon de Valera (1882–1975), became the governing (and largest) party in 1932, favours the independence of the whole of Ireland.
- **Fine Gael**
  Founded in 1933, is slightly more pro-British than Fianna Fail.

Political parties in Northern Ireland
- **Ulster Unionist Party (UUP)**
  Founded in 1921, main party since then; moderately Protestant, wants to maintain union with Britain.
- **Democratic Unionist Party (DUP)**
  Founded in 1971 by Ian Paisley, radically unionist, opposed to any negotiations which involve the Republic of Ireland.
- **Social Democratic and Labour Party (SDLP)**
  Founded in 1970 by Gerry Fitt, moderately Catholic, originates from the Civil Rights movement, and favours consensual reunification of Ireland.
- **Sinn Fein**
  Founded in 1906 by Arthur Griffith ('Irish Republicans'), associated with the demand for Irish independence after 1916, radically Catholic, represents today the Republican movement in Northern Ireland.

Paramilitary groups in Northern Ireland since 1969
- **Provisional Irish Republican Army (IRA)**
  Split from the Official IRA in 1970, fought an armed guerrilla struggle for a united Irish republic, agreed to diverse ceasefires since 1994, to decommission its paramilitaries in 1999 and to scrap its weapons in 2005.
- **Irish National Liberation Army**
  Radical splinter group, which split from the Provisional IRA in 1975.
- **Real IRA**
  Another radical splinter group, which split from the Provisional IRA in 1997.
- **Ulster Defence Association (UDA)**
  Formed in 1972, legal until 1992, loyalist group engaged in sectarian killings of Catholics.
- **Ulster Volunteer Force (UVF)**
  Formed in 1912 to oppose Home Rule, today engaged in sectarian killings of Catholics.

Northern Ireland terminology
- **Nationalists**, moderate or extremist, want to see and bring about a united Ireland.
- **Republicans** are extremely militant nationalists.
- **Catholics** are mostly nationalist.
- **Protestants** are mostly unionist.
- **Unionists**, moderate or extremist, want Northern Ireland to remain part of the United Kingdom.
- **Loyalists** are extremely militant unionists.

guerrilla war against the Royal Irish Constabulary and the British Army. To contain the conflict the government tried two complementary strategies: to defeat the Irish Republican Army by military means and to establish two Home Rule governments in Ireland (Government of Ireland Act, 1920), one for the six counties in the north-east, the other for the rest of the island. The Irish Unionists did not like the Act but, realising that a unified Ireland could no longer be

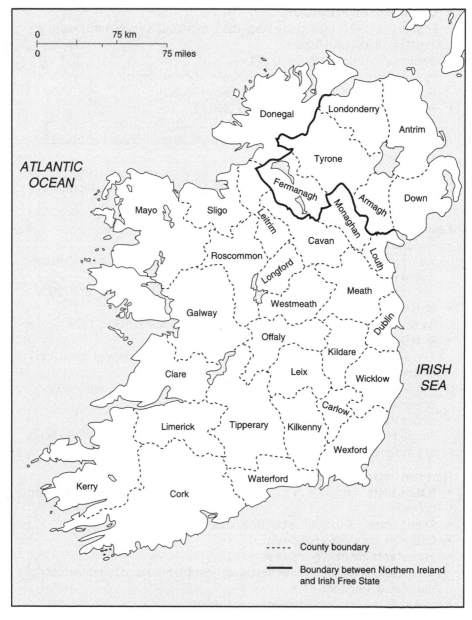

Map 11 The partition of Ireland, 1922

had within the United Kingdom, they accepted Home Rule for Northern Ireland (with the seat of government at Stormont, Belfast); in contrast, Sinn Fein refused to accept the Act. In 1921 the London government changed its policy. Later in the same year, the Anglo-Irish Treaty was negotiated which allowed the twenty-six southern counties to form a self-governing state outside the United Kingdom which, however, was to remain as a dominion within the British Empire. Since 1922, Irish history has run on two different tracks.

Developments within the Empire favoured the Irish Free State's interest in greatest possible independence from the United Kingdom. At the Imperial Conference in 1926, the status of a dominion was agreed upon, and by the Statute of Westminster (1931) the dominions were made autonomous states within the British Commonwealth. When Eamon de Valera became prime minister of the Irish Free State, he began to sever the remaining political links with the United Kingdom and the Commonwealth. He abolished the oath of allegiance for MPs, reduced the position of the governor-general (the monarch's representative) and, in 1937, introduced a new constitution which made Eire (the new name of the state) a 'republic in all but name'. During the Second World War, Eire was the only part of the Empire/Commonwealth which stayed neutral. Even when de Valera was secretly offered the reunification of Ireland if Eire entered the war on the Allied side, he refused. (He may have had good reasons to doubt Churchill's will to honour such an agreement, as the Northern Irish had not been consulted.) After the war, in 1949, Eire became a republic and left the Commonwealth.

In the same year the House of Commons passed the Ireland Act under which, on the one hand, Irish citizens retained considerable rights in the United Kingdom while, on the other, a change of the constitutional position of Northern Ireland was made dependent on the consent of the Northern Irish people. As the Unionists had a clear majority (some two-thirds of the population), this constituted the 'Unionist veto'. As a consequence, the Ulster Unionist Party (UUP) held power continuously from 1921 to 1972, changing the rules of the game (by, for example, gerrymandering, i.e. the redrawing of electoral boundaries) wherever and whenever they could to maintain their majority. The Nationalists rightly felt discriminated against not only in politics – in 1929, for example, proportional representation was replaced by the 'first-past-the-post' system, which disadvantaged them – but also in employment and housing. The Royal Ulster Constabulary (RUC) and the part-time 'B' Specials used their powers to harass the Catholic communities, while successive British governments were apparently indifferent to Irish Nationalism.

Although violence and discrimination must not be condoned, one should at least list some of the Unionist arguments against Irish unification. First, the Unionists feared being forced into a unified Ireland which they did not want. In the 1937 constitution, Eire claimed Northern Ireland as part of its national territory. Second, they argued that because of its historical development (cf.

Chapter 4) Northern Ireland rightly regarded itself as closer to Scotland, north Wales and the north of England than to the rest of Ireland. (In post-Roman times, for example, Christian Irish culture had expanded across the Irish Sea into parts of Wales, Scotland and northern England, and in the post-Viking Middle Ages today's distinction between Ulster and south-west Scotland had not existed because the channel dividing the two areas served as a unifying element for the seafaring society which occupied the coasts of these parts of the British Isles. The systematic 'plantations' of the seventeenth century made this link nigh on unbreakable.) Finally, there were also very mundane fears – loss of privilege, loss of a high(er) standard of living, domination by an 'alien' faith – which fuelled Unionist resistance. All of these fears and arguments do not justify violence and discrimination but they have to be taken into account if a successful solution of the problem is to be arrived at.

By the 1960s, Nationalist/Catholic resentment led to the creation of the Northern Ireland Civil Rights Association (NICRA), which was inspired by the North American civil rights movement. Initially peaceful demonstrations were opposed by the Northern Ireland government and seriously disrupted by various Unionist organisations (most prominently by the Orange Order, which was originally formed in 1795 as a secret society to maintain the Protestant ascendancy in Ireland and to prevent Catholic emancipation). Mounting sectarian violence was the result. (The class aspect of this civil war – the prosperous Unionists versus the needy Nationalists – has often been seriously neglected.) In 1969 the Northern Ireland government felt unable to maintain peace. On 15 August, British troops arrived in a 'peace-keeping role'. Unfortunately, the Army did not live up to this message. With Stormont continuing its Unionist policy, the British troops appeared as its defenders. The Irish Republican Army split, and the Provisional IRA began an 'armed defence' of the Catholics. Over the next two years political violence escalated. On 30 January 1972 an illegal (but peaceful) civil rights march in Londonderry was stopped by the Royal Ulster Constabulary and the Army; fourteen marchers were killed. Six weeks later, Stormont was suspended and direct rule from Westminster was introduced. The next quarter of the century saw repeated attempts by moderate politicians to furnish talks or negotiations between the contending groups, but progress was extremely slow. In 1973 the Sunningdale Agreement wanted to replace direct rule by power-sharing and to involve Eire in the peace process by creating a Council of Ireland. It was opposed by the paramilitary groups on both sides. In 1985 the British and Irish governments concluded the Anglo-Irish Agreement which formally involved the Irish government in Northern Ireland affairs for the first time. When the Irish government conceded that the political status of Northern Ireland could only be changed by the consent of the majority, it officially recognised Northern Ireland's existence and implicitly 'corrected' those parts of its 1937 constitution which regarded the six northern counties as part of Eire's national territory. Still, political violence continued. In

1993 the Irish and British governments issued the Downing Street Declaration, which made clear that Britain no longer had any strategic or economic interest in Northern Ireland. The declaration stressed 'the right of the people on both parts of the island to exercise the right of self-determination on the basis of consent . . . to bring about a united Ireland'. In August 1994 the IRA declared a ceasefire. Peace did not follow because the IRA refused to decommission (destroy) their weapons; the IRA declared an end to the ceasefire in February 1996. In 1997, after the landslide victory of Labour, the IRA announced a second ceasefire. With the help of US senator George Mitchell the Good Friday (or Belfast) Agreement was reached on 10 April 1998. It created a Northern Ireland Assembly, a power-sharing executive and a Council of Ireland (involving North and South). The Agreement was approved by the peoples in both parts of Ireland in subsequent referendums. In the 1998 election, the UUP gained 28 seats, the SDLP 24, the DUP 20, Sinn Fein 18 and others 15. On 1 July 1998 the Assembly met for the first time, and on 1 December 1999 it had certain powers devolved to it. Since then it has been suspended and restored again and again, for shorter and longer terms. In 2003 the UUP gained 27 (−1) seats, the SDLP 18 (−6), the DUP 30 (+10) and Sinn Fein 24 (+6). Clearly, the more moderate parties lost seats, while the more radical won more of them. At the time of writing (September 2005) the Assembly is suspended, but the recent declaration of the IRA leadership that it formally ordered 'an end to the armed campaign' and authorised its representative 'to engage with the IICD [Independent International Commission on Decommissioning] to complete the process to verifiably put its arms beyond use' (25 July 2005) gives hope that the Assembly may soon be restored. (It reconvened in May 2006.)

Both the Republic of Ireland and Northern Ireland joined the European Economic Community in 1973, the latter as part of the United Kingdom, the former as an independent state. Since then, Eire's poor economy has profited from European funding and economic incentives to such an extent that in the 1990s it became known as the 'Celtic Tiger' because it had the fastest-growing economy in the European Union.

Scotland

On and off, there had been Scottish voices demanding 'Home Rule' since the Union (1707). When Home Rule for Ireland was on the political agenda, these voices grew louder. In 1885 the London government established a secretaryship for Scotland, which became a full secretaryship of state in 1926. Furthermore, a reorganisation of the Scottish Office (Edinburgh-based departments of the London government) was begun. At the same time, however, the National Party of Scotland was formed to promote self-government. After mergers with a more separatist and a more moderate party, this party became the Scottish National Party (1934). It remained weak until 1967, when it won its first

Westminster seat (in a by-election). In 1974 (October election), eleven Scottish Nationalists were elected to the House of Commons. This change was most probably due to rising unemployment, on the one hand, and the discovery of North Sea oil off the Scottish coast, on the other. The London Labour government, seriously divided over the issue of devolution and hampered by international economic problems as well as increasing violence in Northern Ireland, introduced a badly prepared bill for Scottish devolution to the House of Commons, which became subject to numerous amendments. One stipulated that over 40 per cent of the electorate had to give their approval; a simple majority would not be enough. So, when 51.6 per cent voted 'yes', as a proportion of the electorate this came to only 32.9 per cent (1979). This setback proved to be only temporary: increasing dispute and acrimony between Scotland and the London government quickly revived and strengthened interest in devolution. (Margaret Thatcher had introduced the community charge, popularly known as the 'poll tax', which was universally attacked as socially inequitable, first in Scotland [1989], then in England and Wales [1990].) The Labour party fought the 1997 election on, amongst others, the issue of devolution. When it was returned to office – the Conservatives did not win a single seat in Scotland – a referendum (without quorum) was held in September. This time 74.3 per cent were in favour. Two years later, a Scottish parliament was elected by a mixed system of majority vote and proportional representation. Its being established did not undo the Act of Union (1707), but it was the first step to Scotland's recognition as an equal partner in the United Kingdom. The Scottish parliament's remit is to control the Scottish executive (i.e. the devolved government) and to deal with matters devolved to it by the United Kingdom parliament, such as education, justice, health and agriculture. It also has the power to pass laws, including (limited) tax-varying measures. In the 1999 election Labour gained 56 seats, the Scottish National Party 35, the Liberal Democrats 17, the Conservatives 18, and others 3. Labour and the Liberal Democrats formed the first Scottish executive. Interestingly, the 2003 Scottish election produced a more pluralist parliament with Labour gaining 50 seats (−6), the SNP 27 (−8), the Liberal Democrats 17, the Conservatives 18, the Scottish Green Party 7 (+6), the Scottish Socialist Party 6 (+5), and others 4.

Wales

Nationalist sentiments have always been strong in Wales, although they may not have always expressed themselves in separatist politics but, rather, in cultural difference. The dedicated adherence to the Welsh language, the fostering of Wales's rich literary and musical traditions, and the practice of religious nonconformity are just three examples of this tendency. At the end of the nineteenth and at the beginning of the twentieth century, Welsh nationalist sentiments were associated with Liberalism, but after the Second World War the Labour party became dominant in Wales, while the Welsh National Party (later Plaid Cymru), founded in 1925, was without success until the 1950s. From 1974 onwards it was modestly successful, holding a few seats in every parliament until the end of the century. In 1964 the Labour government established the Welsh Office in Cardiff, and a new secretary of state for Wales was created. The Welsh Language Act (1967) gave equal status to Welsh in official contexts (documents, road signs, etc.). In the 1979 referendum the Welsh overwhelmingly voted against devolution, but in the 1997 referendum they voted for it, albeit by only the narrowest of margins. A Welsh Assembly was elected in 1999 by proportional representation. It can neither pass its own primary legislation nor raise its own taxes, but it may vary laws passed at Westminster. In the election Labour gained 28 seats, Plaid Cymru 17, the Conservatives 9 and the Liberal Democrats 6. In 2003, Labour gained 30 (+2), Plaid Cymru 12 (−5), the Conservatives 11 (+2), the Liberal Democrats 6 and others 1.

It may appear as a paradox that in both nations, Scotland and Wales, the two parties that have consistently stood for devolution (if not for more) incurred losses in the last election. This may be read as either satisfaction with the work of the new representative institutions on the part of the electorate or a sign of the parties' inability to develop perspectives for the future.

England?

Interestingly, devolution has also become a topic in England. This is perhaps because the devolutionary process has not really been extended to England and the English people. England has neither a parliament nor an assembly. Unlike the Scots, the Welsh and the Northern Irish, the English people have no forum of any kind where they can discuss and decide issues which affect them as the people of England. This situation is further complicated by the fact that, through their members of the United Kingdom parliament, the Scots can legislate for England in every possible area of law and governance, whereas no English MP can participate in the making of any legislation in matters reserved to the Scottish parliament – the so-called 'West Lothian Question'. (A reorganisation of the Scottish constituencies, however, resulted in the fact that from the 2005 general election onwards only fifty-nine instead of seventy-two Scottish MPs take their seats in Westminster.) In contrast to Scotland and Wales, the United Kingdom government did not go for a uniform system of devolution in England but responded to the great variety of demands for directly elected regional governments. It created Regional Development Agencies (to promote economic development) and regional chambers made up of members of local authorities to prepare for the introduction of regional assemblies. In July 2004 the government presented a draft bill and policy statement on eight elected regional assemblies to Parliament.

THE BRITISH ISLES IN EUROPE?

The Second World War wreaked havoc on the European continent. But Britain, although it did not escape destruction, was not occupied by the Nazis. Britain was one of the victors, it still had its Empire and Commonwealth, and it regarded itself as one of the key players in postwar Europe. Churchill's wish to 'build a United States of Europe' (1946) signalled not so much a British initiative to be or become part of a European community as the wish to supervise and guide European development from the outside. When France, West Germany, Italy, the Netherlands, Belgium and Luxembourg (i.e. the 'Six') established the European Coal and Steel Community (1951), they began a process which aimed at economic cooperation and (eventually) at political integration. In 1957 the Six signed the Treaty of Rome, setting up the European Economic Community (EEC), an economic customs union which had all duties between the six countries removed by July 1968. Where the Six saw benefits only (economic growth, political stability, cultural rapprochement), Britain was ambivalent at best. In both instances – 1951 and 1957 – the British considered their options and decided that joining was not in their interest. On the one hand, although trade with Europe increased, economic links with the Empire and Commonwealth were still strong. On the other, the EEC's wish to create a political union was not to Britain's taste: British politicians regarded supranational institutions as an unacceptable challenge to national sovereignty. Instead, they formed the rival European Free Trade Association (EFTA) which worked with intergovernmental rather than supranational structures (1960). Another important, albeit not directly related, factor was the outcome of the Suez crisis (1956), which destroyed good feeling between Britain and France: when the former withdrew under American pressure, the latter felt it had been left in the lurch. Britain turned to the United States to enhance its status; France turned to Europe and had its 'revenge' (as the German chancellor, Konrad Adenauer, said at the time). When Britain eventually realised that it could no longer afford to remain outside the EEC – the Six were enjoying economic growth while Britain's growth was distinctly slowing – it had its membership application vetoed twice by the French president, Charles de Gaulle (1963, 1967), who condemned Britain's application as half-hearted because of its continuing allegiance to the Commonwealth and the United States. Britain was eventually allowed to join the European Community (so renamed in 1967) in 1973, but their relationship was no less burdensome and fractious, although a referendum demonstrated that 67 per cent of Britons were in favour of EC membership (1975). From the very beginning, both political parties have used European questions to score in domestic political issues. The EC has continued to grow (nine members in 1973, fifteen in 1995, twenty-five in 2004), but Britain's relationship to the European Union (so renamed in the Treaty of Maastricht, 1992) has remained ambivalent, contentious and anything but productive. Successive prime ministers (Thatcher, Major, Blair) have felt compelled to commit themselves to certain European Union policies in order not to be sidelined by further developments, but they have also used the first chance to adjust, circumvent or renege on what they had agreed to. While Europe may have socially and culturally arrived in Britain, politically it remains alien.

The case of the Republic of Ireland (Eire) is entirely different. A referendum in 1972 showed that the Irish were five to one for membership. Membership (1973) brought huge benefits to Ireland. Farming and industry gained from access to a wider market. A major inflow of funds helped rebuild the country's infrastructure. More important, Ireland's economic recovery made it less dependent on Britain's economy. In January 1999, Eire was in the first group of member states to move towards monetary union by adopting the euro. Since then growth rates, which were outstanding already, have drastically increased.

8 Twenty-first-century perspectives

Historians are no good at predicting future developments – which is why they usually refrain from drawing lessons for the future from the recent (or not so recent) past. But perhaps one should not think so much of 'drawing lessons' as, rather, of discerning and considering different options, of the possibilities as well as the limits of one's choices and of the ways and means of making these choices felt in the political sphere. Moreover, before focusing on pressing problems of the present, it might do good to look at some past accomplishments in order not to lose heart when facing the future. Here are two examples. Since the end of the Second World War, for one, the people of the West – North Americans, Canadians, Australians, New Zealanders and, in particular, West Europeans – have achieved an unprecedented level of economic prosperity and social security. If current tendencies are not deceiving, a similar development can be expected in the East (China, India) over the next half century or so. Second, the number of states which can rightly be called 'democratic' has increased enormously. In 1950 some twenty of the then eighty sovereign nation states in the world were democracies (i.e. 25 per cent); according to the latest count (2004), today there are 192 nation states out of which 117 (i.e. nearly two-thirds) are democracies and 'only' forty-four are dictatorships. Limited as these achievements may be – and some may even argue that some of them took place at the expense of the 'Rest' (i.e. non-Western countries) – they may still encourage us to face the challenges of the future, to look at the options, to make distinct choices and to let our representatives know of them.

In what follows I should like to sketch mainly in the form of questions seven challenges, the handling of which, in my opinion, will be crucial for the future of the British Isles. The first three challenges are global in nature; they cannot be solved on the local, regional or national level but need international cooperation.

(i) How will it be possible to deal with what some people regard as the 'bright' side of globalisation, i.e. the free flow of trade, capital, communications and labour? And how will it be feasible to deal with its 'dark' side, i.e. the endangered ozone layer, the threat of global warming, the horrendous imbalance of wealth and health in the world? Perhaps a 'war on want' or a 'war on sicknesses' may become more important than the current 'war on terror'.

(ii) What are the possibilities (and limits) of keeping peace in a world in which 1 billion (of 6 billion) inhabitants are rich (with an average income of $70 a day), while 1 billion live on less than $1 and another 1–2 billion on less than $2 a day? How is it possible to redistribute the wealth and resources of the world so that the income gap between rich and poor countries decreases instead of increasing? How can we possibly balance economic growth where it is in dire need with, perhaps, no growth where it is dispensable? Or is growth indispensable, as employers and employees unanimously maintain (although they make a big fuss about their share of it)? If growth is regarded as indispensable, what does that mean for our finite resources?

(iii) What roles are imaginable for the new technologies of information (media), registration (biometrics) and transformation (genetic engineering) in this context? What effect will it have that the amount of visual impressions an average person in 1900 had to cope with in his or her lifetime is equal to the amount we have to cope with today in one week? Does the registration of biometric data make us citizens under the eye of Big Brother? If so, do we want this? Why or why not? How can the advantages and possible dangers of genetic engineering be balanced? No doubt, these global challenges need global answers. They cannot be had without a mixture of intergovernmental and supranational institutions which initiate, implement and evaluate the necessary reforms. If these institutions are to function properly, each and every nation state has to relinquish some of its sovereignty. And why not, if it is for the good of humankind?

The next four challenges are inevitably interdependent with the first three, but focus on the British Isles.

(iv) The first question concerns Britain's – not Ireland's – relationship with Europe. At the beginning of this book the geological process is described in which the British Isles were cut off from the Continent some 7000 years ago. Perhaps it is as well to end the book with the wish that, politically speaking, the British Isles as a whole – two states, four nations – may succeed in docking at the Continent again. In this process, the Republic of Ireland has already taken the lead, which may not make it easier for the United Kingdom to follow. But Europe with only a part of the British Isles, politically speaking, 'in' it is incomplete. Being in Europe would provide Britain with the role it has been seeking since the dismantling of its Empire. Of course, Britain is also inextricably intertwined with the United States. But the more friends (or allies) one has, the more one's friendship is desired. Being an active and reliable partner in the European Union would make Britain more (and not less) attractive to the United States. Why not be an ally and interpreter in both directions?

(v) Supranational and international cooperation needs to be balanced by local and regional participation ('think global, act local'). The process of devolution should go on. Perhaps Wales and Scotland could benefit from regional assemblies (strengthening regional identities) within their borders, as England could benefit not only from regional assemblies but also from a parliament of its own (which need not sit in London). These processes of participatory administration could make political processes more transparent and thereby accessible to the people; they would also make greater demands on the accountability of their representatives. Lest it be forgotten: devolution must not preclude the creation of bigger political entities; the people of both parts of the Irish island should be able to unite if they so wish.

(vi) While some people fear that an intensification of the devolutionary process may lead to the 'break-up' of Britain, others dread that increasing numbers of immigrants will threaten the social cohesion of its population. A recent report from the Institute of Public Policy Research, *Beyond Black and White: Mapping New Immigrant Communities* (2005), shows that the percentage of foreign-born people living in Britain rose from 4.55 per cent (1971) to 5.14 per cent (1981) to 5.75 per cent (1991) and to 7.53 per cent (2001). Between 1991 and 2001, Britain's population increased by 2.2 million; roughly half of them were immigrants. If we look at the various communities of British residents born abroad, we find that the largest consists of nearly half a million people from the Irish Republic (although the figure fell by 100,000 from 1991), followed by 466,416 people from India, 320,767 from Pakistan, 262,276 from Germany (including the offspring of British service personnel in Germany), 254,740 from the Caribbean and 155,030 from the United States. Perhaps more important, over the decade from 1991 to 2001 a sharp rise in European migrants – from Albania, Finland, Greece, Sweden and the former Yugoslavia – occurred. Besides creating permanently peaceful and prosperous communities out of this diverse mix of people, there are at least three challenges in this development which need to be taken up. First, as always, these immigrants are unevenly distributed across the United Kingdom: 41 per cent of the immigrant population were based in London in 2001, making up a quarter of its population. Second, the economic performances of the immigrant groups differ widely and result in differences in standards of living. Third, while some groups of immigrants may have received basic or even good education in their country of birth, others come with little or no education at all.

(vii) It is only consequent that my final point is on education (in particular and in general) because the challenges before us in this century – and I could do no more than point to the tip of the iceberg – demand that we pay them our full attention. We must be inventive, flexible and prepared to take risks and expect change, perhaps rapid change. As we know that educated people are less fearful of change than uneducated people, we should – nay, we have to – do our utmost to provide the best education that we can think of. How successful has Britain been in this respect? One example may suffice. According to one count, at the 'end of the 1970s one in eight eighteen-year-olds was in higher education; by 1990 it was one in five; by 1994 one in three'. So all is going well? According to the same source, student numbers 'went up by 88 per cent between 1989 and 2002, while the money provided per student, having already fallen by 20 per cent between 1976 and 1989, fell a further 37 per cent between 1989 and 2002'. This is, to put it mildly, disastrous.

Reading and speaking about twenty-first-century perspectives may not be very uplifting and encouraging. Sometimes it may cause anger, frustration and contempt. However, before we accuse others – business leaders, politicians or 'the system' – we could remember our own strength and use it, 'for really I think', the Leveller Thomas Rainsborough said in 1647, 'that the poorest he that is in England hath a life to live, as the greatest he; and therefore truly, Sir, I think it's clear, that every man that is to live under a government ought first by his own consent to put himself under that government; and I do think that the poorest man in England is not bound in a strict sense to that government that he hath not had a voice to put himself under'. Those of us who enjoy democratic rights must use them and thereby lend those of us who don't a hand in acquiring them.

Documents

The following documents may help to amplify and illustrate, but also to qualify, criticise and, perhaps, contradict the preceding narrative. The documents are followed by questions which may be used for further thought and discussion.

1 BRITONS, CELTS AND ROMANS, c.4000 BC–AD 410

1 Civilisation or servitude?

Tacitus (c.AD 55–120) is the principal (Roman) historian of the first forty years of Roman Britain, which he describes in the Annals, *the* Histories *and, in greater detail, in the account of the career of his father-in-law, Agricola, the governor of Britain, 77–83.*

Pompous, but points out helplessness

In order to encourage a truculent population that dwelled in scattered settlements (and was thus only too ready to fall to fighting) to live in a peaceful and inactive manner by offering it the pleasures that would follow on such a way of living, Agricola urged these people privately, and helped them officially, to build temples, public squares with public buildings (*fora*), and private houses (*domus*). He praised those who responded quickly, and severely criticised laggards. In this way, competition for public recognition took the place of compulsion. Moreover he had the children of the leading Britons educated in the civilised arts and openly placed the natural ability of the Britons above that of the Gauls, however well trained. The result was that those who had once shunned the Latin language now sought fluency and eloquence in it. Roman dress, too, became popular and the toga was frequently seen. Little by little there was a slide toward the allurements of degeneracy: assembly-rooms (*porticus*), bathing establishments and smart dinner parties. In their inexperience the Britons called it civilisation when it was really all part of their servitude.

(Tacitus, *Civilisation or Servitude?*, in Morgan 1993: 20)

2 SAXONS, DANES AND NORMANS, 410–1154

2 The Code of Edmund

King Edmund I ruled from 939 to 946. His Code is one of a number of statements by Anglo-Saxon kings aimed at controlling violence in general, and family and clan vengeance in particular.

PROLOGUE. King Edmund informs all people, both high and low, who are under his dominion, that I have been inquiring with the advice of my councillors, both ecclesiastical and lay, first of all how I could most advance Christianity.

Prol. 1. First, then, it seemed to us all most necessary that we should keep most firmly our peace and concord among ourselves throughout my dominion.

Prol. 2. The illegal and manifold conflicts which take place among us distress me and all of us greatly. We decreed then:

1. If henceforth anyone slay a man, he is himself to bear the feud; unless he can with the aid of his friends within twelve months pay compensation at the full wergild, whatever class he [the man slain] may belong to.

1.1. If, however, the kindred abandons him, and is not willing to pay compensation for him, it is then my will that all that kindred is to be exempt from the feud, except the actual slayer, if they give him neither food nor protection afterwards.

1.2. If, however, any of his kinsmen harbours him afterwards, he is to be liable to forfeit all that he owns to the king, and to bear the feud as regards the kindred [of the man slain], because they previously abandoned him.

1.3. If, however, any of the other kindred takes vengeance on any man other than the actual slayer, he is to incur the hostility of the king and all his friends, and to forfeit all that he owns.

2. If anyone flees to a church or my residence, and he is attacked or

molested there, those who do it are to be liable to the same penalty as is stated above.

3. And I do not wish that any fine or fighting or compensation to a lord for his man shall be remitted.

4. Further, I make it known that I will allow no resort to my court before he [the slayer] has undergone ecclesiastical penance and undertaken the prescribed compensation to the kindred, and submitted to every legal obligation, as the bishop, in whose diocese it is, instructs him.

5. Further, I thank God and all of you who have well supported me, for the immunity from thefts which we now have; I now trust to you, that you will support this measure so much the better as the need is greater for all of us that it shall be observed.

6. Further, we have declared concerning *mundbryce* [violation of anyone's rights of protection over others; here: the king's rights] and *hamsocn* [attack on a homestead, includes forcible entry and injury of persons inside a house], that anyone who commits it after this is to forfeit all that he owns, and it is to be for the king to decide whether he may preserve his life.

7. Leading men must settle feuds: First, according to the common law the slayer must give a pledge to his advocate, and the advocate to the kinsmen, that the slayer is willing to pay compensation to the kindred.

   7.1. Then afterwards it is fitting that a pledge be given to the slayer's advocate, that the slayer may approach under safe-conduct and himself pledge to pay the wergild.

   7.2. When he has pledged this, he is to find surety for the wergild.

   7.3. When that has been done, the king's *mund* [protection] is to be established; 21 days from that day *healsfang* [a proportion of the wergild which went to the nearest relatives of the slain man] is to be paid; 21 days from then the compensation to the lord for his man; 21 days from then the first instalment of the wergild.

   (Edmund's code concerning the blood-feud [II Edmund, 939–46], in Whitelock 1996: 427–9)

Questions

1 What does Edmund's code tell us about Anglo-Saxon society around 950?
2 Can you think of regions in the world where problems like those described above still prevail?

3 William's reign

The Anglo-Saxon Chronicle *is one of the most important documents of British history. Its compilation started approximately* AD *890, and it was subsequently added to by generations of anonymous writers until the middle of the twelfth century. In this excerpt the reign of the new Norman king of England, William I, is described in detail.*

If anyone wishes to know what sort of a man he was, or what dignity he had, or of how many lands he was lord – then we will write of him even as we, who have looked upon him, and once lived at his court, have perceived him to be.

This King William of whom we speak was a very wise man, and very powerful and more worshipful and stronger than any predecessor of his had been. He was gentle to the good men who loved God, and stern beyond all measure to those people who resisted his will. In the same place where God permitted him to conquer England, he set up a famous monastery and appointed monks for it, and endowed it well. In his days the famous church at Canterbury was built, and also many another over all England. Also, this country was very full of monks, and they lived their life under the rule of St Benedict, and Christianity was such in his day that each man who wished followed out whatever concerned his order. Also, he was very dignified: three times every year he wore his crown, as often as he was in England. At Easter he wore it at Winchester, at Whitsuntide at Westminster, and at Christmas at Gloucester, and then there were with him all the powerful men over all England, archbishops and bishops, abbots and earls, thegns and knights. Also, he was a very stern and violent man, so that no one dared do anything contrary to his will. He had earls in his fetters, who acted against his will. He expelled bishops from their sees, and abbots from their abbacies, and put thegns in prison, and finally he did not spare his own brother, who was called Odo; he was a very powerful bishop in Normandy (his cathedral church was at Bayeux) and was the foremost man next the king, and had an earldom in England. And when the king was in Normandy, then he was master in his country; and he [the king] put *him* in prison. Amongst other things the good security he made in this country is not to be forgotten – so that an honest man could travel over his kingdom without injury with his bosom full of gold; and no one dared strike another, however much wrong he had done him. And if any man had intercourse with a woman against her will, he was forthwith castrated.

He ruled over England, and by his cunning it was so investigated that there was not one hide of land in England that he did not know who owned it, and what it was worth, and then set it down in his record. Wales was in his power, and he built castles there, and he entirely controlled that race. In the same way, he also subdued Scotland to himself, because of his great strength. The land of Normandy was his by natural inheritance, and he ruled over the county called

Maine; and if he could have lived two years more, he would have conquered Ireland by his prudence and without any weapons. Certainly in his time people had much oppression and very many injuries:

> He had castles built
> And poor men hard oppressed.
> The king was so very stark
> And deprived his underlings of many a mark
> Of gold and more hundreds of pounds of silver,
> That he took by weight and with great injustice
> From his people with little need for such a deed.
> Into avarice did he fall
> And loved greediness above all.
> He made great protection for the game
> And imposed laws for the same,
> That who so slew hart or hind
> Should be made blind.
> He preserved the harts and boars
> And loved the stags as much
> As if he were their father.
> Moreover, for their hares did he decree that they should go free.
> Powerful men complained of it and poor men lamented it,
> But so fierce was he that he cared not for the rancour of them all,
> But they had to follow out the king's will entirely
> If they wished to live or hold their land,
> Property or estate, or his favour great.
> Alas! woe, that any man so proud should go,
> And exalt himself and reckon himself above all men!
> May Almighty God show mercy to his soul
> And grant unto him forgiveness for his sins.

These things we have written about him, both good and bad, that good men may imitate their good points, and entirely avoid the bad, and travel on the road that leads us to the kingdom of heaven.

(*The Anglo-Saxon Chronicle* [1087], in Smith and Smith 1993: 29–31)

Questions

1 According to this extract, what was life under William I like?
2 If you were to write an account of William's reign, which aspects would you include (and why)?

3 LATE-MEDIEVAL STRUGGLES: WITHIN THE BRITISH ISLES AND ON THE CONTINENT, 1154–1485

4 Eleventh-century English agrarian society: rights and ranks of people

These definitions are taken from a document which probably belongs to the half century before the Norman Conquest. Its detailed descriptions of agrarian conditions and social ranks in the time of Edward the Confessor make the text remarkable for this period. Its insistence on the significance of regional traditions and rules is also quite striking.

Thegn's law

The law of the thegn is that he be entitled to his book-right, and that he shall contribute three things in respect of his land: armed service, and the repairing of fortresses and work on bridges. Also in respect of many estates, further service arises on the king's order such as service connected with the deer fence at the king's residence, and equipping a guard ship, and guarding the coast, and guarding the lord, and military watch, almsgiving and church dues and many other various things.

Cottar's right

The cottar's right is according to the custom of the estate: in some he must work for his lord each Monday throughout the year, or 3 days each week at harvest-time. . . . He does not make land payment. He should have 5 acres: more if it be the custom on the estate; and it is too little if it ever be less; because his work must be frequent. Let him give his hearth-penny on Ascension day even as each freeman ought to do. Let him also perform services on his lord's demesne-land if he is ordered, by keeping watch on the sea-coast and working at the king's deer fence and such things according to his condition. Let him pay his church dues at Martinmas.

Boor's right

The boor's duties are various, in some places heavy and in others light. On some estates the custom is that he must perform week-work for 2 days in each week of the year as he is directed, and 3 days from the feast of the Purification to Easter. If he perform carrying service he need not work while his horse is out. At Michaelmas he must pay 10 pence for *gafol*, and at Martinmas 23 sesters of barley and 2 hens, and at Easter a young sheep or 2 pence. And he must lie from Martinmas to Easter at his lord's fold as often as it falls to his lot; and from the time when ploughing is first done until Martinmas he must each week plough 1 acre, and himself present the seed in the lord's barn. Also [he must plough] 3 acres as boon work, and 2 for pasturage. If he needs more grass, let him earn it as it may be permitted. Let him plough 3 acres as his tribute land and sow it from his own barn, and pay his hearth-penny. And every pair of boors must maintain 1 hunting dog, and each boor must give 6 loaves to the herdsman of the lord's swine when he drives his herd to the mast-pasture. On the same land to which the customs apply a farmer ought to be given for his occupation of the land 2 oxen, 1 cow, 6 sheep and 7 acres sown him, and let him be given tools for his work and utensils for his house. When death befalls him let the lord take charge of what he leaves.

(Rights and Ranks of People [*Rectitudines Singularum Personarum*], in Douglas and Greenaway 1996: 875–6)

Questions

1 Identify the main tasks of each profession mentioned above.
2 What do these definitions tell us about the general attitude towards 'workers', especially regarding their rights and duties?

5 Land and people

William fitz Stephen: description of the city of London (1170–83)

The following sections are extracts from the prologue of William fitz Stephen's 'Life of Thomas Becket'. The prologue, entitled 'A description of the most noble city of London', gives detailed information about both the structure of the city and the London way of life in the reign of Henry II.

Among the noble and celebrated cities of the world that of London, the capital of the kingdom of the English, is one which extends its glory farther than all the others and sends its wealth and merchandise more widely into distant lands. Higher than all the rest does it lift its head. It is happy in the healthiness of its air; in its observance of Christian practice; in the strength of its fortifications, in its natural situation; in the honour of its citizens; and in the modesty of its matrons. It is cheerful in its sports, and the fruitful mother of noble men. . . .

Of the ordering of the city

Those engaged in business of various kinds, sellers of merchandise, hirers of labour, are distributed every morning into their several localities according to their trade. Besides, there is in London on the river bank among the wines for sale in ships and the cellars of the vintners a public cook-shop. There daily you may find food according to the season, dishes of meat, roast, fried and boiled, large and small fish, coarser meats for the poor and more delicate for the rich, such as venison and big and small birds. If any of the citizens should unexpectedly receive visitors, weary from their journey, who would fain not wait until fresh food is bought and cooked, or until the servants have brought bread or water for washing, they hasten to the river bank and there find all they need. However great the multitude of soldiers and travellers entering the city, or preparing to go out of it, at any hour of the day or night – that these may not fast too long, and those may not go out supperless – they turn aside thither, if they please, where every man can refresh himself in his own way. . . .

(William fitz Stephen: description of London [1170–83], in Douglas and Greenaway 1996: 1024–9)

Questions

How did William fitz Stephen perceive the city of London? Give examples from the text.

---

6 Magna Carta (1225)

After the first charter of liberties had been granted by King John in 1215, a few modifications were added in 1216 and 1217, and a final version was confirmed by Henry III in 1225. The first version was the most radical; the later versions slightly mitigated the conflict between the monarch and his barons. Whenever opponents of the Crown made suggestions of reform they believed they were following the authors of Magna Carta. This was particularly so from the seventeenth century onwards.

Henry by the grace of God, king of England, lord of Ireland, duke of Normandy, Aquitaine, and count of Anjou, to the archbishops, bishops, abbots, priors, earls, barons, sheriffs, stewards, servants and to all his bailiffs and faithful subjects who shall look at the present charter, greeting. Know that we, out of reverence for God and for the salvation of our soul and the souls of our ancestors and successors, for the exaltation of holy church and the reform of our realm, have *of our own spontaneous goodwill given and granted to the archbishops, bishops, abbots, priors, earls, barons and all of our realm* these liberties written below to be held in our kingdom of England for ever.

[1] In the first place we have granted to God, and by this our present charter confirmed for us and our heirs for ever, that the English church shall be free and shall have *all* its rights undiminished and its liberties unimpaired. We have also granted to all free men of our kingdom, for ourselves and our heirs for ever, all the liberties written below to be *had and* held by them and their heirs of us and our heirs *for ever.*

[2] If any of our earls or barons or others holding of us in chief by knight service dies, and at his death his heir be of full age and owe relief he shall have his inheritance on payment of the old relief, namely the heir or heirs of an earl £100 for a whole earl's barony, the heir or heirs of a baron £100 for a whole barony, the heir or heirs of a knight 100s, at most, for a whole knight's fee; and he who owes less shall give less according to the ancient usage of fiefs. . . .

[7] A widow shall have her marriage portion and inheritance forthwith and without any difficulty after the death of her husband, nor shall she pay anything to have her dower or her marriage portion or the inheritance which she and her husband held on the day of her husband's death; and she may remain in the chief house of her husband for forty days after his death, within which time her dower shall be assigned to her, unless it has already been assigned to her or unless the house is a castle; and if she leaves the castle, a suitable house shall be provided for her in which she can stay honourably until her dower is assigned to her in accordance with what is aforesaid, and she shall have meanwhile her reasonable estover of common. There shall be assigned to her for her dower a third of all her husband's land which was his in his lifetime, unless a smaller share was given her at the church door. No widow shall be forced to marry so long as she wishes to live without a husband, provided that she gives security not to marry without consent if she holds of us, or without the consent of her lord if she holds of another.

[8] We or our bailiffs will not seize for any debt any land or rent, so long as the available chattels of the debtor are sufficient to repay the debt and the debtor himself is prepared to have it therefrom; nor will those who have gone surety for the debtor be distrained so long as the principal debtor is himself able to pay the debt; and if the principal debtor fails to pay the debt, having nothing wherewith to pay it or is unwilling to pay, then shall the sureties answer for the debt; and they shall, if they wish, have the land and rents of the debtor until they are reimbursed for the debt which they have paid for him, unless the principal debtor can show that he has dis-charged his obligation in the matter to the said sureties.

[9] The city of London shall have all its ancient liberties and free customs. Furthermore, we will and grant that all other cities, boroughs, towns, the barons of the Cinque Ports, and all ports shall have all their liberties and free customs.

[10] No one shall be compelled to do greater service for a knight's fee or for any other free holding than is due from it.

[11] Common pleas shall not follow our court, but shall be held in some fixed place. . . .

[14] A free man shall not be amerced [to impose a fine] for a trivial offence except in accordance with the degree of the offence and for a grave

215

offence in accordance with its gravity, yet saving his way of living; and a merchant in the same way, saving his stock-in-trade; and a villein other than one of our own shall be amerced in the same way, saving his means of livelihood; if he has fallen into our mercy: and none of the aforesaid amercements shall be imposed except by the *oath* of good and law-worthy men of the neighbourhood. Earls and barons shall not be amerced except by their peers, and only in accordance with the degree of the offence. No ecclesiastical person shall be amerced according to the amount of his ecclesiastical benefice but in accordance with his lay holding and in accordance with the degree of the offence. . . .

[28] No bailiff shall in future put anyone to manifest trial or to oath upon his own bare word without reliable witness produced for this purpose.

[29] No free man shall in *future* be arrested or imprisoned or disseised [to dispossess or deprive] of his freehold, liberties or free customs, or out-lawed or exiled or victimised in any other way, neither will we attack him or send anyone to attack him, except by the lawful judgement of his peers or by the law of the land. To no one will we sell, to no one will we refuse or delay right or justice.

[30] All merchants, unless they have been publicly prohibited beforehand, shall be able to go out of and come into England safely and securely and stay and travel throughout England, as well as by land as by water, for buying and selling by the ancient and right customs free from all evil tolls, except in time of war and if they are of the land that is at war with us. And if such are found in our land at the beginning of a war, they shall be attached without injury to their persons or goods, until we, or our chief justiciar, know how merchants of our land are treated who were found in the land at war with us when war broke out; and if ours are safe there, the others shall be safe in our land. . . .

[32] No free man shall henceforth give or sell to anyone more of his land than will leave enough for the full service due from the fief to be rendered to the lord of the fief. . . .

[34] No one shall be arrested or imprisoned upon the appeal of a woman for the death of anyone except her husband. . . .

[37] . . . All these aforesaid customs and liberties which we have granted to be observed in our kingdom as far as it pertains to us towards our men, all of our kingdom, clerks as well as laymen, shall observe as far as it pertains to them towards their men. *In return for this grant and gift of these liberties and of the other liberties contained in our charter on the liberties of the forest, the archbishops, bishops, abbots, priors, earls, barons, knights, freeholders and all of our realm have given us a fifteenth part of all their movables. We have also granted to them for us and our heirs that neither we nor our heirs will procure anything whereby the liberties contained in this charter shall be infringed or weakened; and if anything contrary to this is procured from anyone, it shall avail*

nothing and be held for nought. These being witness: the lord S. archbishop of Canterbury ... Given at Westminster on the eleventh day of February in the ninth year of our reign.

(Magna Carta [1225], in Rothwell 1996: 341–6)

Questions

1 Sketch the aspects of Magna Carta that seem important to you. Why do you think was it necessary to write this charter?
2 Can you give examples from bills and constitutions nowadays that remind you of the regulations in Magna Carta?

---

4 RENAISSANCE – RECONNAISSANCE – REFORMATION – REVOLUTION, 1485–1688/9

7 Francesco Petrarch: A letter to Boccaccio: literary humanism (1362)

Francesco Petrarch (1304–74) was a well-known humanist trying to revive and refine studies of classical antiquity. In his letter (1362) to his friend Giovanni Boccaccio (1313–75), he responded to charges often made against humanist education.

Neither exhortations [urgent recommendations] to virtue nor the argument of approaching death should divert us from literature; for in a good mind it excites the love of virtue, and dissipates, or at least diminishes, the fear of death. To desert our studies shows want of self-confidence rather than wisdom, for letters do not hinder but aid the properly constituted mind which possesses them; they facilitate our life, they do not retard it. Just as many kinds of food which lie heavy on an enfeebled and nauseated stomach furnish excellent nourishment for one who is well but famishing, so in our studies many things which are deadly to the weak mind may prove most salutary to an acute and healthy intellect, especially if in our use of both food and learning we exercise proper discretion. If it were otherwise, surely the zeal of certain persons who persevered to the end could not have roused such admiration. Cato ['the Elder', aka 'the Censor' 234–149 BC], I never forget, acquainted himself with Latin literature as he was growing old, and Greek when he had really become an old man. Varro [Roman scholar and author, 116–27 BC], who reached his hundredth year still reading and writing, parted from life sooner than from his love of study. Livius Drusus [Roman consul (112 BC) and censor (109 BC)], although weakened by age and afflicted with blindness, did not give up his interpretation of the civil law, which he carried on to the great advantage of the state ...

Besides these and innumerable others like them, have not all those of our own religion whom we should wish most to imitate devoted their whole lives to literature, and grown old and died in the same pursuit? Some, indeed, were overtaken by death while still at work reading or writing. To none of them, so far as I know, did it prove a disadvantage to be noted for secular learning . . .

While I know that many have become famous for piety without learning, at the same time I know of no one who has been prevented by literature from following the path of holiness.

(Francesco Petrarch, A Letter to Boccacio: Literary Humanism [1362])

Questions

1 According to Petrarch, what are the benefits of literary humanism?
2 Which examples and similes does he use to explain his ideas and what are their effects?

8 Johann Tetzel, The Spark for the Reformation: Indulgences

Johann Tetzel (?1465–1519) was a Dominican friar who sold indulgences which granted remission of temporal punishment in Purgatory. This is an excerpt from his sermon on indulgences.

You may obtain letters of safe conduct from the vicar of our Lord Jesus Christ, by means of which you are able to liberate your soul from the hands of the enemy, and convey it by means of contrition and confession, safe and secure from all pains of Purgatory, into the happy kingdom. For know, that in these letters are stamped and engraven all the merits of Christ's passion there laid bare. Consider, that for each and every mortal sin, it is necessary to undergo seven years of penitence after confession and contrition, either in this life or in Purgatory. How many mortal sins are committed in a day, how many in a week, how many in a month, how many in a year, how many in the whole extent of Life! They are well-nigh numberless, and those that commit them must needs suffer endless punishment in the burning pains of Purgatory.

But with these confessional letters you will be able at any time in life to obtain full indulgence for all penalties imposed upon you, in all cases except the four reserved to the Apostolic See. Thence throughout your whole life, whenever you wish to make confession, you may receive the same remission, except in cases reserved to the Pope, and afterwards, at the hour of death, a full indulgence as to all penalties and sins, and your share of all spiritual blessings that exist in the church militant and all its members.

Do you not know that when it is necessary for anyone to go to Rome, or undertake any other dangerous journey, he takes his money to a broker and gives a certain per cent – five or six or ten – in order that at Rome or elsewhere he may receive again his funds intact, by means of the letters of this same broker? Are you not willing, then, for the fourth part of a florin, to obtain these letters, by virtue of which you may bring, not your money, but your divine and immortal soul, safe and sound into the land of Paradise?

(Johann Tetzel, The Spark for the Reformation: Indulgences)

Questions

1 Which arguments does Tetzel present in support of the purchase of indulgences?
2 Tetzel was accused of abusing indulgences for secular purposes. How do you think he might defend himself against such claims?

9 Martin Luther: Justification by faith

Martin Luther (1483–1546) was an Augustinian monk and an early leader of the Protestant Reformation who became involved in a controversy about indulgences with Tetzel because he regarded them as a purchase and sale of salvation. This excerpt deals with beliefs which form the basis of Protestantism.

I greatly longed to understand Paul's Epistle to the Romans and nothing stood in the way but that one great expression, 'the justice of God', because I took it to mean that justice whereby God is just and deals justly in punishing the unjust. My situation was that, although an impeccable monk, I stood before God as a sinner troubled in conscience, and I had no confidence that my merit would assuage [appease] him. Therefore I did not love a just and angry God, but rather hated and murmured against Him. Yet I clung to the dear Paul and had a great yearning to know what he meant.

Night and day I pondered until I saw the connection between the justice of God and the statement that 'the just shall live his faith'. Then I grasped that the justice of God is that righteousness by which through grace and sheer mercy God justifies us through faith. Thereupon I felt myself to be reborn and to have gone through open doors into paradise. The whole of Scripture took on a new meaning, and whereas before the 'justice of God' had filled me with hate, now it became to be inexpressibly sweet in greater love. This passage of Paul became to me a gate to heaven. . . .

If you have a true faith that Christ is your Saviour, then at once you have a gracious God, for faith leads you in and opens up God's heart and will, that you should see pure grace and overflowing love. This it is to behold God in faith that you should look upon His fatherly, friendly heart, in which there is no anger nor ungraciousness. He who sees God as angry does not see Him rightly but looks only on a curtain, as if a dark cloud had been drawn across his face.

(Martin Luther, Justification by Faith)

10 Martin Luther: Address to the Christian nobility of the German nation (1520)

In this address, Martin Luther (see Document 9) points out several ecclesiastical abuses of the Catholic church as well as possible improvements.

It is pure invention that pope, bishop, priests, and monks are called the spiritual estate while princes, lords, artisans, and farmers are called the temporal estate. This is indeed a piece of deceit and hypocrisy. Yet no one need be intimidated by it, and for this reason: all Christians are truly of the spiritual estate, and there is no difference among them except that of office. Paul says in I Corinthians 12 [: 12–13] that we are all one body, yet every member has its own work by which it serves the others. This is because we all have one baptism, one gospel, one faith, and are all Christians alike; for baptism, gospel, and faith alone make us spiritual and a Christian people.

The pope or bishop anoints, shaves heads, ordains, consecrates, and prescribes garb different from that of the laity, but he can never make a man into a Christian or into a spiritual man by so doing. He might well make a man into a hypocrite or a humbug and blockhead, but never a Christian or spiritual man. As far as that goes, we are all consecrated priests through baptism, as St Peter says in I Peter 2 [: 9], 'You are a royal priesthood and a priestly realm.'

(Martin Luther, Address to the Christian Nobility of the German Nation [1520], in Johnston 1996: 87–8)

11 An Act for the King's Highness to Be Supreme Head of the Church of England, and to Have Authority to Reform and Redress All Errors, Heresies, and Abuses in the Same, 1534

The Act of Supremacy established the English monarch as the country's highest spiritual authority.

Albeit the King's Majesty justly and rightfully is and oweth to be the supreme head of the Church of England, and so is recognized by the clergy of this realm in their Convocations; yet nevertheless for corroboration and confirmation thereof, and for increase of virtue in Christ's religion within this realm of England, and to repress and extirp all errors, heresies, and other enormities and abuses heretofore used in the same, Be it enacted . . . that the King our sovereign lord, his heirs and successors kings of this realm, shall be taken, accepted, and reputed the only supreme head in earth of the Church of England called *Anglicana Ecclesia*, and shall have and enjoy annexed and united to the imperial crown of this realm as well the title and style thereof, as all honours, dignities, pre-eminences, jurisdictions, privileges, authorities, immunities, profits, and commodities, to the said dignity of supreme head of the same Church belonging and appertaining: And that our said sovereign lord, his heirs and successors kings of this realm, shall have full power and authority from time to time to visit, repress, redress, reform, order, correct, restrain, and amend all such errors, heresies, abuses, offences, contempts, and enormities, whatsoever they be, which by any manner spiritual authority or jurisdiction ought or may lawfully be reformed, repressed, ordered, redressed, corrected, restrained, or amended, most to the pleasure of Almighty God, the increase of virtue in Christ's religion, and for the conservancy of the peace, unity and tranquillity of this realm: any usage, custom, foreign laws, foreign authority, prescription or any other thing or things to the contrary hereof notwithstanding.

(An Act for the King's Highness to Be Supreme Head of the Church of England, and to Have Authority to Reform and Redress All Errors, Heresies, and Abuses in the Same, 1534, in Williams 1996: 745–6)

Questions

1 What kinds of power are conferred on the monarch?
2 How is the monarch's relationship to God defined?

12 An Exhortation Concerning Good Order, and Obedience to Rulers and Magistrates

The following sermon was delivered in 1563 and describes the concept of a 'godly order', a hierarchical universe.

Almighty God hath created and appointed all things in heaven, earth, and waters in a most excellent and perfect order. In heaven he hath appointed distinct or several orders and states of archangels and angels. In earth he hath assigned and appointed kings, princes, with other governors under them, all in good and necessary order. The water above is kept and raineth in due time and season. The sun, moon, stars, rainbow, thunder, lightning, clouds, and all birds of the air do keep their order. The earth, trees, seeds, plants, herbs, corn, grass, and all manner of beasts keep themselves in their order: all the parts of the whole year, as winter, summer, months, nights and days, continue in their order. All kinds of fishes in the sea, rivers, and waters, with all fountains, springs, yea, the seas themselves keep their comely course and order: and man himself also hath all his parts both within and without, as soul, heart, mind, memory, understanding, reason, speech, with all and singular corporal members of his body in a profitable, necessary, and pleasant order. Every degree of people, in their vocation, calling and office, hath appointed to them their duty and order: some are in high degree, some in low, some kings and princes, some inferiors and subjects, priests and laymen, masters and servants, fathers and children, husbands and wives, rich and poor, and every one have need of other: so that in all things is to be lauded and praised the godly order of God, without the which no house, no city, no commonwealth can continue and endure, or last. For where there is no right order, there reigneth all abuse, carnal liberty, enormity, sin, and babylonical confusion. Take away kings, princes, rulers, magistrates, judges, and such estates of God's order, no man shall ride or go by the highway unrobbed, no man shall sleep in his own house or bed unkilled, no man shall keep his wife, children and possessions in quietness: all things shall be common and there must needs follow all mischief, and utter destruction both of souls, bodies, goods, and common wealths. But blessed be God that we in this realm of England feel not the horrible calamities, miseries, and wretchedness which all they undoubtedly feel and suffer that lack this godly order. And praised be God that we know the great excellent benefit of God shewed towards us in this behalf. God hath sent us his high gift, our most dear sovereign Lady, Queen Elizabeth, with a godly, wise and honourable council, with other superiors and inferiors, in a beautiful order, and godly. Wherefore let us subjects do our bounden duties, giving hearty thanks to God, and praying for the preservation of this godly order.

(*Certain Sermons Appointed by the Queen's Majesty* [London, 1563], in Suerbaum 1991: 512–14)

Questions

1 Try to visualise the 'godly order' explained in the sermon above.
2 What are possible reasons why the Church encouraged the values of this order?

13 James I: Speech to Parliament (1610)

In this speech from 21 March 1610, James I describes the importance of the monarchy and Parliament's proper role in government.

. . . The state of monarchy is the supremest thing upon earth: for kings are not only God's lieutenants upon earth and sit upon God's throne, but even by God himself they are called gods. There be three principal similitudes that illustrate the state of monarchy: one taken out of the word of God, and the two other out of the grounds of policy and philosophy. In the Scriptures kings are called gods, and so their power after a certain relation compared to the divine power. Kings are also compared to fathers of families: for a king is truly *parens patriae*, the politic father of his people. And lastly, kings are compared to the head of this microcosm of the body of man. . . .

I conclude then this point touching the power of kings with this axiom of divinity, That as to dispute what God may do is blasphemy . . . so is it sedition in subjects to dispute what a king may do in the height of his power. But just kings will ever be willing to declare what they will do, if they will not incur the curse of God. I will not be content that my power be disputed upon; but I shall ever be willing to make the reason appear of all my doings, and rule my actions according to my laws. . . .

Now the second general ground whereof I am to speak concerns the matter of grievances. . . . First then, I am not to find fault that you inform yourselves of the particular just grievances of the people; nay I must tell you, ye can neither be just nor faithful to me or to your countries that trust and employ you, if you do it not. . . . But I would wish you to be careful to avoid three things in the matter of grievances.

First, that you do not meddle with the main points of government: that is my craft . . . I am now an old king. . . . I must not be taught my office.

Secondly, I would not have you meddle with such ancient rights of mine as I have received from my predecessors, possessing them *more majorum*: such things I would be sorry should be accounted for grievances. All novelties are dangerous as well in a politic as in a natural body: and therefore I would be loath to be quarrelled in my ancient rights and possessions: for that were to judge me unworthy of that which my predecessors had and left me.

And lastly I pray you, beware to exhibit for grievance anything that is established by a settled law, and whereunto (as you have already had a proof) you know I will never give a plausible answer: for it is an undutiful part in subjects to press their king, wherein they know beforehand he will refuse them. Now if any law or statute be not convenient, let it be amended by Parliament, but in the meantime term it not a grievance; for to be grieved with the law is to be grieved with the king, who is sworn to be the patron and maintainer thereof. But as all men are flesh and may err in the execution of laws, so may ye justly make a grievance of any abuse of the law, distinguishing wisely between the faults of the person and the thing itself. As for example, complaints may be made unto you of the high commissioners: if so be, try the abuse and spare not to complain upon it, but say not there shall be no omission, for that were to abridge the power that is in me. . . .

(James I, Speech to Parliament [1610], in Smith and Smith 1993: 333–4)

Questions

1 According to this speech, how far can a monarchy be regarded as divine?
2 What does James I expect from Parliament?

14 Anthony Van Dyck: Charles I on horseback (1633)

Anthony Van Dyck (1599–1641), a Flemish painter, was the leading court painter in England. In 1633 he painted this portrait of Charles I.

Questions

1 What effect does it have that Charles I is painted on horseback?
2 Which other elements are used in this portrait to represent Charles I and what are their effects?

15 The execution

On 30 January 1649, Charles I was beheaded. His execution is depicted in this contemporary German print, which is surmounted by portraits of Thomas Fairfax, Charles I and Oliver Cromwell.

Question

What do you learn about Charles's execution from this print?

16 Bill of Rights, 1689: An Act of Declaiming the Rights and Liberties of the Subject and Settling the Succession of the Crown

The Bill of Rights is one of the basic documents of English constitutional law. It was passed by Parliament in December 1689 giving statutory form to the Declaration of

Figure 9 Equestrian portrait of Charles I (1600–49), *c.* 1637–38 (oil on canvas) by Sir Anthony Van Dyck (1599–1641), National Gallery, London, UK/ The Bridgeman Art Library

Rights which the Convention Parliament presented to William and Mary in February 1689.

Whereas the Lords Spiritual and Temporal and Commons assembled at Westminster, lawfully, fully and freely representing all the estates of the people of this realm, did upon the thirteenth day of February in the year of

Figure 10 Execution of Charles I (1600–49) at Whitehall, 30 January 1649 (engraving) by German School (17th century). Private Collection/ The Bridgeman Art Library

our Lord one thousand six hundred eighty-eight present unto their Majesties, then called and known by the names and style of William and Mary, prince and princess of Orange, being present in their proper persons, a certain declaration in writing made by the said Lords and Commons in the words following, viz.:

Whereas the late King James the Second, by the assistance of divers evil counsellors, judges and ministers employed by him, did endeavour to subvert and extirpate the Protestant religion and the laws and liberties of this kingdom;

By assuming and exercising a power of dispensing with and suspending of laws and the execution of laws without consent of Parliament;

By committing and prosecuting divers worthy prelates for humbly petitioning to be excused from concurring to the said assumed power;

By issuing and causing to be executed a commission under the great seal for erecting a court called the Court of Commissioners for Ecclesiastical Causes;

By levying money for and to the use of the Crown by pretence of prerogative for other time and in other manner than the same was granted by Parliament;

By raising and keeping a standing army within this kingdom in time of peace without consent of Parliament, and quartering soldiers contrary to law;

By causing several good subjects being Protestants to be disarmed at the same time when papists were both armed and employed contrary to law;

By violating the freedom of election of members to serve in Parliament;

By prosecutions in the Court of King's Bench for matters and causes cognizable only in Parliament, and by divers other arbitrary and illegal courses;

And whereas of late years partial, corrupt and unqualified persons have been returned and served on juries in trials, and particularly divers jurors in trials for high treason which were not freeholders;

And excessive bail hath been required of persons committed in criminal cases to elude the benefit of the laws made for the liberty of the subjects;

And excessive fines have been imposed;

And illegal and cruel punishments inflicted;

And several grants and promises made of fines and forfeitures before any conviction or judgment against the persons upon whom the same were to be levied;

All which are utterly and directly contrary to the known laws and statutes and freedom of this realm;

And whereas the said late King James the Second having abdicated the government and the throne being thereby vacant, his Highness the prince of Orange (whom it hath pleased Almighty God to make the glorious instrument of delivering this kingdom from popery and arbitrary power) did (by the advice of the Lords Spiritual and Temporal and divers principal persons of the Commons) cause letters to be written to the Lords Spiritual and Temporal being Protestants, and other letters to the several counties, cities, universities, boroughs and cinque ports, for the choosing of such persons to represent them as were of right to be sent to Parliament, to meet and sit at Westminster upon the two and twentieth day of January in this year one thousand six hundred eighty and eight, in order to such an establishment as that their religion, laws and liberties might not again be in danger of being subverted, upon which letters elections having been accordingly made;

And thereupon the said Lords Spiritual and Temporal and Commons, pursuant to their respective letters and elections, being now assembled in a full and free representative of this nation, taking into their most serious consideration the best means for attaining the ends aforesaid, do in the first place (as their ancestors in like case have usually done) for the vindicating and asserting their ancient rights and liberties declare

That the pretended power of suspending of laws or the execution of laws by regal authority without consent of Parliament is illegal;

That the pretended power of dispensing with laws or the execution of laws by regal authority, as it hath been assumed and exercised of late, is illegal;

That the commission for erecting the late Court of Commissioners for Ecclesiastical Causes, and all other commissions and courts of like nature, are illegal and pernicious;

That levying money for or to the use of the Crown by pretence of prerogative, without grant of Parliament, for longer time, or in other manner than the same is or shall be granted, is illegal;

That it is the right of the subjects to petition the king, and all commitments and prosecutions for such petitioning are illegal;

That the raising or keeping a standing army within the kingdom in time of peace, unless it be with consent of Parliament, is against law;

That the subjects which are Protestants may have arms for their defence suitable to their conditions and as allowed by law;

That election of members of Parliament ought to be free;

That the freedom of speech and debates or proceedings in Parliament ought not to be impeached or questioned in any court or place out of Parliament;

That excessive bail ought not to be required, nor excessive fines imposed, nor cruel and unusual punishments inflicted;

That jurors ought to be duly impanelled and returned, and jurors which pass upon men in trials for high treason ought to be freeholders;

That all grants and promises of fines and forfeitures of particular persons before conviction are illegal and void;

And that for redress of all grievances, and for the amending, strengthening and preserving of the laws, Parliaments ought to be held frequently.

And they do claim, demand and insist upon all and singular the premises as their undoubted rights and liberties, and that no declarations, judgments, doings or proceedings to the prejudice of the people in any of the said premises ought in any wise to be drawn hereafter into consequence or example; to which demand of their rights they are particularly encouraged by the declaration of his Highness the prince of Orange as being the only means for obtaining a full redress and remedy therein. Having therefore an entire confidence that his said Highness the prince of Orange will perfect the deliverance so far advanced by him, and will still preserve them from the violation of their rights which they have here asserted, and from all other attempts upon their religion, rights and liberties, the said Lords Spiritual and Temporal and Commons assembled at Westminster do resolve that William and Mary, prince and princess of Orange, be and be declared king and queen of England, France and Ireland and the dominions thereunto belonging, to hold the crown and royal dignity of the said kingdoms and dominions to them, the said prince and princess, during their lives and the life of the survivor of them, and that the sole and full exercise of the regal power be only in and executed by the said prince of Orange in the names of the said prince and princess during their joint lives, and after their deceases the said crown and royal dignity of the said kingdoms and dominions to be to the heirs of the body of the said princess, and for default of such issue to the Princess Anne of Denmark and the heirs of her body, and for default of such issue to the heirs of the body of the said prince of Orange. And the Lords Spiritual and Temporal and Commons do pray the said prince and princess to accept the same accordingly.

And that the oaths hereafter mentioned be taken by all persons of whom the oaths of allegiance and supremacy might be required by law, instead of them; and that the said oaths of allegiance and supremacy be abrogated.

I, A.B., do sincerely promise and swear that I will be faithful and bear true allegiance to their Majesties King William and Queen Mary. So help me God.

I, A.B., do swear that I do from my heart abhor, detest and abjure as impious and heretical this damnable doctrine and position, that princes excommunicated or deprived by the Pope or any authority of the see of Rome may be deposed or murdered by their subjects or any other whatsoever. And I do declare that no foreign prince, person, prelate, state or potentate hath or ought to have any jurisdiction, power, superiority, pre-eminence or authority, ecclesiastical or spiritual, within this realm. So help me God.

(Bill of Rights, 1689, in Browning 1996: 122–4)

Questions

1 What are the key aspects of this document, keeping in mind its historical context?
2 Why is the Bill of Rights considered to be a basic document of English constitutional law?
3 Compare this document with other bills of rights such as the first ten amendments to the American Constitution which are also known as the 'Bill of Rights'. How far do they differ?

17 Sir Isaac Newton: *Mathematical Principles of Natural Philosophy*

Sir Isaac Newton (1642–1727) was an English physicist, mathematician, astronomer and philosopher who made important discoveries concerning gravity, motion, light and calculus. Mathematical Principles of Natural Philosophy *(1687) is his most famous work.*

Rule I

We are to admit no more causes of natural things than such as are both true and sufficient to explain their appearances.

To this purpose the philosophers say that Nature does nothing in vain, and more is in vain when less will serve; for Nature is pleased with simplicity, and affects not the pomp of superfluous causes.

Rule II

Therefore to the same natural effects we must, as far as possible, assign the same causes.

As to respiration in a man and in a beast; the descent of stones in *Europe* and in *America*; the light of our culinary fire and of the sun; the reflection of light in the earth, and in the planets.

Rule III

The qualities of bodies, which admit neither intensification nor remission of degrees, and which are found to belong to all bodies within the reach of our experiments, are to be esteemed the universal qualities of all bodies whatsoever.

For since the qualities of bodies are only known to us by experiments, we are to hold for universal all such as universally agree with experiments; and such as are not liable to diminution can never be quite taken away.

Rule IV

In experimental philosophy we are to look upon propositions inferred by general induction from phenomena as accurately or very nearly true, notwithstanding any contrary hypotheses that may be imagined, till such time as other phenomena occur, by which they may either be made more accurate, or liable to exceptions.

This rule we must follow, that the argument of induction may not be evaded by hypotheses.

(Sir Isaac Newton, *Mathematical Principles of Natural Philosophy*, in Latin 1687, trans. 1729; in Newton 1962)

Questions

1 What different aspects do these four rules focus on?
2 Why have Newton's rules for arriving at knowledge been so influential?

5 TOWARDS INTERNAL STABILITY AND EXTERNAL EXPANSION, 1689–1789

18 Act of Settlement, 1701: An Act for the Further Limitation of the Crown and Better Securing the Rights and Liberties of the Subject

This statute was passed 1701 to amend the Bill of Rights. It was designed to regulate the succession of the English crown.

Whereas in the first year of the reign of your Majesty and of our late most gracious Sovereign Lady Queen Mary (of blessed memory) an Act of Parliament was made, entitled, *An Act for declaring the rights and liberties of the subject and for settling the succession of the crown*, wherein it was (amongst other things) enacted, established and declared, that the crown and regal government of the kingdoms of England, France and Ireland and the dominions thereunto belonging should be and continue to your Majesty and the said late queen during the joint lives of your Majesty and the said queen and to the survivor, and that after the decease of your Majesty and of the said queen the said crown and regal government should be and remain to the heirs of the body of the said late queen, and for default of such issue to her Royal Highness the Princess Anne of Denmark and the heirs of her body, and for default of such issue to the heirs of the body of your Majesty; and it was thereby further enacted, that all and every person and persons that then were or afterwards should be reconciled to or shall hold communion with the see or Church of Rome, or should profess the popish religion or marry a papist, should be excluded, and are by that Act made forever incapable to inherit, possess or enjoy the crown and government of this realm and Ireland and the dominions thereunto belonging or any part of the same, or to have, use or exercise any regal power, authority or jurisdiction within the same, and in all and every such case and cases the people of these realms shall be and are thereby absolved of their allegiance; and that the said crown and government shall from time to time descend to and be enjoyed by such person or persons being Protestants as should have inherited and enjoyed the same in case the said person or persons so reconciled, holding communion, professing or marrying as aforesaid were naturally dead; after the making of which statute and the settlement therein contained your Majesty's good subjects, who were restored to the full and free possession and enjoyment of their religion, rights and liberties by the providence of God giving success to your Majesty's just undertakings and unwearied endeavours for that purpose, had no greater temporal felicity to hope or wish for than to see a royal progeny descending from your Majesty, to whom (under God) they owe their tranquillity, and whose ancestors have for many years been principal assertors of the reformed religion and the liberties of Europe, and from our said most gracious sovereign lady, whose memory will always be precious to the subjects of these realms; and it having since pleased Almighty God to take away our said sovereign lady and also the most hopeful Prince William, duke of Gloucester (the only surviving issue of her Royal Highness the Princess Anne of Denmark), to the unspeakable grief and sorrow of your Majesty and your said good subjects, who under such losses being sensibly put in mind that it standeth wholly in the pleasure of Almighty God to prolong the lives of your Majesty and of her Royal Highness, and to grant to your Majesty or to her Royal Highness such issue as may be inheritable to the crown and regal government aforesaid by the respective limitations in the said recited Act contained, do constantly implore the divine mercy for those blessings, and your Majesty's said subjects having daily experience of your royal care and concern for the present and future welfare of these kingdoms, and particularly recommending from your throne a further provision to be made for the succession of the crown in the Protestant line for the happiness of the nation and the security of our religion, and it being absolutely necessary for the safety, peace and quiet of this realm to obviate all doubts and contentions in the same by reason of any pretended titles to the crown, and to maintain a certainty in the succession thereof to which your subjects may safely have recourse for their protection in case the limitations in the said recited Act should determine: therefore for a further provision of the succession of the crown in the Protestant line, we your Majesty's most dutiful and loyal subjects the Lords Spiritual and Temporal and Commons in this present Parliament assembled do beseech your Majesty that it may be enacted and declared, and be it enacted and declared by the king's most excellent Majesty, by and with the advice and consent of the Lords Spiritual and Temporal and Commons in this present Parliament assembled and by the authority of the same, that the most excellent Princess Sophia, electress and duchess dowager of Hanover, daughter of the most excellent Princess Elizabeth, late queen of Bohemia, daughter of our late Sovereign Lord King James the First of happy memory, be and is hereby declared to be the next in succession in the Protestant line to the imperial crown and dignity of the said realms of England, France and Ireland, with the dominions and territories thereunto belonging, after his Majesty and the Princess Anne of Denmark and in default of issue of the said Princess Anne and of his Majesty respectively, and that from and after the deceases of his said Majesty our now sovereign lord, and of her Royal Highness the Princess Anne of Denmark, and for default of issue of the said Princess Anne and of his Majesty respectively, the crown and regal government of the said kingdoms of England, France and Ireland and of the dominions thereunto belonging, with the royal state and dignity of the said realms, and all honours, styles, titles, regalities, prerogatives, powers, jurisdictions and authorities to the same belonging and appertaining, shall be, remain and continue to the said most excellent Princess Sophia and the heirs of her body being Protestants; and thereunto the said Lords Spiritual and Temporal and Commons shall and will in the name of all the people of this realm most humbly and faithfully submit themselves, their heirs and posterities, and do faithfully promise that after the deceases of his Majesty and her Royal Highness, and the failure of the heirs of their respective bodies, to stand to, maintain and defend the said Princess Sophia and the heirs of her body being Protestants, according to the limitation and succession of the crown in this Act specified and contained, to the utmost of their powers with their lives and estates against all persons whatsoever that shall attempt anything to the contrary. . . .

(Act of Settlement, 1701, in Browning 1996: 129–34)

Questions

1 What do the different clauses of this act provide for? Which role does Parliament play in this act as compared to the role of the monarchy?
2 Comment on the name of this statute: 'Act of Settlement'. What are its implications and effects?

19 Habeas Corpus Act, 1679: An Act for the Better Securing the Liberty of the Subject and for Prevention of Imprisonments beyond the Seas

This act of 1679 refers to the old law of 'habeas corpus ad subjiciendum' (Latin for 'You [shall] have the body to be subjected to [examination]'), which means that people who were imprisoned should be brought before the court without delay.

Whereas great delays have been used by sheriffs, gaolers and other officers to whose custody any of the king's subjects have been committed for criminal or supposed criminal matters, in making returns of writs of Habeas Corpus to them directed, by standing out an Alias and Pluries Habeas Corpus and sometimes more, and by other shifts to avoid their yielding obedience to such writs, contrary to their duty and the known laws of the land, whereby many of the king's subjects have been and hereafter may be long detained in prison, in such cases where by law they are bailable, to their great charge and vexation; for the prevention whereof and the more speedy relief of all persons imprisoned for any such criminal or supposed criminal matters, be it enacted . . . that whensoever any person or persons shall bring any Habeas Corpus directed unto any sheriff or sheriffs, gaoler, minister or other person whatsoever, for any person in his or their custody, and the said writ shall be served upon the said officer or left at the gaol or prison with any of the under-officers, under-keepers or deputy of the said of officers or keepers, that the said officer or officers, his or their under-officers, under-keepers or deputies, shall within three days after the service thereof as aforesaid (unless the commitment aforesaid were for treason or felony plainly and specially expressed in the warrant of commitment), upon payment or tender of the charges of bringing the said prisoner, to be ascertained by the judge or court that awarded the same and endorsed upon the said writ, not exceeding twelve pence per mile, and upon security given by his own bond to pay the charges of carrying back the prisoner if he shall be remanded by the court or judge to which he shall be brought according to the true intent of this present Act, and that he will not make any escape by the way, make return of such writ, and bring or cause to be brought the body of the party so committed or restrained unto or before the Lord Chancellor or Lord Keeper of the Great Seal of England for the time being, or the judges or barons of the said court from whence the said writ shall issue, or unto and before such other person or persons before whom the said writ is made returnable according to the command thereof, and shall then likewise certify the true causes of his detainer or imprisonment, unless the commitment of the said party be in any place beyond the distance of twenty miles from the place or places where such court or person is or shall be residing, and if beyond the distance of twenty miles and not above one hundred miles, then within the space of ten days, and if beyond the distance of one hundred miles then within the space of twenty days after such delivery aforesaid and not longer.

II. And to the intent that no sheriff, gaoler or other officer may pretend ignorance of the import of any such writ, be it enacted . . . that all such writs shall be marked in this manner, *Per statutum tricesimo primo Caroli Secundi Regis*, and shall be signed by the person that awards the same; and if any person or persons shall be or stand committed or detained as aforesaid for any crime, unless for treason or felony plainly expressed in the warrant of commitment, in the vacation time and out of term, it shall and may be lawful to and for the person or persons so committed or detained (other than persons convict or in execution by legal process), or anyone on his or their behalf, to appeal or complain to the Lord Chancellor or Lord Keeper or any one of his Majesty's justices, either of the one bench or of the other, or the barons of the Exchequer of the degree of the coif; and the said Lord Chancellor, Lord Keeper, justices or barons or any of them, upon view of the copy or copies of the warrant or warrants of commitment and detainer, or otherwise upon oath made that such copy or copies were denied to be given by such person or persons in whose custody the prisoner or prisoners is or are detained, are hereby authorized and required, upon request made in writing by such person or persons, or any on his, her or their behalf, attested and subscribed by two witnesses who were present at the delivery of the same, to award and grant an Habeas Corpus under the seal of such court whereof he shall then be one of the judges, to be directed to the officer or officers in whose custody the party so committed or detained shall be, returnable *immediate* before the said Lord Chancellor or Lord Keeper, or such justice, baron or any other justice or baron of the degree of the coif of any of the said courts; and upon service thereof as aforesaid the officer or officers, his or their under-officer or under-officers, under-keeper or under-keepers or their deputy, in whose custody the party is so committed or detained, shall within the times respectively before limited bring such prisoner or prisoners before the said Lord Chancellor or Lord Keeper, or such justices, barons or one of them before whom the said writ is made returnable, and in case of his absence before any other of them, with the return of such writ and the true causes of the commitment and detainer: and thereupon within two days after the party shall be brought before them the said Lord Chancellor or Lord Keeper, or such justice or baron before whom the prisoner shall be brought as aforesaid, shall discharge the said prisoner from his imprisonment, taking his or their recognizance with one or more surety or sureties in any sum according to their discretions, having regard to the quality of the prisoner and nature of the offence, for his or their appearance in the Court of King's Bench the term following, or at the next assizes, sessions, or general gaol delivery of and for such county, city or place where the commitment was, or where the offence was committed, or in such other court where the said offence is properly cognizable, as the case shall require, and then shall certify the said writ with the return thereof and the said recognizance or recognizances into the said court where such appearance is to be made, unless it shall appear unto the said Lord Chancellor or Lord Keeper, or justice or justices, or baron or barons, that the party so committed is detained upon a legal process, order or warrant out of some court that hath jurisdiction of criminal matters, or by some warrant signed and sealed with the hand and seal of any of the said justices or barons, or some justice or justices of the peace, for such matters or offences for the which by the law the prisoner is not bailable. . . .

IV. And be it further enacted . . . that if any officer or officers, his or their under-officer or under-officers, under-keeper or under-keepers or deputy, shall neglect or refuse to make the returns aforesaid, or to bring the body or bodies of the prisoner or prisoners according to the command of the said writ within the respective times aforesaid, or upon demand made by the prisoner or person in his behalf shall refuse to deliver, or within the space of six hours after demand shall not deliver, to the person so demanding a true copy of the warrant or warrants of commitment and detainer of such prisoner, which he and they are hereby required to deliver accordingly, all and every the head gaolers and keepers of such prisons, and such other person in whose custody the prisoner shall be detained, shall for the first offence forfeit to the prisoner or party grieved the sum of one hundred pounds; and for the second offence the sum of two hundred pounds, and shall and is hereby made incapable to hold or execute his said office. . . .

(Habeas Corpus Act, 1679, in Browning 1996: 92–4)

Questions

1 What are the benefits of this Act?
2 Comment on the style of the language used in this Act.
3 Compare it to the laws in your own country.

20 Mary Wollstonecraft: *A Vindication of the Rights of Woman*

Mary Wollstonecraft (1759–97) was an early feminist. In 1792 she published A Vindication of the Rights of Woman, *in which she argued for a fundamental change in woman's role in society.*

Contending for the rights of woman, my main argument is built on this simple principle, that if she be not prepared by education to become the companion of man, she will stop the progress of knowledge and virtue; for truth must be common to all, or it will be inefficacious with respect to its influence on general practice. And how can woman be expected to cooperate unless she knows why she ought to be virtuous? unless freedom strengthens her reason till she comprehends her duty, and sees in what manner it is connected with her real good. If children are to be educated to understand the true principle of patriotism, their mother must be a patriot; and the love of mankind, from which an orderly train of virtues spring, can only be produced by considering the moral and civil interest of mankind; but the education and situation of woman at present shuts her out from such investigations.

In this work I have produced many arguments, which to me were conclusive, to prove that the prevailing notion respecting a sexual character was subversive of mortality, and I have contended, that to render the human body and mind more perfect, chastity must more universally prevail, and that chastity will never be respected in the male world till the person of a woman is not, as it were, idolised, when little virtue or sense embellish it with the grand traces of mental beauty, or the interesting simplicity of affection.

Consider, sir, dispassionately these observations, for a glimpse of this truth seemed to open before you when you observed, 'that to see one-half of the human race excluded by the other from all participation of government was a political phenomenon, that, according to abstract principles, it was impossible to explain'. If so, on what does your constitution rest? If the abstract rights of man will bear discussion and explanation, those of woman, by a parity of reasoning, will not shrink from the same test; though a different opinion prevails in this country, built on the very arguments which you use to justify the oppression of woman prescription.

Consider – I address you as a legislator – whether, when men contend for their freedom, and to be allowed to judge for themselves respecting their own happiness, it be not inconsistent and unjust to subjugate women, even though you firmly believe that you are acting in the manner best calculated to promote their happiness? Who made man the exclusive judge, if woman partake with him of the gift of reason?

(Mary Wollstonecraft, *A Vindication of the Rights of Woman* [1792])

Questions

1 What arguments does Wollstonecraft give for changing women's role in society?
2 Imagine you were a philosopher of that time opposing Wollstonecraft's argument. How would you reply to her feminist ideas?

21 Coffee house

This painting depicts an early London coffee house.

Figure 11 An early London coffee house © Copyright the Trustees of The British Museum

Questions

1 Who is depicted in this painting? What are they doing?
2 Why did coffee houses become so popular?

22 William Blake: 'Europe Supported by Africa and America'

This engraving by William Blake (1757–1827) was made for J. G. Stedman, who published it in his book Narrative, of a five years' expedition, against the Revolted Negroes of Surinam, in Guiana, on the Wild coast of South America; from the year 1772, to 1777 *(London, 1796).*

Questions

1 How are the continents Africa, America and Europe represented in this picture?
2 Can you link this painting to the transatlantic economy, the middle passage or the slave trade?

23 The plan of the *Brookes*

The Brookes *was one of the vessels used for shipping slaves across the Atlantic to the West Indies. The following document gives a detailed description of the ship's dimensions.*

During the discussion of the possible regulation of slave vessels, Captain Perry visited Liverpool and examined eighteen vessels, nine of which belonged to James Jones. . . . The dimensions of the *Brookes*, one of the vessels examined, were: 'Length of the lower deck, gratings and bulkheads included, at A A, 100 feet, breadth of beam on lower deck inside, B B, 25 feet 4 inches, depth of Hold, O O O, from ceiling to ceiling, 10 feet, height between decks, from deck to deck, 5 feet 8 inches, length of the men's room, C C, on the lower deck, 46 feet, breadth of the men's room, C C, on the lower deck, 25 feet 4 inches, length of the platforms, D D, in the men's room, 46 feet, breadth of the platforms in the men's room on each side, 6 feet, length of the boy's room, E E, 13 feet 9 inches, breadth of the boy's room, 25 feet, breadth of platforms, F F, in boy's room, 6 feet, length of women's room, G G, 28 feet 6 inches, breadth of women's room, 23 feet 6 inches, length of platforms, H H, in women's room, 28 feet 6 inches, breadth of platforms in women's room, 6 feet, length of the gun-room, I I, on the lower deck, 10 feet 6 inches, breadth of the gun-room on the lower deck, 12 feet, length of the quarter-deck, K K, 33 feet 6 inches, breadth of the quarter-deck, 19 feet 6 inches, length of the cabin, L L, 14 feet, height of the cabin, 6 feet 2 inches, length of the half-deck, M M, 16 feet 6 inches, height of the half-deck, 6 feet 2 inches, length of the platforms, N N, on the half-deck, 16 feet, 6 inches, breadth of the platforms on the half-deck, 6 feet, upper deck, P P.

'Let it now be supposed that the above are the real dimensions of the ship *Brookes*, and further, that every man slave is to be allowed six feet by one foot four inches for room, every woman five feet ten by one foot four, every boy five

Figure 12 'Europe supported by Africa and America', from *Narrative, of a Five Years' Expedition, against the Revolted Negroes of Surinam* by John Gabriel Stedman (1744–97) Private Collection/ The Bridgeman Art Library

feet by one foot two, and every girl four feet six by one foot, it will follow that the annexed plan of a slave vessel will be precisely the representation of the ship *Brookes*, and of the exact number of persons neither more nor less, that could be stowed in the different rooms of it upon these data. These, if counted, (deducting the women stowed in Z, of figures VI and VII,) will be found to amount to *four hundred and fifty-one*. Now, if it be considered that the ship *Brookes* is of three hundred and twenty tons, and that she is allowed to carry by act of Parliament *four hundred and fifty-four persons*, it is evident that if three more could be wedged among the number represented in the plan, this plan would contain precisely the number which the act directs. . . .

(The slave ship *Brookes* of Liverpool, published by J. Robertson, 1791)

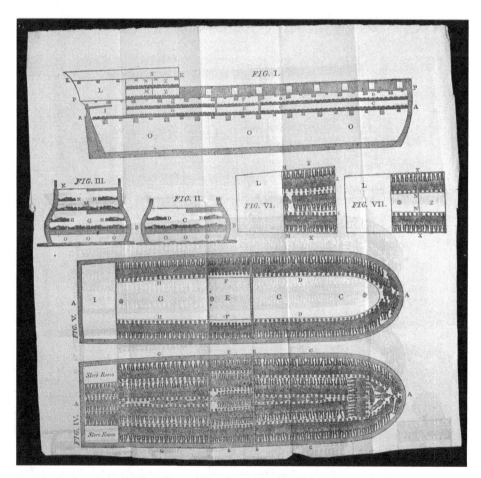

Figure 13 The slave ship *Brookes* of Liverpool, published by J. Robertson, Edinburgh, 1791 (wood engraving and letterpress) by English School (18th century). Private Collection/ © Michael Graham-Stewart/ The Bridgeman Art Library

24 James Thomson: 'Rule, Britannia!'

This poem by James Thomson (1700–48) was set to music by Thomas Arne (1710–78). It is a well-known patriotic song – another British national anthem – which is traditionally performed on the Last Night of the Proms.

When Britain first, at Heaven's command,
Arose from out the azure main,
This was the charter of the land,
And guardian angels sung this strain –
'Rule, Britannia, rule the waves;
Britons never will be slaves.'

The nations, not so blest as thee,
Must in their turns to tyrants fall;
While thou shalt flourish great and free,
The dread and envy of them all.
'Rule,' &c.

Still more majestic shalt thou rise,
More dreadful from each foreign stroke:
As the loud blast that tears the skies
Serves but to root thy native oak.
'Rule,' &c.

Thee haughty tyrants ne'er shall tame;
All their attempts to bend thee down
Will but arouse thy generous flame,
But work their woe and thy renown.
'Rule,' &c.

To thee belongs the rural reign;
Thy cities shall with commerce shine;
All thine shall be the subject main,
And every shore it circles thine.
'Rule,' &c.

The Muses, still with freedom found,
Shall to thy happy coast repair:
Blest isle! with matchless beauty crowned,

And manly hearts to guard the fair.
'Rule, Britannia, rule the waves;
Britons never will be slaves.'

(James Thomson, 'Rule, Britannia!', in Robertson 1971: 422–3)

Questions

1 What image of Great Britain does this song convey? Give examples.
2 What role does this song play in the context of the British Empire and the British slave trade?

25 Edmund Burke: Conciliation with America (1775)

Edmund Burke (1729–97) was an Anglo-Irish statesman and philosopher, and a member of the Whig party sitting in the House of Commons. He is known for opposing the French Revolution (see Document 29) as well as for supporting the American colonies against George III, as in this speech which he delivered on 22 March 1775.

In this character of the Americans, a love of freedom is the predominating feature which marks and distinguishes the whole: and as an ardent is always a jealous affection, your colonies become suspicious, restive, and untractable, whenever they see the least attempt to wrest from them by force, or shuffle from them by chicane, what they think the only advantage worth living for. This fierce spirit of liberty is stronger in the English colonies probably than in any other people of the earth; and this from a great variety of powerful causes which, to understand the true temper of their minds, and the direction which this spirit takes, it will not be amiss to lay open somewhat more largely.

First, the people of the colonies are descendants of Englishmen. England, Sir, is a nation, which still I hope respects, and formerly adored, her freedom. The colonists emigrated from you, when this part of your character was most predominant; and they took this bias and direction the moment they parted from your hands. They are therefore not only devoted to liberty, but to liberty according to English ideas, and on English principles. Abstract liberty, like other mere abstractions, is not to be found. . . . It happened, you know, Sir, that the great contests for freedom in this country were from the earliest times chiefly upon the question of taxing. . . . The colonies draw from you, as with their life-blood, these ideas and principles. Their love of liberty, as with you, fixed and attached on this specific point of taxing. . . .

They were further confirmed in this . . . by the form of their provincial legislative assemblies. Their governments are popular in an high degree; some are merely popular; in all, the popular representative is the most weighty; and this share of the people in their ordinary government never fails to inspire them with lofty sentiments, and with a strong aversion from whatever tends to deprive them of their chief importance.

If any thing were wanting to this necessary operation of the form of government, religion would have given it a complete effect. Religion, always a principle of energy, in this new people, is no way worn out or impaired; and their mode of professing it is also one main cause of this free spirit. The people are Protestants; and of that kind, which is the most adverse to all implicit submission of mind and opinion. This is a persuasion not only favorable to liberty, but built upon it. . . . All Protestantism, even the most cold and passive, is a sort of dissent. But the religion most prevalent in our northern colonies is a refinement on the principle of resistance; it is the dissidence of dissent; and the Protestantism of the Protestant religion. . . .

In the southern colonies the Church of England forms a large body, and has a regular establishment. It is certainly true. There is however a circumstance attending these colonies, which, in my opinion, fully counterbalances this difference, and makes the spirit of liberty still more high and haughty than in those to the northward. It is that in Virginia and the Carolinas, they have a vast multitude of slaves. Where this is the case in any part of the world, those who are free, are by far the most proud and jealous of their freedom. Freedom is to them not only an enjoyment, but a kind of rank and privilege. . . .

Permit me, Sir, to add another circumstance in our colonies, which contributes no mean part towards the growth and effect of this untractable spirit. I mean their education. In no country perhaps in the world is the law so general a study. The profession itself is numerous and powerful; and in most provinces it takes the lead. The greater number of the deputies sent to the Congress were lawyers. But all who read, and most do read, endeavour to obtain some smattering in that science. . . . This study renders men acute, inquisitive, dexterous, prompt in attack, ready in defense, full of resources. In other countries, the people, more simple, and of a less mercurial cast, judge of an ill principle in government only by an actual grievance; here they anticipate the evil, and judge of the pressure of the grievance by the badness of the principle. They augur misgovernment at a distance; and snuff the approach of tyranny in every tainted breeze.

The last cause of this disobedient spirit in the colonies is hardly less powerful than the rest, as it is not merely moral, but laid deep in the natural constitution of things. Three thousand miles of ocean lie between you and them. No contrivance can prevent the effect of this distance, in weakening government. . . .

Then, Sir, from these six capital sources; of descent; of form of government; of religion in the northern provinces; of manners in the southern; of education; of the remoteness of situation from the first mover of government; from all these causes a fierce spirit of liberty has grown up. It has grown with the growth of the people in your colonies, and increased with the increase of their wealth; a spirit, that unhappily meeting with an exercise of power in England, which, however lawful, is not reconcileable to any ideas of liberty, much less with theirs, has kindled this flame, that is ready to consume us.

. . . the question is, not whether their spirit deserves praise or blame; – what, in the name of God, shall we do with it? . . .

If . . . the removal of the causes of this spirit of American liberty be, for the greater part, or rather entirely, impracticable; if the ideas of criminal process be inapplicable, or, if applicable, are in the highest degree inexpedient, what way yet remains? No way is open, but the third and last – to comply with the American spirit as necessary; or, if you please to submit to it, as a necessary evil. . . .

My idea . . . is *to admit the people of our colonies into an interest in the Constitution*; and, by recording that admission in the journals of Parliament, to give them as strong an assurance as the nature of the thing will admit, that we mean for ever to adhere to that solemn declaration of systematic indulgence. . . .

My resolutions therefore mean to establish the equity, and justice of a taxation of America, by *grant*, and not by *imposition*. To mark the *legal competency* of the colony assemblies for the support of their government in peace, and for public aids in time of war. To acknowledge that this legal competency has had a *dutiful and beneficial exercise*; and that experience has shewn the benefit of their grants, and the *futility of parliamentary taxation as a method of supply*. . . .

Magnanimity in politics is not seldom the truest wisdom; and a great empire and little minds go ill together. . . . Our ancestors have turned a savage wilderness into a glorious empire; and have made the most extensive, and the only honourable conquests; not by destroying, but by promoting, the wealth, the number, the happiness of the human race. Let us get an American revenue as we have got an American empire. English privileges have made it all it is; English privileges alone will make it all it can be.

(Edmund Burke, Conciliation with America [1775], in Arnstein 1993: 98–100)

Questions

1 What is the relation between England and America like, according to Burke?
2 What are Burke's arguments supporting a conciliation with America?

26 George III: Speech from the Throne (October 1775)

In this speech, George III describes his position towards the rebellion of the American colonies.

The present situation of America, and my constant desire to have your advice, concurrence, and assistance on every important occasion, have determined me to call you thus early together.

Those who have long too successfully labored to inflame my people in America by gross misrepresentation and to infuse into their minds a system of opinions repugnant to the true constitution of the colonies, and to their subordinate relation to Great Britain, now openly avow their revolt, hostility, and rebellion. They have raised troops, and are collecting a naval force; they have seized the public revenue, and assumed to themselves legislative, executive, and judicial powers, which they already exercise in the most arbitrary manner over the persons and properties of their fellow subjects; and although many of these unhappy people may still retain their loyalty and may be too wise not to see the fatal consequence of this usurpation, and wish to resist it; yet the torrent of violence has been strong enough to compel their acquiescence till a sufficient force shall appear to support them.

The authors and promoters of this desperate conspiracy have in the conduct of it derived great advantage from the difference of our intentions and theirs. They meant only to amuse by vague expressions of attachment to the parent state and the strongest protestations of loyalty to me, whilst they were preparing for a general revolt. On our part, though it was declared in your last session that a rebellion existed within the province of the Massachusetts Bay, yet even that province we wished rather to reclaim than to subdue. The resolutions of Parliament breathed a spirit of moderation and forbearance; conciliatory propositions accompanied the measures taken to enforce authority, and the coercive acts were adapted to cases of criminal combinations amongst subjects not then in arms. I have acted with the same temper; anxious to prevent, if it had been possible, the effusion of the blood of my subjects and the calamities which are inseparable from a state of war; still hoping that my people in America would have discerned the traitorous views of their leaders and have been convinced that to be a subject of Great Britain, with all its consequences, is to be the freest member of any civil society in the known world.

The rebellious war now levied is become more general and is manifestly carried on for the purpose of establishing an independent empire. I need not dwell upon the fatal effects of the success of such a plan. The object is too important, the spirit of the British nation too high, the resources with which God hath blessed her too numerous, to give up so many colonies which she has planted with great industry, nursed with great tenderness, encouraged with many commercial advantages, and protected and defended at much expense of blood and treasure.

It is now become the part of wisdom, and (in its effects) of clemency to put a speedy end to these disorders by the most decisive exertions. For this purpose I have increased my naval establishment, and greatly augmented my land forces, but in such a manner as may be the least burdensome to my kingdoms.

I have also the satisfaction to inform you that I have received the most friendly offers of foreign assistance; and if I shall make any treaties in consequence thereof, they shall be laid before you. And I have, in testimony of my affection for my people who can have no cause in which I am not equally interested, sent to the garrisons of Gibraltar and Port Mahon a part of my Electoral troops in order that a larger number of the established forces of this kingdom may be applied to the maintenance of its authority; and the national militia, planned and regulated with equal regard to the rights, safety, and protection of my crown and people, may give a farther extent and activity to our military operations.

When the unhappy and deluded multitude against whom this force will be directed shall become sensible of their error, I shall be ready to receive the misled with tenderness and mercy; and in order to prevent the inconveniences which may arise from the great distance of their situation, and to remove as soon as possible the calamities which they suffer, I shall give authority to certain persons upon the spot to grant general or particular pardons and indemnities, in such manner and to such persons as they shall think fit, and to receive the submission of any province or colony which shall be disposed to return to its allegiance. It may be also proper to authorize the persons so commissioned to restore such province or colony so returning to its allegiance to the free exercise of its trade and commerce and to the same protection and security as if such province or colony had never revolted.

Gentlemen of the House of Commons:
I have ordered the proper estimates for the ensuing year to be laid before you; and I rely on your affection to me and your resolution to maintain the just rights of this country, for such supplies as the present circumstances of our affairs require. Among the many unavoidable ill consequences of this rebellion none affects me more sensibly than the extraordinary burden which it must create to my faithful subjects.

My Lords and Gentlemen:
I have fully opened to you my views and intentions. The constant employment of my thoughts, and the most earnest wishes of my heart tend wholly to the safety and happiness of all my people, and to the reestablishment of order and tranquillity through the several parts of my dominions, in a close connection and constitutional dependence. You see the tendency of the present disorders and I have stated to you the measures which I mean to pursue for suppressing them. Whatever remains to be done that may farther contribute to this end, I commit to your wisdom. And I am happy to add that as well from the assurances I have received as from the general appearance of affairs in Europe, I see no probability that the measures which you may adopt will be interrupted by disputes with any foreign power.

(George III, Speech from the Throne [October 1775], in Arnstein 1993: 104–6)

Questions

1 How does this speech compare to Burke's 'Conciliation with America' (Doc. 25)? Describe differences and similarities.
2 Whose arguments do you find more convincing, and why?

27 Thomas Paine: *Common Sense*

Thomas Paine (1737–1809) is chiefly remembered for his role as one of the Founding Fathers of the United States of America. His pro-independence pamphlet Common Sense *was published in January 1776 and triggered the move towards independence in the colonies.*

Society in every state is a blessing, but government even in its best state is but a necessary evil; in its worst state it is an intolerable one. Government, like dress, is the badge of lost innocence; the palaces of kings are built on the ruins of the bowers of paradise. For were the impulses of conscience clear, uniform, and irresistibly obeyed, man would need no other law giver. . . .

England, since the conquest, hath known some few good monarchs, but groaned beneath a much larger number of bad ones; yet no man in his senses can say that their claim under William the Conqueror is a very honourable one. A French bastard landing with an armed banditti, and establishing himself King of England against the consent of the natives, is in plain terms a very paltry rascally original. It certainly hath no divinity in it. . . .

We have boasted the protection of Great Britain, without considering, that her motive was interest not attachment; that she did not protect us from our enemies on our account, but from her enemies on her own account, from those who had no quarrel with us on any other account, and who will always be our enemies on the same account. Let Britain waive her protections to the continent, or the continent throw off the dependence, and we should be at peace with France and Spain were they at war with Britain. This new world hath been the asylum for the persecuted lovers of civil and religious liberty from every part of Europe. Hither have they fled, not from the tender embraces of the mother, but from the cruelty of the monster; and it is so far true of England, that the same tyranny which drove the first immigrants from home, pursues their descendants still. . . .

To be always running three or four thousand miles with a tale or a petition, waiting four or five months for an answer, which then obtained requires five or six more to explain it in, will in a few years be looked upon as folly and childishness. . . . Small islands not capable of protecting themselves, are the proper objects of kingdoms to take under their care; but there is something very absurd, in supposing a continent to be perpetually governed by an island. In no instance hath nature made the satellite larger than its primary planet, and as England and America, with respect to each other, reverse the common order of nature, it is evident they belong to different systems; England to Europe, America to itself. . . .

But where, says some, is the King of America? I will tell you. Friend, he reigns above, and doth not make havoc of mankind like the royal brute of Britain. Yet that we may not appear to be effective even in earthly honours, let a day be solemnly set apart for proclaiming the charter; let it be brought forth placed on the divine law, the word of God; let a crown be placed thereon, by which the world may know, that so far we approve of monarchy, that in America the law is king. For as in absolute governments the king is law, so in free countries the law ought to be king; and there ought to be no other.

(Thomas Paine, *Common Sense*, in Williams 1977: 42–3)

Questions

1 How and with what words does Paine describe the relations between Great Britain and America?
2 What is his opinion about government? Do you agree with him? Why (not)?
3 Compare his text to Burke's (Doc. 25).

---

6 POLITICAL REFORMS, INDUSTRIAL REVOLUTION, IMPERIAL RULE, 1789–1914

28 The Declaration of the Rights of Man and Citizen (26 August 1789)

The Declaration of the Rights of Man and Citizen is one of the most important documents of the French Revolution, defining fundamental individual rights such as popular sovereignty and natural equality.

I.   Men are born and remain free and equal in rights. Social distinctions may be founded only upon the general good.

II.   The aim of all political association is the preservation of the natural and imprescriptible rights of man. These rights are liberty, property, security, and resistance to oppression.

III. The principle of all sovereignty resides essentially in the nation. No body nor individual may exercise any authority which does not proceed directly from the nation.

IV.   Liberty consists in the freedom to do everything which injures no one else. . . .

V.   Law can only prohibit such actions as are hurtful to society. Nothing may be prevented which is not forbidden by law, and no one may be forced to do anything not provided for by law.

VI.   Law is the expression of the general will. . . . It must be the same for all, whether it protects or punishes. All citizens, being equal in the eyes of the law, are equally eligible to all dignities and to all public positions and occupations, according to their abilities, and without distinction except that of their virtues and talents.

VII.   No person shall be accused, arrested, or imprisoned except in the cases and according to the forms prescribed by law. Any one soliciting, transmitting, executing, or causing to be executed, any arbitrary order, shall be punished. But any citizen summoned or arrested in virtue of the law shall submit without delay, as resistance constitutes an offense.

VIII.   The law shall provide for such punishments only as are strictly and obviously necessary, and no one shall suffer punishment except it be legally inflicted in virtue of a law passed and promulgated before the commission of the offense.

IX.   As all persons are held innocent until they shall have been declared guilty, if arrest shall be deemed indispensable, all harshness not essential to the securing of the prisoner's person shall be severely repressed by law.

X.   No one shall be disquieted on account of his opinions, including his religious views, provided their manifestation does not disturb the public order established by law.

XI.   The free communication of ideas and opinions is one of the most precious of the rights of man. Every citizen may, accordingly, speak, write, and print with freedom, but shall be responsible for such abuses of this freedom as shall be defined by law.

XII.   The security of the rights of man and of the citizen requires public military forces. These forces are, therefore, established for the good of all and not for the personal advantage of those to whom they shall be intrusted.

XIII.   A common contribution is essential for the maintenance of the public forces and for the cost of administration. This should be equitably distributed among all the citizens in proportion to their means.

XIV.   All the citizens have a right to decide, either personally or by their representatives, as to the necessity of the public contribution; to grant this freely; to know to what uses it is put; and to fix the proportion, the mode of assessment and of collection and the duration of the taxes.

XV.   Society has the right to require of every public agent an account of his administration.

XVI.   A society in which the observance of the law is not assured, nor the separation of powers defined, has no constitution at all.

XVII.   Since property is an inviolable and sacred right, no one shall be deprived thereof except where public necessity, legally determined, shall clearly demand it, and then only on condition that the owner shall have been previously and equitably indemnified.

(The Declaration of the Rights of Man and Citizen [1789], prepared by Gerald Murphy [The Cleveland Free-Net – aa300]. Distributed by the Cybercasting Services Division of the National Public Telecomputing Network [NPTN]).

Questions

1 Sketch the important principles which are set forth in this declaration. Why do you think this declaration is a fundamental document of the French Revolution?
2 Do you think that this declaration is still relevant today?

29 Edmund Burke: *Reflections on the Revolution in France* (1790)

In Reflections on the Revolution in France *Burke expressed his strong opposition to the French Revolution, criticising it as a violent rebellion against tradition and authority.*

Society is indeed a contract. Subordinate contracts for objects of mere occasional interest may be dissolved at pleasure – but the state ought not to be considered as nothing better than a partnership agreement in a trade of pepper and coffee, callico or tobacco, or some other such low concern, to be taken up for a little temporary interest, and to be dissolved by the fancy of the parties. It is to be looked on with other reverence; because it is not a partnership in things subservient only to the gross animal existence of a temporary and perishable nature. It is a partnership in all science; a partnership in all art; a partnership in every virtue, and in all perfection. As then ends of such a partnership cannot be obtained in many generations, it becomes a partnership not only between those who are living, but between those who are living, those who are dead, and those who are to be born. Each contract of each particular state is but a clause in the great primaeval contract of eternal society, linking the lower with the higher natures, connecting the visible and invisible world, according to a fixed compact sanctioned by the inviolable oath which holds all physical and all moral natures, each in their appointed place. This law is not subject to the will of those, who by an obligation above them, and infinitely superior, are bound to submit their will to that law.

(Edmund Burke, *Reflections on the Revolution in France* [1790], in Burke 1973: 194–5)

30 Thomas Paine: *Rights of Man* (1791–2)

Thomas Paine's Rights of Man *is a political tract which is highly critical of monarchies. It was written as an answer to Burke's* Reflections on the Revolution in France, *supporting the French Revolution.*

There never did, there never will, and there never can exist a parliament, or any description of men, or any generation of men, in any country, possessed of the right or the power of binding and controlling posterity to the *'end of time'*, or of commanding for ever how the world shall be governed, or who shall govern it; and therefore, all such clauses, acts or declarations, by which the makers of them attempt to do what they have neither the right nor the power to do, nor the power to execute, are in themselves null and void. – Every age and generation must be as free to act for itself, *in all cases*, as the ages and generations which preceded it. The vanity and presumption of governing beyond the grave is the most ridiculous and insolent of all tyrannies. Man has no property in man; neither has any generation a property in the generations which are to follow. The parliament or the people of 1688, or of any other period, has no more right to dispose of the people of the present day, or to bind or to control them in *any shape whatever*, than the parliament or the people of the present day have to dispose of, bind or control those who are to live in a hundred or a thousand years hence. Every generation is, and must be, competent to all the purposes which its occasions require. It is the living, and not the dead, that are to be accommodated. When man ceases to be, his power and his wants cease with him; and having no longer any participation in the concerns of this world, he has no longer any authority in directing who shall be its governors, or how its government shall be organised, or how administered.

(Thomas Paine, *Rights of Man* [1791–2], in Paine 1971: 63–4)

31 Address of the London Corresponding Society, 19 November 1792

The corresponding societies – the London Corresponding Society, founded in 1792 and suppressed in 1799, was the most famous – spread the ideas of the French Revolution among the British population and favoured parliamentary reform as well as universal male suffrage.

Friends and Fellow Countrymen!

Unless we are greatly deceived, the Time is approaching when the Object for which we struggle is likely to come within our Reach. – That a Nation like Britain should be free, it is requisite only that Britons should will it to become so; that such should be their Will, the Abuses of our Original Constitution, and the Alarm of our Aristocratic Enemies, sufficiently witness. – Confident in the Purity of our Motives, and in the Justice of our Cause, let us meet Falsehood with Proofs, and Hypocrisy with Plainness: Let us persevere in declaring our Principles, and Misrepresentation will meet its due Reward – Contempt.

In this View the Artifices of a late Aristocratic Association, formed on the 20th Instant, call for a few Remarks, on account of the Declaration they have published relative to other Clubs and Societies formed in this Nation. It is true that this Meeting of Gentlemen (for so they style themselves) have mentioned no Names, instanced no Facts, quoted no Authorities; but they take upon themselves to assert, that Bodies of their Countrymen have been associated professing Opinions favourable to the Rights of Man, to Liberty, and Equality; and moreover that those Opinions are conveyed in the Terms No King! No Parliament! – So much for their Assertions.

If this be intended to include the Societies to which we respectively belong, we here in the most solemn Manner deny the latter Part of the Charge; while in admitting the former, we claim the Privilege, and glory in the Character, of Britons. Whoever shall attribute to us (who wish only the Restoration of the lost Liberties of our Country) the expressions of No King! No Parliament! or any Design of invading the Property of other Men, is guilty of a wilful, and impudent, and a malicious Falsehood.

We know and are sensible that the Wages of every Man are his Right; that Difference of Strength, of Talents, and of Industry, do and ought to afford proportional Distinctions of Property, which, when acquired and confirmed by the Laws, is sacred and inviolable. We defy the most slavish and malevolent Man in the Meeting of the 20th Instant, to bring the remotest Proof to the Contrary: If there be no Proof, we call upon them to justify an insidious Calumny, which seems invented only to terrify Independent Britons from reclaiming the Rightful Constitution of their Country.

We admit and we declare, that we are Friends to Civil Liberty, and therefore to Natural Equality, both of which we consider as the Rights of Mankind – Could we believe them to be 'in direct Opposition to the Laws of this Land', we should blush to find ourselves among the Number of its Inhabitants; but we are persuaded that the Abuses of the Constitution will never pass current for its true Principles, since we are told in its first Charter that all are Equal in the Sight of the Law, which 'shall neither be sold, nor refused, nor delayed, to any Free Man whatsoever'. Should it ever happen that 'Right and Justice' are opposed by Expence, by Refusal, or by Delay, *then is this Principle of Equality violated, and we are no longer Freemen.*

(London Corresponding Society, Address of the London Corresponding Society, 19 November 1792)

Question

Which ideas or concepts of the French Revolution are mirrored in this address?

32 Exchanging goods/commodities, using money, and the uses of capital

The following points summarise some central ideas of Karl Marx's critical analysis of capitalist economic thought.

1 As soon as a society is developed to such an extent that it can produce more than it can consume, it is free to exchange this surplus for other goods. This exchange of goods is called *simple exchange of goods* ($G_{oods} <> G_{oods}$). If it becomes necessary, however, to exchange many different goods, it is very useful to have *one* commodity which can be exchanged for *any* other. This commodity then plays the role of a yardstick; today this commodity is, of course, *money* ($G_{oods} > M_{oney} > G_{oods}$). In these processes (in which we exchange goods in order to consume them) no profit worth mentioning is made.

2 This situation changes as soon as money is transformed into *capital*. This happens when it becomes the 'directing agency' of the exchange process, i.e. when the reason for exchanging goods is no longer the exchange of goods in order to consume them but the accumulation of capital ($M_{oney} > G_{oods} > M_{ore\ money}$ [= M']). Capital can be accumulated as merchant capital and as industrial capital.

3 MERCHANT CAPITAL. The merchant buys commodities in a certain market at a certain price. He then either stores them until the price for these goods rises or transports them to another market where they are scarce and their price, as a consequence, is higher: $M > G >=> G > M'$.

4 INDUSTRIAL CAPITAL. An entrepreneur owning a certain amount of capital buys in the *market* certain *means of production* (raw materials, machines, the soil) as well as *labour power* and combines them under his direction in the *sphere of production* (mills, factories, etc.). (i) The *means of production* are

253

bought at their price; they are the object and means of production and do *not* create any value by themselves. The capital invested in them can be called *constant* capital (c) because its value does not change. Through the quality of his labour the worker transfers the value of the means of production on to the new product(s). (ii) The commodity *labour power* is equally bought at its price. However, there is a difference between the *price* of labour power (appearing in wages) and the amount of *value* it can create. Roughly speaking, the worker works for his wages, but in doing so he (or she) also creates a certain surplus; he (or she) produces value and surplus value. As a consequence, the capital invested in labour power changes the totally invested sum; therefore it is called *variable* capital (v). There is but one motive for the above process: *profit*. The origin of this profit is the surplus value the worker produces in the sphere of production. There c+v is transformed into c+v+s (s = surplus value). As the entrepreneur owns the place of production (mill, factory, etc.) and the means of production, he also claims the right to sell the goods produced by the workers. Having had the goods produced by the workers the entrepreneur, so to speak, turns into a merchant to solve the problem of 'realising' the goods in money form. Only if the surplus value, produced and appropriated in the sphere of production, is realised in money is it real. The transformation of the newly produced commodities (G') into money/capital (M') completes the process of transformation of capital. It is in this transformation of G' into M' that out of a certain sum of money (invested capital) *more* money (profit) is 'made': $M > G_{(c+v)} >>$ [Sphere of Production] $>> G'_{(c+v+s)} > M'$. The process $M > M'$ (to 'make' more money out of a certain sum of money) happens through the production and exchange of commodities $(G > G')$. If one transformation is finished, a new one can begin. The rules of commodity exchange have been observed: only equivalents have been exchanged, and yet a certain surplus value has come into existence through the application of labour power exceeding the amount of time necessary for the reproduction of its own price. That is the secret of profit-making.

(Author's contribution)

Questions

1 What is the difference between merchant capital and industrial capital?
2 Describe the creation of surplus value.
3 In this system of thought there is a tendency for the rate of profit to fall. Why is this so?

33 Robert Owen: *Observations on the Effect of the Manufacturing System* (1815)

The Welsh reformer Robert Owen (1771–1858) was the manager of the cotton mills at New Lanark, a Scottish factory village which his father-in-law, David Dale, had built and which was considered to be a profitable community with good working conditions. Owen was also an influential figure in the cooperative movement, advocating mutual economic activity and benefit.

. . . Hitherto, legislators have appeared to regard manufactures only in one point of view, as a source of national wealth.

The other mighty consequences which proceed from extended manufactures *when left to their natural progress*, have never yet engaged the attention of any legislature. Yet the political and moral effects to which we allude, well deserve to occupy the best faculties of the greatest and the wisest statesmen.

The general diffusion of manufactures throughout a country generates a new character in its inhabitants; and as this character is formed upon a principle quite unfavourable to individual or general happiness, it will produce the most lamentable and permanent evils, unless its tendency be counteracted by legislative interference and direction. . . .

The acquisition of wealth, and the desire which it naturally creates for a continued increase, have introduced a fondness for essentially injurious luxuries among a numerous class of individuals who formerly never thought of them, and they have also generated a disposition to sacrifice the best feelings of human nature to this love of accumulation. To succeed in this career, the industry of the lower orders, from whose labour this wealth is now drawn, has been carried by new competitors striving against those of longer standing, to a point of real oppression, reducing them by successive changes, as the spirit of competition increased and the ease of acquiring wealth diminished, to a state more wretched than can be imagined by those who have not attentively observed the changes as they have gradually occurred. In consequence, they are at present in a situation infinitely more degraded and miserable than they were before the introduction of these manufactories, upon the success of which their bare subsistence now depends. . . .

The inhabitants of every country are trained and formed by its great leading existing circumstances, and the character of the lower orders in Britain is now formed chiefly by circumstances arising from trade, manufactures, and commerce; and the governing principle of trade, manufactures, and commerce is immediate pecuniary gain, to which on the great scale every other is made to give way. All are sedulously trained to buy cheap and to sell dear; and to succeed in this art, the parties must be taught to acquire strong powers of deception; and thus a spirit is generated through every class of traders, destructive of that open, honest sincerity, without which man cannot make others happy, nor enjoy happiness himself.

Strictly speaking, however, this defect of character ought not to be attributed to the individuals possessing it, but to the overwhelming effect of the system under which they have been trained.

But the effects of this principle of gain, unrestrained, are still more lamentable on the working classes, those who are employed in the operative parts of the manufactures. . . .

The employer regards the employed as mere instruments of gain, while these acquire a gross ferocity of character, which, if legislative measures shall not be judiciously devised to prevent its increase, and ameliorate the condition of this class, will sooner or later plunge the country into a formidable and perhaps inextricable state of danger.

(Robert Owen, *Observations on the Effect of the Manufacturing System* [1815], in Arnstein 1993: 150–1)

Questions

1 What effects does the introduction of manufactures have on society?
2 Coin a phrase for the policy presented in this excerpt.

34 Samuel Smiles: *Self-Help* (1859)

This document is an excerpt from Smiles' book Self-Help, *in which he advocates individual self-improvement as a means of social advance.*

'Heaven helps those who help themselves' is a well tried maxim, embodying in a small compass the results of vast human experience. The spirit of self-help is the root of all genuine growth in the individual; and, exhibited in the lives of many, it constitutes the true source of national vigour and strength. Help from without is often enfeebling in its effects, but help from within invariably invigorates. Whatever is done *for* men or classes, to a certain extent takes away the stimulus and necessity of doing for themselves; and where men are subjected to over-guidance and over-government, the inevitable tendency is to render them comparatively helpless.

Even the best institutions can give a man no active help. Perhaps the most they can do is, to leave him free to develop himself and to improve his individual condition. But in all times men have been prone to believe that their happiness and well-being were to be secured by means of institutions rather than by their own conduct. Hence the value of legislation as an agent in human advancement has usually been much overestimated. To constitute the millionth part of a Legislature, by voting for one or two men once in three or five years, however conscientiously this duty may be performed, can exercise but little active influence upon any man's life and character. Moreover, it is every day becoming more clearly understood, that the function of Government is negative and restrictive, rather than positive and active; being resolvable principally into protection – protection of life, liberty, and property. Laws, wisely administrated, will secure men in the enjoyment of the fruits of their labour, whether of mind or body, at a comparatively small personal sacrifice; but no laws, however stringent, can make the idle industrious, the shiftless provident, or the drunken sober. Such reforms can only be effected by means of individual action, economy, and self-denial; by better habits, rather than by greater rights. . . .

Indeed, all experience serves to prove that the worth and strength of a State depend far less upon the form of its institutions than upon the character of its men. For the nation is only an aggregate of individual conditions, and civilisation itself is but a question of the personal improvement of the men, women, and children of whom society is composed.

(Samuel Smiles, *Self-Help* [1859, 1882])

Questions

1 Comment on the phrase 'Heaven helps those who help themselves.' What does it imply? What consequences does it have for society? Is it still relevant today?
2 How does this text compare to Owen's *Observations on the Effect of the Manufacturing System*? Describe similarities and differences.

35 Percy Bysshe Shelley: 'England in 1819'

Percy Bysshe Shelley (1792–1822), a British poet, wrote this sonnet about England as well as other political poems while he stayed in Italy.

An old, mad, blind, despised, and dying king –
Princes, the dregs of their dull race, who flow
Through public scorn – mud from a muddy spring;
Rulers who neither see, nor feel, nor know,
But leechlike to their fainting country cling,
Till they drop, blind in blood, without a blow;
A people starved and stabbed in the untilled field –
An army, which liberticide and prey
Makes as a two-edged sword to all who wield;
Golden and sanguine laws which tempt and slay;
Religion Christless, Godless – a book sealed;
A Senate – Time's worst statute unrepealed –
Are graves, from which a glorious Phantom may
Burst, to illumine our tempestuous day.

(Percy Bysshe Shelley, 'England in 1819' [1839])

Questions

1 How and by which literary means are the English monarchy and England in general represented in this sonnet?
2 If you were to give an account of England in 1819, what would it look like?

36 'Land of Hope and Glory'

This song is one of England's favourite patriotic songs (almost an 'unofficial' national anthem). The music was there first – one of five marches in Edward Elgar's 'Pomp and Circumstance' (1901); A. C. Benson later provided the words (allegedly prompted by a remark of Edward VII).

Dear Land of Hope, thy hope is crowned.
God make thee mightier yet!
On Sov'ran brows, beloved, renowned,
Once more thy crown is set.
Thine equal laws, by Freedom gained,
Have ruled thee well and long;
By Freedom gained, by Truth maintained,
Thine Empire shall be strong.

Land of Hope and Glory,
Mother of the Free,
How shall we extol thee,
Who are born of thee?
Wider still and wider
Shall thy bounds be set;
God, who made thee mighty,
Make thee mightier yet.

Thy fame is ancient as the days,
As Ocean large and wide:
A pride that dares, and heeds not praise,
A stern and silent pride:
Not that false joy that dreams content
With what our sires have won;
The blood a hero sire hath spent
Still nerves a hero son.

(A. C. Benson, 'Land of Hope and Glory' [1902])

37 Walter Bagehot: The English Monarchy

Walter Bagehot (1826–77) was a journalist and political writer whose book The
English Constitution *(1867) has been of central importance in the description and
definition of the British monarchy. His distinction between the 'efficient' and 'dignified'
parts of government – the decision-taking political machinery (particularly the
Cabinet) and the monarchy – has been influential until the present day.*

. . . The use of the Queen, in a dignified capacity, is incalculable. Without her in
England, the present English Government would fail and pass away. Most
people when they read that the Queen walked on the slopes at Windsor – that
the Prince of Wales went to the Derby – have imagined that too much thought
and prominence were given to little things. But they have been in error; and it is
nice to trace how the actions of a retired widow and an unemployed youth
become of such importance.

The best reason why Monarchy is a strong government is that it is an
intelligible government. The mass of mankind understand it, and they hardly
anywhere in the world understand any other. It is often said that men are ruled
by their imaginations; but it would be truer to say they are governed by the
weakness of their imaginations. The nature of a constitution, the action of an
assembly, the play of parties, the unseen formation of a guiding opinion, are
complex facts, difficult to know and easy to mistake. But the action of a single
will, the fiat of a single mind, are easy ideas: anybody can make them out, and
no one can ever forget them. . . . To state the matter shortly, royalty is a government in which the attention of the nation is concentrated on one person
doing interesting actions. A Republic is a government in which that attention is
divided between many, who are all doing uninteresting actions. Accordingly, so
long as the human heart is strong and the human reason weak, royalty will be
strong because it appeals to diffused feeling, and Republics weak because they
appeal to the understanding.

Secondly. The English Monarchy strengthens our Government with the
strength of religion. It is not easy to say why it should be so. Every instructed
theologian would say that it was the duty of a person born under a Republic as
much to obey that Republic as it is the duty of one born under a Monarchy to
obey the monarch. But the mass of the English people do not think so; they
agree with the oath of allegiance; they say it is their duty to obey the 'Queen',
and they have but hazy notions as to obeying laws without a queen. . . . If you

ask the immense majority of the Queen's subjects by what right she rules, they would never tell you that she rules by Parliamentary right. . . . They will say she rules by 'God's grace'; they believe that they have a mystic obligation to obey her. When her family came to the Crown it was a sort of treason to maintain the inalienable right of lineal sovereignty, for it was equivalent to saying that the claim of another family was better than hers: but now, in the strange course of human events, that very sentiment has become her surest and best support. . . .

A principal reason why the Monarchy so well consecrates our whole state is to be sought in the peculiarity many Americans and many utilitarians smile at. They laugh at this 'extra', as the Yankee called it, at the solitary transcendent element. . . . When a monarch can bless, it is best that he should not be touched. It should be evident that he does no wrong. He should not be brought too closely to real measurement. He should be aloof and solitary. As the functions of English royalty are for the most part latent, it fulfils this condition. It seems to order, but it never seems to struggle. It is commonly hidden like a mystery, and sometimes paraded like a pageant, but in neither case is it contentious. The nation is divided into parties, but the crown is of no party. Its apparent separation from business is that which removes it both from enmities and from desecration, which preserves its mystery, which enables it to combine the affection of conflicting parties – to be a visible symbol of unity to those still so imperfectly educated as to need a symbol.

Thirdly. The Queen is the head of our society. If she did not exist the Prime Minister would be the first person in the country. He and his wife would have to receive foreign ministers, and occasionally foreign princes, to give the first parties in the country; he and she would be at the head of the pageant of life; they would represent England in the eyes of foreign nations; they would represent the Government of England in the eyes of the English.

It is very easy to imagine a world in which this change would not be a great evil. In a country where people did not care for the outward show of life, where the genius of the people was untheatrical, and they exclusively regarded the substance of things, this matter would be trifling. . . . A nation of unimpressible philosophers would not care at all how the externals of life were managed. Who is the showman is not material unless you care about the show.

But of all nations in the world the English are perhaps the least a nation of pure philosophers. It would be a very serious matter to us to change every four or five years the visible head of our world. We are not now remarkable for the highest sort of ambition; but we are remarkable for having a great deal of the lower sort of ambition and envy. The House of Commons is thronged with people who get there merely for 'social purposes', as the phrase goes; that is, that they and their families may go to parties else impossible. Members of Parliament are envied by thousands merely for this frivolous glory, as a thinker calls it. If the highest post in conspicuous life were thrown open to public competition, this low sort of ambition and envy would be fearfully increased.

Politics would offer a prize too dazzling for mankind; clever base people would strive for it, and stupid base people would envy it. . . .

Fourthly. We have come to regard the Crown as the head of our morality. The virtues of Queen Victoria and the virtues of George III. have sunk deep into the popular heart. We have come to believe that it is natural to have a virtuous sovereign, and that the domestic virtues are as likely to be found on thrones as they are eminent when there. But a little experience and less thought show that royalty cannot take credit for domestic excellence. Neither George I., nor George II., nor William IV. were patterns of family merit; George IV. was a model of family demerit. The plain fact is, that to the disposition of all others most likely to go wrong, to an excitable disposition, the place of a constitutional king has greater temptations than almost any other, and fewer suitable occupations than almost any other. All the world and all the glory of it, whatever is most attractive, whatever is most seductive, has always been offered to the Prince of Wales of the day, and always will be. It is not rational to expect the best virtue where temptation is applied in the most trying form at the frailest time of human life. The occupations of a constitutional monarch are grave, formal, important, but never exciting; they have nothing to stir eager blood, awaken high imagination, work off wild thoughts.

Lastly, constitutional royalty has the function which I insisted on at length in my last essay, and which, though it is by far the greatest, I need not now enlarge upon again. It acts as a DISGUISE. It enables our real rulers to change without heedless people knowing it. The masses of Englishmen are not fit for an elective government; if they knew how near they were to it, they would be surprised, and almost tremble.

Of a like nature is the value of constitutional royalty in times of transition. The greatest of all helps to the substitution of a Cabinet government [constitutional government] for a preceding absolute monarchy is the accession of a king favourable to such a government, and pledged to it. Cabinet government, when new, is weak in time of trouble. The Prime Minister – the chief on whom everything depends, who must take responsibility if any one is to take it, who must use force if any one is to use it – is not fixed in power. He holds his place, by the essence of the Government, with some uncertainty. Among a people well-accustomed to such a Government, such a functionary may be bold: he may rely, if not on the Parliament, on the nation which understands and values him. But when that Government has only recently been introduced, it is difficult for such a Minister to be as bold as he ought to be. His power rests too much on human reason, and too little on human instinct. The traditional strength of the hereditary monarch is at these times of incalculable use. It would have been impossible for England to get through the first years after 1688 but for the singular ability of William III. . . .

(Walter Bagehot, *The English Constitution* [1867])

38 Harriet Taylor: 'Enfranchisement of Women' (1851)

Harriet Taylor (1807–58) was a women's rights advocate. The text, from which the following extract is taken, was published under her husband's name (John Stuart Mill) but was largely written by her.

Many persons think they have sufficiently justified the restrictions on women's field of action, when they have said that the pursuits from which women are excluded are *unfeminine*, and that the *proper sphere* of women is not politics or publicity, but private and domestic life.

We deny the right of any proportion of the species to decide for another portion, or an individual for another individual, what is and what is not their 'proper sphere'. The proper sphere for all human beings is the largest and highest which they are able to attain to. What this is, cannot be ascertained, without complete liberty of choice.

(Harriet Taylor, 'Enfranchisement of women', *Westminster Review*, LV [1851], reprinted in Hollis 1979: 293)

39 'Why Women want the Vote', a pamphlet issued by the Women's Social and Political Union (1903)

Two groups were instrumental in the struggle for women's suffrage: the more moderate National Union of Women's Suffrage Societies (NUWSS) founded in 1897 by Millicent Fawcett, and the more radical Women's Social and Political Union (WSPU) founded in 1903 by Emmeline and Christabel Pankhurst. The latter published the following pamphlet.

Because

No race or class or sex can have its interest properly safeguarded in the Legislature of a country unless it is represented by direct suffrage.

Because

Politics and economics go hand in hand. And so long as woman has no political status she will be the 'bottom-dog' as a wage-earner.

Because

While men who are voters can get their economic grievance listened to, non-voters are disregarded.

Because

The possession of citizenship and the meeting together for political discussion stimulates the faculty of combined action, and gives of itself a greater power of economic resistance.

Because

Women are taxed without being represented, and taxation without representation is tyranny.

Because

Women have to obey the laws equally with men, and they ought to have a voice in deciding what those laws shall be.

Because

The Legislature in the past has not made laws which are equal between men and women; and these laws will not be altered until women get the vote.

Because

Additional laws affecting the labour of women are contemplated, and such laws ought not to be introduced in a Parliament only responsible to men.

Because

All the more important and lucrative positions are barred to women, and opportunities of public service are denied.

Because

Politics have invaded the home, and women must therefore enter politics.

Because

Grave questions, such as the death rate of infants, the waste of child-life, the employment of married women, unemployment, wages, and care of the aged, cannot be satisfactorily settled if the women's point of view is left out.

Because

All the wisest men and women realise that decisions based upon the point of view of men and women together are more valuable than those based upon either singly.

Because

So long as the majority of women of the country have no interest in politics the children grow up ignorant of the meaning of the struggle for freedom, and lessons learnt in school in one generation by bitter experience have to be re-learnt by the next in the same school.

Because

Wherever women have become voters, reform has proceeded more rapidly than before, and even at home our municipal government, in which women have a certain share, is in advance and not behind our Parliament attitudes on many important questions.

Because

Women, like men, need to have some interest outside the home, and will be better comrades to their husbands, better mothers to their children, and better housekeepers of their home, when they get them.

(Women's Social and Political Union, 'Why Women Want the Vote' [1903])

Questions

1 Which of the demands do you regard as radical?
2 Do the demands listed above include the interests of working-class women?
3 For a long time the women's movement was split along class lines, i.e. middle-class women and working-class women could not agree on one particular question. Can you guess which question this was?

40 Workhouses

The diagram opposite demonstrates how workhouses could be constructed.

Questions

1 What do you think of the plan? Does is remind you of any other social institution?
2 Could you think of an alternative?

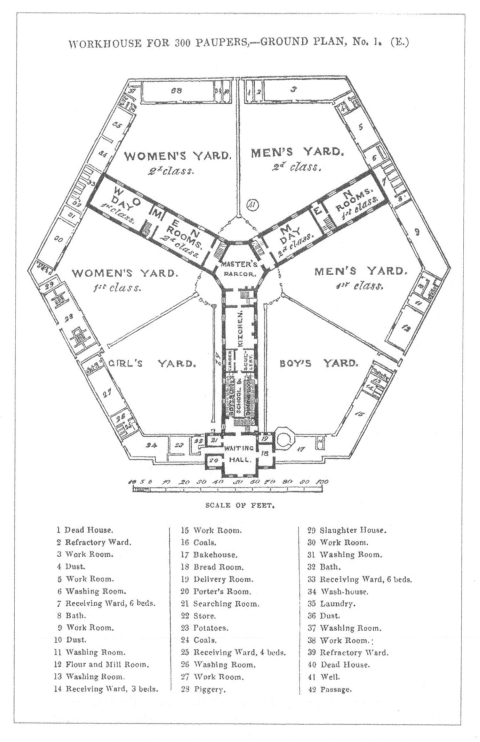

Figure 14 Ground plan of workhouse for 300 paupers, from Trevor May, *The Victorian Workhouse* (Shire Publications, 2000) p. 10. By permission of Shire Publications.

265

41 Isaac Butt: For Irish affairs an Irish Parliament (1874)

This document is taken from a speech by Isaac Butt, the founder and first leader of the Irish Home Rule League, which he delivered in the House of Commons, 30 June 1874.

I am asking . . . for a constitutional government, and the benefit of those free institutions which make England great. If I succeed in showing that Ireland has not a constitutional government, then I think I can rely on the justice and generosity of the English Parliament and of the Commons at large to give it to her. What is constitutional government? It consists of adequate representation in Parliament – a control of the administration of affairs by a representative assembly of the people, so as to bring the government of the country into harmony with the feeling, the wants, and the wishes of the people. Does the representation by 103 Irish members in the English House of Commons amount to that? Can it be said that this House discharges the great function of constitutional government to Ireland? If it does not, then it follows that Ireland is deprived of that constitutional government which is its inherent right. I know it may be said that this involves the question whether Ireland and England are not so blended into one nation, that the same House may discharge the duties of a representative assembly for both. This, again, is a matter of fact. The House may wish that we were all West Britons, but wishes will not alter facts. . . . An Irishman travelling through England, while admiring the people and their manufacturing prosperity, and wishing they may long enjoy it, will think with bitter regret that his own country is not likewise prosperous. The two countries are not blended together, because in every department in Ireland the distinction was marked. We have a separate government, a separate lord lieutenant, separate courts of law; and exceptional laws are passed for Ireland which would never be tolerated for England. How, then, can one representative assembly act for both? . . . Is there a department of the Irish administration which does not consider it is highest policy to thwart the wishes of the Irish people? ('Oh!') That I say deliberately. Apart from the office of lord chancellor there are five great and important administrative offices in Ireland: – that of the chief secretary, the chief of the Irish constabulary – that Irish army of occupation which is not placed in that country for police – the first commissioner of police in Dublin, the chief of the local government board, and the chief of . . . the board of works. How many of these are Irishmen? Not a single one. And these are offices the owner of which are brought into daily contact with the life of the people. They are all filled at this moment by Englishmen and Scotchmen.

The whole record of the legislation for Ireland since the Union [of 1800] is made up of successive Arms Acts, suspensions of the Habeas Corpus Act, two Party Procession Prevention Acts, and Coercion Acts, each one more severe than its predecessor. And this record is the more gloomy because it is a record of the doings of well-intentioned parliaments. Notwithstanding all that has been done, the curfew bell of the Norman conquerors is rung in many parts of the country, and in others blood money is exacted after the example of the Saxons.

(Isaac Butt, For Irish affairs an Irish Parliament [1874], *Hansard's Parliamentary Debates*, 3rd series, CCXX, cols. 700 seq.)

Questions

1 According to this speech, what are the main concerns of the Home Rule League?
2 What reasons does Butt give in order to support Home Rule?

7 THE TWENTIETH CENTURY: DEVASTATION AND DECLINE, RECONSTRUCTION AND REORIENTATION, 1914–99

42 Herbert Henry Asquith: Justification of War (1914)

From 1908 to 1916, Herbert Henry Asquith (1852–1928) served as prime minister. In 1914, when Britain declared war on Germany, he made the following statement.

I am entitled to say, and I do so on behalf of this country – I speak not for a party I speak for the country as a whole – that we made every effort any government could possibly make for peace. But this war has been forced upon us. What is it we are fighting for? Everyone knows, and no one knows better than the government, the terrible, incalculable suffering, economic, social, personal and political, which war, and especially a war between the Great Powers of the world, must entail. There is no man amongst us sitting upon this bench in these trying days – more trying perhaps than any body of statesmen for a hundred years have had to pass through – there is not a man amongst us who has not, during the whole of that time, had clearly before his vision the almost unequalled suffering which war, even in a just cause, must bring about, not only to the peoples who are for the moment living in this country and in the other countries of the world, but to posterity and to the whole prospects of European civilization. Every step we took with that vision before our eyes, and with a sense of responsibility which it is impossible to describe. Unhappily, if in spite of all our efforts to keep the peace, and with what fully and overpowering consciousness of the result, if the issue be decided in favour of war, we have, nevertheless thought it the duty as well as the interest of this country to go to war, the House may be well assured it was because we believe, and I am certain the country will believe, that we are unsheathing our sword in a just cause.

If I am asked what we are fighting for, I reply in two sentences. In the first place to fulfil a solemn international obligation, an obligation which, if it had been entered into between private persons in the ordinary concerns of life, would have been regarded as an obligation not only of law but of honor, which no self-respecting man could have repudiated. I say, secondly we are fighting to vindicate the principle which, in these days when force, material force, sometimes seems to be the dominant influence and factor in the development of mankind, we are fighting to vindicate the principle that small nationalities are not to be crushed, in defiance of international good faith, by the arbitrary will of a strong and overmastering power.

(Herbert Henry Asquith, Justification of War [1914], in Arnstein 1993: 321)

Questions

What arguments does Herbert Henry Asquith put forward in order to justify war?

43 Bertrand Russell: Reflections on Pacifism in Wartime (1914–1918)

The philosopher Bertrand Russell (1872–1970) voiced strong objections against World War One. Because of his pacifist activities and writings as presented in the following document he eventually lost his fellowship at Trinity College, Cambridge.

The great stimulant to herd-instinct is fear; in patriots, the instinct was stimulated by fear of the Germans, but in pacifists fear of the patriots produced a similar result. I can remember sitting in a bus and thinking: 'These people would tear me to pieces if they knew what I think about the war.' The feeling was uncomfortable, and led one to prefer the company of pacifists. Gradually a pacifist herd was formed. When we were all together we felt warm and cozy, and forgot what an insignificant minority we were. We thought of other minorities that had become majorities. We did not know that one of us was to become prime minister, but if we had known we should have supposed that it would be a good thing when he did.

The pacifist herd was a curious one, composed of very diverse elements. There were those who, on religious grounds, considered all warfare wicked; there were many in the I.L.P. [Independent Labour Party] who came to the same conclusion without invoking the authority of the Bible; there were men who subsequently became Communists, who were cynical about capitalist wars but were quite willing to join in a proletarian revolution; and there were men in the Union of Democratic Control, who, without having definite opinions about wars in general, thought that our pre-war diplomacy had been at fault, and that the belief in the sole guilt of Germany was a dangerous falsehood. These different elements did not easily work together. The cynicism of communists-to-be was painful to Quakers, and Quaker gentleness toward the war-mongers was exasperating to those who attributed everything evil to the wickedness of capitalists. The socialism of the I.L.P. repelled many Liberal pacifists, and those who condemned all war were impatient with those who confined their arguments to the particular war then in progress. And so the pacifist herd split into minor herds. In some men, the habit of standing out against the herd became so ingrained that they could not co-operate with anybody about anything.

(Bertrand Russell, Reflections on Pacifism in Wartime (1914–1918) in Arnstein 1993: 325)

Questions

1 How is the 'pacifist herd' represented in this document?
2 Discuss the main aspects of Russell's reflections in comparison to Asquith's key ideas. Which attitude would you have shared in that situation and why?

44 William Beveridge: Social Insurance and Allied Services

In 1942 the social reformer William Beveridge (1879–1963) presented a report on social insurance to Parliament from which the following excerpts are taken. It had a great impact on the Labour Party's welfare policy of the later 1940s.

Three Guiding Principles of Recommendations

6.   In proceeding from this first comprehensive survey of social insurance to the next task – of making recommendations – three guiding principles may be laid down at the outset.

7.   The first principle is that any proposals for the future, while they should use to the full the experience gathered in the past, should not be restricted by consideration of sectional interests established in the obtaining of that experience. Now, when the war is abolishing landmarks of every kind, is the opportunity for using experience in a clear field. A revolutionary moment in the world's history is a time for revolutions, not for patching.

8.   The second principle is that organisation of social insurance should be treated as one part only of a comprehensive policy of social progress. Social insurance fully developed may provide income security; it is an attack upon Want. But Want is one only of five giants on the road of reconstruction and in some ways the easiest to attack. The others are Disease, Ignorance, Squalor and Idleness.

9.   The third principle is that social security must be achieved by co-operation between the State and the individual. The State should offer security for

service and contribution. The State in organising security should not stifle incentive, opportunity, responsibility; in establishing a national minimum, it should leave room and encouragement for voluntary action by each individual to provide more than that minimum for himself and his family.

10. The Plan for Social Security set out in this Report is built upon these principles. It uses experience but is not tied by experience. It is put forward as a limited contribution to a wider social policy, though as something that could be achieved now without waiting for the whole of that policy. It is, first and foremost, a plan of insurance – of giving in return for contributions benefits up to subsistence level, as of right and without means test, so that individuals may build freely upon it. . . .

311. Eight Primary Causes of Need: The primary needs for social security are of eight kinds, reckoning the composite needs of a married woman as one and including also the needs of childhood (Assumption A) and the need for universal comprehensive medical treatment and rehabilitation (Assumption B). These needs are set out below; to each there is attached in the security scheme a distinct insurance benefit or benefits. Assistance may enter to deal with any kind of need, where insurance benefit for any reason is inadequate or absent.

Unemployment: that is to say, inability to obtain employment by a person dependent on it and physically fit for it, met by unemployment benefit with removal and lodging grants.

Disability: that is to say, inability of a person of working age, through illness or accident, to pursue a gainful occupation, met by disability benefit and industrial pension.

Loss of Livelihood by person not dependent on paid employment, met by training benefit.

Retirement from occupation, paid or unpaid, through age, met by retirement pension.

Marriage needs of a woman, met by Housewives' Policy including provision for

(1) Marriage, met by marriage grant.

(2) Maternity, met by maternity grant in all cases, and, in the case of a married woman in gainful occupation, also by maternity benefit for a period before and after confinement.

(3) Interruption or cessation of husband's earnings by his unemployment, disability or retirement, met by share of benefit or pension with husband.

(4) Widowhood, met by provision varying according to circumstances including temporary widow's benefit for readjustment, guardian benefit while caring for children and training benefit if and when there are no children in need of care.

(5) Separation, i.e. end of husband's maintenance by legal separation, or established desertion, met by adaptation of widowhood provisions, including separation benefit, guardian benefit and training benefit.

(6) Incapacity for household duties, met by provision of paid help in illness as part of treatment.

Funeral Expenses of self or any person for whom responsible, met by funeral grant.

Childhood, provided for by children's allowances if in full-time education, till sixteen.

Physical Disease or Incapacity, met by medical treatment, domiciliary and institutional, for self and dependants in comprehensive health service and by post-medical rehabilitation.

(William Beveridge, *The Beveridge Report* [1942])

Questions

1 Describe and comment on this concept of social insurance. What does it consist of and how does it work? Do you regard it as effective, realistic, utopian, etc.? Why?
2 Compare this concept of social insurance to the laws in your country.

45 Statute of Westminster (1931)

On 11 December 1931 this statute was enacted by the British Parliament. It establishes legislative equality between the United Kingdom and the dominions of the British Empire.

. . . NOW, THEREFORE, BE IT ENACTED by the King's Most Excellent Majesty, by and with the advice and consent of the Lords Spiritual and Temporal, and Commons, in this present Parliament assembled, and by the authority of the same, as follows: –

1. In this Act the expression 'Dominion' means any of the following Dominions, that is to say, the Dominion of Canada, the Commonwealth of Australia, the Dominion of New Zealand, the Union of South Africa, the Irish Free State and Newfoundland.

2. (1) The Colonial Laws Validity Act, 1865, shall not apply to any law made after the commencement of this Act by the Parliament of a Dominion.
   (2) No law and no provision of any law made after the commencement of this Act by the Parliament of a Dominion shall be void or inoperative on the ground that it is repugnant to the law of England, or to the provisions

of any existing or future Act of Parliament of the United Kingdom, or to any order, rule, or regulation made under any such Act, and the powers of the Parliament of a Dominion shall include the power to repeal or amend any such Act, order, rule or regulation in so far as the same is part of the law of the Dominion.

3. It is hereby declared and enacted that the Parliament of a Dominion has full power to make laws having extra-territorial operation.

4. *No Act of Parliament of the United Kingdom passed after the commencement of this Act shall extend or be deemed to extend, to a Dominion as part of the law of that Dominion, unless it is expressly declared in that Act that that Dominion has requested, and consented to, the enactment thereof. . . .*

12. This Act may be cited as the Statute of Westminster, 1931.

(Statute of Westminster [1931])

Questions

1 Which paragraphs do you regard as the key passages of this statute, and why? Try to describe their meaning in your own words.
2 Why and how far is this statute of historical and political importance? Is it still relevant today?

46 Clement Attlee: The End of British Rule in India (1947)

On 20 February 1947, Prime Minister Clement Attlee (1883–1967), head of the Labour government, declared that Britain intended to transfer power to Indian authorities and government.

It has long been the policy of successive British governments to work toward the realization of self-government in India. In pursuance of this policy an increasing measure of responsibility has been devolved on Indians and today the civil administration and the Indian Armed Forces rely to a very large extent on Indian civilians and officers. In the constitutional field the Acts of 1919 and 1935 passed by the British Parliament each represented a substantial transfer of political power. In 1940 the Coalition Government recognized the principle that Indians should themselves frame a new constitution for a fully autonomous India, and in the offer of 1942 they invited them to set up a Constituent Assembly for this purpose as soon as the war was over.

His Majesty's government believe this policy to have been right and in accordance with sound democratic principles. Since they came into office, they have done their utmost to carry it forward to its fulfillment. The declaration of the prime minister of 15th March last, which met with general approval in Parliament and the country, made it clear that it was for the Indian people themselves to choose their future status and constitution and that in the opinion of His Majesty's government the time had come for responsibility for the government of India to pass into Indian hands. . . .

His Majesty's government desire to hand over their responsibility to authorities established by a constitution approved by all parties in India in accordance with the Cabinet Mission's plan, but unfortunately there is at present no clear prospect that such a constitution and such authorities will emerge. The present state of uncertainty is fraught with danger and cannot be indefinitely prolonged. His Majesty's government wish to make it clear that it is their definite intention to take the necessary steps to effect the transference of power into responsible Indian hands by a date not later than June, 1948. . . .

His Majesty's government are anxious to hand over their responsibilities to a government which, resting on the sure foundation of the support of the people, is capable of maintaining peace and administering India with justice and efficiency. It is therefore essential that all parties should sink their differences in order that they may be ready to shoulder the great responsibilities which will come upon them next year. . . .

His Majesty's government believe that British commercial and industrial interests in India can look forward to a fair field for their enterprise under the new conditions. The commercial connection between India and the United Kingdom has been long and friendly, and will continue to be to their mutual advantage.

His Majesty's government cannot conclude this statement without expressing on behalf of the people of this country their goodwill and good wishes toward the people of India as they go forward to this final stage in their achievement of self-government. It will be the wish of everyone in these islands that, notwithstanding constitutional changes, the association of the British and Indian peoples should not be brought to an end; and they will wish to continue to do all that is in their power to further the well-being of India.

(Clement Attlee, The End of British Rule in India [1947], in Arnstein 1993: 382–3)

Questions

What reasons did Attlee give for bringing British rule in India to an end? Do they sound convincing to you?

47 Winston Churchill: A Protest Against Britain's 'Shameful Flight' from India (1947)

On 6 March 1947, Winston Churchill (1874–1965), leader of the Conservative opposition, responded to Attlee's declaration (Document 46) and protested against the Labour government's policy towards India.

Everyone knows that the 14-months' time limit is fatal to any orderly transference of power, and I am bound to say that the whole thing wears the aspect of an attempt by the government to make use of brilliant war figures in order to cover up a melancholy and disastrous transaction. One thing seems to me absolutely certain. The government, by their 14-months' time limit, have put an end to all prospect of Indian unity. I myself have never believed that that could be preserved after the departure of the British Raj, but the last chance has been extinguished by the government's action. How can one suppose that the thousand-year gulf which yawns between Muslims and Hindus will be bridged in 14 months? Here are these people, in many cases, of the same race, charming people, lightly clad, crowded together in all the streets and bazaars and so forth, and yet there is no intermarriage. It is astounding. Religion has raised a bar which not even the strongest impulses of nature can overleap. It is an astounding thing. Yet the government expect in 14 months that there will be an agreement on these subjects between these races. . . .

Let the House remember this. The Indian political parties and political classes do not represent the Indian masses. It is a delusion to believe that they do. I wish they did. They are not as representative of them as the movements in Britain represent the surges and impulses of the British nation. This has been proved in the war, and I can show the House how it was proved. The Congress Party declared noncooperation with Great Britain and the Allies. The other great political party, to whom all main power is to be given, the Muslim League, sought to make a bargain about it, but no bargain was made. So both great political parties in India, the only forces that have been dealt with so far, stood aside. Nevertheless, the only great volunteer army in the world that fought on either side in that struggle was formed in India. More than three and a half million men came forward to support the king-emperor and the cause of Britain; they came forward not by conscription or compulsion, but out of their loyalty to Britain and to all that Britain stood for in their lives. In handing over the government of India to these so-called political classes we are handing over to men of straw, of whom, in a few years, no trace will remain. . . .

We are told that we cannot walk out of Palestine because we should leave behind us a war between 600,000 Jews and 200,000 Arabs. How, then, can we walk out of India in 14 months and leave behind us a war between 90 million Muslims and 200 million caste Hindus, and all the other tribulations which will fall upon the helpless population of 400 million? Will it not be a terrible disgrace to our name and record if, after our 14-months' time limit, we allow one-fifth of the population of the globe, occupying a region nearly as large as Europe, to fall into chaos and into carnage? Would it not be a world crime that we should be committing, a crime that would stain – not merely strip us, as we are being stripped, in the material position – but would stain our good name for ever?

Yesterday, the president of the Board of Trade and other speakers brought into great prominence our physical and military weakness. How can we keep a large army in India for 15 or 20 years? He and other speakers stressed that point; and, certainly, it is a very grave point. But he might as well have urged that in our present forlorn condition we have, not only not the physical strength, but not the moral strength and will power. If we, through lack of physical and moral strength, cannot wind up our affairs in a responsible and humane and honorable fashion, ought we not to consider invoking the aid or, at least, the advice of the world international organization, which is now clothed with reality, and on which so many of us, in all parts of the House, base our hopes for the peaceful progress, freedom and, indeed, the salvation of all mankind? . . .

I thank the House for listening so long and so attentively to what I have said. I have spoken with a lifetime of thought and contact with these topics. It is with deep grief I watch the clattering down of the British Empire, with all its glories and all the services it has rendered to mankind. I am sure that in the hour of our victory, now not so long ago, we had the power, or could have had the power, to make a solution of our difficulties which would have been honourable and lasting. Many have defended Britain against her foes. None can defend her against herself. We must face the evils that are coming upon us, and that we are powerless to avert. We must do our best in all these circumstances, and not exclude any expedient that may help to mitigate the ruin and disaster that will follow the disappearance of Britain from the East. But, at least, let us not add – by shameful flight, by a premature, hurried scuttle – at least, let us not add, to the pangs of sorrow so many of us feel, the taint and smear of shame. . . .

(Winston Churchill, A Protest against Britain's 'Shameful Flight' from India [1947], in Arnstein 1993: 385–6)

Questions

1 Why did Churchill protest against the end of British rule in India?
2 How does Churchill's protest compare to Document 46? Describe differences as well as similarities. Which argument seems more convincing, and why?
3 Imagine you were an Indian politician of that time. How would you argue for or against the end of British rule?

Chronology

Year	Britain and Ireland	Europe and beyond	Society and culture	Arts and science
5000 BC	**c.5000 BC** Rising sea levels cut the British Isles off from the rest of Europe **c.2000 BC** The main stage of Stonehenge is completed			
AD 1		**753 BC** Traditional date for the foundation of Rome		
AD 100	**43** The Romans begin to invade Britain **79–84** Agricola's campaign in Scotland **122–33** Construction of Hadrian's Wall **c.415** End of Roman dominance			
AD 500	**c.500** Romano-British troops stop Anglo-Saxon invaders near Mt Badon		**563** St Columba founds the monastery of Iona	**Early 6th century** Gildas, *On the Ruin of Britain*
AD 600		**622** Muhammad's flight from Mecca marks the beginning of the Muslim era	**635** Aidan founds the monastery of Lindisfarne **644** Synod of Whitby	

Year	Britain and Ireland	Europe and beyond	Society and culture	Arts and science
AD 700	793 Vikings sack Lindisfarne 795 Viking raids on Scotland and Ireland			731 Bede, *Ecclesiastical History of the English People* c.796 Nennius, *Historia Brittonum* ('History of the Britons')
800	878 Alfred, king of Wessex, defeats the Danes at Edington	800 Charlemagne is crowned Holy Roman Emperor		
1000	1016 Danes conquer England: Cnut becomes king 1042 Edward the Confessor restores the Wessex dynasty in England 1066 Battle of Hastings: the Normans, under William the Conqueror, invade England	c.1000 Leif Eriksson becomes the first European to land in the Americas 1054 The Great Schism between the Latin (western) and Greek churches 1099 The First Crusade captures Jerusalem		
1100	1171 Irish kings submit to Henry II of England	1187 Saladin recaptures Jerusalem		1136 Geoffrey of Monmouth, *History of the Kings of Britain* 1142–4 Adelard of Bath writes treatise on the astrolabe
1200	1215 King John accepts Magna Carta 1284 Statute of Wales establishes the Principality of Wales	1291 The last Christian states in the Holy Land are recaptured by the Muslims	1290 The Jews are expelled from England	

Year	Britain and Ireland	Europe and beyond	Society and culture	Arts and science
1300	**1348–50** The Black Death		**Early 14th century** Hanseatic League office established at the Steelyard (London) **1351** The Statute of Labourers attempts to fix wages in England	
	1381 English Peasants' Revolt	**1378–1417** Great Schism of the Papacy		**1390** Lollards produce the first English translation of the Bible
1400			**1430** 40-shilling freehold franchise introduced for English county elections	
		1453 Fall of the Byzantine empire: Ottoman Turks capture Constantinople		**1469–70** Thomas Malory, *Le Morte D'Arthur*
	1485 End of the War of the Roses: Henry Tudor becomes king	**1492** Columbus' first voyage to the Americas		
	1494 Poynings' Law: Ireland's legislation subordinated to the English parliament	**1498** John Cabot reaches Newfoundland		
1500		**1517** Martin Luther begins Protestant Reformation **1519–22** First circumnavigation of the world		**1509** Niccolò Machiavelli, *The Prince* **1516** Sir Thomas More, *Utopia*

Year	Britain and Ireland	Europe and beyond	Society and culture	Arts and science
	1534 Act of Supremacy			
	1534–9 Dissolution of the monasteries			
	1536 Welsh Act of Union			
	1541 Henry VIII declared king of Ireland			
		1545–63 Council of Trent launches the Counter-Reformation		
			1569 Mercator map	
		1572 St Bartholomew's Day Massacre of French Huguenots		
		1577–80 Sir Francis Drake circumnavigates the globe		
		1582 First English colony in Newfoundland established	**1582** University of Edinburgh founded	
	1588 Spanish Armada defeated			**1589–1600** Richard Hakluyt, *Principal Navigations*
1600	**1603** Union of the Crowns: James VI of Scotland becomes James I of England	**1607** First successful English colony in North America at Jamestown	**1600** East India Company founded	
				1611 King James Bible
				1616 Death of Shakespeare and of Cervantes
		1618–48 Thirty Years War		
		1620 Voyage of the *Mayflower*		**1627** Francis Bacon, *Nova Atlantis*
			1633 Galileo's trial	**1636** Anthony Van Dyck, *Charles I on Horseback*
	1642–6 First War of the Three Kingdoms			
	1648–9 Second War of the Three Kingdoms			
	1649 Execution of Charles I			

Year	Britain and Ireland	Europe and beyond	Society and culture	Arts and science
	1651 Navigation Act		1650 Tea first drunk in England	1651 Thomas Hobbes, *Leviathan*
			1655 Jews readmitted into England	1656 First opera house in London opened
			1657 Drinking chocolate introduced to England	
				c.1660 Actresses appear on English stage
			1665 Great Plague	
			1666 Great Fire (London)	
	1679–81 Exclusion Crisis; Whig and Tory parties emerge			
		1685 Edict of Nantes revoked: Huguenot emigration to Britain		1687 Sir Isaac Newton, *The Mathematical Principles of Natural Philosophy*
	1689 Bill of Rights			1689 John Locke, *Two Treatises of Government*; Henry Purcell, *Dido and Aeneas*
	1690 Battle of the Boyne			
		1694 Bank of England founded		
		1698–9 Scotland fails to found a colony at Darien		
1700	1701 Act of Settlement to ensure Protestant succession	1713 Treaty of Utrecht		1717 Handel's *Water Music* first performed
	1707 Act of Union between England and Scotland			1719 Daniel Defoe, *Robinson Crusoe*
				1726 Jonathan Swift, *Gulliver's Travels*
	1745 Jacobite rebellion		1730 Methodism founded	
		1756–63 Seven Years War		
		1768–71 James Cook's first circumnavigation of the globe	1769 James Watt invents the condensing steam engine	1771 First edition of the *Encyclopedia Britannica*

Year	Britain and Ireland	Europe and beyond	Society and culture	Arts and science
			1773 First cast-iron bridge at Coalbrookdale	1776 Adam Smith, *The Wealth of Nations*
		1776 American Declaration of Independence		
		1789 French Revolution		
1800	1801 Act of Union of Britain and Ireland			
	1807 Slave trade abolished			
			1825 Stockton and Darlington railway opened	
	1832 First Reform Act			
		1833 Slavery abolished in the British Empire		
	1838 People's Charter drawn up by Working Men's Associations			
		1840 Treaty of Waitangi: New Zealand becomes a British colony		
			1844 Cooperative Society founded	
	1845–6 Potato blight causes famine in Ireland			1847 Charlotte Brontë, *Jane Eyre*; Emily Brontë, *Wuthering Heights*
				1848 W. M. Thackeray, *Vanity Fair*
				1850 Charles Dickens, *David Copperfield*
			1851 Great Exhibition in London	
		1857–8 Indian Mutiny		1859 Charles Darwin, *The Origin of Species*; J. S. Mill, *On Liberty*
		1861–5 American Civil War		
	1867 Second Reform Act		1863 Football Association founded	
			1868 First Trade Union Congress	1871 George Eliot, *Middlemarch*

Year	Britain and Ireland	Europe and beyond	Society and culture	Arts and science
	1876 Queen Victoria made empress of India			
			1883 Fabian Society founded	
	1884 Third Reform Act			
	1897 Queen Victoria's Diamond Jubilee			1895 Oscar Wilde, *The Importance of Being Earnest*
				1899 Joseph Conrad, *Heart of Darkness*
				Sir Edward Elgar, *Enigma Variations*
1900		1908 Olympic Games in London		1903 G. B. Shaw, *Man and Superman*
		1914–18 First World War		
	1916 Easter Rising in Dublin	1917 Russian Revolution		
	1921 Anglo-Irish Treaty			1922 James Joyce, *Ulysses*
				1927 Virginia Woolf, *To the Lighthouse*
	1928 Universal suffrage for all over 21			1928 D. H. Lawrence, *Lady Chatterley's Lover*
			1930 First Empire Games	
		1939–45 Second World War		
	1948 Ireland becomes a republic	1949 NATO formed		1949 George Orwell, *1984*
			1951 Festival of Britain	
			1953 Hillary and Tenzing climb Mt Everest	1954 William Golding, *Lord of the Flies*
		1956 Suez Crisis	1956 Campaign for Nuclear Disarmament	
				1960–70 The Beatles' decade

Year	Britain and Ireland	Europe and beyond	Society and culture	Arts and science
	1964–9 Civil Rights protests lead to 'the troubles' in Northern Ireland			1965 Harold Pinter, *The Homecoming*
	1972 'Bloody Sunday'			
	1980–1 Rioting in Bristol, Toxteth and Brixton			1981 Salman Rushdie, *Midnight's Children*
		1982 Falklands War		
	1984–5 Miners' Strike			
		1989 Fall of the Berlin Wall		
		1990–1 First Persian Gulf War		
			1994 Channel Tunnel opened	
		1997 Hong Kong returned to China	1997 Dolly the sheep cloned	
	1998 Good Friday peace agreement			
	1999 Devolution for Scotland and Wales	1999 NATO intervenes in Kosovo		
		2001 Terrorist attacks on the World Trade Center, New York		
		2003 Second Persian Gulf War		

Glossary

calico plain-woven cotton cloth, named after the Indian city of Calicut from which it was originally exported

cottar, cottier in the feudal system a serf or bond tenant who held a cottage by service rather than rent

crown colony colony administered exclusively by the monarch (and his/her government in London)

demesne land belonging to a lord; an estate

devolution sometimes also called 'home rule': the transfer of power from a central to a regional (or local) government

dominion originally 'sovereign authority'; characterisation of formerly self-governed parts of the British Empire (Canada, Australia, New Zealand, the Cape Colony, the Irish Free State)

ealdorman also *Alderman*: the chief magistrate of a county (shire), later an elected member of a borough or county council

fealty fidelity to a lord; a vassal had to swear fealty (a vow of allegiance and loyalty) to his lord

fief fee (Scottish: *feu*), or estate in land, held by a tenant of a feudal lord

gentry also 'landed gentry', the lesser nobility (baronets, knights, esquires, gentlemen)

Gross Domestic Product (GDP) the total value of goods and services produced in a country

JP Justice of the Peace: a local public officer who has jurisdiction in minor civil and criminal cases

MP Member of Parliament

national debt the excess of government expenditure over revenue

peerage the higher nobility (dukes, marquesses, earls, viscounts, barons)

Privy Council a body of advisers to the monarch

Purgatory in Roman Catholic belief, a place of temporary punishment and purification of venial sins

reeve a person commissioned by a lord to administer his land

royal proclamation formal announcement by the monarch

serf a person required to work for his/her lord with no right to leave his/her lord's estate without permission; unlike slaves, a serf was allowed to work some fields for his/her own needs

shilling British coin until 1971, worth 12 old pennies, is one-twentieth of a pound

sokeman a tenant holding land in socage (specified services which did not include military service)

T.R.E. Latin: *tempore regis Edwardi* = during the reign of Edward the Confessor

thegn Anglo-Saxon name for vassal

tithe (Old English: *teogotha* = 'tenth'): the tenth of the yield given to the Church for works of mercy

vassal a person who swears loyalty to a lord and in return receives land and protection from him

villein another word for serf

A guide to further reading

A. GENERAL: HISTORICAL OVERVIEWS

(a) The British Isles

Black, Jeremy (1996), *A History of the British Isles*, Basingstoke: Palgrave.

Cunliffe, Barry *et al.* (eds) (2001), *The Penguin Atlas of British and Irish History*, London: Penguin.

Davies, Norman (1999), *The Isles: A History*, Basingstoke: Macmillan.

Foster, Roy F. (ed.) (1989), *The Oxford Illustrated History of Ireland*, Oxford: Oxford University Press.

Gilbert, Martin (2003), *The Routledge Atlas of British History*, 3rd edn, London/New York: Routledge.

Haigh, Christopher (ed.) (1985), *The Cambridge Historical Encyclopedia of Great Britain and Ireland*, Cambridge: Cambridge University Press.

Hill, Christopher (1969), *Reformation to Industrial Revolution*, Harmondsworth: Penguin.

Hobsbawm, Eric J. ([1968] 1999), *Industry and Empire: From 1750 to the Present Day*, London: Penguin.

Kearney, Hugh (1989), *The British Isles: A History of Four Nations*, Cambridge: Cambridge University Press.

Lynch, Michael (1992), *Scotland: A New History*, London: Pimlico.

Morgan, Kenneth O. (ed.) (1984), *The Oxford Illustrated History of Britain*, Oxford: Oxford University Press.

Paor, Liam de (1986), *The Peoples of Ireland: From Prehistory to Modern Times*, London: Hutchinson.

Schama, Simon (2000), *A History of Britain*, 3 vols, London: BBC.

Schultz, Harold J. (1992), *British History*, 4th edn, New York: HarperCollins.

Welsh, Frank (2002), *The Four Nations: A History of the United Kingdom*, London: HarperCollins.

(b) Europe and beyond

Allen, J. Michael and James B. Allen (1993), *World History from 1500*, New York: HarperCollins.

Anglin, Jay Pascal and William J. Hamblin (1993), *World History to 1648*, New York: HarperCollins.

Blackburn, Robin (1997), *The Making of New World Slavery: From the Baroque to the Modern, 1492–1800*, London/New York: Verso.

Davies, Norman (1996), *Europe: A History*, Oxford/New York: Oxford University Press, 1996.

Delouche, Frédéric (ed.) (1993), *Illustrated History of Europe*, London: Weidenfeld & Nicolson.

Hobson, John M. (2004), *The Eastern Origins of Western Civilisation*, Cambridge: Cambridge University Press.

Kagan, Donald *et al.* (2002), *The Western Heritage* [Brief Edition, Combined Volume], 3rd edn, Upper Saddle River, NJ: Prentice-Hall.

Marshall, P. J. (ed.) (1996), *The Cambridge Illustrated History of the British Empire*, Cambridge: Cambridge University Press.

Merriman, John (2004), *A History of Europe: From the Renaissance to the Present*, 2nd edn, New York/London: W. W. Norton.

Porter, A. N. (ed.) (1991), *Atlas of British Overseas Expansion*, London: Routledge.

B. CHAPTER 1: BRITONS, CELTS AND ROMANS

Cunliffe, Barry (1997), *The Ancient Celts*, Oxford/New York: Oxford University Press.

Salway, Peter (2002), *The Roman Era*, Short Oxford History of the British Isles, Oxford/New York: Oxford University Press.

C. CHAPTER 2: SAXONS, DANES AND NORMANS

Charles-Edwards, Thomas (ed.) (2004), *After Rome*, Short Oxford History of the British Isles, Oxford/New York: Oxford University Press.

Davies, Wendy (ed.) (2003), *From the Vikings to the Normans*, Short Oxford History of the British Isles, Oxford/New York: Oxford University Press.

D. CHAPTER 3: LATE-MEDIEVAL STRUGGLES

Griffiths, Ralph (ed.) (2003), *The Fourteenth and Fifteenth Centuries*, Short Oxford History of the British Isles, Oxford/New York: Oxford University Press.

Harvey, Barbara F. (ed.) (2001), *The 12th and 13th Centuries: 1066–c.1280*, Short Oxford History of the British Isles, Oxford/New York: Oxford University Press.

E. CHAPTER 4: RENAISSANCE – RECONNAISSANCE – REFORMATION – REVOLUTION

Collison, Patrick (ed.) (2002), *The Sixteenth Century, 1485–1603*, Short Oxford History of the British Isles, Oxford/New York: Oxford University Press.

MacCulloch, Diarmaid (2004), *Reformation: Europe's House Divided, 1490–1700*, London: Penguin.

Wormald, Jenny (ed.) (2006), *The Seventeenth Century*, Short Oxford History of the British Isles, Oxford/New York: Oxford University Press.

F. CHAPTER 5: TOWARDS INTERNAL STABILITY

Hobsbawm, Eric J. ([1962] 1993), *The Age of Revolution, 1789–1848*, London: Abacus.

Langford, Paul (ed.) (2002), *The Eighteenth Century, 1688–1815*, Short Oxford History of the British Isles, Oxford/New York: Oxford University Press.

G. CHAPTER 6: POLITICAL REFORMS, INDUSTRIAL REVOLUTION, IMPERIAL RULE

Hobsbawm, Eric J. ([1975] 1993), *The Age of Capital, 1848–1875*, London: Abacus.

Hobsbawm, Eric J. (1987), *The Age of Empire, 1875–1914*, London: Weidenfeld & Nicolson.

Matthew, Colin (ed.) (2000), *The Nineteenth Century: The British Isles, 1815–1901*, Short Oxford History of the British Isles, Oxford/New York: Oxford University Press.

H. CHAPTER 7: THE TWENTIETH CENTURY

Burke, Kathleen (ed.) (2003), *The British Isles since 1945*, Short Oxford History of the British Isles, Oxford/New York: Oxford University Press.

Hobsbawm, Eric J. (1994), *Age of Extremes: The Short Twentieth Century, 1914–1991*, London: Michael Joseph.

Robbins, Keith (ed.) (2003), *The British Isles, 1901–1951*, Short Oxford History of the British Isles, Oxford/New York: Oxford University Press.

I. CHAPTER 8: TWENTY-FIRST-CENTURY PERSPECTIVES

Ash, Timothy Garton (2004), *Free World*, London: Allen Lane.

J. DICTIONARIES, ENCYCLOPEDIAS, HANDBOOKS

Cannon, John (ed.) (1997), *The Oxford Companion to British History*, Oxford/New York: Oxford University Press.

Connolly, S. J. (ed.) (2002), *The Oxford Companion to Irish History*, 2nd edn, Oxford: Oxford University Press.

Cook, Chris and John Stevenson (2001), *The Longman Handbook of Modern British History, 1714–2001*, 4th edn, Harlow/London: Longman.

Gardiner, Juliet (ed.) (2000), *The History Today Who's Who in British History*, London: Collins & Brown/Cima Books.

Gardiner, Juliet and Neil Wenborn (eds) (1995), *The History Today Companion to British History*, London: Collins & Brown.

Lynch, Michael (ed.) (2001), *The Oxford Companion to Scottish History*, Oxford: Oxford University Press.

Thane, Pat (2001), *Cassell's Companion to Twentieth Century Britain*, London: Cassell & Co.

K. DOCUMENTS

Arnstein, Walter L. (ed.) (1993), *The Past Speaks, Vol. II: Since 1688*, Lexington, Mass.: D. C. Heath.

Douglas, David C. (ed.) (1996), *English Historical Documents*, 10 vols, London: Routledge.

Sherman, D. (ed.) (1995) *Western Civilization. Sources, Images, and Interpretations. From the Renaissance to the Present*, New York: McGraw-Hill.

Smith, Lacey Baldwin and Jean Reeder Smith (eds) (1993), *The Past Speaks, Vol. I: To 1688*, Lexington, Mass.: D. C. Heath.

Wiener, J. H. (ed.) (1974) *Great Britain, The Lion at Home, A Documentary History of Domestic Policy 1689–1973*, London/New York: Chelsea House Publishers.

Documentary sources

Arnstein, W. L. (ed.) (1993) *The Past Speaks, Vol II: Since 1688*, Lexington, Mass.: D.C. Heath.

Bagehot, Walter, *The English Constitution*, London: Chapman and Hall, 1867.

Benson, A. C., 'Land of Hope and Glory', 1902. (http://en.wikipedia.org/wiki/Land_of_Hope_and_Glory; 15.09.2006)

Beveridge, W., 'Social Insurance and Allied Services', report by Sir William Beveridge. Presented to Parliament November 1942. *Parliamentary Papers*, Session 1942–3, vol. 6.

Browning, A. (ed.) (1996) *English Historical Documents, Vol. VI, 1660–1714*, London: Routledge.

Burke, E. (1973) *Reflections on the Revolution in France and on the Proceedings in Certain Societies in London Relative to that Event*, Harmondsworth: Penguin.

Butt, I. (1874) *Hansard's Parliamentary Debates*, 3rd series, CCXX, cols. 700 seq.

Chippindale, C. (1994) *Stonehenge Complete*, London: Thames & Hudson.

Cunliffe, B. (1997) *The Ancient Celts*, Oxford: Oxford University Press.

Cunliffe, B. (ed.) (2002) *The Penguin Atlas of British and Irish History*, London: Penguin.

The Declaration of the Rights of Man and Citizen, 1789, prepared by Gerald Murphy (The Cleveland Free-Net – aa300). Distributed by the Cybercasting Services Division of the National Public Telecomputing Network (NPTN).

Delouche, F. (ed.) (1993) *Illustrated History of Europe*, London: Weidenfeld & Nicolson.

Douglas, D. C. and G. W. Greenaway (eds) (1993) *English Historical Documents, Vol. II, 1042–1189*, London: Routledge.

Hollis, P. (ed.) (1979) *Women in Public 1850–1900: Documents of the Victorian Women's Movement*, London Boston, Mass./Sydney: George Allen & Unwin.

Hoppen, K. T. (1998) *The Mid-Victorian Generation, 1846–1886*, Oxford: Oxford University Press.

Johnston, A. (1996) *The Protestant Reformation in Europe*, London/New York: Longman.

London Corresponding Society, *Address of the London Corresponding Society, 19 November 1792*. (http://www.napoleon-series.org/research/government/british/c_habeus.html#address; 15.09.2006)

May, T. (2000) *The Victorian Workhouse*, Princes Risborough: Shire Publications.

McDowall, D. (1989) *An Illustrated History of Britain*, Harlow: Longman.

Morgan, K. (ed.) (1993) *The Oxford Illustrated History of Britain*, London: Book Club Associates.

Newton, I. (1962) *The Principia: Mathematical Principles of Natural Philosophy*, California: University of California Press.

Paine, T. (1971) *Rights of Man*, Harmondsworth: Penguin.

Rand McNally Historical Atlas of the World (1994), New York: Houghton Mifflin.

Robertson, J. L. (ed.) (1971) *The Complete Poetical Works of James Thomson*, Oxford: Oxford University Press.

Rothwell, H. (ed.) (1996) *English Historical Documents, Vol. III, 1189–1327*, London: Routledge.

Shelley, P. B., 'England in 1819', 1839. (http://rpo.library.utoronto.ca/poem/1885.html; 14.09.2006)

Sherman, D. (ed.) (1995) *Western Civilization: Sources, Images, and Interpretations. From the Renaissance to the Present*, New York: McGraw-Hill.

Smiles, Samuel, *Self-Help*, London: Murray, 1859.

Smith, L. B. and J. R. Smith (eds) (1993) *The Past Speaks, Vol. I: To 1688*, Lexington, Mass.: D.C. Heath.

Statute of Westminster, 1931. (http://solon.org/Constitutions/Canada/English/StatuteofWestminster.html; 15.09.06)

Suerbaum, U. (1991) *Das elisabethanische Zeitalter*, Stuttgart: Reclam.

Tetzel, J., *The Spark for the Reformation: Indulgences*, 1465, reprinted by the Department of History of the University of Pennsylvania.

Treharne, R. F. and H. Fullard (eds) (1976) *Muir's Historical Atlas: Ancient, Medieval and Modern*, London: Book Club Associates.

Whitelock, D. (ed.) (1996) *English Historical Documents, Vol. I, c.500–1042*, London: Routledge.

Williams, M. (ed.) (1977) *Revolutions 1775–1830*, Harmondsworth: Penguin.

Williams, C. H. (ed.) (1996) *English Historical Documents, Vol. V, 1485–1558*, London: Routledge.

Wollstonecraft, M., *A Vindication of the Rights of Woman*, 1792. (http://oregonstate.edu/instruct/phl302/texts/wollstonecraft/woman-a.html; 15.09.2006)

Women's Social and Political Union, *Why Women Want the Vote*, 1903.

Routledge History

British Civilization
6th Edition
John Oakland

The sixth edition of this highly-praised textbook has been substantially updated and revised.

British Civilization provides a comprehensive introduction to a wide range of aspects of contemporary Britain, including its country and people, politics and government, education, the economy, the media, arts and religion.

It includes:

- discussion of recent developments and areas of topical interest in British society such as immigration, asylum seekers, the war against terror, the changing welfare state and Britain's relationships with the US and the EU
- new illustrations, maps, diagrams and graphs, and tables
- expanded chapters
- a companion website.

British Civilization is a vital introduction to the crucial and complex identities of Britain.

For supplementary exercises, questions and tutor guidance, go to www.routledge.com/textbooks/0415365228.

ISBN10: 0–415–36521–X (hbk)
ISBN10: 0–415–36522–8 (pbk)
ISBN13: 978–0–415–36521–5 (hbk)
ISBN13: 978–0–415–36522–2 (pbk)

Available at all good bookshops
For ordering and further information please visit:
www.routledge.com

Routledge History

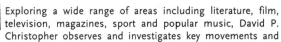

British Culture: An Introduction
2nd Edition
David P. Christopher

Exploring a wide range of areas including literature, film, television, magazines, sport and popular music, David P. Christopher observes and investigates key movements and issues, placing them in a clear, historical context. This second edition offers a wider range of topics, and gives special emphasis to outstanding artists and developments in the field. Also included are:

- fully revised and updated chapters
- new chapters on sport, newspapers and magazines
- authentic extracts from novels, plays and television series
- discussion of recent developments such as the greater commercialisation of cultural life and wider public participation through increased exposure in the mass media
- follow-up activities and suggestions for further reading to strengthen study skills.

This book is an engaging study of contemporary life and arts, and is essential reading for every student of modern Britain.

ISBN10: 0–415–35396–3 (hbk)
ISBN10: 0–415–35397–1 (pbk)
ISBN13: 978–0–415–35396–0 (hbk)
ISBN13: 978–0–415–35397–7 (pbk)

Available at all good bookshops
For ordering and further information please visit:
www.routledge.com

Routledge History

Contemporary Britain
John Oakland

Contemporary Britain is the latest book from the bestselling author of British Civilization and American Civilization. It is a wide-ranging collection of sources concerning every important aspect of life in Britain today, from national identity to moral panics and offers an accurate snapshot of life in Britain at the beginning of the twenty-first century.

Topics covered include:

- Britain's role in world affairs
- British national identity
- constitutional reform within Britain
- social institutions including the NHS
- political parties
- morality and religion.

Lively and accessible *Contemporary Britain* is the essential companion for anyone studying current British civilization.

ISBN10: 0–415–15037–X (hbk)
ISBN10: 0–415–15038–8 (pbk)
ISBN13: 978–0–415–15037–8 (hbk)
ISBN13: 978–0–415–15038–5 (pbk)

Available at all good bookshops
For ordering and further information please visit:
www.routledge.com